Business Accounting

An Introduction to Financial and Management Accounting

2nd edition

By

Jill Collis
Andrew Holt
Roger Hussey

palgrave
macmillan

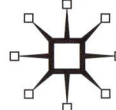

First edition 2007
Second edition published 2012 by
PALGRAVE MACMILLAN

Palgrave Macmillan in the UK is an imprint of Macmillan Publishers Limited, registered in England, company number 785998, of Houndmills, Basingstoke, Hampshire RG21 6XS.

Palgrave Macmillan in the US is a division of St Martin's Press LLC, 175 Fifth Avenue, New York, NY 10010.

Palgrave Macmillan is the global academic imprint of the above companies and has companies and representatives throughout the world.

Palgrave® and Macmillan® are registered trademarks in the United States, the United Kingdom, Europe and other countries

ISBN-13: 978–0–230–27623–9 paperback

This book is printed on paper suitable for recycling and made from fully managed and sustained forest sources. Logging, pulping and manufacturing processes are expected to conform to the environmental regulations of the country of origin.

A catalogue record for this book is available from the British Library.

Library of Congress Cataloging-in-Publication Data

Collis, Jill.
  Business accounting : an introduction to financial and management
    accounting / Jill Collis, Andrew Holt, Roger Hussey. -- 2nd ed.
        p. cm.
    Summary: "Business Accounting, 2Ecovers financial and management
    accounting in an accessible, non-technical style that is
    particularly suitable for undergraduate students of business and
    finance and MBAs. The active learning approach seeks to convey the
    ability to understand and evaluate financial information for a
    range of business services. The book has well developed
    pedagogical features with each chapter including learning
    objectives and activities within the text to illustrate the
    principles and introduce the next learning point. The text includes
    exam-style practice questions at the end of each chapter to test
    the learning outcomes" -- Provided by publisher.
    ISBN 978-0-230-27623-9 (pbk.)
  1. Accounting.   I. Holt, Andrew. II. Hussey, Roger. III. Title.
  HF5605.C655 2012
    657--dc23   2012012340

10   9   8   7   6   5   4   3
21 20 19 18 17 16 15 14

Printed in China

Contents

List of figures   xi
List of tables   xiii
Preface   xv
Acknowledgements   xvii
Acronyms   xviii

Part I   The world of accounting and finance   1

1.   Introduction to business accounting   **3**
1.1   Introduction   3
1.2   Business entities   4
1.3   The accountancy profession   12
1.4   Nature and purpose of accounting   13
1.5   Overview of financial accounting   15
1.6   Overview of management accounting   18
1.7   Accounting principles   23
1.8   Conclusions   27
Practice questions   28

2.   The importance of cash   **30**
2.1   Introduction   30
2.2   The finance gap   31
2.3   Main sources of finance   34
2.4   Need for cash flow information   39
2.5   Preparing a cash flow forecast   41
2.6   Planning capital requirements   46
2.7   Preparing a cash flow statement for management   48
2.8   Conclusions   51
Practice questions   51

Part II   Financial accounting   55

3.   The accounting system   **57**
3.1   Introduction   57
3.2   Main sources of data   58
3.3   Double-entry bookkeeping   59
3.4   Recording transactions   62

3.5	Preparing a trial balance	71
3.6	Limitations of a trial balance	77
3.7	Conclusions	78
	Practice questions	78
4.	**Regulatory framework for financial reporting**	**81**
4.1	Introduction	81
4.2	Need for regulation	82
4.3	International harmonization and convergence	89
4.4	Company law	93
4.5	UK accounting standards	98
4.6	International financial reporting standards	101
4.7	The future of UK GAAP	107
4.8	Conclusions	109
	Practice questions	109
5.	**Conceptual framework for financial reporting**	**112**
5.1	Introduction	112
5.2	Need for a conceptual framework	113
5.3	Objective of general purpose financial reporting	115
5.4	Qualitative characteristics of usefulness	118
5.5	Elements of financial statements	121
5.6	Recognition and measurement of elements	124
5.7	Concepts of capital and capital maintenance	125
5.8	Conclusions	127
	Practice questions	127
6.	**Statement of comprehensive income**	**129**
6.1	Introduction	129
6.2	Purpose of the statement of comprehensive income	130
6.3	Preparing a draft statement of comprehensive income	133
6.4	Difference between cash and profit	139
6.5	Inventory, accruals and prepayments	142
6.6	Depreciation of property, plant and equipment	144
6.7	Bad debts and doubtful receivables	148
6.8	Finalizing the statement of comprehensive income	149
6.9	Conclusions	152
	Practice questions	153
7.	**Statement of financial position**	**157**
7.1	Introduction	157
7.2	Purpose of the statement of financial position	158
7.3	Preparing a draft statement of financial position	159
7.4	Inventory, accruals and prepayments	168
7.5	Depreciation of property, plant and equipment	169
7.6	Bad debts and doubtful receivables	172

7.7 Finalizing the statement of financial position   173
7.8 Conclusions   177
Practice questions   178

8.   Consolidated financial statements   **183**
8.1 Introduction   183
8.2 Group structure of companies   184
8.3 Consolidated statement of financial position at acquisition 188
8.4 Consolidated statement of financial position after acquisition 196
8.5 Consolidated statements of comprehensive income and changes
     in equity   198
8.6 Associates   201
8.7 Joint arrangements   205
8.8 Conclusions   211
Practice questions   211

9.   Financial statement analysis   **214**
9.1 Introduction   214
9.2 Ratio analysis   215
9.3 Investment ratios   216
9.4 Profitability ratios   222
9.5 Liquidity and efficiency ratios   227
9.6 Gearing ratios   231
9.7 Trend analysis   233
9.8 Limitations of ratio analysis   234
9.9 Conclusions   235
Practice questions   236

10. Ethics, governance and corporate social responsibility **241**
10.1 Introduction   241
10.2 Ethics and the professional accountant   242
10.3 Corporate governance   246
10.4 Development of the corporate governance code in the UK 248
10.5 The UK Corporate Governance Code (2010)   250
10.6 Overview of international corporate governance codes   253
10.7 Environmental and corporate social responsibility   255
10.8 Conclusions   260
Practice questions   261

Part III Management accounting   **265**

11. Importance of cost information   **267**
11.1 Introduction   267
11.2 Management's need for information   268
11.3 Cost accounting   270
11.4 Classifying costs and expenses   273

11.5	Elements of total cost	277
11.6	Conclusions	280
Practice questions		280

12.	**Costing for product direct costs**	**283**
12.1	Introduction	283
12.2	Material control	284
12.3	Costing direct materials	286
12.4	Advantages and disadvantages of different costing methods	291
12.5	Costing direct labour	292
12.6	Costing direct expenses	295
12.7	Conclusions	296
Practice questions		296

13.	**Costing for indirect costs**	**298**
13.1	Introduction	298
13.2	Absorption costing	299
13.3	Allocating and apportioning production overheads	301
13.4	Calculating the production overhead absorption rate	304
13.5	Calculating the production cost per unit	306
13.6	Apportioning service cost centre overheads	307
13.7	Predetermined overhead absorption rates	310
13.8	Conclusions	311
Practice questions		312

14.	**Activity-based costing**	**314**
14.1	Introduction	314
14.2	Need for an alternative to absorption costing	315
14.3	Main stages in activity-based costing	317
14.4	Activities and cost drivers	318
14.5	The decision to adopt activity-based costing	320
14.6	Costing for marketing and administration overheads	321
14.7	Advantages and disadvantages of activity-based costing	322
14.8	Conclusions	324
Practice questions		324

15.	**Marginal costing**	**327**
15.1	Introduction	327
15.2	Classifying costs by behaviour	328
15.3	Calculating contribution	331
15.4	Breakeven analysis	332
15.5	Contribution analysis	335
15.6	Limiting factors	338
15.7	Limitations and the relevant range	340
15.8	Conclusions	341
Practice questions		341

16.   Budgetary planning and control   **344**
16.1   Introduction   344
16.2   Importance of business planning   345
16.3   Main stages in budgetary control   346
16.4   Purpose of budgetary control   349
16.5   Budget setting   351
16.6   Fixed and flexible budgets   356
16.7   Advantages and disadvantages of budgetary control systems   360
16.8   Conclusions   361
Practice questions   362

17.   Standard costing   **364**
17.1   Introduction   364
17.2   Standard costs and revenues   365
17.3   Variance analysis   366
17.4   Direct materials variance   367
17.5   Direct labour variance   370
17.6   Advantages and disadvantages of standard costing   372
17.7   Conclusions   373
Practice questions   373

18.   Capital investment appraisal   **375**
18.1   Introduction   375
18.2   Purpose of capital investment appraisal   376
18.3   Simple payback period method   378
18.4   Advantages and disadvantages of the simple payback method   382
18.5   Accounting rate of return   383
18.6   Advantages and disadvantages of the accounting rate of return   386
18.7   Conclusions   388
Practice questions   389

19.   Discounting methods of investment appraisal   **391**
19.1   Introduction   391
19.2   Time value of money   392
19.3   Net present value   394
19.4   Internal rate of return   396
19.5   Discounted payback period   398
19.6   Advantages and disadvantages of discounted cash flow methods   401
19.7   Conclusions   402
Practice questions   403

20.   Issues in management accounting   **405**
20.1   Introduction   405
20.2   Strategic management accounting   406
20.3   Market-orientated accounting   411
20.4   Target costing   415
20.5   Balanced scorecard   418

20.6 Accounting for quality   425
20.7 Environmental management accounting   428
20.8 Conclusions   431
Practice questions   432

Appendix: Present value table for £1 at compound interest   436
Glossary of terms   437
Index   447

List of figures

1.1	UK private sector enterprises by legal status	4
1.2	The concept of limited liability	9
1.3	Development of incorporated entities in the UK	10
1.4	Types of business entity	11
1.5	History of accounting	13
1.6	Accounting concepts	27
2.1	The finance gap	32
2.2	Limitations on ability to meet business objectives in 2008	34
2.3	Main sources of finance by term and purpose	35
2.4	Main sources of external finance by type	38
2.5	Ease of obtaining types of finance in 2008 compared to 2004	39
2.6	Cash flow forecast formulae	45
2.7	Checklist for interpreting cash flow information	48
3.1	Overview of the accounting process	59
3.2	History of double-entry bookkeeping	60
3.3	Pearls of wisdom	71
4.1	Contents of Ted Baker PLC Annual Report and Accounts 2010/2011	86
4.2	Auditors' report for Ted Baker PLC 2010/2011	87
4.3	Members of the European Union (EU-27)	90
4.4	International understanding on rules	92
4.5	Reasons for international differences in GAAP	92
4.6	Organization of the Financial Reporting Council	100
4.7	Proposed structure of the Financial Reporting Council from 2012	101
4.8	Organization of the IFRS Foundation	103
4.9	The IASB's standard-setting process	106
5.1	Primary users of general purpose financial reports	116
5.2	Qualitative characteristics of useful financial information	120
7.1	Classifying assets, equity and liabilities	160
9.1	Examples of main types of ratio	216
9.2	Ted Baker Report and Accounts 2010/11 (abridged extracts)	217
9.3	Five-year analysis of Ted Baker's operating profit margin	233
9.4	Five-year trend in Ted Baker's operating profit margin	234

10.1 Factors influencing disclosures in the annual report and accounts of UK companies   243
10.2 Examples of statements of compliance with the UK Code   252
10.3 Examples of disclosures about non-executive directors and their independence   252
10.4 Example of disclosure on communications with shareholders   253
10.5 Example of disclosure on the audit committee   254
10.6 Example of disclosure on the remuneration committee   254
10.7 Example of corporate social reporting   257
10.8 Example of website CSR   259

11.1 Typical cost centres in a factory   273
11.2 Classifying expenditure   275

12.1 Illustration of formulae in an Excel Workbook   290

13.1 Main stages in absorption costing   300

14.1 Main stages in ABC   317
14.2 Comparison of the main stages in absorption costing and ABC   318

15.1 Mementos Ltd, breakeven graph   334

16.1 Main stages in budgetary control   349
16.2 Example of non-financial and financial budgets   351
16.3 Early Crops Ltd budget report for May   360

17.1 Total direct costs variance   367
17.2 Total direct materials variance   368
17.3 Total direct labour variance   371

18.1 Non-discounting methods of investment appraisal   378

19.1 Main methods of investment appraisal   392
19.2 Keith Hackett: Internal rate of return   398

20.1 Four perspectives of the balanced scorecard   419
20.2 Cause-and-effect relationships within the balanced scorecard   419
20.3 Balanced scorecard for Southwest Airlines   420

List of tables

1.1	Worldwide membership of UK and Irish accountancy bodies, 2010	12
4.1	Financial reporting size thresholds	96
4.2	Proposals for the future of UK GAAP	108
5.1	Set of financial statements under IAS 1 (2007)	121
6.1	Examples of fair value	146
8.1	Accounting methods for different types of investee	206
11.1	Typical characteristics of small and large firms	268
13.1	Main bases for apportioning production overheads	303
14.1	Analysis of costing systems used in the UK	323
18.1	Short-term decisions and long-term capital investment decisions	377
18.2	Comparison of non-discounting methods for capital investment appraisal	388
19.1	Present value table for £1 at compound interest (extract)	393
19.2	Comparison of discounted cash flow methods of investment appraisal	402
20.1	Characteristics of traditional and strategic management accounting	407

Preface

Accounting information lies at the heart of business, regardless of whether the user of the information is the owner, the manager or an external party, and irrespective of the size of the business. Therefore, it is not surprising that accounting is a core module on programmes that include the study of business. *Business Accounting* provides an introduction to financial and management accounting in an accessible, non-technical style that is suitable for non-specialist undergraduate and postgraduate students. The active-learning approach seeks to convey an understanding of the subjectivity inherent in accounting and the ability to evaluate financial information for a range of business purposes.

The chapters are presented in a logical teaching sequence and each chapter has a clear structure with learning objectives, key definitions and activities within the text. The latter are used to illustrate the principles, encourage reflection and introduce the next learning point. At the end of each chapter there are exam-style practice questions to test the learning outcomes. Answers to these questions, together with additional materials, PowerPoint slides and interactive quizzes for use in a virtual learning environment are available on the companion website (www.palgrave.com/business/collis/ba2).

Part I of the book sets the scene with two chapters that introduce the student to the world of accounting and finance in a business context, whilst Parts II and III cover the key aspects of financial and management accounting respectively. The wide range of topics offered allows the lecturer to select those that are relevant to the syllabus and the level of study. On some programmes, the two main branches of accounting are studied at different stages (for example, in consecutive semesters or consecutive years); on other programmes, the topics are drawn from both branches (for example, introduction to accounting) in year 1 and a follow-up module as a core or elective in year 2 or 3). The use of the book on consecutive modules offers the advantage of continuity as well as cost savings for students. The following examples illustrate some of the ways in which the book can be used.

Example 1. Two branches of accounting are taught separately

Module 1
Introduction to financial accounting

Part I The world of accounting and finance
1 Introduction to business accounting
2 The importance of cash

Part II Financial accounting
3 The accounting system
4 Regulatory framework for financial reporting
5 Conceptual framework for financial reporting
6 Statement of comprehensive income
7 Statement of financial position
8 Consolidated financial statements
9 Financial statement analysis

Module 2
Introduction to management accounting

Part III Management accounting
11 Importance of cost information
12 Costing for product direct costs
13 Costing for indirect costs
14 Activity-based costing
15 Marginal costing
16 Budgetary control
17 Standard costing
18 Capital investment appraisal
19 Discounting methods of investment appraisal

Example 2. Both branches of accounting are taught together

Module 1
Introduction to accounting

Part I The world of accounting and finance
1 Introduction to accounting
2 The importance of cash

Part II Financial accounting
3 The accounting system
4 Regulatory framework for financial reporting
5 Conceptual framework for financial reporting
6 Statement of comprehensive income
7 Statement of financial position

Part III Management accounting
11 Importance of cost information
15 Marginal costing
18 Capital investment appraisal

Module 2
Advanced accounting

Part II Financial accounting
8 Consolidated financial statements
9 Financial statement analysis
10 Ethics, governance and corporate social responsibility

Part III Management accounting
12 Costing for product direct costs
13 Costing for indirect costs
14 Activity-based costing
16 Budgetary control
17 Standard costing
19 Discounting methods of investment appraisal
20 Issues in management accounting

Acknowledgements

We would like to acknowledge the invaluable help we have received from our students, who have given us their opinions on this book and its associated learning resources. We are also grateful to the anonymous reviewers for their thoughtful feedback on the second edition.

We are indebted to a number of friends and colleagues, who have given us the benefit of their experience – in particular Rachel Jones and Bian Tan in relation to the first edition, and Mark Farmer in connection with the second edition. Thanks are also due to Geoffrey George for contributing the ethical dilemma exercise in Chapter 10, and to the Palgrave team and our copy-editor, Caroline Richards.

Acronyms

AADB	Accountancy and Actuarial Discipline Board
ABC	activity-based costing
ACCA	Association of Chartered Certified Accountants
AGM	annual general meeting
AIM	Alternative Investment Market
APB	Auditing Practices Board
ARR	accounting rate of return
ASB	Accounting Standards Board
ASC	Accounting Standards Committee
BBAA	British Business Angels Association
BEP	breakeven point
b/f	brought forward
BIS	(Department for) Business, Innovation and Skills
BSC	balanced scorecard
BVCA	British Private Equity & Venture Capital Association
CA2006	Companies Act 2006
c/f	carried forward
CIMA	Chartered Institute of Management Accountants
CIPFA	Chartered Institute of Public Finance and Accountancy
CSR	corporate social reporting
CWA	continuous weighted average
DCF	discounted cash flow
EC	European Commission
EEA	European Economic Area
EFRAG	European Financial Reporting Advisory Group
EMA	environmental management accounting
EMS	environmental management system
EPS	earnings per share
EU	European Union
FASB	Financial Accounting Standards Board
FIFO	first in, first out
FRC	Financial Reporting Council
FRS	Financial Reporting Standard
FRSSE	Financial Reporting Standard for Smaller Entities
FSA	Financial Services Authority
GAAP	generally accepted accounting principles

HP	hire purchase
IAASB	International Auditing and Assurance Standards Board
IAESB	International Accounting Education Standards Board
IAS	International Accounting Standard
IASB	International Accounting Standards Board
IASC	International Accounting Standards Committee
ICAEW	Institute of Chartered Accountants in England and Wales
ICAI	Institute of Chartered Accountants in Ireland
ICAS	Institute of Chartered Accountants in Scotland
IESBA	International Ethics Standards Board for Accountants
IFAC	International Federation of Accountants
IFRIC	International Financial Reporting Interpretations Committee
IFRS	International Financial Reporting Standard
IOSCO	International Organization for Securities Commissions
IRR	internal rate of return
ISA	International Standard on Auditing
JIT	just-in-time
LLP	limited liability partnership
LSE	London Stock Exchange
Ltd	limited
MBO	management buyout
MOA	market-orientated accounting
NBV	net book value
NPV	net present value
NRV	net realizable value
OAR	overhead absorption rate
OECD	Organization for Economic Co-operation and Development
PAT	profit after tax
PBIT	profit before interest and tax
PCAOB	Public Company Accounting Oversight Board
P/E	price/earnings
PLC	public limited company
POB	Professional Oversight Board
PPE	property, plant and equipment
PV	present value
ROCE	return on capital employed
ROE	return on equity
SAC	Standards Advisory Committee
SBS	Small Business Service
SEC	Securities and Exchange Commission
SMA	strategic management accounting
SMEs	small and medium-sized entities
SoP	Statement of Principles for Financial Reporting

SSAP	Statement of Standard Accounting Practice
STRGL	Statement of Total Recognized Gains and Losses
TQM	total quality management
UK	United Kingdom [of Great Britain and Northern Ireland]
UN	United Nations
WIP	work-in-progress

The world of accounting and finance

1 Introduction to business accounting

Learning objectives

When you have studied this chapter, you should be able to:

- compare different types of business entity
- explain the concept of limited liability
- explain the nature and purpose of accounting
- distinguish between management accounting and financial accounting
- describe the fundamental accounting principles.

1.1 Introduction

This book focuses on accounting in a business context. Everyone knows that business is about trying to make money and in this chapter we will start by looking at the different types of business entity. Whether you decide to start your own business when you complete your studies or you find a job in a large, small or medium-sized entity, you will need a basic understanding of accounting. In this chapter we provide an overview of the different types of business entity and explain the purpose of accounting, the role of the accountant and the two main branches of accounting. We also introduce you to the conventions that represent the fundamental accounting principles that are used by accountants.

1.2 Business entities

1.2.1 Legal form and size

In the UK the legal form of businesses in the *private sector* can be classified into one of three main types:

- sole proprietorships
- partnerships
- companies (and other incorporated entities).

Figure 1.1 shows how the 4.5 million private sector enterprises in the UK at the start of 2010 were dispersed among these categories.

Figure 1.1 UK private sector enterprises by legal status

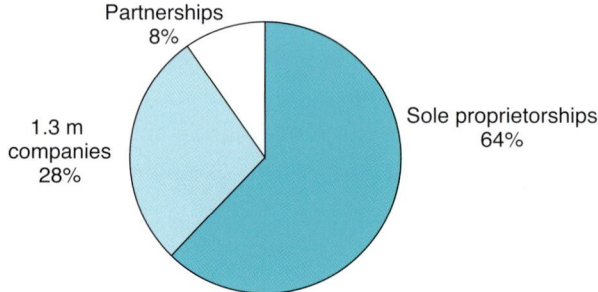

Source: Adapted from BIS (2011a, Table 3).

The private sector comprises business entities and can be distinguished from the public sector (entities under state control) and the voluntary sector (public benefit entities such as charities and other not-for-profit entities). The size of private sector enterprises ranges from very small businesses, such as a sole proprietorship or one-person company with no employees, to a large international company with thousands of owners and thousands of employees. Of the total of 4.5 million businesses in the UK, 99.9% were small (fewer than 50 employees) or medium-sized (fewer than 250 employees) (BIS, 2011b, p. 1). In addition to providing a living for their owners, these SMEs contributed to the economy by providing 59% of employment and 49% of turnover in the private sector. Of the 20 million active enterprises in the European Union, small and medium-sized enterprises (SMEs) accounted for 99% and provided 67% of jobs (Eurostat, 2008). Not surprisingly, they are considered the backbone of the European economy. At a global level, the contribution to employment made by smaller enterprises varies. For example, those with fewer than 20 employees account for around 11% of the business population in the USA and the Czech Republic, but as much as 35% in Greece (OECD, 2010, p. 60).

The majority of smaller entities are owner-managed and family-owned (SBS, 2004; Collis, 2008). In larger businesses, it is more likely that ownership and control will become separated, and the owners will appoint managers to run the business on their behalf. Businesses also differ in terms of their legal status and in the groups of people who are likely to be interested in financial information about them.

To a large extent, the range of users of the financial information depends on the size of the business. For example, financial information relating to a small shop is likely to be used only by the owner-manager and the tax authorities, whereas financial information relating to a large international company will be of interest not only to managers within the business but also to investors, lenders, suppliers, customers and other external parties, such as competitors. For example, a manager working in a division of a large company is likely to require detailed information in order to run the department; a bank lending officer contemplating lending £1 million to a business is likely to need information for assessing the lending risk; and a supplier will need information for assessing the risk of supplying goods and/or services on credit to the business.

Accounting provides important financial information that helps businesses achieve their objectives. All entities strive to ensure that the income generated and the costs incurred are at acceptable levels, but what is an acceptable level varies. In the private sector the economic objective of some business owners is to maximize their wealth by following profit maximization strategies. Others simply want to make sufficient profit to maintain a certain lifestyle and can be described as following satisficing strategies. Research shows that 53% of SMEs[1] do not intend to grow (SBS, 2004) and less than 1% plan to seek a stock exchange listing (Collis, 2003). Although we are looking at accounting in a business context, you should be aware that the economic objective of organizations in the public sector and the voluntary sector is to break even. This means that their managers focus on generating enough income to cover costs and thus avoid making a profit or a loss.

1.2.2   Sole proprietorships

The majority of businesses are *sole proprietorships*. A sole proprietorship is an unincorporated entity because it has not gone through a process of incorporation by which it is registered as a limited liability entity. It is owned by one person, who is in business with a view to making a profit. A sole proprietor may be providing a service (for example, a window cleaner, a hairdresser or a business consultant), trading goods (for example, a newsagent, florist or grocer) or making goods (for example, a cabinet maker, potter or a dress designer). Alternatively, the business may have activities in the primary sector (agriculture, forestry or fishing).

A sole proprietor may run the business alone or employ full-time or part-time staff. The owner of this type of business may experience difficulty in obtaining the finance to start the enterprise, as the capital is restricted to what he or she has available to invest plus any loans. However, there are no legal formalities to set up this type of business and no obligation to disclose financial information to the public. One key characteristic is that a sole proprietor has *unlimited liability*, which means that the owner is personally liable for any debts the business may incur. This liability extends beyond any original investment and could mean the loss of personal assets.

---

1. The study defined a small enterprise as one with fewer than 50 employees and a medium-sized enterprise as one with fewer than 250 employees.

1.2.3 Partnerships

There are two types of *partnership* in the UK:

- unincorporated partnerships
- limited liability partnerships (LLPs).

We will start by looking at *unincorporated partnerships*. This type of partnership is an entity in which two or more people join together in business with a view to making a profit. They are a popular form of business for professional firms offering services, such as accountants, doctors, dentists and solicitors. In the UK, there has been no restriction on the maximum number of partners since 2002.

In an unincorporated partnership the partners have 'joint and several' liability. This means that the partners have unlimited liability for each other's acts in terms of any debts the business may incur. The capital invested in the business is restricted to what the partners have to invest, supplemented by what they can borrow. The partners may run the business alone or employ full-time or part-time staff. The Business Names Act 1985 requires the names of the partners to be shown on business stationery, but they need not be used in the business name. The partners must keep accounting records and in the absence of a written or verbal *partnership agreement*, the Partnership Act 1890 applies. A partnership agreement is a deed of contract relating to the agreement to form a partnership.

Activity

What sort of financial matters do you think partners ought to agree before forming an unincorporated partnership?

The most obvious points on which they should reach agreement are:

- how to divide the profit
- how much money (capital) each partner will invest in the business
- whether any of the partners will be entitled to a salary
- whether any interest will be payable on the capital invested by the partners
- whether any interest will be payable on any loan made to the partnership by any of the partners.

In the absence of a partnership agreement, or if the agreement does not cover a point in dispute, the Partnership Act 1890 provides the following rules:

- Partners share equally in the profits or losses of the partnership.
- Partners are not entitled to receive salaries.
- Partners are not entitled to interest on their capital.
- Partners may receive interest at 5% per annum on any advances over and above their agreed capital.
- A new partner may not be introduced unless all the existing partners consent.

- A retiring partner is entitled to receive interest at 5% per annum on his or her share of the partnership assets retained in the partnership after his or her retirement.
- On dissolution of the partnership, the assets of the firm must be used first to repay outside creditors, second to repay partners' advances, and third to repay partners' capital. Any residue on dissolution should be distributed to the partners in the profit-sharing ratio (equally unless specified otherwise in the partnership agreement).

Activity

To help you identify the similarities and differences between the two types of business organization, decide whether the following characteristics apply to a sole proprietor, an unincorporated partnership, or both:

	Sole proprietorship	Partnership
(a) The entity is an unincorporated business	❑	❑
(b) There is only one owner	❑	❑
(c) There is no maximum number of owners	❑	❑
(d) There are no formalities involved when starting the business	❑	❑
(e) There should be a contract of agreement	❑	❑

What sole proprietorships and unincorporated partnerships have in common is that their owners have unlimited liability for the debts of the business. The first important difference to note is that a sole proprietor is the sole owner of the business, whereas a partnership has at least two owners with no maximum. Another difference is that there are no formalities involved in setting up a business as a sole proprietor, whereas the relationship between partners in an unincorporated partnership must be formalized in a partnership agreement. You might argue that partners do not need an agreement, because in the absence of such a contract the Partnership Act 1890 sets out the relationship. This means that a standard agreement is applied, although this may not be appropriate in all circumstances. You may have thought of some other differences such as:

- A partnership can raise more capital than a sole proprietorship to start the business because there is more than one owner.
- For the same reason, a greater range of skills is likely to be available in a partnership.
- The pressures of managing the business are shared in a partnership, whereas a sole trader must bear them alone.
- Any loss made by an unincorporated partnership is shared among the partners, whereas a sole trader suffers the whole of the loss made by the business.
- In an unincorporated partnership the partners share responsibility for the debts incurred by individual partners or the business as a whole, whereas a sole trader must carry responsibility for the debts of the business alone.
- In an unincorporated partnership the individual partners are responsible for the actions of the other partners, whereas a sole trader has none of these worries.

One of the major disadvantages of an incorporated partnership is the financial risk to individual partners due to the actions of other partners carried out in the normal course of business. In other words, if you are a partner and one of the other partners is incompetent and incurs large debts, you will have responsibility for those debts even if it means bankruptcy. If the partnership has only two or three partners it may be possible to monitor the activities of all partners, but this would be impossible in a large international firm with hundreds of partners spread throughout the world. Moreover, it would not be very agreeable to accept personal liability for their actions.

This issue is resolved by allowing a partnership to obtain limited liability by incorporating as a *limited liability partnership (LLP)*. LLPs were introduced in the UK by the Limited Liability Partnership Act 2000 and the Limited Liability Partnership Regulations 2001. All LLPs must be registered at Companies House, which is part of the Department for Business, Innovation and Skills (BIS). By 2009 35,457 LLPs had been registered (Companies House, 2010, Table E4). LLPs are allowed to organize themselves internally in the same way as an unincorporated partnership, but the regulations that apply to them are similar to the requirements for companies.

With an unincorporated partnership, the partners are liable for the debts of the business, even if they were not personally responsible for incurring them. However, an important advantage of an LLP is that each partner's liability is limited to the amount of his or her investment in the business. There are two main exceptions to this limited liability:

- If a partner of an LLP is personally at fault, he or she may have unlimited liability if he or she accepted a personal duty of care or a personal contractual obligation.
- If an LLP becomes insolvent, the partners can be required to repay any property withdrawn from the LLP (including profits and interest) in the 2 years prior to insolvency. This is applies where it is reasonable that the partner could not have concluded that insolvency was likely.

Another advantage of an LLP is that if one of the partners dies, his or her shares can be transferred to someone else and the firm continues. On the other hand, when a partner in an unincorporated partnership dies, the partnership ceases. If they want the business to continue, the surviving partners will need to form a new partnership, with or without additional partners. Thus, LLPs have an unlimited life, whereas an unincorporated partnership has a finite life.

1.2.4   Limited companies

The majority of limited liability entities are *limited companies*. A limited company is a business that through the process of incorporation acquires a legal status that is separate from that of its owners. Historically, corporation status was achieved by royal charter or letters patent (a chartered company), by Act of Parliament (a statutory company) and, since 1844, by registration (a registered company). Under the various

Companies Acts since that time, registration has become the most common form of incorporation and today nearly all commercial companies are registered companies.

The capital invested in the business is raised by selling shares to investors, who are known as members (hence the term *shareholder*). This equity can be supplemented by loans and other forms of finance. Members have *limited liability*, which means that even if the business goes into liquidation owing significant amounts to lenders and creditors, the owners' liability for those debts is limited. Figure 1.2 explains the concept of limited liability.

Figure 1.2 The concept of limited liability

'The Limited Liability Act 1855 was the first to establish the principle of limited liability subject to certain safeguards, but it was only in force a few months before the Joint Stock Companies Act 1856 superseded it and became the first in the line of statutes which culminated in the concept of limited liability as we know it today.

The concept of limited liability relates to the members of a company being liable to contribute towards payment of its debts only to a limited extent. The amount of members' liability is determined by the liability clause contained in a company's memorandum of association, and differs in its nature according to whether the company is one which is limited by shares, limited by guarantee, or unlimited.

The vast majority of companies registered under the Companies Act are companies "limited by shares". This means that the shareholders or members have a limited liability to pay the debts of the company. When new shares are issued by a company the person who takes the shares must agree to pay for them. Usually payment will be made immediately but sometimes shares will be issued 'unpaid' or 'partly paid', in which case payment must be made later. If the company goes into liquidation and is insolvent, the members are liable to pay for their shares in full if they have not already done so ...

Complementary to the concept of limitation of the members' liability is the notion that the company is a separate "legal person" distinct from the members and the directors. It is the company that buys and sells, owns land, employs workers, makes profits or losses, and not the individuals who make up the company. The company itself is owned by the members, and its directors act on its behalf, but the debts are the debts of the company and the only assets which can be used to satisfy those debts are the assets owned by the company ... These complementary rules of limited liability and legal personality, therefore, combine to confer enormous advantages on the sole proprietor who turns his [or her] business into a company.'

Source: Mallet and Brumwell (1994, pp. 6–7).

The need for limited companies developed in the eighteenth century when the Industrial Revolution in Europe began to change many countries from rural economies to urban economies and the new industrialists needed investors to fund their entrepreneurial endeavours. In the nineteenth century new commercial and industrial technologies, such as engineering and applied science, and industrialization spread to other continents through the colonial activities of the more powerful European nations as they competed for raw materials, new markets and political advantage. In the UK the Joint Stock Companies Registration and Regulation Act 1844 was important because not only did it introduce incorporation by registration, but it introduced the requirement that companies present a balance sheet to shareholders. Figure 1.3 summarizes the developments that led to legislation that created companies with limited liability.

Figure 1.3   Development of incorporated entities in the UK

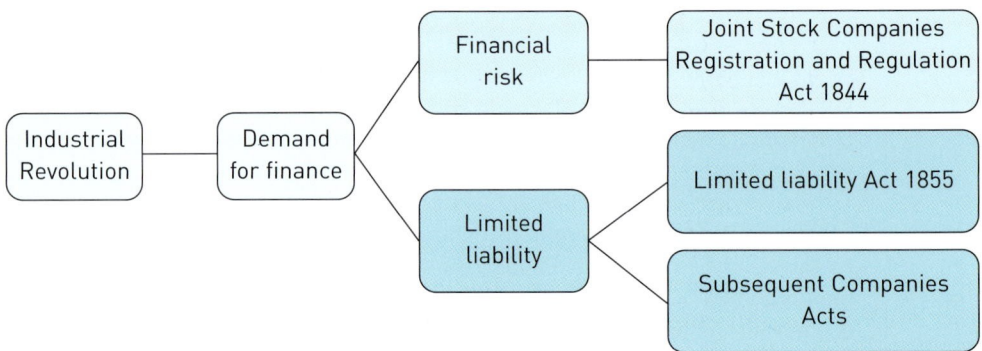

The Companies Act 2006 (CA2006) defines a company as a *limited company* if the liability of its members is limited by its constitution. It may be limited by shares or by guarantee. The company is limited by shares if the members' liability is limited to the amount (if any) unpaid on the shares held by them. If the members' liability is limited to such amount as they undertake to contribute to the assets of the company in the event of it being wound up, the company is limited by guarantee.

Limited companies can be divided into *private companies* and *public companies*. A private company is any company that is not a public company. A public company is a company limited by shares or limited by guarantee and having share capital. Of the population of 1.3m companies on the register in 2009, 99.95% were private companies and the remainder (0.05%) were public limited companies (BIS, 2010). Most companies are started as a private limited company and, if they are successful and grow large, their owners may decide to convert them into a public company under the re-registration procedure in CA2006. This allows them to obtain a listing on a stock exchange and make an *initial public offering* (IPO). This allows public companies to raise large amounts of capital to fund their activities. Public limited companies often have familiar names and a higher public profile than private companies. They can also pay high salaries to attract the best staff and negotiate favourable terms with lenders and suppliers because of their size and status. It is an offence for a private limited company to offer its shares to the public.

The main differences between a private company and a public company are:

- A public company must state in its memorandum of association that it is a public company.
- A public limited company's name must end with the words 'Public Limited Company' or the abbreviation 'PLC' (or the Welsh equivalent), whereas a private limited company's name must end with the word 'Limited' or the abbreviation 'Ltd' (or the Welsh equivalent).
- A public limited company can advertise its shares for sale to the public and, if the company is listed on the stock exchange, its shares can be traded in the stock market. However, a private limited company's shares cannot be advertised and can only be offered for sale privately.

The shares of a UK public limited company are listed on the *London Stock Exchange* (LSE) and may also be listed on any of the international stock exchanges. Investors can buy and sell shares in person through a broker, a bank, a share shop or on the Internet. When shares are issued, an advertisement is placed in the newspapers in the form of a prospectus and application coupon. Most investors take professional advice before buying shares, since all investments carry some risk as well as the possibility of financial rewards. Because limited companies are so important to the economy, information about them, particularly public companies, is readily available. This is because all companies must comply with the regulatory framework for financial reporting which requires them to publish an annual report and accounts. We discuss this in Chapter 4.

Activity

What are the advantages of a private company over a public company?

Figure 1.4 Types of business entity

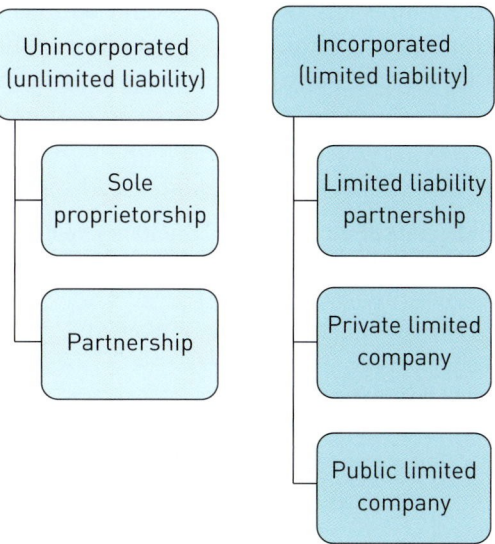

One of the advantages you may have thought of is that private companies are not obliged to comply with stock exchange regulations and most small private companies do not have to disclose as much financial information as a public company. In addition, the formalities for setting up a private limited company are somewhat easier than for a public company.

Figure 1.4 summarizes the different types of business entity we have described.

1.3   The accountancy profession

A professional accountant in the UK must pass a number of rigorous examinations set by one of the recognized accountancy bodies and pay an annual subscription to become a member of that body. The examinations cover a wide range of topics such as business and finance, financial and management accounting, financial reporting, auditing, taxation, law, business strategy and financial management.

An accountant can set up in practice as a sole practitioner or partnership, or seek employment in a partnership or larger firm of accountants. He or she can also look for a job in one of the other industries in the private sector, in the public sector (e.g. the National Health Service or local government), or the voluntary sector (e.g. a charity). Table 1.1 shows the worldwide membership of the six chartered accountancy bodies in the UK and the Republic of Ireland at 31 December 2009.

The ACCA has now overtaken the ICAEW as the largest chartered accountancy body in terms of total membership and has the highest proportion of members outside the UK (50%) and the highest proportion of female members (43%). Although all the accountancy bodies have shown steady increases in the number of qualified female members, women are still outnumbered by men.

An accountant in a professional practice is likely to be a member of ICAEW, ACCA, ICAS or ICAI. Membership of CIMA would be most appropriate for a management accountant in industry. Membership of ACCA or CIPFA would be appropriate for a treasurer in a local authority, or an accountant in the National Health Service or other public sector organization with funding from national or local government.

Table 1.1   Worldwide membership of UK and Irish accountancy bodies, 2010

	Number	%
Association of Chartered Certified Accountants (ACCA)	144,397	35
Institute of Chartered Accountants in England and Wales (ICAEW)	136,615	33
Chartered Institute of Management Accountants (CIMA)	83,487	20
Institute of Chartered Accountants in Ireland (ICAI)	20,010	5
Institute of Chartered Accountants in Scotland (ICAS)	18,780	5
Chartered Institute of Public Finance and Accountancy (CIPFA)	13,668	3
Total	416,957	100

Source: Adapted from POB (2011, p. 8).

A large entity is likely to have sufficient resources to employ a number of accounting and finance specialists, whereas a medium-sized entity may have one accountant who carries out both financial and management accounting functions, supported by other staff, such as a credit controller and bookkeeper. A small entity may find it more cost effective to employ an external accountant to provide most of its accounting needs.

1.4 Nature and purpose of accounting

In its broadest form, we might say that accounting is a service provided to those who need financial information. In everyday language, *accounting* for something means giving an explanation or report on something, and this lies at the heart of the subject, as the brief history in Figure 1.5 shows.

Figure 1.5 History of accounting

'The earliest records of financial information, in Mesopotamia and later in Egypt, date from the fourth millennium BC. Records are more abundant from Greek and Roman times. They are often merely lists of expenditure on major projects or lists of income from taxation. However, even before sophisticated accounting had been invented, some of the functions of accountants had become well established. 'Keeping account' has always been part of ordered society. 'Giving account' has always been the duty of chancellors and stewards to whom responsibility has been delegated. From time to time, the kings or lords would *audit*, or hear the accounts. Sometimes the lord was illiterate and innumerate and relied considerably on the skills of his steward, or accountant.

The essential purpose of accounting is still to communicate relevant financial information to interested persons. Today, the owners of companies (the shareholders) expect to see an account from their stewards (the directors), which has already been audited by independent accountants (the auditors). The original purpose of accounting was to explain what had been going on – how the stewards had collected and used their lord's money. This accountability or stewardship role still applies, though there are now additional roles for accounting information.'

Source: Nobes and Kellas (1990, p. 10).

The following definition is taken from the *Oxford Dictionary of Accounting*.

Key definition

Accounting is the process of identifying, measuring, recording and communicating economic transactions.

Source: Law (2010, p. 6).

In this context the term *economic transactions* refers to the money-making activities of the business that are concerned with creating wealth for the owner(s). We will now examine each stage in the accounting process:

- *Identifying* economic transactions in most cases is fairly straightforward. Examples include selling goods and services to customers, paying employees, purchasing inventories (goods for resale) and buying equipment (for use in the business) from suppliers. It is also important to distinguish between the economic transactions of the business and the personal economic transactions of the owner(s) and manager(s). Thus, the first stage in the accounting process leads to the classification of the economic transactions of the business into categories, such as purchase, sales revenue and salaries.
- *Measuring* economic transactions is done in monetary terms. This convention began when more people learned to read and write, and society moved from a bartering system in which goods and services were exchanged without using money. For example, a farmer might have exchanged 10 pigs for 1 dairy cow and the sale recorded in those very simple quantitative terms. Under a monetary system, the farmer might sell 10 pigs at £20 each, recorded as revenue of £200; 1 cow purchased at £200 and recorded as purchases of £200. Not only is a monetary system convenient for suppliers and customers, but measuring transactions in monetary terms makes it easier to aggregate, summarize and compare financial transactions.
- *Recording* economic transactions is essential. Traditionally transactions were recorded in handwritten books of accounts known as ledgers, but today most businesses record transactions in a computerized accounting system. Small businesses may be able to use a relatively simple accounting system based on spreadsheets, but larger businesses with a wider range and volume of transactions will need to use sophisticated accounting software.
- *Communicating* economic transactions is achieved by generating a variety of financial statements from the records in the accounting system. These are presented in a format that summarizes a particular financial aspect of the business. We will be looking at the layout and content of the main financial statements in Part II.

The following activity allows you to carry out the basic accounting procedures of identifying, measuring and recording the economic transactions involved in building some office shelves.

Activity

A business buys 5 litres of paint, 20 metres of timber and employs a carpenter for 2 days to build shelves in an office. Paint costs £4 per litre, timber costs £2.50 per metre and the carpenter charges £50 per day. What is the total cost of the shelves?

The cost can be calculated in a number of stages. You need to multiply the cost of paint per litre by the amount used. You also need to multiply the cost of timber per metre by the amount used. Finally, you need to calculate the cost of employing the carpenter by multiplying his daily rate by the number of days. The order in which you work out the figures does not matter, as long as you arrive at three figures which, when added together, make up the total cost of the job:

	£
Cost of paint (£4 × 5 litres)	20
Cost of timber (£2.50 × 20 metres)	50
Cost of labour (£50 × 2 days)	100
Total cost of the shelves	170

In more complex examples it is not so easy to identify and measure the economic events in monetary terms. We will be looking at some of these problems in subsequent chapters.

You have seen from the definition of accounting that it is a process that results in the communication of financial information. There are two main branches of accounting: financial accounting, which is concerned with providing financial information to *external* users (those not involved in managing the business), and management accounting, which is concerned with providing financial information to *internal* users. Although accounting can be divided into financial and management accounting, you should not be misled into thinking that there is no relationship between these two activities, since they both draw on the same data sources to generate financial information.

1.5 Overview of financial accounting

1.5.1 Purpose of financial accounting

As you can see from the following definition, the purpose of *financial accounting* is to provide financial information to meet the needs of external users.

Key definition

Financial accounting is the branch of accounting concerned with classifying, measuring and recording the economic transactions of an entity in accordance with established principles, legal requirements and accounting standards. It is primarily concerned with communicating a true and fair view of the financial performance and financial position of an entity to external parties at the end of the accounting period.

The term *true and fair view* implies that the financial statements produced at the end of an accounting period (usually one year) are a faithful representation of the entity's economic activities. The financial statements of limited liability entities are drawn up within a regulatory framework and are prepared using a number of accounting concepts which have been established as general principles. We will examine the fundamental accounting principles in the next section, but will postpone a detailed discussion of the regulatory framework until Chapter 4. Generally, an entity's financial statements are considered to give a true and fair view if they comply with the regulatory framework and accounting principles. However, in a few cases, the preparers may have to ignore specific rules to ensure that the financial statements give a true and fair view and do not mislead the users.

1.5.2 Importance of financial information to external parties

The *annual report and accounts* is a comprehensive source of financial information on a limited liability entity and includes narrative reports as well as the annual financial statements. This statutory disclosure of general purpose financial information by limited liability entities to external parties is known as *financial reporting*. According to the *Conceptual Framework for Financial Reporting* (IASB, 2010), the objective of financial reporting is to provide information that is useful to users.

Key definition

Financial reporting refers to the statutory disclosure of general purpose financial information by limited liability entities via the annual report and accounts.

The following activity will help you understand the importance of financial information to external parties in the context of a small business.

Activity

For some years, Sally Lunn has owned and managed a small coffee shop which is a limited company. List the various external parties who might find financial information about the business useful and say how they would use it.

You may have started by thinking about the bank that provides Sally's business banking needs. These are likely to include a current account with overdraft facilities, debit and credit cards and even a small loan or a mortgage on the business premises. The bank and other lenders are likely to be interested in detailed financial information about Sally's business in order to assess and monitor their lending risk. In addition, you may have thought of suppliers and trade creditors who supply goods or services to the business, who will want to assess their credit risk. Of course, the tax authorities will need financial information about the business in order to assess how much tax needs to be paid and Companies House will be interested in whether the annual report and accounts has been filed on time (there is a penalty for late filing).

You may also have thought of competitors as being interested parties, but they would have to rely on the information filed at Companies House, which is available on the website for a small fee. If Sally's business had been set up as a sole proprietorship, competitors would find it difficult to obtain any financial information about the business, since only limited liability entities have a statutory obligation to publish annual financial statements. The primary users of financial information published by limited liability entities are:

- existing and potential investors
- lenders and other creditors.

We will look at the information needs of these users in Part II.

1.5.3 Role of the financial accountant

Financial accounting can be divided into a number of specific activities, such as the following:

- *Bookkeeping* focuses on the recording of business transactions. Some small businesses keep a simple cash-based system, but the majority of businesses record transactions using an accounting system known as *double-entry bookkeeping,* which provides an arithmetical check on the accuracy of the records. Most small businesses use spreadsheets or standard accounting software, while large businesses are more likely to need tailor-made accountancy software.
- *Accounts preparation* involves the compilation of general purpose financial statements by limited liability entities that must be registered at Companies House and sent to members. Special purpose financial statements are required for the tax authorities. Detailed sets of special purpose financial statements may also be prepared for lenders, suppliers and customers.
- *Auditing* involves a thorough examination of the entity's financial systems and records, tangible assets, management and employees, suppliers, customers and other business contacts. Auditors conduct compliance tests to assess the effectiveness of the systems of financial control and substantive tests to assess the completeness, ownership, existence, valuation and disclosure of the information in the accounting records and financial statements.

Key definition

An audit is an independent examination of, and the subsequent expression of opinion on, the financial statements of an organization. This involves the auditor in collecting evidence by means of compliance tests (tests of control) and substantive tests (tests of detail).

Source: Law (2010, p. 37).

In addition to providing accounting and auditing services, firms of accountants may offer general advice on running the business. They may also provide specialist advice on taxation, raising finance, insolvency, investment, pension planning, treasury management, IT and human resource management.

Activity

A financial accountant can give advice on the following matters (*tick the appropriate box*):

	True	False
(a) How to arrange financial affairs so that the least amount of tax is incurred	☐	☐
(b) The best way to borrow money for a specific project	☐	☐
(c) The likely profit to be made on a music festival	☐	☐
(d) Carrying out financial transactions in foreign currencies	☐	☐
(e) Deciding on the best way to provide for a pension	☐	☐
(f) Calculating the amount to be paid to the tax authorities	☐	☐
(g) Trading in stocks and shares	☐	☐

You may have been puzzled by some of these statements, but you would be right if you said that they are all the concern of the financial accountant. However, as in other professions, there are specialists who may concentrate on specific areas within financial accounting.

1.6 Overview of management accounting

1.6.1 Purpose of management accounting

Whereas financial accounting focuses on providing financial information to external users, you can see from the following definition that the purpose of *management accounting* is to provide managers with financial and other quantitative information to help them carry out their responsibilities. Therefore, it focuses on the needs of internal users. Unlike financial accounting, management accounting is not governed by the regulatory framework, and the emphasis is on providing information that will help the business achieve its financial objectives.

Key definition

Management accounting is the branch of accounting concerned with collecting and analysing financial and other quantitative information. It is primarily concerned with communicating information to management to help effective performance measurement, planning, controlling and decision making.

Performance measurement involves developing financial and non-financial indicators of progress towards the organization's goals and regularly reviewing progress. Non-financial measures might include delivery time, customer retention and staff turnover. *Planning* includes developing budgets for future activities and operations, and *controlling* involves using techniques for highlighting variances once the actual figures are known and ensuring that costs fall within acceptable levels and revenue targets are achieved. Costing techniques provide information that will help management set the selling prices of products and services.

The financial and other quantitative information that managers require helps them to control the resources for which they are responsible, plan how those resources can be most effectively used and decide what course of action they should take when a number of options are open.

Activity

Imagine you are a manager and decide whether you would require the following information for planning, controlling or decision making:

(a) The amount claimed for taxi fares by staff last month.
(b) The prices charged by a new supplier for services or materials.
(c) The cost of running the office photocopier.
(d) The cost of employing subcontracted staff, compared with your own employees.
(e) The cost of making a component, compared with buying it from a supplier.

Items (d) and (e) should be easy to define because in both circumstances you are choosing between alternatives and therefore you are making decisions. With items (a) and (c) you are mainly concerned with controlling costs, although you might want the information to make plans for future expenditure. Item (b) could be concerned with planning future costs or you may be about to decide whether to change to another supplier. This decision may have arisen because you are trying to control costs. Although the boundaries between planning, controlling and decision making are blurred, financial and statistical information has a very important role to play and it is the management accountant who provides this information.

Management accounting offers a number of general advantages, such as helping the business to become more profitable.

Activity

What other advantages do you consider management accounting information offers to managers? Draw up a list of the ways in which management accounting information can be used by managers under the headings of planning, controlling and decision making.

Your list may include some of the following advantages:

Planning:

- the selling price of products or services
- the number of employees and what they should be paid
- the quantity of each product or service that must be sold to achieve the desired level of profit.

Controlling:

- unnecessary expense and waste
- the amount of investment in machinery or equipment
- the cost of running different departments.

Decision making:

- whether to make or buy a particular component
- whether it is worth investing in new technology
- which products or services to offer if there is a shortage of skilled labour.

1.6.2 Importance of financial information to internal parties

To understand how financial information can be useful to internal parties, we need to identify the uses to which it can be put. One way of doing this is to define the responsibilities involved in a particular job or activity.

Activity

Here is a list of the responsibilities of Sally Lunn, who is the owner-manager of a small coffee shop:

- ordering and controlling inventories of food and drink to sell in the shop
- supervising two full-time and two part-time staff
- ensuring the security of premises
- keeping cash records and daily banking
- general display and maintenance of the shop
- serving customers
- dealing with customers' complaints.

Think of your current job or one you have had in the past and jot down a list of your responsibilities. If you have not had any work experience, think about any voluntary job you may have done, such as helping in a charity or organizing a student event.

No matter what work you are describing, it is likely that your responsibilities can be classified under one of the following major activities:

- Planning – Without plans and policies a business has no sense of direction or purpose. Financial information allows plans and policies to be formulated and helps people in the organization understand the targets and standards it intends to achieve. For example, a manager needs to know what profit it is hoped the business will make; on a personal level, you need information in order to plan holidays, decide whether you need to take a weekend job, and so on.
- Controlling – A large number of responsibilities at work are concerned with ensuring that the organization makes progress towards its objectives. For control to be effectively maintained, financial information is required on such matters as the cost of products and processes, monitoring labour efficiency and identifying the sources

and purpose of all expenditure. Similarly for social activities, such as organizing a student ball, information is needed to ensure that a loss is not made.

- Decision making – In establishing plans, it is necessary to decide which of the various courses of action should be taken. We need to know the financial implications of our actions in order to select the most appropriate plan. In business, a manager may need to make a decision between using machinery and labour on an activity; on a personal level, we may need to make a decision between buying a car and using public transport.

Activity

Consider any financial information you currently receive and classify it according to whether it helps you in controlling, planning or decision making. The information can be financial information you receive at work or at home, such as your bank statement, household bills, etc. You may find that some types of information help with more than one activity.

Once you have completed your list, compare it with the one you drew up for the previous activity. The information should match. For example, if you decided that most of your responsibilities are concerned with controlling, then most of the information you receive will be ticked under that heading in your list. On the other hand, you may have identified financial information that you need but do not currently receive, or financial information you receive but cannot use because you do not understand it. In subsequent chapters we will look at different types of financial information and identify those that are most relevant to your responsibilities.

1.6.3 Role of the management accountant

A management accountant is concerned with identifying why the information is required, so that the most appropriate technique can be used to supply information to managers. Managers need this information to enable them to plan the progress of the business, control the activities and understand the financial implications of any decisions they may take.

Management accounting can be divided into the following main activities:

- *Cost accounting* focuses on techniques for recording costs that help mangers ascertain the cost of cost units, such as products and services, and cost centres. This allows management to make important decisions, such as setting selling prices and production/sales targets, and deciding which products or services are the most profitable to produce/sell. Another important aspect of cost accounting is establishing budgets and standard costs, and comparing them with the actual costs incurred. Large organizations may employ a cost accountant; smaller businesses may use the services of an external accountant. Cost accounting provides the cost and expenditure figures that are needed by the financial accountant when the business prepares its annual financial statements.

- *Managerial accounting* focuses on the processing and reporting component of management accounting. Although most small businesses are owner-managed, the large majority use monthly or quarterly management accounts and budgets in addition to cash flow information and bank statements to help them manage the business (Collis and Jarvis, 2002).

To illustrate the difference between financial accounting and management accounting we will return to the example of the office shelves we used earlier in the chapter:

- A financial accountant would be interested in the total cost of £170 so that it can be recorded as the economic transaction.
- A management accountant would be more concerned with informing managers how much the individual elements cost, such as the paint, the timber and the labour. A management accountant would also want to calculate how much the shelves actually cost and compare it with the budgeted figure that represented the estimated cost.

Activity

Classify the following accounting activities (*tick the appropriate box*):

	Financial accounting	Management accounting
(a) Auditing the accounting systems and records of a business	❑	❑
(b) Managing the tax affairs of a business	❑	❑
(c) Analysing the financial implications of management decisions	❑	❑
(d) Preparing financial statements at the end of the financial year	❑	❑
(e) Ensuring compliance with legal and other regulations	❑	❑
(f) Providing financial information for managers	❑	❑
(g) Keeping the accounting records of the business	❑	❑

By now you are probably more confident about deciding which activities involve financial accounting and which can be classified as management accounting. With the exception of (c) and (f), all the above activities are concerned with financial accounting.

Although accounting can be divided into financial and management accounting, you should not be misled into thinking that there is no relationship between these two activities, since they both draw on the same data sources and both generate financial information. However, there are some important differences, which relate to the level of detail and timing of the information produced.

Financial accounting operates on the basis of an annual reporting cycle and, as you will see in Chapter 4, the preparation of the financial statements of limited liability entities is highly regulated in order to ensure that external users receive accurate and reliable information. However, the annual report and accounts is not published until some months after the end of the financial year. By contrast, management accounting is not regulated at all, which means the information can be provided to internal users in the form they want it and as often as they want it. In both large and small businesses, detailed management accounting information for each activity in each part of the business is produced on a weekly, monthly or quarterly basis. If the periodic management accounts for the different parts of a business were aggregated, the totals would be very similar to the figures in the financial accounts, but there would be some differences. For example, the financial accounts would contain information on finance costs (e.g. interest paid on loans) and taxation, whereas the management accounts are likely to contain more estimated figures.

1.7   Accounting principles

It is important to remember that accounting has its roots in best practice, from which a number of *accounting principles* (or *accounting concepts*) developed. These conventions tend to focus on the whole of the accounting process and some are still in use today. Several are so fundamental that they have been incorporated in the more detailed rules and regulations that form the modern regulatory framework for financial reporting. We will look at the regulatory framework in more detail in Chapter 4.

Key definition

Accounting principles are the basic theoretical concepts that guide financial accounting and financial reporting.

1.7.1   Underlying assumption of going concern

The underlying assumption is that financial statements are normally prepared on a 'going concern' basis. *The going concern concept* is based on the principle that the entity is a going concern and will continue in operation for the foreseeable future. Therefore, unless it is known otherwise, it is assumed that the entity is not intending to close down or significantly reduce its activities (IASB, 2010). If that presumption is not valid, the financial statements will need to show the assets of the business at their break-up value and any liabilities that are applicable on liquidation. The going concern assumption is confirmed by IAS 1, *Presentation of Financial Statements* (IASB, 2011), which requires management to look at least 12 months ahead to assess this and, if there is significant doubt over the entity's ability to continue as a going concern, those uncertainties must be disclosed, together with the basis used.

Activity

A company bought a machine for the production department at the beginning of the year for £3,000. It is estimated that the machine will contribute to the profits of the business for the next 10 years. Six months later the chief accountant finds out that if

the machine had to be sold it would be worth only £2,000. Using the going concern concept, which of these two amounts should be shown in the accounts?

The clue to answering this question lies in understanding what we mean by a going concern. As we have already seen, a going concern is a business that will continue to operate for the foreseeable future. In other words, the business does not have to sell its machine and it will be shown in the accounts at £3,000, as it is anticipated that it will continue to contribute to the profits of the business.

Next, we consider what situation a business might be in if it were not a going concern. You are probably aware of the consequences of a business closing or going into liquidation. The activities of the business cease, the workforce is made redundant and any assets the business owns, such as buildings, vehicles, equipment and so on, are liquidated. This means that they are sold and the proceeds are used to pay any outstanding debts. If the business is a going concern, the correct figure for the machine is the price which was paid for it: £3,000. If the business is not a going concern, the figure would be the estimated market value of the machine: £2,000. However, if there was no going concern concept, either of these figures might be used, which would be very confusing for the users of the financial information.

When a business is closing down it needs to prepare the financial statements on a *break-up basis*. Essentially, this means all assets (what the business owns) and liabilities (what it owes) will be classified as current in the sense that they do not relate beyond the next accounting year. In addition, all the assets will be valued at their net realizable value (the disposal value less any direct selling costs), which is likely to be substantially lower than the carrying amount under historical cost accounting.

A wide range of stakeholders in the company, such as investors, lenders, suppliers, customers and employees are interested in whether it is a going concern. For example, if it is intending to close down or significantly reduce its activities:

- Existing investors would try to sell their shares and potential investors would be deterred from investing in the company.
- Existing lenders would demand repayment of loans, increase interest rates on over-draft facilities or even withdraw such facilities.
- Suppliers would be unwilling to supply goods and services on credit.
- Customers would be anxious about the continuity of supply of goods and services and switch to alternative providers. They would also be concerned if they have bought goods that are still under warranty or those that require specialist replacement parts.
- Employees will be concerned about their job security, remuneration and future benefits.

1.7.2   Accrual accounting

Apart from cash flow information, limited liability entities must prepare their annual financial statements using the *accrual* basis of accounting, which shows the effects of economic transactions and events in the period in which those effects occur, even if the resulting cash receipts and payments occur in a different period. The *accruals concept* is the principle that revenue and costs are recognized as they are earned and incurred, not as cash is received or paid (the *realization concept*), and they are matched with one another (the *matching concept*) and dealt with in the income statement of the period to which they relate (the *period concept*).

Accrual accounting can be contrasted with cash accounting, which recognizes transactions and events only when cash has been received or paid.

Activity

During the month of August your friend, who buys and sells cars, sold a vehicle for £7,500 that he had purchased at the beginning of the month for only £6,000. He paid cash for the car, but has not yet received the cash from the buyer. What is his financial position at the end of August?

Using the accruals concept, we can calculate the profit he has made as revenue minus purchases:[2]

	£
Revenue	7,500
Purchases	(6,000)
Profit	1,500

However, that is only part of the story. At the end of the month he has £6,000 less than he had at the start of the month because he has paid for the car, but has not yet received the cash from the buyer. We can show his cash position as follows:

	£
Cash at the start of the month	6,000
Purchases	(6,000)
Cash at the end of the month	0

It is because of the accruals concept that we need to use more than one financial statement to give a complete picture of the financial performance and wealth of a business.

1.7.3 Other basic accounting principles

- The *business entity concept* is the principle that the financial statements reflect the economic activities of the entity and not those of the owner(s). This means that the accounting records for a business like Cut Above must be kept separately from the personal accounting records for the owner of the hair salon, Roberto Garibaldi.
- The *monetary measurement concept* is the principle that transactions are only recognized in the financial statements if they can be measured in monetary

---

2. We are using brackets to indicate figures that will be subtracted in the calculation.

terms. For example, rather than recording the number of haircuts in a year, the owner-manager of the hair salon, Cut Above, must record the value of the haircuts. Thus, 1,500 haircuts at £50 each becomes a sales revenue figure of £75,000. Related to this concept is the assumption that currency is stable and holds its value over time (for example, there is no inflation or deflation and no fluctuations in foreign exchange rates).

- The *materiality concept* is the principle that only items of information that are material (significant) are included in the financial statements. An item of information is material if its omission or misstatement could influence the economic decisions of those using the financial statements. We will look at this again in Chapter 5.

- The *historical cost concept* is the principle that the values of assets are based on their original acquisition cost, unadjusted for subsequent changes in price or value. This presents some problems. For example, four years ago a business may have had to pay £50 for a box of printed stationery, but due to advances in printing technology the business would only have to pay £45 today. On the other hand, the business may have paid £2,500 for office furniture four years ago, but replacing it might cost £3,250 due to higher manufacturing costs. Some assets, such as property in a prime location, increase in value over time. Historical cost is widely used, but is usually combined with *fair value*. The four main bases of fair value are current cost, net realizable value (selling price less costs of selling), value in use and replacement cost. We will refer to this again in Part II.

- The *consistency concept* is the principle that there is consistency in the accounting treatment of items of a similar nature within each accounting period and from one period to the next.

- The *prudence concept* is the principle that revenue and profits should be included only if there is reasonable certainty they will be received. However, provision for all known expenses and losses must be made, whether the amount is known with certainty or is a best estimate based on the information available. The prudence concept is less important in modern accounting as it conflicts with the notion that the financial statements need to be free of bias if they are to give a faithful representation of the underlying transactions and events.

Figure 1.6 summarizes the accounting principles we have discussed.

Although you may find the accounting principles we have described fairly difficult to understand at this stage, they lie at the heart of the preparation of financial statements and it is important that you become familiar with them before you study Part II.

Figure 1.6 Accounting concepts

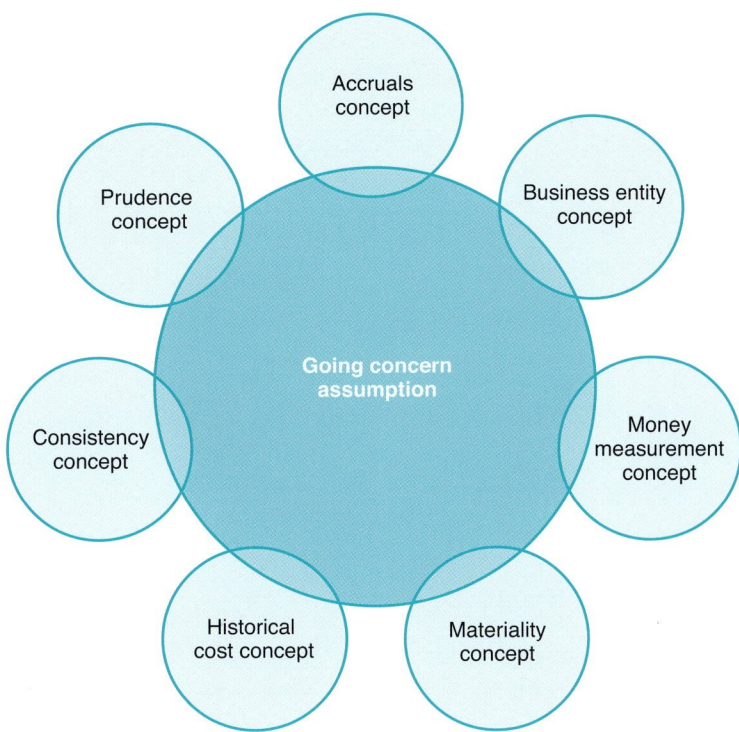

1.8 Conclusions

In this first chapter we have examined and contrasted the main characteristics of two types of unincorporated business (sole proprietorships and partnerships) and two types of incorporated business (limited liability partnerships and limited liability companies). We have also compared a private limited company with a public limited company. This has allowed us to draw out the financial implications resulting from the choice of business form, with a particular focus on raising capital and disclosure of financial information. We have also looked at the role of the accountant and the two main branches of accounting.

Our discussion of the importance of management accounting in providing financial information to internal users allowed us to draw the general conclusion that it aids managers in their responsibilities for planning, controlling and decision making. Our discussion of the importance of financial accounting in providing financial information to external users allowed us to draw the general conclusion that financial reporting needs to be regulated in order to ensure that the financial statements provide a true and fair view to those not involved in managing the business. The final section of the chapter has introduced you to the fundamental accounting principles that guide the general process of accounting and the underlying assumptions that underpin financial accounting.

Practice questions

1 Describe the advantages and disadvantages of the money measurement concept and explain why students studying business and management should learn about accounting.

2 Define the term *accounting* and explain the difference between the two main branches of accounting.

3 Explain the concept of limited liability and the advantages of a company over an unincorporated business.

4 Compare and contrast the advantages and disadvantages of public and private companies.

5 Describe the two underlying assumptions that underpin financial accounting and reporting, providing examples to illustrate your explanations.

References

BIS (2011a) *Business Population Estimates for the UK and Regions 2010*. Available at: http://www.bis.gov.uk/analysis/statistics/business-population-estimates (accessed 30 November 2011).

BIS (2011b) *Statistical Release*, URN11/92, 24 May. Available at: http://www.bis.gov.uk/analysis/statistics/business-population-estimates (accessed 30 November 2011]).

Collis, J. (2003) *Directors' Views on Exemption from Statutory Audit*, URN 03/1342, October. London: DTI. Available at: http://www.bis.gov.uk/files/file25971.pdf (accessed 30 November 2011).

Collis, J. (2008) *Directors' Views on Accounting and Auditing Requirements for SMEs*. London: BERR. Available at: http://www.berr.gov.uk/whatwedo/businesslaw/corp-gov-research/current-research-proj/page18121.html (accessed 30 November 2011).

Collis, J. and Jarvis, R. (2002) Financial information and the management of small private companies. *Journal of Small Business and Enterprise Development* 9(2), 100–10.

Companies House (2010) *Statistical Tables on Companies Registration Activities 2009–10*. Available at: http://www.companieshouse.gov.uk/about/pdf/companies RegActivities2009_2010.pdf (accessed 30 November 2011).

European Communities (2004) *Highlights from the 2003 Observatory*, 2003/8. Luxembourg: Office for Official Publications of the European Communities.

Eurostat (2008) Enterprises by size class – overview of SMEs in the EU. *Statistics in Focus 31/2008*. Available at: http://epp.eurostat.ec.europa.eu/portal/page/portal/publications/collections/sif_dif (accessed 30 November 2011).

IASB (2010) *The Conceptual Framework for Financial Reporting*, September. London: International Accounting Standards Board.

IASB (2011) IAS 1, *Presentation of Financial Statements*. London: International Accounting Standards Board.

Law, J. (ed.) (2010) *Dictionary of Accounting*, 4th edition. Oxford: Oxford University Press.

Mallet, N. and Brumwell, J. (1994) The concept of limited liability. *Credit Control* 15(10), 6–9.

Nobes, C. and Kellas, J. (1990) *Accountancy Explained*. London: Penguin Books.

OECD (2010) *OECD Factbook 2010*. Available at: http://www.oecd.org/site/0,3407, en_21571361_34374092_1_1_1_1_1,00.html (accessed 30 November 2011).

POB (Professional Oversight Board) (2011) *Key Facts and Trends in the Accountancy Profession*, June. Available at: http://www.frc.org.uk/pob/publications/index.cfm? mode=list&cID=3 (accessed 30 November 2011).

SBS (2004) *Annual Small Business Survey 2003*. URN 04/390.

2 The importance of cash

Learning objectives

When you have studied this chapter, you should be able to:

- explain the theory of a finance gap for small and medium-sized enterprises
- describe and classify potential sources of business finance
- explain the need for cash flow information
- prepare and interpret a cash flow forecast and a cash flow statement
- describe the principles for monitoring and controlling cash.

2.1 Introduction

In Chapter 1 we explained that the objective of some business owners is to maximize their wealth, while others simply want to make enough money to maintain a certain lifestyle. Before an owner can start making money, he or she needs to have enough to set up or acquire a business and enough cash to run the business. Once the business has started, irrespective of whether it has been set up as a sole proprietorship, partnership or company, the cash position must be monitored closely. There are many reasons why businesses close and they are not all associated with failure. The main reason for failure is that the business does not have sufficient cash or credit. Typically, the business will have fallen behind with payments for goods or services received, leading to supplies being cut off. Insufficient cash also means that employees cannot be paid and must be laid off. Thus, cash is crucial to the survival of the business.

Because of the importance of cash, would-be entrepreneurs and the owners and managers of existing businesses need information about the current and future cash position. This allows them to check that there will be sufficient finance in terms of cash or credit facilities to meet the needs of the business, and also allows them to plan the investment of any surplus cash. In this chapter we describe the main sources of finance in the UK for small and medium-sized enterprises (SMEs) and discuss the difficulties entrepreneurs may face in seeking finance to start and develop a business. We also introduce you to two simple financial statements that provide information about the cash position of a business: the cash flow forecast, which predicts the future position, and the cash flow statement, which looks at the past position. The majority of well-managed businesses prepare these statements because they are an essential source of information for running the business. You will learn the layout for the statement of cash flows required by IAS 7 in a later chapter.

2.2   The finance gap

In general, the term *finance* refers to the management of money and this is a subject that may form part of your future studies. There are two further ways in which the term can be used and we will now look at all three definitions.

Key definition

Finance is:

- **the practice of manipulating and managing money**
- **the capital involved in a project, especially the capital needed to start a new business**
- **a loan of money for a particular purpose, especially by a financial house.**

Source: Law (2010, p. 185).

You can see from the second and third definitions that finance is not used to refer to small amounts of money, such as the cost of £170 for the materials and labour used to make a set of office shelves (the example we looked at in Chapter 1). Instead, it refers to large sums of money, such as the amount invested in the business by the owner(s) or borrowed from a financial institution such as a bank, or from some other provider of finance for the purpose of buying land, premises, vehicles, equipment, etc. From this we can deduce that one of the key considerations when planning a business is to ensure that the owner has sufficient finance in place to launch the enterprise and allow it to grow to the desired size.

Unfortunately, some entrepreneurs who have an idea for a new business or want to expand an existing business cannot raise sufficient finance. The situation where a business has profitable opportunities, but is unable to raise the funds to exploit them, can be described as a *finance gap* (Jarvis, forthcoming 2012). Figure 2.1 gives further details.

The main argument supporting the notion of a finance gap is that because the majority of SMEs are sole proprietorships, partnerships and private companies, they cannot raise equity finance by selling shares to the public. In other words, there is no

Figure 2.1 The finance gap

'Historically, the existence of a "finance gap" was formally recognised 80 years ago. In 1931 the government-sponsored Macmillan Committee reported that the financing needs of small business were not well served by the then existing financial services institutions. The committee consisting of such eminent academics as John Maynard Keynes and politicians such as Ernest Bevin illustrates the importance given to the subject of financing small firms by government in the 1930s. Since then this criticism of financial institutions has been echoed by other important inquiries (e.g. Bolton, 1971; Wilson 1979). In response to this criticism successive governments have introduced a number of initiatives with varying success. For example, the Enterprise Finance Guarantee (formerly Small Firms Loan Guarantee) is a guarantee scheme for firms which can only offer limited security as collateral for bank loans ... In recent years financial services institutions have broadened their scope and for commercial reasons have introduced new products that have made access to funds easier for smaller firms. It has been argued that if a finance gap still exists, it has been substantially narrowed because of these initiatives and subsequent responses by the market since the 1930s (Deakins, 1996). However, others dispute this claim on both empirical and theoretical grounds (for example, Harrison and Mason, 1995) ...

A particular problem for policymakers wishing to support growth firms is the low levels of supply and take-up of equity capital (HMT and BIS, 2010). The problem is that businesses can only increase loan capital in proportion to assets held and the equity interest prevailing. Therefore, these firms are effectively constrained in accessing debt finance and the only way the firm can increase capital is through injections of equity.'

Source: Jarvis, forthcoming 2012.

capital market for privately held businesses, as only public listed companies can raise capital on a stock exchange. This aspect of the finance gap is sometimes referred to as the *equity gap*.

Activity

In addition to the equity gap, there are a number of other reasons why smaller entities may have difficulty in accessing finance when they need it. Draw up a list of other possible explanations.

Some of the explanations you may have listed relate to the start-up stage when there is no evidence of:

- the quality of the business idea
- the entrepreneur's management skills
- a financial track record that demonstrates ability to service a loan (pay the interest and repay the amount borrowed) or pay suppliers for goods and services provided on credit.

At any stage there may be obstacles such as:

- the cost of borrowing when interest rates are high
- an information gap due to insufficient knowledge of potential sources of finance
- lack of skills to present a convincing proposal to investors or lenders
- lack of collateral to offset risk, which may be particularly relevant in the service sector.

During times of recession, access to appropriate finance is the key to ensuring that small and growing businesses are able to survive and expand, and in 2011 access to finance was considered as one of the most important problems for SMEs in Europe (UEAPME, 2011). In view of the importance of SMEs to the economy, governments have conducted consultations and commissioned studies to suggest remedies. In the UK, one such remedy was to set up the *Business Growth Fund* in 2011. This £2.5 billion fund helps companies struggling to find long-term growth finance in amounts ranging from £2 million to £10 million. The fund seeks sound investments where it can make minority investments and build long-term positive relationships with the companies it helps. A second remedy was to establish a mentoring programme to provide SMEs with free access to bankers and others in their locality with the skills and experience to help them grow. The mentor can advise on how the business can make the most of its relationship with the bank and where to find further financial and business support. These funding, mentoring and information schemes for SMEs are supported by the British Bankers' Association, and a dedicated website (www.betterbusinessfinance.co.uk) provides a 'one-stop shop' to address the information gap.

To put the finance gap into perspective, it is useful to look at the growth aspirations of smaller entities and the other problems they face. A survey of 818 SMEs at the start of the financial crisis and recession in the UK (Cosh et al., 2009) found that 11% intended to become smaller, 31% wanted to stay the same size and 59% had ambitions to grow over the next three years. Figure 2.2 shows that fewer than 20% of SMEs stated that the availability and cost of finance for expansion or the availability and cost of overdraft finance was a crucial limitation on their business objectives, compared with 39% who reported that market demand was a very significant constraint.

When interpreting the results of surveys examining the problem of access to finance, you need to remember that the respondents are likely to be owners or managers of existing businesses; they may not include entrepreneurs who could be having difficulty in obtaining start-up finance. In addition, businesses require finance for particular purposes and therefore owners and managers seek finance on a contingency basis. Consequently unremitting or regular problems such as poor sales may be considered to be a more important problem during an economic recession.

Figure 2.2   Limitations on ability to meet business objectives in 2008

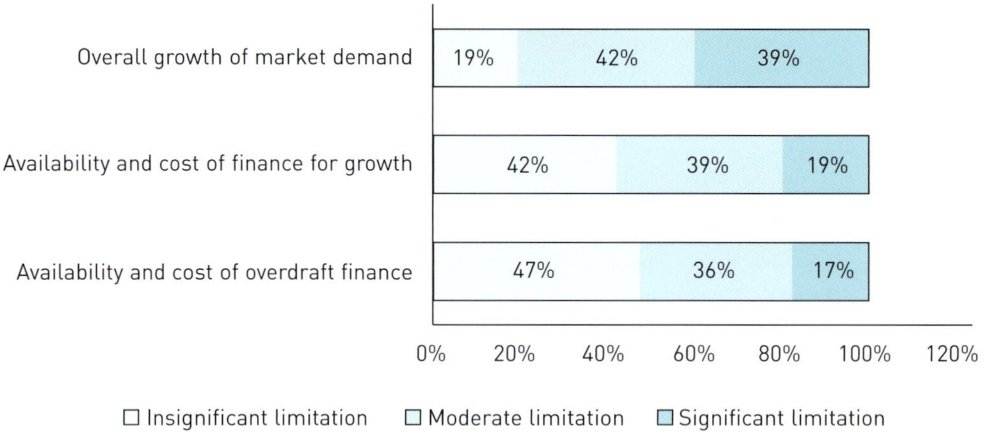

Source: Adapted from Cosh et al. (2009, p. 7).

2.3   Main sources of finance

The cash invested by the owner to start a business is known as *capital*. Sources include money from savings, redundancy, inheritance, investments, winnings, etc. Once the business is established, the capital can be increased by retaining some of the profit (earnings) in the business. You will also see capital referred to as *owners' equity*.

Key definition

Capital is the money contributed by the proprietors to an organisation to enable it to function.

Source: Law (2010, p. 74).

If these internal sources are not sufficient, the owner or manager may need to consider external sources of finance. These sources can be classified according to the length of time the finance is required and this, in turn, depends on the purpose for which it is required. Figure 2.3 shows this classification.

Short-term finance is used to provide the *working capital* needed to fund the day-to-day activities of the business. For example, cash is needed to purchase inventory that is sold and turned back into cash, and used to buy more inventory. Thus, short-term finance is required for periods of less than a year and examples include the following:

- An *overdraft* is a form of bank loan that is set up for a short period (usually one year and renegotiated annually) to cover the possibility of a cash deficit up to an agreed amount. This situation would arise if there was insufficient cash in the bank account to cover the cash going out. An overdraft facility is an 'on demand' form

Figure 2.3 Main sources of finance by term and purpose

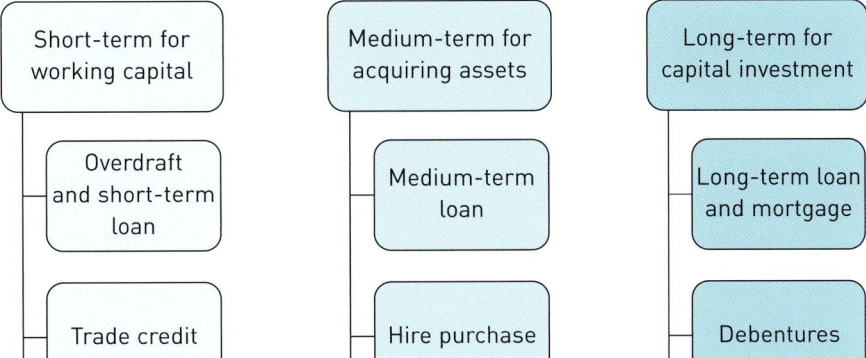

of borrowing. This means the bank can withdraw the facility and/or demand immediate repayment of the overdrawn amount, together with any interest fees and charges due.

- If the business needs money for a fixed period of time (of less than a year), a *short-term loan* from a bank, family or friends may be more appropriate. Banks may charge a setting-up fee. Interest is charged at a rate that varies according to the risk, which is often measured by a credit rating score. Loans are repaid in instalments or at the end of the term according to the loan agreement. Lenders normally require some form of collateral or guarantee to provide security for a loan, so that they can recover any amounts outstanding should the business default on the loan agreement.

- *Trade credit* is finance provided by a *trade creditor*. Amounts owed by trade creditors are known as *trade payables*. A trade creditor is a supplier from whom the business has purchased goods or services on credit. This means that the business does not need to pay for the goods or services until the end of the *credit period*. This is a specified length of time after they have been received (typically between 30 and 90 days) and is dependent on the purchaser's credit rating. Discounts may be offered for prompt payment on the due date. Trade credit does not provide additional cash, but allows money already in the business to be used for other purposes until it is needed to pay creditors.

- *Invoice finance* includes factoring and invoice discounting. *Factoring* is finance provided by a factoring firm (usually a bank or other financial institution) which buys the trade debts of the business. Trade debts are known as *trade receivables*. They are the amounts owed by customers to whom the business has sold goods or services on credit but who have not yet paid. The factoring firm assesses the credit-worthiness of the debtors and collects the debts in return for a fee that represents the risk. The advantage to the business is that it receives up to 90% of the value of the invoices immediately (depending on the terms agreed) and the balance after the debt has been collected. *Invoice discounting* is where the business sells its invoices to a factoring firm at a discount for immediate cash.

Medium-term finance is used to provide assets that are expected to generate cash for the business in the medium term, such as fixtures and fittings, equipment and vehicles. Since the finance is secured on an asset, this type of finance can be referred to as *asset-based finance*. Examples of medium-term finance include the following:

- A *medium-term loan* from a bank, government scheme, friends or family to purchase an asset over a fixed period of time that is linked to the economic life of the asset. The conditions of the loan are similar to those described above for overdrafts and short-term loans.
- A more flexible alternative to borrowing is to use *hire purchase* (HP). HP allows the purchaser to start using the asset as soon as a deposit has been paid. The deposit represents the first of a number of instalments spread over a specified period of time. Ownership does not pass to the purchaser until the final instalment has been paid.
- *Leasing* is also a more flexible alternative to taking out a loan. Essentially, a *finance lease* is a financing agreement, whereas an *operating lease* is a rental agreement. Under an operating lease the lessee hires the asset for a period of time that is normally substantially shorter than the life of the asset. Therefore, ownership of the asset remains with the lessor. Operating leases are commonly used for assets where the *residual value* of the asset is uncertain. The residual value is an estimate of the amount that will be received on disposal of the asset at the end of its expected useful life. The residual value of the asset is likely to be uncertain where technological advances are rapid (such as office equipment) or there is extensive wear and tear on the asset (such as fleet vehicles). Operating leases are also used where the assets are required for a particular project (such as plant and machinery in a construction industry). Leases may be packaged with other services, such as maintenance and servicing of the asset.

Long-term finance is used to provide assets that are expected to give economic benefits to the business in the long-term. Long-term finance can be divided into *debt finance* and *equity finance*. We will start by looking at the main sources of debt finance:

- A *long-term loan* is a suitable form of finance for capital investment in assets that are not acquired for trading purposes but intended to be kept in the business in the long term, such investment in plant and machinery.
- A *mortgage* is a long-term loan for purchasing land or premises. Mortgages are usually supplied by financial institutions, such as banks and building societies, for a specified number of years (in the UK the maximum period is usually 25–30 years)

at a fixed or variable rate of interest. Repayment may be in instalments or at the end of the term.

- A *debenture* (or *loan stock*) is the most common type of long-term loan taken by large companies. Debentures are usually repayable at a fixed date, a long time in the future. The debenture holder may be a private investor or a corporate investor and normally receives a fixed rate of interest, which is lower than the rate charged for an overdraft. Debentures involve less risk to the investor than equities and can be sold on a stock exchange.

The last category is *equity finance*, which refers to finance raised from the sale of ordinary shares, as opposed to preference shares (which are classified as non-equity shares) and to debt finance. This type of finance is only available to companies and other limited liability entities:

- Public companies can raise capital on the main market of the *London Stock Exchange* (LSE). Small, fast-growing public companies can obtain access to the market at an earlier stage in their development through a listing on the *Alternative Investment Market* (AIM), which was set up as a subsidiary market in 1995. The listing rules for AIM are less onerous and, therefore, less expensive. To give you some idea of the size of these markets, in March 2011 there were 1,174 companies listed on AIM and 1,416 UK and international companies listed on the main market (LSE, 2011).
- *Formal venture capital* from corporate investors, such as pension funds, typically provides equity finance for certain new businesses, such as an initial public offering (IPO) or a management buyout (MBO). Venture capitalists are interested in investing in businesses with potential for above-average returns to offset the high risks. The average size of the investment is likely to be over £50,000. The British Private Equity & Venture Capital Association (BVCA) represents 230 firms with approximately £32 billion funds under management, and more than 220 professional advisory firms based in regions throughout the world.
- *Informal venture capital* from *business angels* is a valuable source of equity finance for SMEs. Business angels are wealthy individuals who wish to invest in profitable privately owned businesses (usually private companies). Businesses seeking angel finance often rely on firms of accountants and other professionals to introduce them to investors. The British Business Angels Association (BBAA) represents the vast majority of business angel networks across the UK. In 2009 there were an estimated 4,000 to 6,000 business angels in the UK and the average size of the investment was £42,000 (Wiltbank, 2009).

Activity

Classify the following sources of finance into debt finance, asset-based finance and equity finance by ticking the appropriate box:

	Debt finance	Asset-based finance	Equity finance
(a) Share capital	❏	❏	❏
(b) Debenture	❏	❏	❏
(c) Hire purchase	❏	❏	❏
(d) Invoice finance	❏	❏	❏
(e) Leasing	❏	❏	❏
(f) Loan	❏	❏	❏
(g) Overdraft	❏	❏	❏
(h) Mortgage	❏	❏	❏
(i) Venture capital	❏	❏	❏
(j) Trade credit	❏	❏	❏

You can check your answers against Figure 2.4, which summarizes the main sources of external finance.

Figure 2.4   Main sources of external finance by type

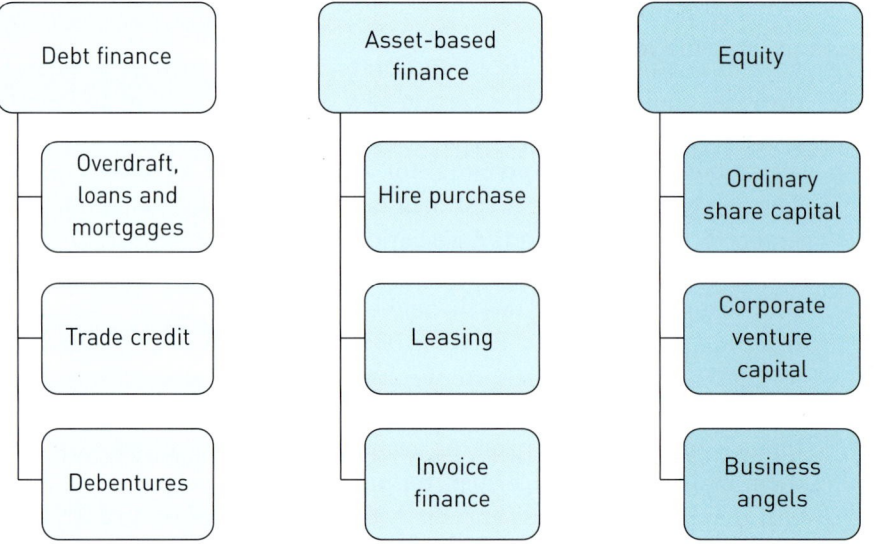

Despite a wide range of potential sources of finance, as we have already explained, there are a number of obstacles for smaller businesses in terms of access to finance. Figure 2.5 shows the ease with which the SMEs that took part in the survey by Cosh et al. (2009) were able to obtain different types of finance compared to four years earlier. Not surprisingly, bank overdrafts, commercial loans and mortgages became harder to obtain as a result of the 'credit crunch' due to the financial crisis at that time. You can see that some businesses did not try to obtain some of the sources,

Figure 2.5   Ease of obtaining types of finance in 2008 compared to 2004

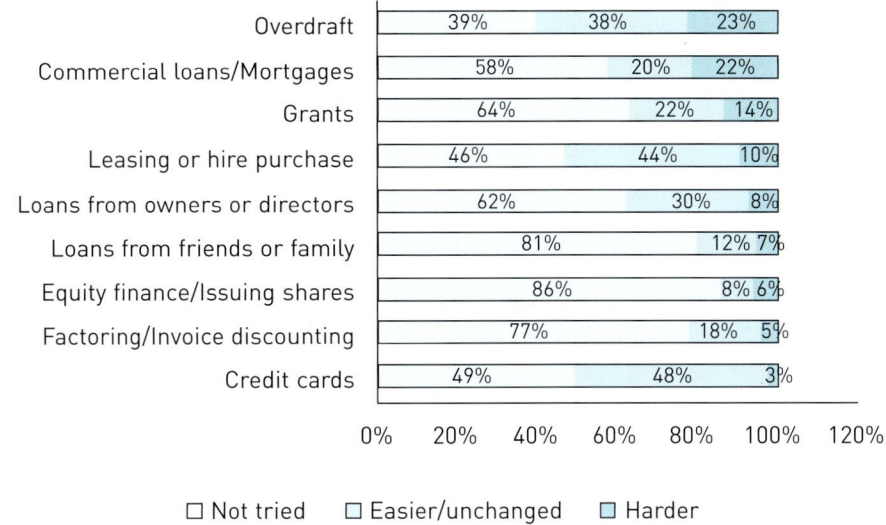

Source: Adapted from Cosh et al. (2009, p. 7).

which may be an indication of choice, lack of suitability for their purpose or evidence of an information gap.

2.4   Need for cash flow information

Since business is about money, information about cash is very important. Without sufficient cash an individual or organization may become insolvent, which in many cases leads to a state of *bankruptcy* for an individual or *liquidation* for an organization. In business, economic transactions are based on the immediate payment of cash (a cash transaction) or payment after an agreed period (a credit transaction). The term *cash* refers to all money, whether in the form of coins, notes, cheques or any other way of making payment that does not involve the use of credit. Businesses need to keep a careful record of all cash receipts and payments in order to keep track of the money. These records are kept as part of the accounting system we describe in Chapter 3.

Activity

Imagine you have £200 cash that you use to buy a computer from another student. You are a bit of an opportunist and see a chance to make some money. You decide to advertise the computer for sale, which costs £10, and you sell the computer for £300 cash. You have no other business transactions. Calculate the cash position of your business at the end of the month.

You should have found the answer by deducting all the cash outflows for the month from all the cash inflows for the month, something you might have been able to do in your head. However, you will not have arrived at the correct answer of £290 if you overlooked the recording of the capital of £200, which was the amount you invested in your business at the start. The following simple statement shows how we arrived at the correct answer:

Your business	
Cash flow statement for the month	
	£
Cash inflows	
Capital	200.00
Revenue	300.00
	500.00
Cash outflows	
Purchases	200.00
Advertising	10.00
	210.00
Net cash flow (500 – 210)	290.00

Starting at the top of the statement, you see the term *capital*, which we have already explained is the term used to describe the money contributed by the owner to enable the business to function; *revenue* is cash flowing into the business from sales to customers. *Purchases* is cash flowing out of the business to suppliers for goods that are purchased for resale. *Advertising* represents cash flowing out of the business when that expense is paid.

Activity

Using the same example, imagine that this time you agreed to sell the computer on credit, but a few days later you receive a letter from your telephone service provider that you will be disconnected unless you pay an overdue invoice. Which of the following actions do you think is the best one to take and which is the worst? Give your reasons.

(a) Allow the connection to be cut and have it reconnected after you have received the cash from the sale of the computer.
(b) Use your savings to pay the bill.
(c) Take out a loan to pay the bill.
(d) Ask the person who bought the computer to pay you immediately.

You may be able to think of other courses of action, but all the alternatives have advantages and disadvantages. If the connection is disconnected, it is likely to prevent you from carrying out your business activities. Although using your savings remedies the situation, you will lose any interest your investment might be earning. Borrowing money would also prevent the connection being cut, but you would incur interest charges and have to repay the loan. You may think that the best solution is to ask the buyer to pay you immediately, but he or she may not be able to do so. From this example you can appreciate that not only do we require a record of what has happened to cash in the past, but also information that will show us what is likely to happen to cash in the future.

2.5   Preparing a cash flow forecast

A financial statement that shows what is likely to happen to cash in the future is known as a *cash flow forecast* and is used for the following purposes:

- to plan capital requirements at the start-up stage, where it helps establish whether the proposed capital will be sufficient to finance the activities of the new business
- to plan a forthcoming accounting period in an existing business, where it helps anticipate the need for additional finance if the cash going out of the business is expected to exceed the cash in the business (a *cash deficit*) and the investment of cash if the cash in the business is expected to exceed the cash going out (a *cash surplus*).

A cash flow forecast shows the predicted movement of cash over a specified accounting period (usually one year, but it could be 6 months or a quarter). It is divided into months, with a total column at the end to provide a summary for the period. It predicts as accurately as possible the amount of cash that is expected to come in and go out of the business, and when these movements are expected to take place. The expected timings of the cash transactions might be monthly, quarterly or annually. We will use an example to examine this in more detail.

Sarah Wick is planning to set up a company selling candles in January 2012. She has £10,000 capital to invest in the business, which she is going to register as Candlewick Ltd. She will buy candles from a local supplier and sell them via the Internet. She will work from a small unit on an industrial estate near her home. She plans to purchase the candles for £15 per box and sell them at £20 per box. Her supplier will allow her one month's credit. Sales revenue from a market stall will represent 25% of total sales revenue and these customers will pay cash. The remaining 75% of sales revenue will come from the mail order part of the business, where customers will be given 2 months' credit.

The following table shows the number of boxes of candles Sarah expects the business to purchase at £15 each during the first 6 months of trading. It also shows the amount of cash she expects to pay each month, taking into account that her supplier allows one month's credit.

	January	February	March	April	May	June	Total
Quantity	400	400	500	560	600	600	3,060
Cost of purchases	£0	£6,000	£6,000	£7,500	£8,400	£9,000	£36,900

Having looked at the expected purchases, we can now look at the sales figures Sarah hopes Candlewick Ltd will achieve. The next table shows the number of candles

Sarah expects the business to sell at £20 each during the first 6 months of trading. It also shows the anticipated amount of cash received each month, taking into account that 25% of customers will pay cash and the remaining 75% will be given 2 months' credit.

	January	February	March	April	May	June	Total
Quantity	400	400	500	560	600	600	3,060
Revenue (cash sales)	£2,000	£2,000	£2,500	£2,800	£3,000	£3,000	£15,300
Revenue (credit sales)	£0	£0	£6,000	£6,000	£7,500	£8,400	£27,900

The movements of cash are given specific names and it is important to use them correctly to avoid confusing them with other terms you will learn in connection with other financial statements that we will be looking at in Part II:

- *Cash inflows* are cash transactions that bring money into the business. They are described as *positive cash flow*. They include capital, loans, revenue and interest received. The forecast cash inflows for Candlewick Ltd are the capital Sarah plans to invest and the expected revenue.
- *Cash outflows* are cash transactions that take money out of the business. They are described as *negative cash flow*. They include purchases of inventory and overheads such as wages, rent, rates, electricity, telephone, insurance, interest payable, and cash payments made in connection with loans, HP and leasing agreements. At this stage we know that the forecast cash outflows for Candlewick Ltd are what Sarah expects to pay for purchasing candles.
- *Net cash flow* is the difference between the cash inflows and the cash outflows. If the net cash flow is a *cash deficit*, it is shown in brackets.
- The *cumulative cash brought forward (b/f)* refers to the cash surplus or deficit at the start of the month (the first day of the month). It is the cash position that has been brought forward from the last day of the previous month. In the first month of a new business there is no cash to bring forward so this is always zero.
- The *cumulative cash carried forward (c/f)* refers to the cash surplus or deficit at the end of the month. It consists of the cumulative cash brought forward from the previous month plus the net cash flow that has taken place during the month. It shows the *cash position* at the end of the month, which is carried forward to become the *cumulative cash brought forward* at the start of the next month.

Activity

The following cash flow forecast has been partially completed using the predicted figures for purchases and revenue that we calculated above. Calculate the subtotals for cash inflows and outflows and use them to work out the expected net cash flow each month and the cumulative cash position at the start and end of each month.

Candlewick Ltd Draft cash flow forecast for January–June 2012	January £	February £	March £	April £	May £	June £	Total £
Cash inflows							
Capital	10,000	0	0	0	0	0	10,000
Revenue (cash sales)	2,000	2,000	2,500	2,800	3,000	3,000	15,300
Revenue (credit sales)	0	0	6,000	6,000	7,500	8,400	27,900
Cash outflows							
Purchases	0	6,000	6,000	7,500	8,400	9,000	36,900
Net cash flow							
Cumulative cash b/f							
Cumulative cash c/f							

Your forecast should look like this.

Candlewick Ltd Draft cash flow forecast for January–June 2012	January £	February £	March £	April £	May £	June £	Total £
Cash inflows							
Capital	10,000	0	0	0	0	0	10,000
Revenue (cash sales)	2,000	2,000	2,500	2,800	3,000	3,000	15,300
Revenue (credit sales)	0	0	6,000	6,000	7,500	8,400	27,900
	12,000	2,000	8,500	8,800	10,500	11,400	53,200
Cash outflows							
Purchases	0	6,000	6,000	7,500	8,400	9,000	36,900
	0	6,000	6,000	7,500	8,400	9,000	36,900
Net cash flow	12,000	(4,000)	2,500	1,300	2,100	2,400	16,300
Cumulative cash b/f	0	12,000	8,000	10,500	11,800	13,900	0
Cumulative cash c/f	12,000	8,000	10,500	11,800	13,900	16,300	16,300

You may find the following points helpful:

- The 'Total' column shows the cash receipts and cash payments for the entire 6 months. If we deduct the expected payments for the 6 months, which total £36,900, from the expected receipts, which total £53,200, you can see that there is a forecast cash surplus of £16,300.
- The figures shown in brackets in the cash flow forecast represent cash deficits.
- In a continuing business, the Total column should also show any cumulative cash b/f at the beginning of the accounting period (in a new business, such as this, it is nil).
- The cumulative cash c/f in the total column should agree with the equivalent cumulative cash c/f at the end of the last month of the accounting period. This acts as a crosscheck on the accuracy of the calculation of the cash position.

Key definitions

- Cash inflows are cash transactions that bring money into the business.
- Cash outflows are cash transactions that take money out of the business.
- A cash surplus describes the cash position at the end of the accounting period when the accumulated cash in the business exceeds the cash outflows.
- A cash deficit describes the cash position at the end of the accounting period when the cash outflows exceed the accumulated cash in the business.
- Cumulative cash brought forward (b/f) is the cash surplus or deficit at the start of the accounting period that has been brought forward from the previous period.
- Cumulative cash carried forward (c/f) is the cash surplus or deficit at the end of the accounting period that is carried forward to the next period.

It may have occurred to you that the purchase of candles is not the only cost the business will incur. This is the reason why the heading refers to the forecast as a draft forecast. Accountants use the term 'purchases' to mean the purchase of goods that will be sold as part of the trading cycle. Other costs incurred are given specific names. The other costs Candlewick Ltd is expected to incur are as follows:

- Office and other equipment will be bought on 1 January, but the cost of £13,000 will not have to be paid for until February, as Sarah will make use of the one month's interest-free credit period on the business credit card.
- Rent will be £150 per month, payable by the end of each month.
- Advertising will be £250 per month, payable one month in arrears.
- Telephone and Internet expenses will be £450 per quarter, payable at the end of each quarter.
- Printing, postage and stationery, which include packaging, are estimated at £600 per month apart from January and will be payable in cash.

We now have all the information we need to complete the cash flow forecast for Candlewick Ltd.

Most accountants adopt the layout we have illustrated on the top of page 45 when preparing a cash flow forecast, but you may come across other variations. Do not let this confuse you because the principles are exactly the same. The main points to remember are:

- The heading should state the name of the business and the accounting period to which the forecast refers.
- The columns should be labelled with the months to which they relate and the currency. You should include a total column at the end to provide summary figures for the whole period.
- The cash inflows are itemized separately under that heading and subtotalled.
- Next, the cash outflows are itemized separately under that heading and subtotalled.
- The subtotal for the cash outflows are deducted from the subtotal for the cash inflows to give the net cash flow. If this represents a predicted cash deficit (a negative figure), it is shown in brackets.

Candlewick Ltd
For January–June 2012

	January	February	March	April	May	June	Total
	£	£	£	£	£	£	£
Cash inflows							
Capital	10,000	0	0	0	0	0	10,000
Revenue (cash sales)	2,000	2,000	2,500	2,800	3,000	3,000	15,300
Revenue (credit sales)	0	0	6,000	6,000	7,500	8,400	27,900
	12,000	2,000	8,500	8,800	10,500	11,400	53,200
Cash outflows							
Purchases	0	6,000	6,000	7,500	8,400	9,000	36,900
Equipment	0	13,000	0	0	0	0	13,000
Rent	150	150	150	150	150	150	900
Advertising	0	250	250	250	250	250	1,250
Telephone and Internet	0	0	450	0	0	450	900
Printing, postage and stationery	0	600	600	600	600	600	3,000
	150	20,000	7,450	8,500	9,400	10,450	55,950
Net cash flow	11,850	(18,000)	1,050	300	1,100	950	(2,750)
Cumulative cash b/f	0	11,850	(6,150)	(5,100)	(4,800)	(3,700)	0
Cumulative cash c/f	11,850	(6,150)	(5,100)	(4,800)	(3,700)	(2,750)	(2,750)

Figure 2.6   Cash flow forecast formulae

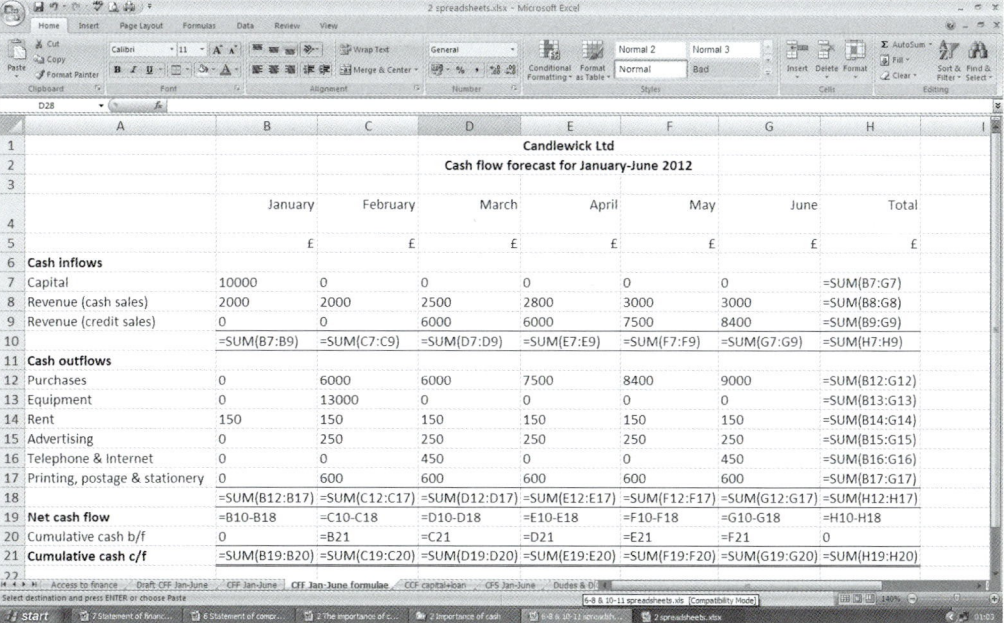

- The next row shows the cumulative cash brought forward (b/f) at the start of each period.
- The final row calculates the cumulative cash carried forward (c/f) at the end of each period. This is the 'bottom line' that shows whether a cash deficit (shown in brackets) or a cash surplus is predicted at the end of each month. The last figure in this row shows the predicted cash deficit or surplus at the end of the whole period and should be the same as the cumulative cash c/f at the end of the last month of the period.

Once you have learned the layout for a cash flow forecast, you should be able to construct one manually (with the aid of a calculator or using mental arithmetic) or using a spreadsheet. The only difference is that negative figures are entered with a minus sign rather than in brackets and formulae are entered to perform the arithmetic. We used Excel to prepare the forecast for Candlewick Ltd and Figure 2.6 shows you the formulae we used. To reveal the formulae in an Excel Workbook (a file with the suffix .xlsx), click on Formulas in the main menu, then select Show Formulas in the Formula Auditing tab. Deselect Show Formulas when you want to return to data view.

2.6 Planning capital requirements

The first step for anyone thinking of starting a new business is to consider how much finance is needed and the source(s) of that finance – in other words, to plan the capital requirements of setting up the enterprise. We already know that Sarah is planning to invest £10,000 of her own money in Candlewick Ltd when it starts on 1 January, but the cash flow forecast shows that by the end of February this will turn into a cash deficit as the cumulative cash position is negative. Based on these predictions, Sarah would go out of business by February and it is clear that she must make some plans to avoid this before starting the business.

Activity

Sarah has decided she needs to look for external finance to ensure the company is solvent for the first 6 months. How much cash does the business need to borrow to ensure there is no cash deficit in any month?

(a) £18,000
(b) £6,150
(c) £5,100
(d) £4,800
(e) £3,700

The correct answer is that Sarah needs £6,150 to give her sufficient cash to start the business and ensure that it does not have a deficit during the first 6 months. Her main choices are:

- to obtain a bank overdraft or loan
- to allow only one month's credit to the mail order customers
- to see if her supplier will allow 2 or 3 months' credit
- to lease some of the equipment or buy it on HP
- to control the cash expected to go out on telephone and Internet, printing, postage and stationery
- to look for a cheaper unit to rent
- a combination of these solutions.

After discussing her cash flow forecast with the bank lending officer, Sarah takes out a bank loan for £6,500 over two years and arranges a £2,500 overdraft facility for short-term cash deficits. The loan has a fixed rate of interest of 7.4%, which works out at £40 per month. Having made these arrangements, Sarah prepares the following revised cash flow forecast.

Candlewick Ltd Revised cash flow forecast for January–June 2012							
	January	February	March	April	May	June	Total
	£	£	£	£	£	£	£
Cash inflows							
Capital	10,000	0	0	0	0	0	10,000
Loan	6,500	0	0	0	0	0	6,500
Revenue (cash sales)	2,000	2,000	2,500	2,800	3,000	3,000	15,300
Revenue (credit sales)	0	0	6,000	6,000	7,500	8,400	27,900
	18,500	2,000	8,500	8,800	10,500	11,400	59,700
Cash outflows							
Purchases	0	6,000	6,000	7,500	8,400	9,000	36,900
Equipment	0	13,000	0	0	0	0	13,000
Rent	150	150	150	150	150	150	900
Advertising	0	250	250	250	250	250	1,250
Telephone and Internet	0	0	450	0	0	450	900
Printing, postage and stationery	0	60	60	60	60	60	300
Interest on loan	40	40	40	40	40	40	240
	190	20,040	7,490	8,540	9,440	10,490	56,190
Net cash flow	18,310	(18,040)	1,010	260	1,060	910	3,510
Cumulative cash b/f	0	18,310	270	1,280	1,540	2,600	0
Cumulative cash c/f	18,310	270	1,280	1,540	2,600	3,510	3,510

It is difficult to make general rules about interpreting a cash flow forecast, because it depends on the particular business. The checklist in Figure 2.7 includes questions you need to consider.

Figure 2.7 Checklist for interpreting cash flow information

- Is all the cash due to the business being collected as early as possible? Although it may be necessary to give credit to customers, the credit period should not be so long as to result in cash flow problems for the business. Alternatively, can invoice finance be arranged?
- Are all payments being made by the due date and not before? To pay sooner than necessary represents poor cash management, but to pay too late runs the risk of not being allowed credit in future and/or being sued for non-payment.
- Can credit agreements be arranged with suppliers who are being paid immediately, or can longer credit periods be agreed that will further delay payments?
- Can hire purchase or leasing be arranged to spread the cost of acquiring large items, such as equipment and vehicles?
- Is there sufficient cash to ensure that the business does not become insolvent?
- Have overdraft facilities been arranged to cover relatively small amounts of cash deficit?
- Has a decision been made to invest any cash surplus where it will receive interest?

2.7   Preparing a cash flow statement for management

A simple *cash flow statement* for management shows the actual movements of cash. The financial information provided can be used to help make decisions about whether to revise planned activities and this helps make the cash flow forecast more realistic. Having realistic plans increases the chance that the business will be successful in meeting its economic objectives, whether the business is pursuing profit maximization or satisficing strategies. Since events seldom turn out exactly as predicted, it is important to establish control of the cash on a regular basis by comparing the actual movements of cash against the predicted movements. If things are not turning out as planned, corrective action can then be taken. Without this comparison of the actual results with the plan, there will be no control.

The following simple cash flow statement on the top of page 49 shows the actual cash flows for Candlewick Ltd for the first 6 months. As this is being prepared for management, there are no rules about how it should be constructed. The following layout is one used by accountants and reflects the layout for the cash flow forecast, but note that the heading reflects the fact that it is now a statement of the (actual) cash flows rather than a forecast.

As you can see, things have not turned out entirely as planned: the revenue from cash sales is slightly higher than planned, but revenue from credit sales is lower than anticipated. In addition, the rent is much higher because Sarah had underestimated the cost, and it looks as though she is paying the company's advertising expenses in the month in which they are incurred, rather than taking the one month's credit allowed.

	January £	February £	March £	April £	May £	June £	Total £
Candlewick Ltd							
Cash flow statement for January–June 2012							
Cash inflows							
Capital	10,000	0	0	0	0	0	10,000
Loan	6,500	0	0	0	0	0	6,500
Revenue (cash sales)	1,600	1,800	2,000	3,500	4,100	4,500	17,500
Revenue (credit sales)	0	0	4,800	5,400	6,000	7,800	24,000
	18,100	1,800	6,800	8,900	10,100	12,300	58,000
Cash outflows							
Purchases	0	6,000	6,000	7,500	8,400	9,000	36,900
Equipment	0	13,000	0	0	0	0	13,000
Rent	500	500	500	500	500	500	3,000
Advertising	50	50	50	50	50	50	300
Telephone and Internet	0	0	450	0	0	450	1,060
Printing, postage and stationery	0	100	100	100	100	100	500
Interest on loan	40	40	40	40	40	40	240
Salaries	0	500	500	500	500	660	2,500
	590	20,190	7,640	8,690	9,590	10,800	57,500
Net cash flow	17,510	(18,390)	(840)	210	510	1.500	500
Cumulative cash b/f	0	17,510	(880)	(1,720)	(1,510)	(1,000)	0
Cumulative cash c/f	17,510	(880)	(1,720)	(1,510)	(1,000)	500	500

However, the advertising expenses are much lower than expected. You may also have noticed that the business has only paid £100 per month for printing, postage and stationery since February instead of the predicted figure of £600, as these expenses were lower than predicted. In addition, Sarah took on a part-time employee in February to help with packing and dispatching the orders and this employee receives a salary of £500 per month, rising to £660 in June.[1] Despite introducing £10,000 capital and taking out a loan for £6,500, you can see that the cumulative cash position at the end of February shows a cash deficit of £880 and by the end of March it has gone up to £1,720. This reduces over the next 3 months and by the end of June there is a cash surplus of £500. Fortunately, the business has not gone into liquidation because the cash deficits between February and May were covered by the overdraft Sarah arranged with the bank.

Activity

Sarah must revise her plans for the next 6 months. Suggest what actions she might take.

You may think that Sarah would be in a better position if she compared her actual cash flow with her plan on a monthly basis, instead of waiting for 6 months. Certainly,

---

1. Sarah will wait until the end of the financial year before deciding whether to take any money from the business. If the business is sufficiently profitable, she will pay herself cash; this is known as a *dividend*.

control is improved with frequency and most businesses carry out this sort of exercise every month. Given the position Sarah is now in, you should have suggested that:

- she introduces more capital than planned
- she revises her planned sales figures for the next 6 months to reflect the level of sales she achieved in the first 6 months and any variations she expects during the forthcoming festive season
- she revises the number of candles she will purchase to reduce the amount of inventory
- she takes up the offer of one month's credit on advertising
- she revises the planned spending on printing, postage and stationery to reflect the mail order sales more closely
- she tries to negotiate more favourable terms from the suppliers of candles and packaging
- she looks for a cheaper unit to rent.

If Sarah revises the cash flow forecast, she may decide it is not worthwhile continuing the business. We have not yet allowed for the interest that must be paid on the overdraft or the increase in drawings she will need to provide a living. Cash flow statements sometimes show unpleasant information, but are essential to the effective running of a business.

Cash flow information is useful in a number of ways. You have seen that planned cash flow information can be used to prepare what is called a *cash flow forecast* that predicts the monthly cash flows for the first accounting period (usually one year) for a new business. Exactly the same construction is used by existing businesses for subsequent periods, but it is usually called a *cash flow budget*. A cash flow budget is prepared in advance of the accounting period and predicts the cash flows for the following year as accurately as possible. Once that year starts, the actual figures in the *cash flow statement* are compared with the budgeted figures to check that the business is meeting its targets. If targets are not being met, the owner or manager can take whatever action is necessary to make sure the business meets its economic objectives. We will be looking at budgets in Chapter 16.

Preparing cash flow forecasts and statements and making revisions to plans can be very tedious if done by hand. The task is made considerably easier and more efficient if you use a spreadsheet. Nevertheless, it is important to remember that even if it is prepared using a spreadsheet, a cash flow forecast is only as good as the quality of the predicted figures it contains.

Activity

Using your own bank statement, prepare a cash flow forecast for yourself for the next 6 months using a spreadsheet. When you have completed your forecast, reflect on the decisions you need to make using the checklist given in section 2.6 as a guide.

2.8 Conclusions

In this chapter we have considered the importance of cash and the need all businesses have for finance. We have examined the theory of a finance gap for small and medium-sized entities, explored some of the evidence and classified the potential sources of finance. We have also looked at the need for financial information in a business and introduced you to two financial statements. The first is the cash flow forecast (or budget), which uses estimated figures to predict the cash position at the end of a future accounting period; and the second is the cash flow statement, which uses actual figures to show the actual cash position at the end of an accounting period. Cash flow information aids planning, control and decision making. In particular, it helps owners and managers to:

- ensure that the business has sufficient cash to carry out planned activities
- anticipate the need for additional finance, such as a bank overdraft or loan
- plan the investment of any cash surplus
- control cash flows by comparing actual figures against the plan or budget
- take decisions to modify activities to ensure the business remains solvent.

Practice questions

1 Define finance and explain why students studying business or management should learn about the management of money.

2 Explain the theory of the finance gap.

3 Describe the potential sources of long-term finance available to a sole proprietorship or traditional partnership.

4 Francesca Diva is planning to start a shoe shop called Dudes & Divas Ltd on 1 July 2012 with £25,000 she has inherited. She is going to be a sole proprietor and plans to open a small shop in the town centre. She has found suitable premises and has arranged for professional shop fitters to refurbish them. The new fixtures and fittings will cost £30,000, but will not have to be paid for until September. In addition, she estimates the following transactions will take place during the first 3 months of trading:

Revenue (cash sales)	£10,000 per month
Revenue (credit sales)	£2,000 per month (customers will have one month's credit)
Purchases	£5,000 per month (suppliers will give 2 months' credit)
Overheads	£5,000 per month
Salaries	£1,500 per month

Required

(a) Prepare a cash flow forecast for Dudes & Divas Ltd for the 3 months 1 July to 30 September 2012.

(b) Interpret the cash flow forecast you have prepared and comment on the cumulative cash position at 30 September 2012.

5 Phil Trigg is the owner of Trigg Electronics Ltd. He has negotiated with two manufacturers of electric circuit boards to carry out assembly work for them and anticipates assembling the following numbers of circuit boards for each manufacturer during 2012.

Sales volume	Jan	Feb	Mar	Apr	May	Jun	Jul	Aug	Sep	Oct	Nov	Dec
Customer A	120	130	130	150	140	140	160	160	170	140	140	120
Customer B	200	240	240	240	220	220	220	270	270	270	230	210

Customer A has agreed to pay £6.60 for each board assembled and Customer B will pay £6.50. Customer A will pay 2 months after the work has been done, but Customer B will pay one month after the work has been done. Phil anticipates the following expenses:

Rent and rates	£6,000 per annum, payable at the beginning of each quarter
Electricity	£120 per month, payable one month in arrears
Telephone and Internet	£50 per quarter, payable at the end of each quarter
Printing, postage and stationery	10% of sales revenue, payable the month after the cash for the sale is received
General expenses	£25 per month
Tools and equipment	£2,500 in January, £1,000 in February and £500 in March

Required

(a) Prepare a cash flow forecast for Trigg Electronics Ltd for 6 months, 1 January to 30 June 2012.
(b) Calculate the amount of capital Phil needs to invest in the business to prevent a cash deficit at any time during the 6 months.

References

Bolton, J. E. (1971) *Report of the Committee of Inquiry on Small Firms*, Cmnd. 4811. London: HMSO.

Cosh, A., Hughes, A, Bullock, A. and Milner, I. (2009) *SME Finance and Innovation in the Current Economic Crisis*. Cambridge: Centre for Business Research, University of Cambridge.

Deakins, D. (1996) *Entrepreneurs and Small Firms*. London: Butterworth.

Harrison, R. and Mason, C. (1995) The role of informal venture capital in financing the growing firm. In R. Buckland and E. W. Davis (eds), *Finance for Growing Enterprises*. London: Routledge.

HMT and BIS (2010) *Financing a Private Sector Recovery*, Cm 7923. London: HMSO.

Jarvis, R. (2012) Finance and the small firm. In S. Carter and D. Jones Evans (eds), *Enterprise and Small Business: Principles, Practice and Policy*, 3rd edition. Harlow: Pearson Education.

Law, J. (ed.) (2010) *Dictionary of Accounting*, 4th edition. Oxford: Oxford University Press.

LSE (2011) *Market Statistics*. London Stock Exchange. Available from: http://www.londonstockexchange.com/statistics/markets/markets.htm (accessed 20 November 2011).

UEAPME (2011) SMEs' access to finance. Available from: http://www.ueapme.com/spip.php?rubrique46 (accessed 20 November 2011).

Wilson Committee (1979) *The Financing of Small Firms: Interim Report of the Committee to Review the Functioning of the Financial Institutions*, Cmnd 7503. London: HMSO.

Wiltbank, R. E. (2009) *Siding with the Angels*. BBA NESTA Research Report, May. Available from: http://www.nesta.org.uk/publications/reports/assets/features/siding_with_the_angels (accessed 20 November 2011).

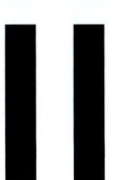

Financial accounting

3 The accounting system

Learning objectives

When you have studied this chapter, you should be able to:

- explain the accounting equation
- describe and apply the principles of double-entry bookkeeping
- balance the ledger accounts and prepare a trial balance
- explain the limitations of a trial balance.

3.1 Introduction

In the preceding chapters we discussed the importance of financial information, together with the main users and uses. Although it is not necessary for students who are not specializing in accounting to learn about bookkeeping, it is useful to provide some understanding, since all businesses are required to keep accounting records of all the economic transactions and events.

In order to generate financial information, a business needs to establish an *accounting system*. The nature of the system depends on the type of business and the size of the organization, but there are common features since procedures must be established to allow all financial transactions to be recorded. These procedures involve raising source documents, such as invoices, purchase orders and credit notes, so that those responsible in the business are made aware that a transaction has taken place and the details of the transaction can be recorded. The most commonly used accounting system is known as *double-entry bookkeeping*. In this chapter we describe a simple double-entry bookkeeping system and explain how the records are used to construct a trial balance.

3.2 Main sources of data

Some business transactions are for immediate cash, but many business transactions are credit transactions. Therefore, owners and managers need a system for recording both types of transaction and documents that give details of the transactions made. Such documents are known as *source documents* and are the foundation on which the financial records of the business are built. The main documents that provide the data recorded in the accounting system can be summarized as follows:

- sales orders, delivery notes, invoices paid by customers and credit notes issued for goods returned by customers
- purchase orders, invoices received from suppliers and credit notes received for goods returned to suppliers
- payroll information, inventory records, banking records and other documents.

We will now look at the process of raising source documents in more detail. In many businesses, goods are purchased on credit and a number of external and internal documents are produced to record the activities. First, the business purchasing the goods issues a *purchase order* and sends it to the supplier. This document specifies the quantity, type and price of the goods ordered. When the purchaser receives the goods, they are examined to ensure that they match the items on the purchase order and a *goods received note* is raised. Copies of the goods received note are sent to the accounts department, the purchase department and the stores department. When the stores department receives the goods, the details are recorded on a *stores record card* so that the manager of the stores has a record of the goods available. Items are released by the stores department only on receipt of a properly authorized *stores requisition*, the fourth document in this chain. When the items are issued, the *stores record card* is adjusted to show the decrease in inventory.

On receipt of the purchase order, the supplier sends the goods to the purchaser with an accompanying *delivery note*. The purchaser signs the delivery note and returns it to the supplier as proof of receipt. Next, the supplier issues an *invoice* showing the amount the purchaser will have to pay. If the purchaser is dissatisfied with any of the goods and returns them, the supplier issues a *credit note*. This shows the value of the goods returned, which the purchaser will not have to pay. If the supplier receives many orders from the same purchaser, rather than requiring payment of each invoice individually, the supplier may issue a monthly statement summarizing the invoices and credit notes during the month and showing the balance due.

In addition to recording transactions for goods, a business must record labour costs. In the manufacturing industry it was traditional to use *clock cards* to record the time spent at work by employees and *job cards* to record the amount of time spent on each job. The job cards were then reconciled with the clock cards. The wages office then prepared the *payroll* by calculating the wages from the time clock cards for the workers paid on a time basis and from the job cards if there was an incentive scheme. Today the information is likely to be recorded in a computerized information system.

In the service industry, *time sheets* may be used to record how much time has been spent on each job so that clients can be charged for the time spent on their work.

Activity

Design a flow diagram to illustrate the external and internal movement of source documents that are raised when a business purchases goods from a supplier on credit.

In constructing your diagram you will have experienced some of the difficulties in establishing and maintaining business information systems. It is necessary to ensure that each stage of the process is monitored, that the appropriate personnel are kept informed and that the records are correctly referenced and dated. The system needs to be designed so that if there is an error or a query, the appropriate source document can be traced and the problem resolved.

You are already family with the first stage in the process of accounting from the definition of accounting you learned in Chapter 1. Figure 3.1 provides an overview of the subsequent stages. In this chapter we will cover the second and third stages, and the remainder in the chapters that follow.

Figure 3.1 Overview of the accounting process

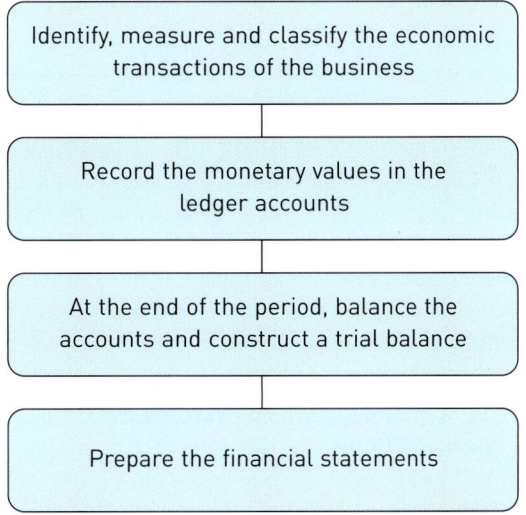

Identify, measure and classify the economic transactions of the business

Record the monetary values in the ledger accounts

At the end of the period, balance the accounts and construct a trial balance

Prepare the financial statements

3.3 Double-entry bookkeeping

Some small entities keep a simple cash-based accounting system, but many businesses record transactions using a system known as *double-entry bookkeeping*. A double-entry bookkeeping system is based on the principle that every financial transaction involves the simultaneous receiving and giving of value. Therefore, every transaction needs to be recorded at least twice in the accounting system. This reflects the dual nature of economic transactions and ensures that an arithmetical check is made on the accuracy of the records. It widely used because it is the most efficient and effective method for recording financial transactions in a way that allows financial statements to be prepared easily.

Key definition

Double-entry bookkeeping is a method of recording the transactions of a business in a set of accounts, such that every transaction has a dual aspect and therefore needs to be recorded in at least two accounts.

Source: Law (2010, p. 158).

The financial statements summarize the transactions that have taken place during any particular period of time. Large organizations carry out thousands of transactions every day and need sophisticated, tailor-made computerized accounting systems. Most small businesses use spreadsheets such as Excel or an accounting package such as SAGE. A few may still use a manual system, but whether the system is manual or computerized, it is normally based on the principles of double-entry bookkeeping and the bookkeeper will apply the relevant fundamental accounting principles described in Chapter 1 (Figure 3.2).

Figure 3.2   History of double-entry bookkeeping

'The first certain records of double-entry bookkeeping come from the early fourteenth century and relate to Italian merchant firms in Provence and in London, and to the city of Genoa. This system of double entry, which is still used in a similar manner throughout the western world, became known as the *Italian method* ... The Italian method was popularized by the first book to include a substantial treatise on it, which was published in Venice in 1494 by Luca Pacioli, a Franciscan friar who was a mathematics professor and good friend of the artist, Leonardo da Vinci. His influential book *Summa de arithmetica, geometria, proportioni e proportionalità* was copied in other countries and helped to spread double entry throughout Europe.'

Source: Nobes and Kellas (1990, pp. 10–11, 14–15).

In order to understand accounting and the principles of double-entry bookkeeping, you need to remember that the business is a separate entity from its owner(s) when it carries out transactions. Therefore, it can have dealings with the owner(s). All businesses need resources and these are known as *assets*. Assets are what the business owns, such as premises, machinery, vehicles, equipment, inventory (stock) and cash. *Liabilities* are what the business owes to others apart from the owners, such as money owed to lenders and suppliers. What remains once the liabilities are subtracted from the assets is known as *equity*. Equity represents the owners' interest in the business and can be divided into the capital invested in the business by the owner(s) plus retained earnings (profits left in the business to help it grow).

The relationship between the assets, liabilities and equity forms what is known as the *accounting equation*:

$$\textbf{Assets = Equity + Liabilities}$$

The accounting equation reflects the dual nature of business transactions by stating that the assets of the entity are always equal to the claims against them: the equity and other liabilities. The point about any equation is that it balances; in other words, the total of the values on each side of the equation are equal. The accounting equation lies at the heart of double-entry bookkeeping.

Activity

A business has capital of £20,000 and assets of £20,000. It then borrows £10,000 from the bank to finance the purchase of some new office equipment. How does this affect the accounting equation?

In this case the business has assets of £20,000 which will increase by £10,000 (the new equipment), making total assets of £30,000. At the same time it will increase its liabilities by £10,000 (the bank loan) whilst the equity, representing the capital of £20,000, remains unchanged. The accounting equation still balances as shown below:

Assets	=	Equity	+	Liabilities
£		£		£
20,000		20,000		10,000
10,000				
30,000		20,000		10,000

You need to remember that in double-entry bookkeeping, every economic transaction of the business is recorded twice to keep the accounting equation balanced. This provides an arithmetical check on the records, which enables the business to be controlled. If a manual system is kept, the bookkeeper records the business transactions in the *ledgers*, which are books of accounts (hence, the term *bookkeeping*). Accounts for each different type of transaction are kept on separate pages in the ledger. The bookkeeper records every transaction as a *debit* entry in an account that receives the value of the transaction and as a *credit* entry in an account that gives the value of the transaction. The following illustration of one page shows the layout.

Name of the account

Date	Details of *debit* entries	Amount £	Date	Details of *credit* entries	Amount £

As you can see, the page is divided into two, with three columns on each side. Debit entries are shown on the left-hand side of the account and credit entries on the right. On each side there is a column for the date, details of the transaction and the amount involved. Because of their layout, ledger accounts are often referred to as *T accounts*.

3.4 Recording transactions

3.4.1 Recording assets and liabilities

The double-entry bookkeeping system provides rules for recording each different type of transaction in the ledger accounts. The rules for recording transactions concerning assets and liabilities are recorded; therefore you need to learn formal definitions so you can be sure you are classifying them correctly.

Key definitions

- An asset is a resource controlled by the entity as a result of past events and from which future economic benefits are expected to flow to the entity.
- A liability is a present obligation of the entity resulting from past events, the settlement of which is expected to result in an outflow from the entity of resources embodying economic benefits.
- Equity is the residual interest in the assets of the entity after deducting all its liabilities.

Source: IASB (2010, para 4.25).

The rules for recording transactions concerning assets and liabilities are as follows:

- To show an increase in an asset account, debit the account.
- To show a decrease in an asset account, credit the account.
- To show an increase in a capital or liability account, credit the account.
- To show a decrease in a capital or liability account, debit the account.

To illustrate these rules we will use an example of a business that commenced on 1 January 2005. The owner of the business is Nick Mulch and he has invested £5,000 in the business, which he has called Mulch Garden Design Ltd. His girlfriend, Louise, has given the business a loan of £2,000. All the money is kept in the bank. To record these transactions, we need to open three accounts: a *capital account* for the money invested by the owner; a *loan account* for the loan; and a *bank account* to show the bank transactions. There are two transactions to record: the amount invested by Nick and the loan given by Louise. Each transaction will require a debit entry to be made to one account and a corresponding credit entry of the same amount in another account.

Capital account

		£			£
			1 January	Bank	5,000

Loan account

		£			£
			1 January	Bank	2,000

Bank account

		£			£
1 January	Capital	5,000			
1 January	Loan	2,000			

If you study these accounts, you can see that the rules for recording transactions have been stringently applied. The investment of £5,000 by the owner has been shown as a credit in the capital account. Because the assets of the business have increased by this amount, the corresponding debit entry is in the bank account. When Louise gave the £2,000 loan to the business, its liabilities increased, so the loan account was credited with this amount. The corresponding debit entry is in the bank account, since the loan means an increase in the assets of the business. As you can see, for each transaction you need to record the date, the name of the account where the corresponding entry is made and the amount. This allows you to trace it at a later date if you have any problems with the records.

We will now extend our example by showing the transactions entered into on 2 January 2005. Using the business chequebook, Nick pays £3,000 for the premises, £1,000 for machinery and £500 for office equipment. The bank account is already open, but we need to open three new asset accounts to record these transactions:

Bank account

		£			£
1 January	Capital	5,000	2 January	Premises	3,000
1 January	Loan	2,000	2 January	Machinery	1,000
			2 January	Equipment	500

Premises account

		£			£
2 January	Bank	3,000			

Machinery account

		£			£
2 January	Bank	1,000			

Office equipment account

		£			£
2 January	Bank	500			

These records reflect the transactions that have taken place. For example, the bank account is an asset account. When the business received the investment of £5,000 from

Nick and the loan from Louise, these amounts were debited to the bank account to show the increase in assets represented by the amount of money held at the bank. When the business paid for items such as the machinery, the bank account was credited. If you take the total of all the debit entries in the bank account and deduct the total of all the credit entries, the resulting figure is £2,500, which is the amount of money the business now has left at the bank.

Activity

Mulch Garden Design Ltd repays £1,500 of the loan to Louise on 3 January and on the same day returns £250 worth of faulty equipment to the supplier and receives a refund, which is paid into the bank. Make the necessary entries in the ledger accounts.

The updated accounts should look like this:

Bank account

		£			£
1 January	Capital	5,000	2 January	Premises	3,000
1 January	Loan	2,000	2 January	Machinery	1,000
3 January	Equipment	250	2 January	Equipment	500
			3 January	Loan	1,500

Loan account

		£			£
3 January	Bank	1,500	1 January	Bank	2,000

Office equipment account

		£			£
2 January	Bank	500	3 January	Bank	250

3.4.2   Recording revenue and expenses

A business also needs ledger accounts for recording *revenue* and *expenses*. Revenue is the income the business receives from its activities. In addition to sales revenue (the monetary value of the sale of goods or services to customers), the business may receive non-sales revenue, such as interest and dividends on investments or rent received from letting part of the business premises. Expenses are the monetary value of the costs and other expenditure incurred by the business in order to obtain its income. You need to learn the formal definitions for these terms.

Key definitions

- Income is increases in economic benefits during the accounting period in the form of inflows or enhancements of assets or decreases of liabilities that result in increases in equity, other than those relating to contributions from equity participants.

> ▪ **Expenses are decreases in economic benefits during the accounting period in the form of outflows or depletions of assets or incurrences of liabilities that result in decreases in equity, other than those relating to distributions to equity participants.**
>
> *Source*: IASB (2010, para 4.25).

The double-entry bookkeeping rules for recording transactions involving revenue and expenses are as follows:

- To show an increase in an expense account, debit the account.
- To show a decrease in an expense account, credit the account.
- To show an increase in a revenue account, credit the account.
- To show a decrease in a revenue account, debit the account.

As required in double-entry bookkeeping, every transaction will involve making a credit entry to one account and a debit entry to another account. We will start by explaining what is meant by an increase in an expense account and an increase in a revenue account. On 4 January Mulch Garden Design Ltd spends £200 on advertising in the form of printed leaflets and £20 on posting them to potential customers. Prior to this date the business has not incurred any expenses, so the monetary value was nil. Now, it has incurred some expenses and we need to show the increase in the appropriate accounts.

Bank account

		£			£
1 January	Capital	5,000	2 January	Premises	3,000
1 January	Loan	2,000	2 January	Machinery	1,000
3 January	Equipment	250	2 January	Equipment	500
			3 January	Loan	1,500
			4 January	Advertising	200
			4 January	Postage	20

Advertising account

		£			£
4 January	Bank	200			

Postage account

		£			£
4 January	Bank	20			

As the business has paid for the advertising leaflets and postage, its cash assets at the bank must have decreased by the amount of these expenses. Therefore, these two transactions resulted in debit entries to the expense accounts and both were credited to the bank account.

You should not have had too much difficulty with this activity. The cleaning expenses were a pair of straightforward entries. The receipt of rent may have caused you to think because we have not illustrated any similar transactions. However, as long as you remembered the rule that you show an increase in revenues by crediting the revenue account (in this case, rent received), the corresponding entry had to be to debit the bank account to show an increase in cash assets of £350. The updated accounts should look like this:

Bank account

		£			£
1 January	Capital	5,000	2 January	Premises	3,000
1 January	Loan	2,000	2 January	Machinery	1,000
3 January	Equipment	250	2 January	Equipment	500
6 January	Rent received	350	3 January	Loan	1,500
			4 January	Advertising	200
			4 January	Postage	20
			5 January	Cleaning	50

Cleaning account

		£			£
5 January	Bank	50			

Rent received account

		£			£
			6 January	Bank	350

3.4.3 Recording purchases, sales and inventory

In a trading business, it is not much use advertising goods for sale unless the business has purchased a stock of goods to sell, and it is necessary to open a *purchases* account, where purchases of stock are recorded as a debit entry. However, when the business sells the goods they are not shown as a credit entry in the purchases account for two reasons. First, they will not be sold at the price for which they were purchased, as the business adds a mark-up in order to make a profit and therefore we do not want to lose this information. The second reason is that at the end of an accounting period it is likely that there will be some *inventory* (unsold goods). This inventory requires special treatment, which we shall be describing at the end of this section.

Instead of crediting sales to the purchases account, a sales account is opened. If the goods are sold to customers for cash, the sale is shown as a credit in the sales account and the corresponding entry is a debit in the bank account. The latter entry reflects the increase in cash assets held at the bank.

We need to look at a new example to show how this is done. Katey Burton opens a boutique called Kool Kate Ltd on 1 July by investing £10,000 in the business. On that day the business buys equipment costing £1,000, purchases of inventory costing £4,000 and pays £500 in advertising expenses. On 2 July she makes sales amounting to £2,800 and buys a second-hand car for business use for £4,000. On 3 July she makes sales totalling of £3,500 and purchases further inventory for £2,000. The entries in the accounts are shown below.

Capital account

		£			£
			1 July	Bank	10,000

Bank account

		£			£
1 July	Capital	10,000	1 July	Equipment	1,000
2 July	Sales	2,800	1 July	Purchases	4,000
3 July	Sales	3,500	1 July	Advertising	500
			2 July	Vehicles	4,000
			3 July	Purchases	2,000

Equipment account

		£			£
1 July	Bank	1,000			

Advertising account

		£			£
1 July	Bank	500			

Purchases account

		£			£
1 July	Bank	4,000			
3 July	Bank	2,000			

Sales account

		£			£
			2 July	Bank	2,800
			3 July	Bank	3,500

Vehicles account

		£			£
2 July	Bank	4,000			

In this example we have referred to the goods that the business is buying and selling as *inventory*. However, we will not use an inventory account until the end of the accounting period, as we will explain in a moment. Instead, the purchases and sales of goods have been recorded in separate accounts, named the *purchases account* and the *sales account*, respectively. Accountants use the term *purchases* to refer only to the purchase of goods for resale in a trading business or to the purchase of materials used to produce goods for sale in a manufacturing business. Do not confuse this with the acquisition of other assets, such as vehicles and equipment, which are not intended for resale but will stay in the business in the long term to help generate revenue.

There is one final aspect of the purchase and sale of goods that we need to consider. Sometimes a business purchases goods, but has returned some of them to the supplier because they are faulty, or for other reasons. Alternatively, a customer sometimes returns goods to the business. The first transaction requires a *returns outward account* (also known as a *purchases returns account*) to be opened. The second transaction requires a *returns inward account* (also known as a *sales returns account*) to be opened.

The following example illustrates the returns outward account. On 1 July Kool Kate Ltd purchases goods from a supplier, but later a £200 suit was found to be faulty. It was returned to the supplier on 12 July and a refund of £200 was received the same day. These transactions are recorded as follows:

Bank account

		£			£
1 July	Capital	10,000	1 July	Equipment	1,000
2 July	Sales	2,800	1 July	Purchases	4,000
3 July	Sales	3,500	1 July	Advertising	500
12 July	Returns outward	200	2 July	Vehicles	4,000
			3 July	Purchases	2,000

Returns outward account

		£			£
			12 July	Bank	200

As you can see, the bank account has been debited to show the increase in cash assets due to the cash refund by the supplier, but rather than crediting the purchases account to record the goods which were returned, a returns outward account has been opened and this provides an accurate record of what has happened. This information will be used when the profit and loss account is drawn up later.

Activity

The same principles are applied if one of the customers returns goods. Show how the transactions would be recorded in the ledger accounts if a customer returns £500 worth of goods to Kool Kate Ltd on 14 July and is given a refund the same day.

The transaction would be recorded as follows:

Bank account

		£			£
1 July	Capital	10,000	1 July	Equipment	1,000
2 July	Sales	2,800	1 July	Purchases	4,000
3 July	Sales	3,500	1 July	Advertising	500
12 July	Returns outward	200	2 July	Vehicles	4,000
			3 July	Purchases	2,000
			14 July	Returns inward	500

Returns inward account

		£			£
14 July	Bank	500			

3.4.4 Credit transactions

All the receipts and payments in the examples we have used so far have been for cash. However, many economic transactions are *credit transactions* and the receipt or payment of cash does not take place until a later date. This requires accounts to be opened for *trade receivables* to record the amounts owed by customers who have bought goods or services on credit and who owe the business money. Accounts also need to be opened for *trade payables* to record the amounts due to be paid to suppliers from whom the business has bought goods or services on credit and to whom the business owes money. Trade receivables are classified as assets of the business and trade payables are classified as liabilities. Therefore, the rules of double-entry book-keeping for making entries in asset and liability accounts apply to trade receivables and trade payables respectively.

First we will consider an example where a customer has been sold goods on credit. Suppose the clothes sold by Kool Kate Ltd for £2,800 on 2 July were credit sales to a customer called Pippa Merton. The entry in the sales account will still be a credit, but instead of debiting the bank account to show an increase in cash assets, we need to open an account for Pippa Merton and debit that account to show an increase in the trade receivables asset. The entries in the accounts are as follows:

Sales account

		£			£
			2 July	Pippa Merton	2,800

Pippa Merton account (trade receivables)

		£			£
2 July	Sales	2,800			

Because Pippa Merton is a trade receivable account, we have followed the rules for all asset accounts. Before 2 July, Pippa owed the business nothing, but after the sales transaction on that date, she owed Kool Kate Ltd £2,800. The increase in trade receivables is shown by debiting the Pippa Merton account. The trade receivables account has been opened in Pippa Merton's name so that a record can be kept of who owes money to Kool Kate Ltd.

Activity

On 20 July Pippa Merton pays £750 of the money she owed to Kool Kate Ltd. Show how this transaction will be recorded in the accounts.

The accounts will be amended as follows:

Bank account

		£			£
1 July	Capital	10,000	1 July	Equipment	1,000
3 July	Sales	3,500	1 July	Purchases	4,000
12 July	Returns outward	200	1 July	Advertising	500
20 July	Pippa Merton	750	2 July	Vehicles	4,000
			3 July	Purchases	2,000
			14 July	Returns inward	500

Pippa Merton account (trade receivables)

		£			£
2 July	Sales	2,800	20 July	Bank	750

As you can see, cash assets have increased by £750 and the asset of trade receivables have decreased by the same amount. Note that in the bank account we have deleted the entry on 2 July for sales of £2,800 because Pippa Merton did not pay cash but took the goods on credit. Therefore, the debit entry is to the Pippa Merton account and the sales account remains unchanged.

Next we consider a case where the business has not paid cash but has obtained goods or services on credit. In such a case the business has acquired a liability and you will need to use the double-entry rules for increasing and decreasing liability accounts. On 26 July Kool Kate Ltd purchases goods for £1,500 on credit from a supplier, Patel & Co. On 28 July Kool Kate Ltd pays the amount in full. The transactions are recorded as follows:

Purchases account

		£			£
1 July	Bank	4,000			
3 July	Bank	2,000			
26 July	Patel & Co	1,500			

Patel & Co account (trade payables)

		£			£
28 July	Bank	1,500	26 July	Purchases	1,500

Bank account

		£			£
1 July	Capital	10,000	1 July	Equipment	1,000
3 July	Sales	3,500	1 July	Purchases	4,000
12 July	Returns outward	200	1 July	Advertising expenses	500
20 July	Pippa Merton	750	2 July	Vehicles	4,000
			3 July	Purchases	2,000
			14 July	Returns inward	500
			28 July	Patel & Co	1,500

While working through the activities in this chapter, you may have noticed how easy it is to make a mistake and enter a transaction on the wrong side of an account. Although you may have found the process somewhat tedious, the activities should help you understand the principles of double-entry bookkeeping, which can be summarized as follows:

- A transaction that represents an increase in purchases, expenses or assets is recorded as a debit entry on the left-hand side of the ledger account.
- A transaction that represents an increase in revenue, liabilities or sales is recorded as a credit entry on the right-hand side of the ledger account.

The pearls of wisdom shown in Figure 3.3 have been passed on by students across the decades. They will help you remember the rules of double-entry bookkeeping.

Figure 3.3   Pearls of wisdom

This mnemonic is set out as a T account and reminds you that an increase in **P**urchases, **E**xpenses or **A**ssets is a **debit** entry shown on the left-hand, whilst an increase in Revenue, Liabilities or Sales is a **credit** entry shown on the right-hand side.

P E A | R L S

3.5   Preparing a trial balance

3.5.1   Balancing the accounts

At the end of the accounting period the ledger accounts are balanced and the balances are used to construct a trial balance, which lists the debit balances in one column and the credit balances in the other. The rules for balancing the ledger accounts are very straightforward:

1. If the total amounts on each side of the account are equal, they are double underlined to close the account. This means that there is no outstanding balance on the account at the end of the accounting period. Kool Kate Ltd's trade payables account for Patel & Co account is an example of this.

Patel & Co account

		£			£
28 July	Bank	1,500	26 July	Purchases	1,500

2. If the account contains only one entry, insert the figure required to make the account balance on the opposite side and label it *carried forward* (or the abbreviation c/f). Insert the same balancing figure on the same side as the original entry to start the next period, labelling it *brought forward* (or the abbreviation b/f). Kool Kate Ltd's vehicle account provides an example of this. We are still complying with the rules of double-entry bookkeeping since, as you can see, for every debit entry there is a corresponding credit entry. Therefore, to balance the account, we have credited the account with a closing balance of £4,000 and debited the account an opening balance of the same amount.

Vehicle account

		£			£
2 July	Bank	4,000	31 July	Balance c/f	4,000
1 August	Balance b/f	4,000			

3. If the account contains a number of entries, add up both sides. If both sides are the same, insert the totals and double underline them. This means that there is no outstanding balance on the account. An extension of Kool Kate Ltd's trade receivable account for Pippa Merton provides an example of this.

Pippa Merton account

		£			£
2 July	Sales	2,800	20 July	Bank	750
5 July	Sales	200	28 July	Bank	2,550
12 July	Sales	300			
		3,300			3,300

4. If both sides are not the same when you add them up, use the larger figure as the total for both sides and then insert the balancing figure to the side that originally had the smaller total. Complete the entry by bringing forward the balancing figure on the opposite side to become the opening balance for the next accounting period. Kool Kate Ltd's bank account is an example of this.

Bank account

		£			£
1 July	Capital	10,000	1 July	Equipment	1,000
3 July	Sales	3,500	1 July	Purchases	4,000
12 July	Returns outward	200	1 July	Advertising	500
20 July	Pippa Merton	750	2 July	Car	4,000
28 July	Pippa Merton	2,550	3 July	Purchases	2,000
			14 July	Returns inward	500
			28 July	Patel & Co	1,500
			31 July	Balance c/f	3,500
		17,000			17,000
1 August	Balance b/f	3,500			

You can see that the balance c/f refers to the balance at the end of the accounting period (in this case, at the end of July) and the balance b/f refers to the balance at the start of the next period (in this case, the start of August).

Activity

Calculate the closing balances of the remaining accounts for Kool Kate Ltd from Chapter 3. These are the capital account, the sales account, the purchases account, the equipment account, the returns inward account, the returns outward account and the advertising account.

You should not have had too much difficulty with this activity if you followed the rules. You can check your closing balances below, where they are used to construct the trial balance.

When all the ledger accounts have been balanced off, some of them will have been closed completely and will show no balance brought down to commence the next accounting period, whereas others will show either a debit or a credit balance. The debit balances normally represent the assets and expenses of the business and the credit balances normally represent the capital, revenue and liabilities of the business. The list of balances is, at a particular point in time, known as a *trial balance*.

Key definition

A trial balance is a listing of the balances on all the accounts of an organization with debit balances in one column and credit balances in the other. If the rules of double-entry bookkeeping have been accurately applied, the totals of each column should be the same.

Source: Law (2010, p. 420).

If you have made a debit entry for every credit entry and vice versa, the total of the debit balances should be equal to the total of the credit balances; in other words, your trial balance should balance. If they are not the same, you will need to look for the cause by checking the bookkeeping entries in the ledger accounts. It may require a number of trials to get the two columns to balance. When you have achieved this, you will have evidence of the arithmetical accuracy of the record keeping. Some adjustments to the trial balance figures may be necessary to take account of closing inventory, accruals, prepayments, depreciation and doubtful debts, after which the figures are used to prepare the financial statements. We will explain how this is done in subsequent chapters.

Continuing to use the example of Kool Kate Ltd, we can now calculate the closing balances for the accounts at the end of the month and construct a trial balance. As you can see, if the balance b/f on the account is a debit balance, it is shown in the debit column in the trial balance; if the balance b/f on the account is a credit balance, it is shown in the credit column in the trial balance.

Kool Kate Ltd

Trial balance as at 31 July 2012

	Debit	Credit
	£	£
Capital at 1 July 2012		10,000
Sales revenue		6,800
Purchases	7,500	
Cash at bank	3,500	
Vehicles	4,000	
Equipment	1,000	
Returns inward	500	
Returns outward		200
Advertising	500	
	17,000	17,000

Note: Inventory at 31 July 2012 was £4,000

You will see that at the end of the trial balance there is a note stating that the business has *closing inventory* of £4,000 at 31 July. This is not surprising because the business needs to have a certain amount of inventory on the last day of the accounting period ready to sell on the first day of the next accounting period. Thus, closing inventory at the end of one period becomes the *opening inventory* at the beginning of the next period.

In order to value closing inventory, a physical count of goods is carried out (usually at the year end or on a random basis throughout the year) to compare the quantities counted with the records. This is referred to as *stocktaking*. Once the quantity of each type of goods in stock is known, the value of this inventory can be calculated by multiplying the quantity by the original purchase price. This complies with the *historical cost concept* (see Chapter 1). However, some goods may be worth less than their original cost due to changes in taste, technological obsolescence or other factors that have reduced market demand. In such cases the goods should be valued at the *net realizable value*. The net realizable value is the price the business expects to get for the inventory less any costs incurred in selling it. We look at this again in Chapter 6.

You may have calculated the closing inventory as 20 items at £2 each (£40) but the value of the closing inventory is 20 items at £1.50 each (£30) because this represents the net realizable value, which is lower than the original cost.

3.5.2   Other transactions

You will remember that Kool Kate Ltd was started on 1 July and we drew up the trial balance at the end of the first month's trading on 31 July. We are now going to extend that simple example and prepare a trial balance at the end of the first 6 months of trading. This allows us to introduce a number of other transactions. Instead of drawing up separate accounts using double-entry bookkeeping, we are going to focus on the nature of the transaction. However, the principles of double-entry bookkeeping still apply.

- *Carriage inward* The business may have to pay delivery charges for raw materials or goods, and this is sometimes referred to as *carriage inward*. It is an expense of the business and therefore appears in the debit column of the trial balance. It is regarded as part of the cost of purchasing the raw materials or goods. Sometimes the business has to bear the cost of delivery of its goods to customers, and this is known as *carriage outward*. This is also an expense and appears in the debit column of the trial balance.
- *Discounts allowed* and *received* When a business purchases goods, it may be able to negotiate a trade discount and pay slightly less than the normal price. In such a case only the net price (the price after discount) is entered into the accounts. Another form of discount sometimes available is a cash discount to encourage customers to pay promptly. When a business offers a cash discount to customers it is referred to in the supplier's accounts as *discounts allowed*. It is treated as an expense of the business and appears in the debit column of the trial balance. When a business receives cash discounts from its suppliers it is referred to in the customer's accounts as *discounts received* and appears in the credit column of the trial balance.
- *Petty cash* As well as maintaining a bank account, a business may keep a very small amount of cash on the premises, known as petty cash. This is used to pay miscellaneous expenses, such as window cleaning, travelling expenses or the milk bill. A cash account must always appear in the debit column of the trial balance because it is an asset. The balance shown on the ledger account for bank transactions appears in the debit column of the trial balance if the business has cash at the bank,

as it is an asset. However, if the business has an overdraft, the balance appears in the credit column of the trial balance because it is a liability.

- *Non-sales revenue* In addition to sales revenue arising from the sale of goods and services, a business may have income in the form of interest, royalties and dividends. It is important that these items are recorded separately. They are not aggregated or included with sales revenue. You will remember that all revenue is shown in the credit column of the trial balance. Earlier, we mentioned that the inventory account is somewhat special and that separate accounts are maintained for purchases and sales revenue. When constructing a trial balance, it is usual to show the figure for *closing inventory* as a footnote because it will be needed for preparing the financial statements.

Activity

On 31 December 2012, after the first 6 months of trading, Kool Kate Ltd has 180 items that cost £20 each and can be sold for £45 each, and 200 items that cost £14 each and can be sold for £16 each. The account balances at 31 December 2012 were as follows:

	£
Capital at 1 July 2012	10,000
Sales revenue	52,400
Salaries	14,400
Purchases	38,700
Cash in hand	300
Bank overdraft	2,800
Vehicles	4,000
Equipment	1,000
Returns inward	900
Returns outward	800
Advertising	3,400
Carriage inward	960
Discounts allowed	1,200
Discounts received	680
Telephone and Internet	600
Shop overheads	1,220

Required
Prepare a trial balance for Kool Kate Ltd at 31 December 2012.

Your completed trial balance should look like this:

```
                     Kool Kate Ltd
           Trial balance at 31 December 2012
                                  Debit       Credit
                                    £            £
  Capital at 1 July 2012                      10,000
  Sales revenue                              52,400
  Salaries                        14,400
  Purchases                       38,700
  Cash                               300
  Bank                                         2,800
  Vehicles                         4,000
  Equipment                        1,000
  Returns inward                     900
  Returns outward                                800
  Advertising                      3,400
  Carriage inward                    960
  Discounts allowed                1,200
  Discounts received                             680
  Telephone and Internet             600
  Shop overheads                   1,220
                                  66,680      66,680

  Note: Inventory at 31 December 2012 was £6,400
```

If you had any difficulty with this activity, you may find it useful to think of the mnemonic **PEARLS** again.

3.6   Limitations of a trial balance

A trial balance can only detect arithmetical errors as it is simply a list of the debit balances and credit balances on the ledger accounts at the end of the accounting period. If the principles of double-entry bookkeeping have been followed, with a debit entry for every credit entry, the sum of the debit column in the trial balance will be the same as the sum of the credit column. If they do not balance, checks must be made to identify any discrepancy. A common error is to transpose numbers; for example, writing £320 instead of £230. To find out whether this is the reason for your trial balance not balancing, calculate the difference between the total of the debit and credit columns on the trial balance. If this figure is divisible by 9, you have probably transposed a number somewhere and you should check for this error.

Activity

If the trial balance balances, it does not necessarily mean that the figures are correct. What other mistakes could have been made in the recording of transactions that would not be revealed by a trial balance?

You may have thought of the following errors that are not revealed in a trial balance:

- Omission – the transaction has not been recorded in the accounts at all.
- Wrong account – the transaction has been recorded in the wrong account (for example, in the vehicles account instead of the equipment account or in an asset account instead of a liability account).
- Wrong amount – the transaction has been recorded in the correct accounts, but the wrong amount was entered.
- Reverse entry – the transaction has been recorded in the correct accounts, but on the wrong side of both accounts.

The accuracy of the records in the accounting system is important, as they are used as the basis for preparing financial statements, which summarize the transactions that have taken place during the accounting period. This period is usually one year.

3.7 Conclusions

Large organizations carry out thousands of transactions every day and need sophisticated, computerized accounting systems. Most small and medium-sized businesses use spreadsheets, such as Excel, or an accounting package, such as SAGE, but some use a manual system. Whether the system is computerized or manual, it is normally based on the principles of double-entry bookkeeping. This is the most efficient and effective method for recording transactions and events in a way that allows the balances on each ledger account at the end of the accounting period to be summarized in a trial balance.

The trial balance acts as a check on the mathematical accuracy of the record keeping. However, there are some limitations to the trial balance since it does not show other errors that might have occurred during the accounting system. Once all errors have been checked and corrected and the two columns agree, the trial balance is used as the basis for preparing the financial statements, which summarize the transactions that have taken place during the accounting period. After we have given you an overview of the regulations and theoretical concepts that underpin financial reporting in the next two chapters, we will show you how to prepare the financial statements.

Practice questions

1 Rex Wellworth started Wellworth Fencing Ltd with £50,000 he inherited from his uncle. On 1 June he opened a bank account for the business and paid in the capital he has invested in the business. On the same day he wrote business cheques to buy a lorry for £16,000, to pay £1,400 to insure the lorry and to pay £4,500 for 3 months' rent on premises in advance. On 2 June he wrote three business cheques: £5,400 to pay for equipment; £850 to pay for fencing materials from Timber Supplies; and £420 to pay for advertising expenses. On 4 June the business bought a further £120 of fencing materials on credit from Timber Supplies Ltd.

Required

Write up the ledger accounts for Wellworth Fencing Ltd.

2 Mrs Lawley owns a gift shop business called Lavender & Lace Ltd. On 4 July the company's cash account looked like this:

Cash account

		£			£
1 July	Opening balance	500	1 July	Postage	25
2 July	Cash sales	138	1 July	Window cleaning	10
3 July	Cash sales	192	1 July	Stationery	15
			1 July	Parking	2
			1 July	Stationery	36
			1 July	Petrol	18
			2 July	Parking	2
			2 July	Postage	31
			2 July	Purchases	104
			3 July	Parking	2
			3 July	Petrol	18
			3 July	Purchases	89

Required

Write up the ledger accounts for Lavender & Lace Ltd to show the corresponding entries.

3 The following bank account shows transactions for Burton's Books Ltd for the month of October.

Bank account

		£			£
1 October	Balance b/f	6,400	2 October	Purchases	750
12 October	Sales	1,800	3 October	Advertising	1,120
15 October	Jones Ltd	950	16 October	Purchases	2,300
18 October	Jones Ltd	950	18 October	Davies Ltd	780
30 October	Sales revenue	1,450	25 October	Purchases	3,400

Required

Balance the account at 31 October and show the balance c/f at 1 November.

4 The following account is that of O'Neill Ltd, a credit customer of Burtons Books Ltd.

O'Neill Ltd

		£			£
2 November	Sales	850			
12 November	Sales	1,650			
18 November	Sales	260			
21 November	Sales	400			
25 November	Sales	640			

Required

On 30 November O'Neill Ltd pays 50% of the amount due. Record this transaction and balance the account.

5 The following list of balances at 30 June 2012 is taken from the accounts of Hampton Health Food Ltd.

Hampton Health Food Ltd

	£
Revenue	26,200
Purchases	?
Returns inward	900
Returns outward	460
Discounts allowed	720
Discounts received	620
Equipment	2,000
Bank	1,500
Salaries	1,600
Rent	1,400
General expenses	390
Capital at 1 July 2011	18,000

Required

Calculate the figure for purchases and prepare a trial balance at 30 June 2012 for Hampton Health Food Ltd.

6 During the year ending 31 December 2012 Country Furniture Ltd achieved sales that were three times higher than total purchases. Trading expenses were 25% of total purchases. On 31 December 2012 the business had £4,000 in the bank and this was half the amount it had incurred in operating expenses. Premises were acquired for £75,000 and 33% of this was funded by a bank loan. Inventory at the beginning of the year was the equivalent of 2 months' sales revenue.

Required

Calculate the figure for capital and prepare a trial balance for Country Furniture Ltd at 31 December 2012.

7 Explain the advantages of a double-entry bookkeeping system and the purpose of a trial balance. In addition, describe the limitations of a trial balance, giving examples to illustrate your answer.

References

IASB (2010) *The Conceptual Framework for Financial Reporting*, September. London: International Accounting Standards Board.

Law, J. (ed.) (2010) *Dictionary of Accounting*, 4th edition. Oxford: Oxford University Press.

Nobes, C. and Kellas, J. (1990) *Accountancy Explained*. London: Penguin Books.

4 Regulatory framework for financial reporting

Learning objectives

When you have studied this chapter, you should be able to:

- explain the need for the regulatory framework for financial reporting
- discuss the need for international convergence in financial reporting practices
- describe the key elements of the regulatory framework for financial reporting in the UK
- describe the IASB's standard-setting process.

4.1 Introduction

In Chapter 1 we explained that *financial accounting* is the branch of accounting concerned with classifying, measuring and recording the economic transactions of an entity in accordance with established principles, legal requirements and accounting standards. It is primarily concerned with communicating a true and fair view of the financial performance and financial position of an entity to external parties at the end of the accounting period. *Financial reporting* is a key part of financial accounting and refers to the statutory disclosure of general purpose financial information by limited liability entities via the annual report and accounts.

In this chapter we examine the *regulatory framework* for financial reporting in the UK, which is part of the European Union (EU). We start by looking at the need for regulation and the reasons for international differences in accounting practices. This is followed by an examination of company law and the role of *international accounting standards*, which have a major influence on financial reporting since they specify how particular economic transactions and events should be reflected in the financial statements in more than 100 countries around the world.

4.2   Need for regulation

Financial accounting is guided by a number of accounting principles based on convention and best practice, but over the years it has been found that a *regulatory framework* is needed to guide corporate financial reporting. The regulatory framework for financial reporting in the UK comprises general rules, which have been codified in company law, and more detailed regulations, which are contained in accounting standards. In addition, public companies with a listing on the London Stock Exchange must comply with stock exchange rules. The term *Generally Accepted Accounting Practice* (GAPP) refers to the regulatory framework for financial reporting that applies in a particular jurisdiction, hence the terms Belgium GAAP, French GAAP, German GAAP, Greek GAAP, Italian GAAP, Portuguese GAAP, Spanish GAAP, UK GAAP, Australian GAAP, Canadian GAAP, Indian GAAP, Japanese GAAP, US GAAP, and so on.

The regulatory framework for financial reporting ensures that the financial statements are prepared in a standard way and that they provide high-quality, reliable information for external users. You will remember from Chapter 1 that *financial reporting* refers to the statutory disclosure of general purpose financial information by limited liability entities via the annual report and accounts. The majority of limited liability entities are limited companies, which can be registered as private or public companies.

4.2.1   Accountability and stewardship

Many small private companies are owner-managed, but investors in large private and public companies have no day-to-day involvement in the business and appoint directors to manage the company on their behalf. This separation of ownership and control leads to an *agency relationship* in which there is information asymmetry between the directors (the agents), who are *accountable* to the investors (the principals), who have delegated authority to the directors for managing the resources they own. Some monitoring is necessary since it cannot be assumed that the directors will always act in the best interests of the investors. The *annual report and accounts* supports the agency relationship between the directors and the investors by providing financial and other information. Not only is the annual report and accounts an important source of information about the company for existing and potential investors, it is also of interest to other user groups such as existing and potential lenders and creditors. Investors, lenders and creditors rely on the integrity and judgement of the directors to provide high-quality information and we will discuss their information needs in the next chapter.

The annual report and accounts allows users to assess the financial performance, financial position and changes in financial position of the entity. It also allows investors to assess how effectively and efficiently the directors have discharged their responsibilities; in other words, it helps them assess the *stewardship* of the directors who manage the business on their behalf.

Key definition

Stewardship is a traditional approach to accounting that placed an obligation on stewards or agents, such as directors, to provide relevant and reliable financial information relating to the resources over which they have control but which are owned by others, such as shareholders.

Source: Law (2010, p. 398).

One way in which the investors can trust that the financial statements the directors have prepared are a fair representation of the economic activities of the entity is to have the accounts audited.

Key definition

An audit is an independent examination of, and the subsequent expression of opinion on, the financial statements of an organization. This involves the auditor in collecting evidence by means of compliance tests (tests of control) and substantive tests (tests of detail).

Source: Law (2010, p. 37).

In the UK the auditor is required to report on whether the financial statements give a *true and fair view* and have been prepared in accordance with Companies Act 2006 (CA2006), and to report on consistency with the directors' report. At present in the UK, non-publicly accountable companies that qualify as small are exempt from statutory audit. The process of auditing is guided by *International Standards on Auditing (ISAs)*, which are developed by the *International Auditing and Assurance Standards Board (IAASB)* of the *International Federation of Accountants (IFAC)*. These are referred to as the *Clarified ISAs* because they are written using a new drafting convention called the 'clarity format' to make them clear, consistent and easy to understand. The UK's *Auditing Practices Board (APB)* has supplemented the Clarified ISAs with additional requirements and guidance to meet the requirements of company law in the UK and Ireland.

The auditor's report must include an opinion as to whether or not the financial statements give a *true and fair view* of the company's profit or loss for the accounting period, and of its state of affairs at the end of the period. It must also state whether the financial statements have been prepared consistently using appropriate accounting policies that are in accordance with company law and accounting standards. In addition, it must state whether there is adequate disclosure of information relevant to the proper understanding of the financial statements. We will look at an example in the next section.

The auditor can issue a qualified or adverse opinion if he or she is not satisfied. It is an offence under the CA2006 for an auditor to knowingly or recklessly cause an auditor's report to contain a statement that is misleading, false or deceptive or cause that report to omit a statement relating to problems with the accounts. The APB has not adopted *Clarified ISA 700, 'Forming an Opinion and Reporting on Financial Statements'*, but has issued a clarified version of *ISA (UK and Ireland) 700, 'The Auditor's Report on Financial Statements'*, which reflects the requirements of company law and provides a more concise auditor's report. This does not prevent the auditor from being able to assert compliance with the Clarified ISAs.

Having a regulatory framework gives guidance to the directors and reduces the choice of accounting policies the company can adopt. It also allows the auditors to point out the relevant regulations if they consider the directors' choices are inappropriate. If there were no regulatory framework, the directors might choose unsuitable accounting policies and the auditors might be reluctant to raise objections since they risk losing future business if the directors decide not to recommend their reappointment.

4.2.2 The annual report and accounts

The *annual report and accounts* contains narrative reports (such as a report from the directors that explains its activities and operations throughout the year and the auditors' report) and the accounts (the financial statements). It is the most useful source of financial information issued by private and public companies. Many public limited companies are well-known high street retailers or banks such as Boots Alliance, Marks & Spencer, J Sainsbury, Tesco, HMV, WHSmith, Barclays, Lloyds TSB, Halifax, HSBC and NatWest. Because of the economic importance of public limited companies in terms of employment and the monetary value of goods and services they produce, information on them is by far the easiest to obtain. If you look in the business pages of newspapers such as *The Times*, *Financial Times*, *Independent* or *Guardian*, you will find news on the financial performance and share prices of major public limited companies and articles about their directors.

At present in the UK, all incorporated bodies (except some unlimited companies) are required by CA2006 to register their annual report and accounts at Companies House. Once filed with the registrar, the annual report and accounts is available to the public. Anyone can download a copy for a small fee from www.companieshouse. gov.uk. If you are interested in the annual report and accounts of a public limited company, you can obtain a free copy from its website or from www.orderannualreports.com, which is a free service provided by the *Financial Times*. In addition to publishing printed and PDF copies of their annual report and accounts, some companies provide Braille, audio and video versions.

Activity

Download a copy of the latest annual report and accounts for Ted Baker PLC from http://ww7.investorrelations.co.uk/tedbaker/ and look at the information disclosed.

The website explains that the entrepreneur behind Ted Baker is designer Ray Kelvin, who left school at the age of 18 and started a business manufacturing menswear. After supplying the high street retailer Burton for 10 years, Ray sold his business to the management team in 1997 and founded Ted Baker with a partner. That year they opened a shirt store in Glasgow. The business has flourished and today Ted Baker PLC has stores in the UK, Continental Europe, USA, the Middle East and Asia, selling trendy designer clothes for men, women and children, in additional to footwear, eyewear, accessories, watches and fragrance. At the time of the 2011 annual report and accounts, Ted Baker PLC was a parent company with five subsidiaries:

- No Ordinary Designer Label Ltd: a design, wholesale and retail company in the UK, owned 100%
- Ted Baker Investments (Jersey) Ltd: an investment holding company in Jersey, owned 100%
- Ted Baker (France) SARL: a retail company in France, owned 100%
- Ted Baker Ltd: a retail company in the USA, owned 100%
- Ted Baker (New York) Inc: a retail company in the USA, owned 66%.

Figure 4.1 presents the contents page of Ted Baker's annual report and accounts for 2010/2011. As you can see, it contains a wide range of narrative reports in addition to the financial statements.

To allow shareholders to appreciate the activities of the entire group, Ted Baker's financial statements not only show information for the parent company, but also for the group. The information from the individual financial statements of the parent and its subsidiaries is adjusted and combined in a process called consolidation and the resulting *group accounts* are presented as those of a single economic entity. This might sound very complicated, but we will show you how it is done in a later chapter.

If you look at pages 35 and 36 in Ted's annual report for 2010/2011, you will find the auditors' report (see Figure 4.2). Because companies differ in their activities and the amount of information they volunteer, no two annual reports are identical. Voluntary disclosures may include information about the company's products, employees and corporate social responsibilities. There is some debate over the extent to which some of this information clutters the annual report, obscuring relevant information and making it harder for users to find the main points about the performance of the business and its future prospects.

Financial reporting is a dynamic and expensive activity. As new issues of public interest arise (for example, environmental issues, fair trade, directors' remuneration and corporate governance), companies must attempt to address them in their annual report and accounts, either voluntarily or as required by the regulations. This has resulted in the annual report and accounts of major companies expanding greatly:

Figure 4.1   Contents of Ted Baker PLC Annual Report and Accounts 2010/2011

Contents

DIRECTORS' REPORT: OVERVIEW

05   Chairman's Statement

07   Business Review

10   Financial Review

12   Principal Risks and Uncertainties

DIRECTORS' REPORT: GOVERNANCE

17   Corporate Governance Statements

20   Sustainability and The Environment

21   People

DIRECTORS' REPORT: OTHER STATUTORY DISCLOSURES

25   Board of Directors

26   Directors' Remuneration Report

31   Other Disclosures

34   Statement of Directors' Responsibilities

35   Independent Auditors' Report to the Members of Ted Baker PLC

FINANCIAL STATEMENTS

41   Group and Company Primary Financial Statements

47   Notes to the Financial Statements

77   Five Year Summary

Ted's advisers

Registered Office: The Ugly Brown Building, 6a St. Pancras Way, London NW1 0TB

Secretary: Charles Anderson ACMA

Financial Advisers and Stockbrokers: Espirito Santo Investment Bank, 10 Paternoster Square, London, EC4M 7AL

Solicitors: Jones Day, 21 Tudor Street, London EC4Y 0DJ

Auditors: KPMG Audit Plc, 15 Canada Square, Canary Wharf, E14 5GL

Bankers: Barclays Bank PLC, 1 Churchill Place, London E14 5HP

             The Royal Bank of Scotland PLC, 62-63 Threadneedle Street, London EC2R 8LA

Registrars: Capita Registrars, 34 Beckenham Road, Beckenham, Kent BR3 4TU

Ted Baker PLC - Registered in England No: 03393836

Figure 4.2 Auditors' report for Ted Baker PLC 2010/2011 (*continued overleaf*)

INDEPENDENT AUDITORS' REPORT TO THE MEMBERS OF TED BAKER PLC

We have audited the financial statements of Ted Baker PLC for the 52 weeks ended 29 January 2011 which comprise the Group Income Statement, the Group Statement of Comprehensive Income, the Group and Parent Company Statement of Changes in Equity, the Group and Parent Company Balance Sheets, the Group and Parent Cash Flow Statement and the related notes. The financial reporting framework that has been applied in their preparation is applicable law and International Financial Reporting Standards (IFRSs) as adopted by the EU and, as regards the parent company financial statements, as applied in accordance with the provisions of the Companies Act 2006.

This report is made solely to the company's members, as a body, in accordance with Chapter 3 of Part 16 of the Companies Act 2006. Our audit work has been undertaken so that we might state to the company's members those matters we are required to state to them in an auditor's report and for no other purpose. To the fullest extent permitted by law, we do not accept or assume responsibility to anyone other than the company and the company's members, as a body, for our audit work, for this report, or for the opinions we have formed.

Respective responsibilities of directors and auditor

As explained more fully in the Directors' Responsibilities Statement set out on page 34, the directors are responsible for the preparation of the financial statements and for being satisfied that they give a true and fair view. Our responsibility is to audit, and express an opinion on, the financial statements in accordance with applicable law and International Standards on Auditing (UK and Ireland). Those standards require us to comply with the Auditing Practices Board's (APB's) Ethical Standards for Auditors.

Scope of the audit of the financial statements

A description of the scope of an audit of financial statements is provided on the APB's website at www.frc.org.uk/apb/scope/private.cfm.

Opinion on financial statements

In our opinion:

- the financial statements give a true and fair view of the state of the group's and of the parent company's affairs as at 29 January 2011 and of the group's profit for the period then ended;

- the group financial statements have been properly prepared in accordance with IFRSs as adopted by the EU;

- the parent company financial statements have been properly prepared in accordance with IFRSs as adopted by the EU and as applied in accordance with the provisions of the Companies Act 2006; and

- the financial statements have been prepared in accordance with the requirements of the Companies Act 2006 and, as regards the group financial statements, Article 4 of the IAS Regulation.

Opinion on other matter prescribed by the Companies Act 2006

In our opinion:

- the part of the Directors' Remuneration Report to be audited has been properly prepared in accordance with the Companies Act 2006; and

- the information given in the Directors' Report for the financial year for which the financial statements are prepared is consistent with the financial statements.

Figure 4.2 *continued*

INDEPENDENT AUDITORS' REPORT TO THE MEMBERS OF TED BAKER PLC continued

Matters on which we are required to report by exception

We have nothing to report in respect of the following:

Under the Companies Act 2006 we are required to report to you if, in our opinion:

- adequate accounting records have not been kept by the parent company, or returns adequate for our audit have not been received from branches not visited by us; or

- the parent company financial statements and the part of the Directors' Remuneration Report to be audited are not in agreement with the accounting records and returns; or

- certain disclosures of directors' remuneration specified by law are not made; or

- we have not received all the information and explanations we require for our audit; or

- a Corporate Governance Statement has not been prepared by the company.

Under the Listing Rules we are required to review:

- the directors' statement, set out on page 32, in relation to going concern;

- the part of the Corporate Governance Statement on page 17 relating to the company's compliance with the nine provisions of the June 2008 Combined Code specified for our review; and

- certain elements of the report to shareholders by the Board on directors' remuneration.

Mike Barradell (Senior Statutory Auditor)

for and on behalf of KPMG Audit Plc, Statutory Auditor

Chartered Accountants
15 Canada Square
London
E14 5GL

24 March 2011

'In 1996, the average length of the annual report of a listed company was 44 pages. By 2000 it was 56 pages. In 2005, the average was 71 pages, increasing to 85 in 2006. From there, it increased steadily to 99 pages in the 2009 survey. It is now 101 pages. Yes, that's a 250% increase in the number of pages in an average annual report over a 14 year span!' (Deloitte, 2010)

It is interesting to look at some contrasting cases from 2008. The length of Ted Baker's annual report and accounts was 68 pages compared with 454 pages for HSBC. HSBC's annual report weighed 1.5 kg and was so heavy that Royal Mail had to restrict the number a postman could carry on a delivery round for health and safety reasons. You can see that quite apart from the cost of complying with the regulatory framework for financial reporting, some companies choose to spend a lot of extra money on publishing additional material in their annual report and accounts.

4.3   International harmonization and convergence

As companies like Ted Baker have become larger and increasingly international in their ownership and activities, there has been growing pressure for international *harmonization* and *convergence* in the regulation of financial reporting. The internationalization of business began to escalate in the 1970s and 1980s when the reduced cost of computer hardware and software helped bring about a revolution in the use of information technology. By the mid-1990s, many entities had created websites on the Internet, thus creating a global market place. Other significant influences on the internationalization of business in Europe were the *Treaties of Rome (1957)* which created the European Economic Community (EEC) and laid the foundation for a common market to stimulate economic development and prevent recurrence of war through closer cooperation. This developed into today's European Union (EU), which by 2009 had 27 Member States. Figure 4.3 shows the year in which each jurisdiction was admitted to the EU.

These changes, together with the establishment of international capital markets for raising finance, have meant that instead of operating in local or national markets, many businesses now operate in a global economy. Indeed, some have become large conglomerates with complex activities and international operations that were unimaginable in the days when transactions were based on simple bartering.

The internationalization of business and the capital markets raises problems because some countries in the developing world have minimal financial reporting regulations, while countries like the USA have highly developed and prescriptive systems. Not surprisingly, financial accounting and reporting has developed in response to these changes in the business environment. In addition, the prevailing view in some countries is that the responsibility for controlling accounting should rest with the accountancy profession rather than governments and their agencies. In Europe, this view became more apparent among the early members of the EU.

Figure 4.3   Members of the European Union (EU-27)

Year	Member state
1957	France, Federal Republic of Germany, Italy, Belgium, the Netherlands, Luxembourg
1973	UK, Ireland, Denmark
1981	Greece
1986	Spain, Portugal
1990	East Germany
1995	Austria, Finland, Sweden
2004	Cyprus, Malta, Hungary, Poland, Slovakia, Latvia, Estonia, Lithuania, Czech Republic, Slovenia
2007	Romania, Bulgaria

Note: By 2007 there were 27 member states (the unification of East and West Germany means that Germany is only counted once).

4.3.1   EU harmonization

Under the terms of the Treaties of Rome, the government of the member state agrees to obey EU Directives, which are issued by the European Commission (EC) and must be approved by the Members of the European Parliament (MEPs). The purpose of the following three company law directives, known as the Accounting Directives, was to remove barriers between EU Member States and bring about *harmonization* in financial reporting:

- The *Fourth Directive* (1978) covers single entity accounts and contains substantial and detailed requirements with standardized formats for the financial statements. As far as the UK was concerned, this represented a more prescriptive European approach, but the UK's influence on the directive meant that other member states had to adopt the 'true and fair' concept which lies at the heart of UK GAAP.
- The *Seventh Directive* (1983) covers group (consolidated) accounts.
- The *Eighth Directive* (1984) covers the statutory audit.

A major review of these accounting and auditing directives is currently underway, with a focus on simplifications for smaller entities. Once the changes have been finalized, the member states will incorporate them in their national legislation.

4.3.2 Reasons for national differences

Over the years many countries have developed their own regulatory frameworks for financial reporting, so in Europe you will see references to Belgium GAAP, French GAAP, German GAAP, Greek GAAP, Italian GAAP, Portuguese GAAP, Spanish GAAP, UK GAAP etc. Further afield you will see Australian GAAP, Canadian GAAP, Indian GAAP, Japanese GAAP, US GAAP, etc. Not surprisingly, this has resulted in significant differences in accounting practices, which mean that a company can show one figure of profit when the financial statements are drawn up under one country's rules and a completely different figure when drawn up under another country's rules. These differences are important when a company is seeking a listing on a stock exchange in another country. For example, if a UK company wanted its shares to be traded on the New York Stock Exchange as well as on the London Stock Exchange, it would have needed to prepare two sets of accounts: one complying with US GAAP and the other complying with UK GAAP, or a reconciliation statement.

Activity

What do you think are the main reasons for the development of different regulatory frameworks for financial reporting in different countries?

It is difficult to summarize the complex social, economic and cultural reasons for national differences in financial reporting practices, but there is general consensus that one important factor is the *legal system*.[1] In some countries the legal system is based on the Roman laws of the 6th century. This tends to result in a rules-based approach to the regulation of financial reporting with detailed 'codified' rules (e.g. Belgium, France, Germany, Greece, Italy, Portugal and Spain). Requirements are more likely to be controlled by the government, but there may still be some contribution from the accountancy profession (e.g. the Netherlands). In other countries, the legal system may be based on the English common law system whereby a limited number of statutes are interpreted by the courts to produce supplementary case law. This tends to result in a principles-based approach to the regulation of financial reporting, with minimal legal requirements supported by accounting principles (e.g. Australia, India, UK and USA). Therefore, the accountancy profession tends to play a key role in developing requirements and the regulations can be changed more frequently. Of course, the size and strength of the accountancy profession in a particular country also has a bearing on its ability to contribute to the regulatory framework. Therefore, a large, strong profession is associated with countries where there is a requirement for the financial statements to be audited.

A country's regulatory framework for financial reporting is likely to consist of accounting practices that have evolved over time and legal requirements that are added to from time to time. These legal requirements arise on a contingency basis as a response to an unusual event such as a financial scandal, or to a change in the economic environment. Of course, countries are not likely to experience the same

1. This discussion draws on Haller and Walton (2003) and Alexander and Nobes (2010).

unusual events and, if they do, the events are not likely to occur at the same time or lead to the same changes in legal requirements. There are also differences due to different attitudes. In some countries it is taken for granted that a law should be obeyed, whereas in other countries there is a subtle understanding about which laws are obeyed and the degree to which they are obeyed. Some people illustrate the problem with the joke shown in Figure 4.4.

Figure 4.4 International understanding on rules

'International understanding on rules is very difficult because the rules have different meanings: in Germany everything is forbidden unless it is explicitly allowed by the law, whereas in England everything is allowed except what is explicitly forbidden in the law. In China, on the other hand, everything is forbidden, even though it is allowed by the law, whereas in Italy everything is allowed, especially if it is forbidden.'

Source: Haller and Walton (2003, p. 4).

A second factor that contributes to international differences in financial reporting practices stems from differences in what is seen as the objective of financial reporting. In some countries the focus of financial reporting is on meeting the needs of investors for decision making, but in other countries it is on the provision of financial information for creditor protection and taxation. This difference arises because in some countries the main source of finance is the equity finance raised on the stock market (for example the UK and the USA), and in others it is debt finance supplied by banks and other financial institutions (for example Germany). A further complication is that in some countries there

Figure 4.5 Reasons for international differences in GAAP

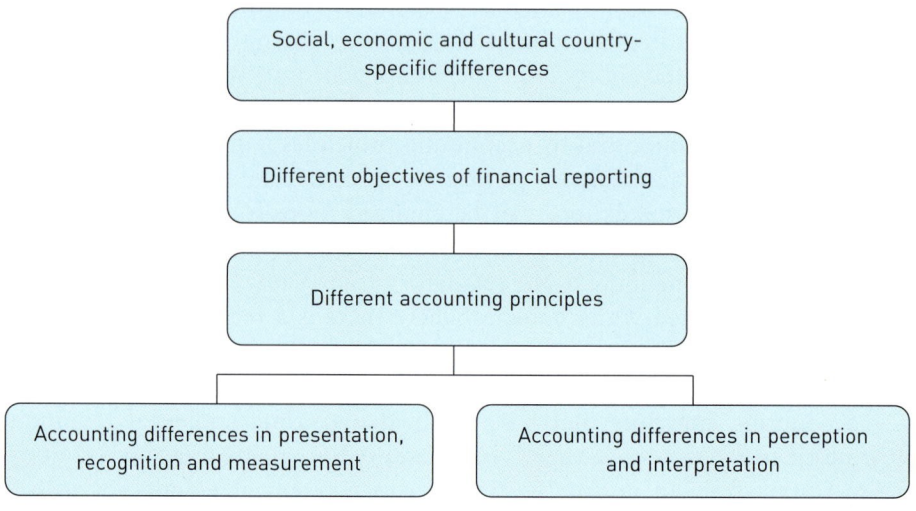

Source: Adapted from Haller and Walton (2003, p. 2).

are separate rules for financial reporting and tax purposes (for example the UK and the USA), requiring two sets of financial statements to be prepared, while in others there is one set of rules for both purposes and therefore a single set of financial statements is sufficient. Figure 4.5 summarizes the various reasons we have discussed.

4.3.3 Main elements of the regulatory framework in the UK

Having set the context, we are now ready to examine the *regulatory framework* in the UK. The key elements are:

- company law as represented by the Companies Act 2006 (CA2006) and subsequent statutory instruments
- national and international accounting standards issued by independent (non-government) bodies
- stock exchange rules, which are issued by an independent regulator.

We are going to look at company law and accounting standards in some detail in the next two sections, but a detailed discussion of stock exchange rules is beyond the scope of this book. It is sufficient for you to know that the London Stock Exchange (LSE) is regulated independently by the *Financial Services Authority (FSA)*. Public companies must meet stringent requirements to obtain a listing on the LSE and these are contained in the *Stock Exchange (Listing) Regulations* and the *Admission of Securities to Listing*. Less information is required for a listing on the *Alternative Investment Market (AIM)*, which is a subsidiary market for smaller, growing public companies. Neither private companies nor unlisted public limited companies need to comply with stock exchange rules.

4.4 Company law

We explained in Chapter 1 that the regulatory framework for financial reporting in the UK is rooted in *accounting principles* based on best practice and early company law in the form of the *Joint Stock Companies Registration and Regulation Act 1844*, the *Limited Liability Act 1855* and subsequent Companies Acts. Modern company law in the UK is embodied in the *Companies Act 2006 (CA2006)*, the development of which is the responsibility of the Department for Business, Innovation and Skills (BIS).

The requirement to make accounts available at a registry is included in the *Fourth Directive* (78/660/EEC) on the basis that anyone dealing with a limited liability company should be able to see the financial statements. This publicity doctrine asserts that the publication of the annual report and accounts is part of the price companies pay for having limited liability. The official Registrar of Companies operates under the name of *Companies House*, which has regional offices and is an executive agency of BIS. Companies House has responsibility for incorporating and dissolving limited companies, examining and storing company information delivered under CA2006 and related legislation, and making that information available to the public.

4.4.1 Companies limited by shares

According to CA2006, the general characteristics of a company limited by shares are as follows:[2]

- The company has a legal identity separate from its members.
- It has perpetual existence because it continues to exist even though a member may die or sell his or her shares to another individual or institutional shareholder.
- It can sue and be sued and, on liquidation, members have limited liability for its debts (limited to the amount they have invested).
- Members of the company appoint the directors (one vote per share).

On formation the company must register three documents:

- The *memorandum of association* defines the company's constitution and provides a record of facts at the time of incorporation. There is no need to state the objects of the company; hence no restriction on its activities.
- The *articles of association* is a document that gives details about the internal regulation of the business, including the voting rights of shareholders, how shareholders' and directors' meetings will be conducted, and the powers of management. This is the core document approved by members that gives directors their operational parameters.
- The *statement of capital* provides information on the number of shares issued and the company's share capital. The concept of authorized capital referred to in previous Companies Acts has been removed.

4.4.2 Main requirements of CA2006

Some of the main requirements of CA2006 are:

- In a one-member company there must be at least one 'natural person' who must be aged 16 or over, which gives ultimate accountability to a human being.
- Companies must keep adequate accounting records to show and explain the company's transactions, to disclose with reasonable accuracy the financial position of the company and to enable the directors to ensure that any accounts required to be prepared comply with CA2006 and International Financial Reporting Standards (where applicable).
- The directors must prepare annual financial statements comprising a profit and loss account (statement of comprehensive income) and balance sheet (statement of financial position), with group accounts as appropriate. Additional information must be disclosed in the notes to the accounts and the form and content of the financial statements must comply with the provisions. There are simplifications for most non-publically accountable entities, which we will discuss in the next section.
- The annual accounts must be accompanied by a *directors' report*, signed by a director or company secretary. The directors must not approve the accounts unless they are satisfied that they give a *true and fair view* of the assets, liabilities, financial

2. See Chapter 1 for an explanation of the difference between a company limited by shares and a company limited by guarantee.

position and profit or loss. There is no legal definition of the term, but essentially 'true' means the financial statements are in accordance with the facts (accurately reflect the underlying transactions) and 'fair' means they are not misleading. The true and fair view concept is important in the UK and may be used as an override to depart from legal requirements. If such departure is necessary, the directors must disclose the reason and the effect of the departure in the notes to the accounts.

- The annual accounts must also be accompanied by an *auditors' report*, signed by the auditors. Unless the company qualifies for exemption from statutory audit, external auditors must be appointed to audit the accounts and their report consists of an opinion on whether the accounts show a true and fair view of the financial performance and position of the business. Exemption from statutory audit is offered to qualifying small non-publically accountable entities.

- Public companies are required to hold an *annual general meeting (AGM)* for members. A 21-day notice period is required. The main items are the presentation of the annual report and accounts, the recommendations of the payment of dividends, the election of directors, and the appointment and remuneration of the auditors. Private companies do not need to hold an AGM, but members can demand one if it is required by at least 10% of shareholders (5% in certain circumstances) and a 14-day notice period is required.

- Public companies must submit a copy of their annual report and accounts to Companies House and lay them before members at an AGM within 6 months of the year end.[3] Private companies must submit a copy of their annual report and accounts to Companies House and distribute them to members within 9 months of the year end.

- Public companies must appoint a *company secretary*, who is required to have certain qualifications. His or her duties include the submission of the annual report and accounts to Companies House and keeping the minutes of meetings. Private companies may choose to appoint a company secretary if they wish.

- Once approved by members, the company's website can be used to transmit all corporate documentation. Electronic communications, including emails and websites, must include the company's name, number, registered office and other particulars (as business letters are required to do).

To help reduce the complexity of the annual report and accounts for individual investors, who may prefer to take professional advice rather than analyse the information themselves, listed companies can give private shareholders (as opposed to corporate shareholders) the option of receiving *summary financial statements*, providing certain conditions are met. Summary financial statements contain a minimum amount of financial information in a few pages. However, many companies incorporate the summary financial statements with other voluntary information, which expands the document. Companies providing summary financial statements to private shareholders must still prepare the full annual report and accounts for institutional shareholders and for filing at Companies House.

---

3. Stock exchange rules require a listed company to reduce this period to 4 months.

4.4.3   Differential reporting

Traditionally, company law has provided a broad framework only. However, in 1973 the UK joined what was to become the EU and this led to a significant increase in the complexity of UK company law due to the need to incorporate the requirements of the Fourth, Seventh and Eighth Directives (the Accounting Directives). For many years the focus of UK GAAP was on financial reporting by large companies (*Big GAAP*), but the Accounting Directives meant incorporating options that simplify requirements for small and medium-sized entities[4] (*Little GAAP*) in recognition of their importance in the European economy.

The *Fourth Directive* specifies the maximum thresholds that EU Member States can set for small entities to qualify for audit exemption and filing abbreviated accounts. It also specifies the thresholds for medium-sized entities to qualify for filing the slightly fuller version of abbreviated accounts that apply to them. The size criteria specify the maximum levels of net turnover (revenue), balance sheet total (aggregate of the amounts shown as assets in the balance sheet) and average number of employees during the financial year. In general, the entity must satisfy two of the three tests for two consecutive years.[5]

A current debate is whether micro entities (very small companies) should be excluded from some of the requirements of the Fourth Directive. This would affect some 5.3 million micro entities, which represent approximately 75% of companies within the scope of the Fourth Directive (EC, 2008). This proposal stems from a 'think small first' approach, which rests on the assumption that the requirements of the Fourth Directive are an administrative burden, the reduction of which would boost Europe's economy. Table 4.1 shows the EU maxima for a small or medium-sized entity which have been adopted by the UK, together with the proposed thresholds for a micro entity.

Under CA2006, unless the entity is excluded for reasons of public interest,[6] it will generally qualify as small if it meets two or more of three size criteria shown in Table 4.1 in its first year.[7] In a subsequent financial year, the entity must qualify or satisfy the

Table 4.1   Financial reporting size thresholds

Criteria	Proposed micro entity	Small entity	Medium entity
Turnover	£0.616m (€0.5m)	£6.5m (€8.8m)	£25.9m (€35.0m)
Total assets	£0.308m (€0.25m)	£3.26m (€4.4m)	£12.9m (€17.5m)
Average employees	10	50	250

Source: European Parliament (2011) and Companies House (2008, n.d.).

4. In this context the term *entity* refers to a single-entity company or a group company.
5. Thresholds are revised periodically to take account of indexation (monetary and economic trends).
6. Under the Companies Act 2006, 'an entity is excluded from the small companies regime if it is a public company, a company that is an authorized insurance company, a banking company, an e-money issuer, an ISD investment firm or a UCITS management company, or carries on insurance market activity, or is a member of an ineligible group' (c. 46, Part 15, Chapter 1, p. 178).
7. These are the EU maxima from April 2008, which were adopted by the UK from the same date.

size tests in that year and the preceding year. An entity that qualifies as small or medium can choose to file *abbreviated accounts* at Companies House, but they must still prepare full accounts for their shareholders. In the case of small entities, this option gives relief from the requirement to file an income statement and a directors' report. This means they only have to file an abbreviated balance sheet and related notes.[8] However, they must still distribute full accounts to their shareholders. Although drawn from the full accounts, abbreviated accounts cannot give a true and fair view because they omit financial information that is necessary to giving a true and fair view.

Auditors of entities submitting abbreviated accounts are required to make a special report that the entity is entitled to deliver abbreviated accounts and that the abbreviated accounts have been properly prepared (APB, 2006). Where the auditor's report on the full accounts is qualified, UK company law requires the special report on the abbreviated accounts to set out this qualification. Where the auditor's report on the full accounts is unqualified but contains an 'emphasis of matter' paragraph, this must be included in the special report, together with any further materials needed to understand it.

Activity

What are the advantages and disadvantages of filing abbreviated accounts?

The main advantage is that abbreviated accounts reduce the disclosure of financial information about the company that might be useful to competitors. This helps the company if it has activities in competitive markets rather than a niche market. The main disadvantages you may have thought of are:

- Users of the financial statements may think the company has something to hide.
- Users will find inter-company comparison is difficult, as fewer figures are available for analysis.
- The company may incur additional accountancy costs in producing this slightly different set of accounts for filing. Any additional costs are not likely to be very significant because accounting software makes it easy to generate abbreviated accounts from the full accounts prepared for shareholders.

The conditions for exemption from audit are that the entity qualifies as small in relation to that year and meets both financial criteria for that year, as shown in Table 4.1.[9] However, if audit is required by shareholders holding at least 10% of issued share capital, the company cannot forgo the statutory audit. When the concessions were first introduced in the UK, the size tests were set lower than the EU maxima and the turnover threshold was set at a lower level for audit exemption than that for the abbreviated accounts option. Subsequently the thresholds were raised in steps, and by 2004 they had been standardized for all accounting and auditing options and harmonized with the EU maxima. In April 2008, the UK thresholds were raised once more to align them with the revised EU maxima. The UK was not alone in adopting the EU

---

8. Abbreviated accounts for medium-sized entities require a higher level of disclosure.
9. The detailed rules are in the Companies Act 2006, c. 45, Parts 15 and 16.

maxima and research suggests that 47% of Member States had fully implemented the filing options in the Fourth Directive by 2003 (EC 2005).[10]

Activity

What are the advantages and disadvantages of audit exemption?

The main advantage is that it will reduce cost burdens because there will be no auditor's fee to be paid. In addition, there will be no working time lost or inconvenience because no auditor will come to the business to conduct compliance tests (to assess the effectiveness of the systems of financial control) and substantive tests (to assess the completeness, ownership, existence, valuation and disclosure of the information in the accounting records and financial statements). The main disadvantages you may have thought of are:

- There will be no independent assurance for external users of the financial statements. An independent audit gives users confidence that the financial statements give a true and fair view and this is particularly important to external investors and to lenders and creditors for making economic decisions.
- In addition, there will be no assurance for management since audit provides an independent check on the accounting systems and records, which helps prevent material error and acts as a deterrent to fraud.

4.5 UK accounting standards

Since the Companies Registration and Regulation Act 1844 introduced the first requirement that companies present a balance sheet to shareholders, there has been a steady pressure on companies to increase the amount of information they disclose. Prior to 1970 the regulation of financial reporting in the UK was relatively light. It was governed solely by company law, with additional rules laid down by the Stock Exchange for listed companies. The Companies Acts of 1948 and 1967 provided general requirements in connection with the preparation, distribution and filing of financial statements, but the detail was left to the practices of accountants.

There was little concern with developing standards on accounting until the Institute of Chartered Accountants in England and Wales (ICAEW) began drafting pronouncements on accounting principles in 1942. Between 1942 and 1969 a total of 29 guidance statements were issued. They had been subjected to a complex exposure process among ICAEW members and had to be approved by an overwhelming majority of its Council, which meant that the ICAEW held considerable influence over accounting practices. This basic framework was widely considered to be insufficient for the purpose of achieving a satisfactory standard of financial reporting. The main problems were the amount of flexibility permitted to companies in the way that they could account for transactions and the minimum amount of information they could disclose. In the 1960s there were a number of major financial scandals involving companies

---

10. There were only 19 Member States at that time.

reporting misleading profit figures,[11] which could be attributed in part to perceptions of the inadequacy of accounting regulations. Similar problems were being experienced in other jurisdictions and some of the wealthier countries addressed them by setting *accounting standards* which gave detailed guidance on how a particular type of economic transaction or event should be reflected in the financial statements.

Key definition

An accounting standard is an authoritative statement on how a particular type of transaction or other event should be reflected in the financial statements. In the UK, compliance with accounting standards is normally necessary for the financial statements to give a true and fair view.

Activity

What are the advantages and disadvantages of accounting standards?

Looking first at the advantages, accounting standards offer a number of benefits to the users and preparers of accounts. The preparers have an authoritative guide to the most appropriate method for accounting for many of the important activities undertaken by companies. The users have additional financial information to that required by legislation alone, as well as information about the basis on which the accounts have been drawn up. This allows comparison of a company's results with other companies and between one year and another. The main disadvantages are:

- They impose additional costs for the company, but to some extent this is offset by the availability of accounting software.
- Standard setters must decide which accounting methods are appropriate for all companies in all industries and in all circumstances.

In 1970 the *Accounting Standards Committee (ASC)* was established as the first standard setter in the UK, with the objective of reducing flexibility by requiring all members of the accountancy bodies to apply accounting standards or face disciplinary action. Over the next 20 years, the ASC issued 25 accounting standards known as *Statements of Standard Accounting Practice (SSAPs)*. The ASC did much to improve the quality of financial reporting, but it did not have the authority or resources to deal with all the problems. Following recommendations made by the Dearing Committee (Dearing, 1988), the ASC was dissolved in 1990. At the same time the *Financial Reporting Council (FRC)* was set up to promote confidence in financial reporting and corporate governance. For many years the *Committee on Corporate Governance* has assisted the FRC in its work on corporate governance and the main functions of the FRC have been carried out by six operating bodies (see Figure 4.6):

- The *Accounting Standards Board* issues financial reporting standards with the support of the *Urgent Issues Task Force*, which gives guidance on interpretation and matters not covered by an accounting standard.

---

11. Two examples include the collapse in 1964 of Rolls Razor Ltd after publishing 'clean' accounts, and the difference between AEI's profit forecast for 1967 and the large loss reported after it was taken over by GEC (partly due to the use of different accounting principles).

- The *Auditing Practices Board* issues standards for auditors.
- The *Board for Actuarial Standards* issues standards for actuaries.
- The *Professional Oversight Board* is responsible for the regulation of the accountancy profession.
- The *Financial Reporting Review Panel* is responsible for investigating material departures from accounting standards.
- The *Accountancy and Actuarial Discipline Board* is responsible for investigating and disciplining accountants and actuaries.

Figure 4.6

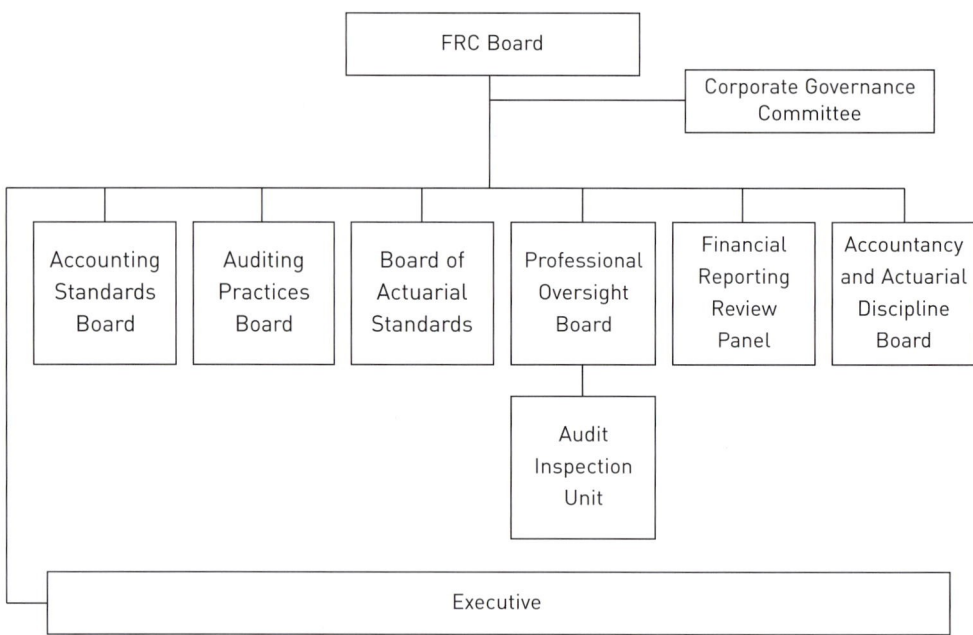

Source: FRC (2011, n.p.).

In 1990 the Accounting Standards Board (ASB) adopted all the SSAPs issued by its predecessor (the ASC) and began issuing *Financial Reporting Standards (FRSs)* that would be applicable to all public and private companies. Some of these replaced earlier accounting standards. In 1997 the ASB issued the *Financial Reporting Standard for Smaller Entities (FRSSE)*, with a view to reducing the financial reporting burden on non-publicly accountable small companies. The FRSSE draws together in a single document all the guidance from the full range of accounting standards that is most likely to be relevant to a small company. The measurement bases are the same as, or a simplification of, those in the accounting standards, and the definitions and accounting treatments are consistent with the requirements of CA2006. The FRSSE is updated on a regular basis and since 2005 has also included relevant requirements of the Companies Act, thus making it a 'one-stop shop' for small companies.

However, you should be aware that the structure of the FRC it is likely to be much more streamlined by the time you read this chapter. In October 2011 a consultation paper (BIS/FRC, 2011) was issued to gather views on a proposal with the intention of:

- reinforcing the FRC's independence from those it regulates
- improving its efficiency and effectiveness
- rationalizing and minimizing the regulatory burdens on large companies.

Figure 4.7 shows the proposed organizational chart for the FRC that is likely to come into effect from April 2012.

Figure 4.7

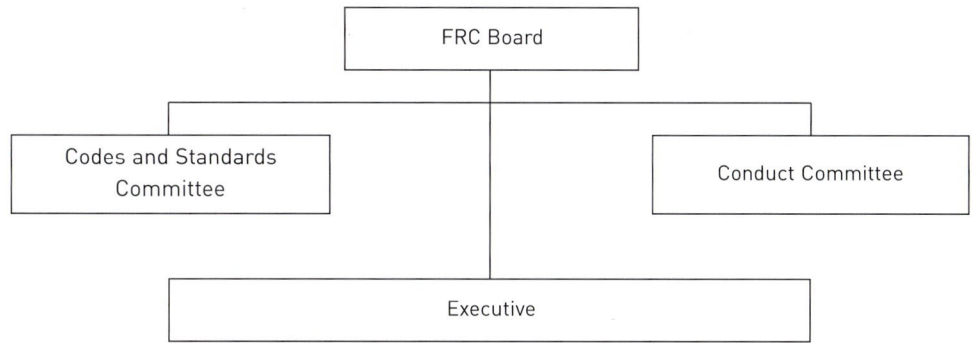

Source: FRC (2011, n.p.).

4.6   International financial reporting standards

As discussed earlier in this chapter, accounting practices developed differently in different countries. Some countries have minimal legislation, whilst other countries have a highly developed and prescriptive system. Clearly this imbalance is highly unsatisfactory today in the context of increased cross-border integration of markets and politics. In addition, the prevailing view in some countries is that the responsibility for controlling accounting should rest with the accountancy profession rather than government and this view became more apparent among the early members of the EU. These are examples of the pressures that led to demand for international accounting standards to bring about convergence by reducing differences in financial reporting due to the variation in accounting practices.

An important step towards this goal took place in 1987 when the *International Organization for Securities Commissions (IOSCO)* was formed. By 1995 it had been agreed that the *International Accounting Standards Committee (IASC)* should be established to develop a basic set of accounting standards that IOSCO would endorse as internationally acceptable. Therefore, the IASC was set up in London in 1973 and began issuing *International Accounting Standards (IASs)* that could be followed by all countries.[12] However, IASC had no power to impose the standards and countries with their own accounting standards were reluctant to relinquish them. In addition, the IASC also found it difficult to agree standards that would be appropriate for all companies, in all countries and in all circumstances. This is not surprising because by the time it was dissolved in 2001, it had grown from 10 members to 153 members in 112 countries.

In 2001 the *International Accounting Standards Board (IASB)* was set up with an independent oversight organization, the name of which was changed to the *IFRS Foundation* in 2010. The IFRS Foundation is 'an independent, not-for-profit private sector organization working in the public interest' (IFRS Foundation, 2011). The principal objectives of the IFRS Foundation are:

- to develop a single set of high-quality, understandable, enforceable and globally accepted international financial reporting standards through its standard-setting body, the International Accounting Standards Board (IASB)
- to promote the use and rigorous application of those standards
- to take account of the financial reporting needs of emerging economies and small and medium-sized entities (SMEs)
- to bring about convergence of national accounting standards and IFRSs to high-quality solutions.

Governance and oversight of the IFRS Foundation rests with a geographically and professionally diverse body of 20 trustees, who are publicly accountable to a monitoring board of public capital market authorities. One crucial element in establishing the IASB was that it would have sufficient resources to carry out its responsibilities. Today, the task of securing those funds rests with the IFRS Foundation. This is achieved through mandatory levies for listed and non-listed companies in a growing number of countries.

The IASB currently has 15 full-time members and is responsible for the development and publication of IFRSs (including *IFRS for SMEs*) and for approving the interpretations of those IFRSs given by the IFRS Interpretations Committee. The IASB engages closely with stakeholders around the world, including investors, analysts, regulators, business leaders, accounting standard setters and the accountancy profession. The IFRS Interpretations Committee is the interpretative body of the IASB and currently has 14 voting members. Their task is to review widespread accounting issues relating to current IFRSs and to provide authoritative guidance on those issues. These interpretations are known as IFRICs. The IFRS Interpretations Committee works closely with similar national committees. Figure 4.8 shows the organization of the IFRS Foundation.

In 2001 the IASB adopted all the IASs issued by its predecessor and began issuing new *International Financial Reporting Standards (IFRSs)*, some of which replaced earlier standards. IFRSs set out the procedures and methods for the measurement, valuation and disclosure of an accounting transaction or event (IFRS is the term used to refer to any of the accounting standards issued by the IASB since 2001).

---

12. It was no coincidence that 1973 was also the year that the UK joined what became the EU and the USA established its own standard setter, the Financial Accounting Standards Board (FASB).

Figure 4.8 Organization of the IFRS Foundation

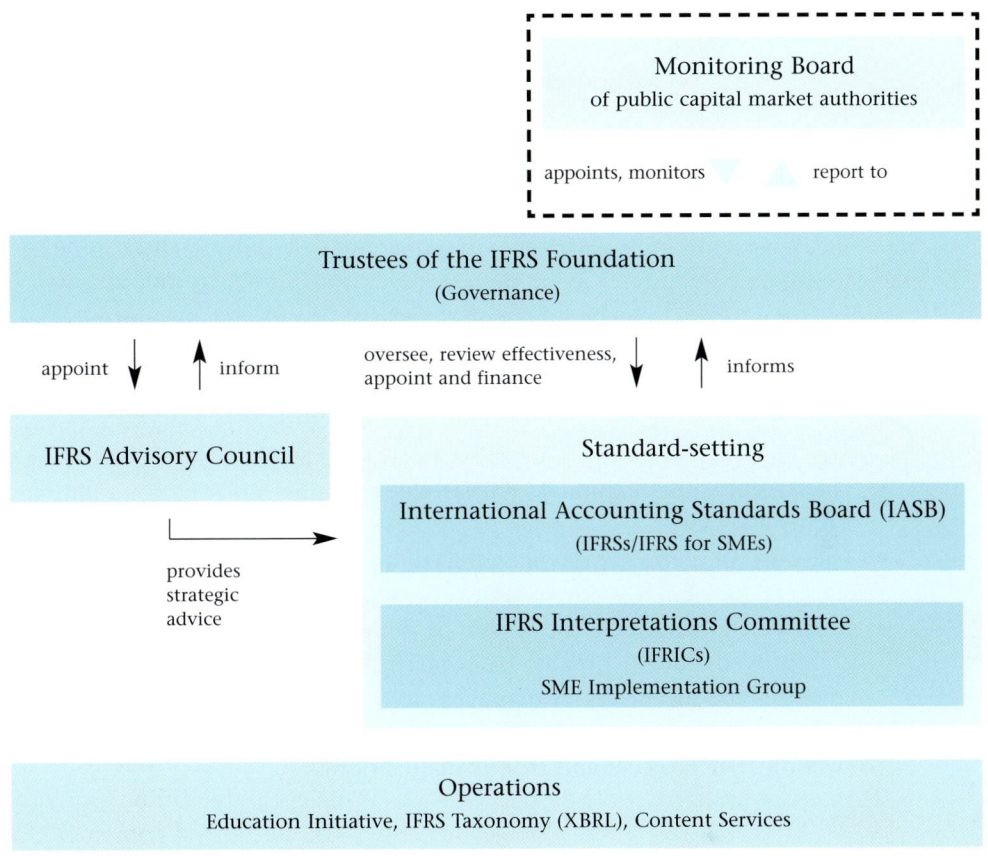

Source: IFRS Foundation (2011, n.p.).

Activity

What are the advantages and disadvantages of IFRSs?

The following pros and cons are drawn from Ball (2006), who was considering the issues in the run-up to the adoption of IFRSs by the EU in 2005. He divides the advantages into direct and indirect, and the disadvantages into immediate and longer-term.

Direct advantages of IFRSs:

- IFRSs provide more accurate, comprehensive and timely financial statement information relative to the national standards they replace in many countries.
- There are reduced costs arising from being informed in a timely fashion (mainly benefits small investors who, unlike investment analysts, do not have access to other sources of information).

- The cost of processing financial information is reduced, since no adjustments are needed for differences in GAAP. This benefits institutions creating standardized financial databases and should increase the efficiency with which the stock market incorporates the information in prices.
- Most assets can be reported using fair value accounting (e.g. replacement cost, market value, net realizable value, value in use), which contains more information than historical cost accounting.
- Companies can compete for capital on equal terms since there are reduced compliance costs for multinational companies, which only need to prepare one set of accounts.
- Transparency is achieved through the use of one global accounting language, which aids inter-company comparison and reduces information costs and information risk to investors, but only if IFRSs are implemented consistently.

Indirect advantages of IFRSs:

- The cost of equity capital is reduced due to higher information quality reducing the risk to investors.
- The cost of debt capital is reduced due to more efficient contracting in debt markets, particularly due to timelier loss recognition.
- Corporate governance (the system by which companies are directed and controlled) is improved due to greater transparency. In particular, timelier loss recognition increases the incentives of managers to attend to existing loss-making investments and strategies more quickly and to undertake fewer unprofitable investments (for example, pet projects and trophy acquisitions).

Immediate disadvantages of IFRSs:

- It is hard to agree on a global accounting language and whether it should be based on principles or rules. It will mean that national models of best practice may be lost.
- There will be initial training costs for preparers, auditors and enforcers.
- Fair value accounting leads to volatility and may reflect estimation noise or managerial manipulation.
- Despite some regulatory coordination, political and economic forces will lead to inconsistency in implementation.

Longer-term disadvantages of IFRSs:

- Allowing all countries to use the IFRS brand name discards information about reporting quality differences. There may also be free-rider problem where low-quality countries may adopt IFRSs in name only.
- Competition encourages innovation and discourages complacency, and bureaucracy and imposing global standards is risky centralization.
- At present IFRSs have a strong common law orientation, but over time the IASB risks becoming a politicized, bureaucratic UN-style body.

Initially the IASB focused on a full range of IFRSs for large, listed companies, but in 2009 it issued the *IFRS for SMEs*. This is a self-contained standard in a single document, designed to meet the needs and capabilities of small and medium-sized entities (SMEs), which are estimated to account for over 95% of companies around the world (IFRS Foundation, 2011). The standard is less complex than full IFRSs and simpler than many national GAAPS. It is available for any jurisdiction to adopt, irrespective of whether it has adopted full IFRSs. Any jurisdiction deciding to adopt the *IFRS for SMEs* can decide which non-publicly accountable entities should use it. The IASB states that it must not be used by listed companies or financial institutions.

The main ways in which the IASB explains that it has reduced complexity in the *IFRS for SMEs* are:

- Topics not relevant for SMEs are omitted (for example, earnings per share, interim financial reporting, and segment reporting).
- Where full IFRSs allow accounting policy choices, the *IFRS for SMEs* allows only the easier option (for example, no option to revalue property, equipment or intangibles; a cost-depreciation model for investment property unless fair value is readily available without undue cost or effort; no 'corridor approach' for actuarial gains and losses).
- Many principles for recognizing and measuring assets, liabilities, income and expenses in full IFRSs are simplified (for example, amortize goodwill; expense all borrowing and R&D costs; cost model for associates and jointly controlled entities; no available-for-sale or held-to-maturity classes of financial assets).
- Significantly fewer disclosures are required (roughly 300 versus 3,000).
- The standard has been written in clear, easily translatable language (by 2011, it was published in 11 languages).
- To reduce costs for preparers, revisions will be limited to once every 3 years.

Activity

What are the advantages and disadvantages of the *IFRS for SMEs*?

Apart from contributing to international convergence, some of the advantages you may have thought of are:

- The *IFRS for SMEs* reduces the financial reporting burden where full IFRSs or full national GAAP are required (for example, developing countries and transition economies).
- It reduces information costs and information risk to users.
- It improves access to capital.
- It aids comparison if it is applied consistently.
- In some jurisdictions it improves the quality of financial reporting compared to national GAAP.
- It reduces the risk of many different national GAAPs for SMEs, all loosely based on full IFRSs.

- It allows easy transition to full IFRSs if the company grows, as it is based on the same principles.

The main disadvantages are:

- It is hard to agree a definition of an SME that is appropriate and acceptable throughout the developed and developing world, in both market economies and in transition economies (those that have only recently moved to market economies).
- It is based on full IFRSs, which have been designed for large, listed companies.
- The unique features of any little GAAP in a particular jurisdiction may be lost.
- There will be initial training costs for preparers, auditors and enforcers, although implementation guidance released with the standard includes illustrative financial statements, presentation and disclosure checklist, guidance in the form of Q&As and free training materials in many languages.

The IASB's *standard-setting process* includes the publication of consultative documents on the accounting issue for public comment. These usually take the form of discussion papers and exposure drafts, as shown in Figure 4.9. This is a lengthy procedure to ensure

Figure 4.9 The IASB's standard-setting process

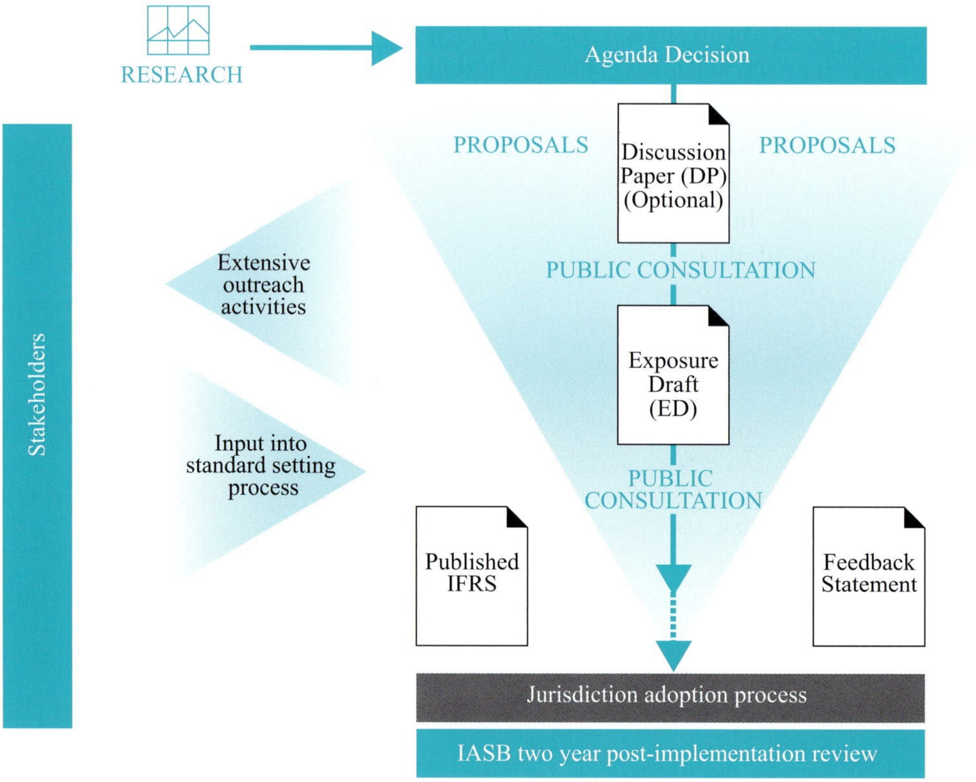

Source: IFRS Foundation (2011, n.p.).

wide consultation and full consideration of problems and alternative solutions. After all comments have been examined and field tests have been conducted, the IASB publishes an *exposure draft* for public comment. The exposure draft takes the same form and content as the proposed standard. After considering all comments and making any amendments, the IASB issues the IFRS. This process means the IASB engages closely with stakeholders around the world, including investors, analysts, regulators, business leaders, accounting standard setters and the accountancy profession. These include:

- European Commission
- European Financial Reporting Advisory Group (EFRAG)
- International Organization of Securities Commissions (IOSCO)
- International Federation of Accountants (IFAC)
- Financial Accounting Standards Board (FASB) in the USA
- Securities and Exchange Commission (SEC) in the USA
- Public Company Accounting Oversight Board (PCAOB) in the USA.

4.7   The future of UK GAAP

The EC supports the work of the IASB and since 2005 all public companies that are listed on an EU stock exchange (approximately 8,000) have been required to use IFRSs for preparing their consolidated (group) financial statements. In addition to the 27 EU Member States, this applies to the three European Economic Area (EEA) jurisdictions. Although Switzerland is not an EU or EEA member, most large companies in that country also use IFRS. This is a big step forward in the harmonization of financial reporting in Europe. However, as mentioned earlier in this chapter, this move towards convergence goes further and by 2011 more than 120 countries have adopted or permit the use of IFRSs. Some of those using full IFRSs and/or the *IFRS for SMEs* are those in the developing world or in emerging market economies which do not have national accounting standards. Other jurisdictions likely to adopt or permit IFRS in the near future include Korea, India and Japan, and most countries in Central and South America. A convergence project between IFRS and US GAAP has been started, but the USA has yet to make a decision about adopting IFRS.

An important recent development is the extent to which IFRS is affected by politics. The credit crunch, the problems in the banking sector and the attempts of politicians to resolve these questions have resulted in pressure on standard setters to amend their standards, primarily those on financial instruments. This pressure is unlikely to disappear, at least in the short term. The IASB is working hard to respond to this; we can therefore expect a continuous stream of changes to the standards in the next few months and years. (PWC, 2010, p. 1). This comment focuses on financial reporting by large companies, but at the other end of the scale there is growing pressure on the

IASB to develop a simpler set of standards for micro entities than the *IFRS for SMEs* (Cairns, 2011).

In 2009 the ASB published a consultation document on the future of financial reporting in the UK. This contained a proposal to move to an IFRS framework with three tiers, as shown in Table 4.2. The proposed IFRS framework would apply to all entities required to prepare financial statements that give a true and fair view and they would be allowed to adopt a higher tier if they wish. Regulation would continue to be based on differential reporting, but the focus would be on *public accountability* rather than size. According to the ASB (2010, p. 7), an entity has public accountability if:

- as at the reporting date, its debt or equity instruments are traded in a public market or it is in the process of issuing such instruments for trading in a public market (a domestic or foreign stock exchange or an over-the-counter market, including local and regional markets); or
- as one of its primary businesses, it holds assets in a fiduciary capacity for a broad group of outsiders and/or it is a deposit-taking entity for a broad group of outsiders. This is typically the case for banks, credit unions, insurance companies, securities brokers/dealers, mutual funds or investment banks.

EU-adopted IFRSs (Tier 1) would apply to listed group companies and any single entities with public accountability. The proposed *Financial Reporting Standard for Medium-sized Entities (FRSME)* (Tier 2) would apply to large and medium-sized non-publicly accountable entities and the smallest financial services businesses, such as small credit unions. The proposed FRSME would be a modified version of the *IFRS for SMEs*, which would avoid any conflict with CA2006 and the Fourth Directive. The FRSSE (Tier 3) would continue to apply to non-publicly accountable entities that qualify as small under CA2006. At the time of writing in 2011, the future is still a matter for debate and it is not yet clear whether the European Commission will endorse the *IFRS for SMEs* or issue an EU-adaption for use by Member States once it has completed the simplification of the Accounting Directives.

Table 4.2　Proposals for the future of UK GAAP

Tier	Accounting regime	Nature of entity	Reduced disclosure for
1	EU-adopted IFRS	Publicly accountable entities	Qualifying subsidiaries
2	FRSME	Entities without public accountability	Qualifying subsidiaries
3	FRSSE	Smaller entities without public accountability	

Source: ASB (2010, p. 6).

4.8 Conclusions

Financial accounting is primarily concerned with providing a true and fair view of the activities of a business to external parties. The regulatory framework for financial reporting in the UK has three main elements: company law, accounting standards and stock exchange rules. The latter only apply to listed companies, which are the most stringently regulated businesses because of the public interest in their financial statements. Listed companies are important because they make a substantial contribution to the economy. They are also important because the accounting practices they follow have been shaping financial accounting and reporting for all businesses, whether large or small. The regulatory framework ensures that the annual report and accounts are prepared in a standard way and provide high-quality, reliable information for external users. At present all public and private companies in the UK must file their annual report and accounts with Companies House, where they are available to the public.

We have examined the regulation of financial reporting in the context of the historical reasons for national differences in accounting practices and the need for harmonization among EU Member States and wider international convergence through the use of IFRSs. We have looked at some of the advantages and disadvantages of accounting standards in general and by focusing on the pros and cons of full IFRS and the *IFRS for SMEs*. We have touched upon two important proposals that have not been decided at the time of going to print: the suggestion that micro entities should be exempt from some of the financial reporting requirements in the Fourth Directive, and the ASB's proposals for a three-tier approach to the future of UK GAAP.

The increase in the number of jurisdictions adopting or permitting the use of IFRS is a very important development and this chapter has provided an overview of the way in which the IASB sets IFRSs. In the next chapter we will examine the conceptual framework that provides the principles the IASB follows when setting an accounting standard.

Practice questions

1 Describe the key elements of the regulatory framework for public and private companies in the UK.

2 Define the term *financial reporting*. In addition, explain the need for the regulation of financial reporting and the purpose of the regulatory framework.

3 Explain the acronym GAAP and outline the historical reasons why one country's GAAP could develop differently from another.

4 Explain what an accounting standard is and discuss the advantages and disadvantages of IFRS. Draw conclusions from your analysis.

5 Search the ASB's website (http://www.frc.org.uk/asb/) to get up-to-date information on the future of UK GAAP and find articles on the subject in the accountancy press (for example *Accountancy Age, Accountancy* magazine or *Accounting & Business*). Then write a brief essay on the advantages and disadvantages of the new regime.

References

Alexander, D. and Nobes, C. (2010) *Financial Accounting – An International Introduction*, 4th edition. Harlow: Pearson (FT Prentice Hall).

APB (2006) *The Special Auditor's Report on Abbreviated Accounts in the United Kingdom*. London: Auditing Practices Board, Bulletin 2006/3.

ASB (2009) *Policy Proposal: The Future of UK GAAP*. Consultation Paper, August.

ASB (2010) *The future of financial reporting in the United Kingdom and the Republic of Ireland – The Key Facts*. October.

Ball, R. (2006) International Financial Reporting Standards (IFRS): pros and cons for investors. *Accounting and Business Research*, International Accounting Policy forum, pp. 5–27.

BIS/FRC (2011) *Proposals to Reform the Financial Reporting Council*, Consultation Paper, October. Available at: http://www.frc.org.uk/press/pub2653.html (accessed 21 November 2011).

Cairns, D. (2011) Financial reporting by micro-entities. *Accountancy*, November, p. 57.

Companies House (n.d.) *Companies Act 2006 Accounts Exemption Thresholds for companies with accounting periods starting on or after 6th April 2008*. Available at: http://www.companieshouse.gov.uk/companiesAct/implementations/apr2008 ExemptionThreshold.shtml (accessed 30 November 2011).

Dearing, R. (1988) *The Making of Accounting Standards*. Report of the Review Committee (The Dearing Report). London: ICAEW.

Deloitte (2010) *Swimming in Words – Surveying Narrative Reporting in Annual Reports*. Available from: http://www.iasplus.com/uk/1010ukswimminginwords.pdf (accessed 30 November 2011).

European Parliament (2011) *Draft Recommendation for Second Reading on the Council position at first reading with a view to the adoption of a directive of the European Parliament and of the Council amending Council Directive 78/660/EEC on the annual accounts of certain types of companies as regards micro-entities*, (10765/1/2011 – C7-0323/2011 – 2009/0035(COD)).

FRC (2011) Email to Palgrave Macmillan re FRC structure, 31 October.

Haller, A. and Walton, P. (2003) Country differences and harmonization. In P. Walton, A. Haller and B. Raffournier (eds), *International Accounting*, 2nd edition. London: International Thomson Business Press.

IFRS Foundation (2011) *About the IFRS Foundation and the IASB*, May. Available from: http://www.ifrs.org/The+organisation/IASCF+and+IASB.htm (accessed 21 November 2011).

Law, J. (ed.) (2010) *Dictionary of Accounting*, 4th edition. Oxford: Oxford University Press.

PwC (2010) *International Financial Reporting Standards – Pocket Guide 2010*, August, PricewaterhouseCoopers. Available from: http://www.pwc.com/gx/en/ifrs-reporting/pocket-guide-to-ifrs.jhtml (accessed 21 November 2011).

5 Conceptual framework for financial reporting

Learning objectives

When you have studied this chapter, you should be able to:

- explain the need for a conceptual framework for financial reporting
- describe the objective of general purpose financial reporting and the needs of the primary user groups
- discuss the qualitative characteristics of useful financial information
- define the elements of financial statements and explain the recognition and measurement criteria
- explain the concepts of capital and capital maintenance.

5.1   Introduction

In Chapter 4 we examined the regulatory framework for financial reporting and discussed the context in which financial reporting takes place. Companies around the world prepare financial statements for external users, but there are likely to be national differences caused by social, economic and legal circumstances. In addition, there are likely to be differences caused by national regulators focusing on the needs of different user groups.

Financial accounting is primarily concerned with providing a true and fair view of the activities of a business to external parties. Financial statements are prepared in accordance with a regulatory framework, which in many countries comprises company law, accounting standards and stock exchange rules for listed companies. In this chapter we will explain how the development of accounting standards is underpinned by a *conceptual framework*, which assists in improving the quality of financial reporting. Since more than 120 countries have adopted or permit the use of International Financial Reporting Standards (IFRSs) issued by the International Accounting Standards Board (IASB), we will focus on the IASB's conceptual framework.

This chapter is important because the principles contained in the conceptual framework are those reflected in the IFRSs we will examine in the next few chapters. We start by looking at the need for such a framework and go on to discuss some of the key principles and definitions.

5.2 Need for a conceptual framework

Prior to the 1970s, the way in which accountants in the USA and UK had tried to achieve consistency in financial accounting was to take an inductive approach based on rationalizing what happened in practice. However, this was criticized because problems were only dealt with as they arose, which caused overlaps, contradictions and loopholes. They then tried a deductive approach based on theoretical assumptions, but this was considered to be unrealistic because it challenged best practice. This led to demand for a conceptual framework to provide a set of coherent underlying principles for financial reporting that would address questions such as:

- What is the objective of financial reporting?
- Who are the users of the financial statements?
- What information does each group of users need?
- What type of financial statements will best satisfy their needs?

Key definition

A conceptual framework is a statement of theoretical principles that provides guidance for financial accounting and reporting.

Source: Law (2010, p. 102).

In the USA, the Financial Accounting Standards Board (FASB) published *Concept Statements* between 1978 and 2000. These were a strong influence on developments at the international level, and in 1989 the *International Accounting Standards Committee (IASC)* issued the *Framework for the Preparation and Presentation of Financial Statements*, which was subsequently adopted by its successor, the IASB. These formed the basis of the UK's *Statement of Principles for Financial Reporting*, which was published by the ASB in 1999. This sets out the concepts that underlie the preparation and presentation of financial statements for external users. We are going to focus on the IASB's Framework.

The IASB is currently updating the Framework and as each chapter is completed, it replaces the relevant paragraphs in the *Framework for the Preparation and Presentation of Financial Statements* that was published in 1989. The updated Framework is called the *Conceptual Framework for Financial Reporting* and the first version (IASB, 2010) includes revised Chapters 1 and 3. Our discussion will focus on that first version, which we will refer to as 'the Framework'.

Activity

What are the advantages of having a conceptual framework for financial reporting?

You might start by thinking about the deficiencies in the inductive and deductive approaches taken previously and then go on to consider who will benefit from a conceptual framework. The main advantage of a conceptual framework is that it clarifies the conceptual underpinnings of accounting standards and allows standard setters to develop accounting standards on a consistent basis. It also assists preparers, auditors and users of financial statements to understand the approach to standard setting, and the nature and function of the financial information reported. Another advantage is that it gives guidance to preparers resolving accounting issues that are not specifically addressed by an existing IFRS or interpretation.

The IASB has not yet revised the purpose of the Framework, but the introduction carried forward from the 1989 publication describes the seven purposes of the Framework (IASB, 2010, A25). These are:

- to assist the Board in the development of future IFRSs and in its review of existing IFRSs
- to assist the IASB in promoting harmonization of regulations, accounting standards and procedures relating to the presentation of financial statements by providing a basis for reducing the number of alternative accounting treatments permitted by IFRSs
- to assist national standard-setting bodies in developing national standards
- to assist preparers of financial statements in applying IFRSs and in dealing with topics that have yet to form the subject of an IFRS
- to assist auditors in forming an opinion on whether financial statements comply with IFRSs
- to assist users of financial statements in interpreting the information contained in financial statements prepared in compliance with IFRSs
- to provide those who are interested in the work of the IASB with information about its approach to the formulation of IFRSs.

The Framework is not an IFRS. It does not define standards for any particular measurement or disclosure issue or override any specific IFRS. The various chapters of the Framework deal with the following concepts:

- the objective of financial reporting (Chapter 1)
- the reporting entity (Chapter 2, which has not yet been issued)
- qualitative characteristics of useful financial information (Chapter 3)
- the underlying assumption, the elements of financial statements, the recognition and measurement of the elements of financial statements, and concepts of capital and capital maintenance (Chapter 4, which has not yet been revised).

Having looked at the scope of the Framework, we will now examine the main principles contained in each chapter.

5.3 Objective of general purpose financial reporting

The Framework is a set of principles that underpins the preparation of *general purpose* financial statements intended to meet the needs of a range of external users. General purpose financial statements can be distinguished from *special purpose* financial statements, such as those prepared specifically for share offerings, borrowing or tax purposes.

5.3.1 Objective

The Framework states that the *objective* of general purpose financial reporting is 'to provide information about the reporting entity that is useful to existing and potential investors, lenders and other creditors in making decisions about providing resources to the entity. Those decisions involve buying, selling or holding equity and debt instruments and providing or settling loans and other forms of credit' (OB2). This principle forms the foundation of the Framework and other aspects of the Framework flow logically from it.

5.3.2 Users and their needs

The Framework defines the primary users of general purpose financial reports (the narrative reports, the financial statements and the related notes) as existing and potential investors, lenders and other creditors (OB3). These users require financial information for economic decision-making purposes.

- *Existing and potential investors* need financial information to help them make investment decisions such as buying, selling or holding equity and debt instruments. These decisions depend on the investment risks and returns. Returns might include dividends payable on shares, principal and interest payments or market price increases in equity and debt instruments.
- *Existing and potential lenders* need financial information to help them make lending decisions. These decisions depend on the lending risks and returns. They need to assess whether loans can be repaid and whether the interest they expect to receive will be paid when it is due. As expectations depend on their assessment of the amount, timing and uncertainty of payments, they need information that will help them assess the prospects for future net cash inflows to an entity.
- *Existing and potential creditors* need financial information to help them make credit decisions. These decisions will depend on the credit risks and returns. The latter usually take the form of interest payments. As in the case of lenders, their

expectations depend on their assessment of the amount, timing and uncertainty of receiving the amounts owed to them, and therefore they need information that will help them assess the prospects for future net cash inflows to an entity.

You can see from this discussion that one of the main purposes of financial reporting is to provide information to help users make economic decisions. Investors also need relevant and reliable financial information to assess the *stewardship* of management. The Framework goes on to explain that in order to assess an entity's prospects for future net cash inflows, users need information about the resources of the entity, claims against the entity, and information on how efficiently and effectively the entity's management and governing board have discharged their responsibilities to use the entity's resources. Examples of such responsibilities include protecting the resources of the business from unfavourable effects of economic factors such as price and technological changes and ensuring that the entity complies with applicable laws, regulations and contractual provisions. Information about how management has discharged its responsibilities is also useful for decisions by existing investors, lenders and other creditors who have the right to vote on or otherwise influence management's actions (OB4). Figure 5.1 summarizes the primary users and their needs.

Figure 5.1 Primary users of general purpose financial reports

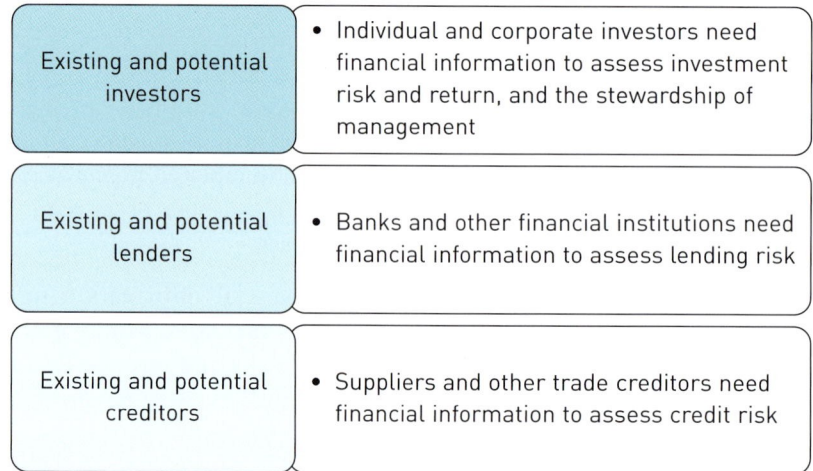

The Framework acknowledges that general purpose financial reports cannot meet all the information needs of the primary users, many of whom are not in a position to demand special purpose financial reports. Therefore, they will also need to obtain information from other sources such as reports on general economic conditions and expectations, political events and political climate, and industry and company outlooks (OB6). For example, if you were an investor, you could make use of information supplied by investment analysts or conduct your own analysis of the economy from International Monetary Fund reports. You could analyse the industry from market reports and compare the entity's performance against that of its competitors or industry benchmarks using data from trade associations or financial databases.

You need to remember that general purpose financial reports are not designed to show the value of a reporting entity. The Framework points out that these financial reports are intended to provide information to help existing and potential investors, lenders and other creditors to estimate the value of the reporting entity (OB7). Although these primary user groups have different, and possibly conflicting, information needs, the IASB will seek to provide information that will meet the needs of the maximum number of primary users. However, focusing on common information needs does not prevent the reporting entity from including additional information that is most useful to a particular subset of primary users (OB8).

The Framework notes that the needs of *management* are not considered because managers can obtain the information they need internally. Although other external parties, including *regulators* (for example prudential and market regulators) and members of the *public* may also find general purpose financial reports useful, such reports are not directed at meeting their specific needs (OB9–10).

Activity

What do you think would be the effect on users if a large company did not supply full information about its financial position, financial performance and changes in financial position to the primary user groups?

One way to tackle this question is to remember that existing and potential investors need financial reports in order to assess investment risk and return, and to assess the stewardship of management. The other primary user group comprises existing and potential lenders and other creditors. You may have thought of some of the following factors:

- Investors will be suspicious that the directors had something to hide and are running the company for their own benefits rather than in the best interests of investors. Therefore, existing and potential investors would be unwilling to invest in the business.
- Lenders would be unable to assess and monitor the lending risk. Therefore they might withdraw existing sources of finance, raise the interest rates, shorten the term of the loan or ask for personal guarantees from the directors. The company would find it harder to obtain access to new sources of finance.
- Suppliers would also be unable to assess risk and might refuse to give credit terms to the company or require the company to insure against the risk of being unable to pay for goods and services supplied on credit.

Investors, lenders and other creditors have a common interest in information about the entity's economic resources and the claims against the reporting entity. This information is shown in the *statement of financial position*. They are also interested in information about the effects of transactions and other events that change a reporting entity's economic resources and claims. This is shown in the *statement of comprehensive income*. Finally, they have a common interest in the changes in the entity's cash flows, which are presented in the *statement of cash flows* (OB12–16). However, one point of difference is that while lenders and major suppliers have the economic power to demand special purpose financial statements, investors have no such power and must rely on general purpose financial statements.

The Framework asserts that information about the nature and amounts of the entity's economic resources and claims can help users identify its financial strengths and weaknesses. This can help users to assess its liquidity and solvency, its needs for additional finance and how successful it is likely to be in obtaining that finance. It goes on to contend that information about priorities and payment requirements of existing claims helps users to predict how future cash flows will be distributed among those with a claim against the business (OB13).

5.4 Qualitative characteristics of usefulness

As already mentioned, the objective of financial reporting is to provide information that is useful to users. In Chapter 3 of the Framework (IASB, 2010) the *qualitative characteristics* that are likely to make the financial information useful to users are divided into *fundamental* qualitative characteristics and *enhancing* qualitative characteristics. These accounting principles flow naturally from the objective of financial reporting and apply to financial information provided in financial statements, as well as to financial information provided in other ways. The Framework acknowledges that cost, which is a constraint on the entity's ability to provide useful financial information, also applies to financial information provided in financial statements, as well as to financial information provided in other ways. However, the considerations in applying the qualitative characteristics and the cost constraint may be different for different types of information. For example, applying them to forward-looking information may be different from applying them to information about existing economic resources and claims and to changes in those resources and claims (QC3).

The fundamental qualitative characteristics are (QC5–16):

- *Relevance* Relevant financial information is capable of making a difference to users' decisions. Financial information is capable of making a difference to decisions if it has predictive value and/or confirmatory value. These two are interrelated. *Materiality* is an entity-specific aspect of relevance based on the nature or magnitude (or both) of the items to which the information relates in the context of an individual entity's financial report. The *materiality concept* is the principle that only items of information that are material (significant) are included in the financial statements. An item of information is material if its omission or misstatement could influence the economic decisions of those using the financial statements. Materiality depends on the size of the item or error and the circumstances of its omission or misstatement (for example, an omission of revenue of £10 versus an omission of £10,000).

- *Faithful representation* General purpose financial reports represent economic phenomena in words as well as numbers. To be useful, the information must not only represent relevant phenomena but it must also be a faithful representation of the phenomena. Ideally it should be complete, neutral and free from error. Free from error does not mean perfectly accurate. For example, an estimate of an unobservable value cannot be perfectly accurate, but it is a faithful representation if is clearly described as being an estimate and the nature and limitations of the estimating process are explained, and no errors have been made in selecting and applying an appropriate process for developing the estimate.

Subject to the effects of enhancing characteristics and the cost constraint, the Framework suggests that the most efficient and effective process for applying the fundamental qualitative characteristics would usually be (QC18):

1. Identify an economic phenomenon that has the potential to be useful to users of the reporting entity's financial information.
2. Identify the type of information about that phenomenon that would be most relevant if it is available and can be faithfully represented.
3. Determine whether that information is available and can be faithfully represented. If so, the process of satisfying the fundamental qualitative characteristics ends at that point. If not, the process is repeated with the next most relevant type of information.

The enhancing qualitative characteristics are (QC19–32):

- *Comparability* The information is more useful if it can be compared with similar information for the entity in other periods, or similar information for other entities. A comparison requires at least two items. Consistency helps achieve comparability and refers to the use of the same methods for the same items, either from period to period within a reporting entity or in a single period across entities.
- *Verifiability* The financial information is more useful if it is verifiable. Verifiability helps to assure users that the information is a faithful representation. It means that different knowledgeable and independent observers could reach consensus, although not necessarily complete agreement, that a particular depiction is a faithful representation.
- *Timeliness* The financial information is more useful if it is timely. Timeliness means that information is available to users in time to be capable of influencing their decisions.
- *Understandability* The financial information is more useful if is readily understandable. Classifying, characterizing and presenting information clearly and concisely makes it understandable. While some phenomena are inherently complex and cannot be made easy to understand, to exclude such information would make financial reports incomplete and potentially misleading. Financial reports are

prepared for users who have a reasonable knowledge of business and economic activities and who review and analyse the information with diligence.

The Framework explains that enhancing qualitative characteristics should be maximized to the extent possible. However, either individually or as a group, they cannot make information useful if that information is irrelevant or is not faithfully represented. Applying the enhancing qualitative characteristics is an iterative process that does not follow a prescribed order (QC33–34). Figure 5.2 summarizes the qualitative characteristics of usefulness we have discussed.

Figure 5.2   Qualitative characteristics of useful financial information

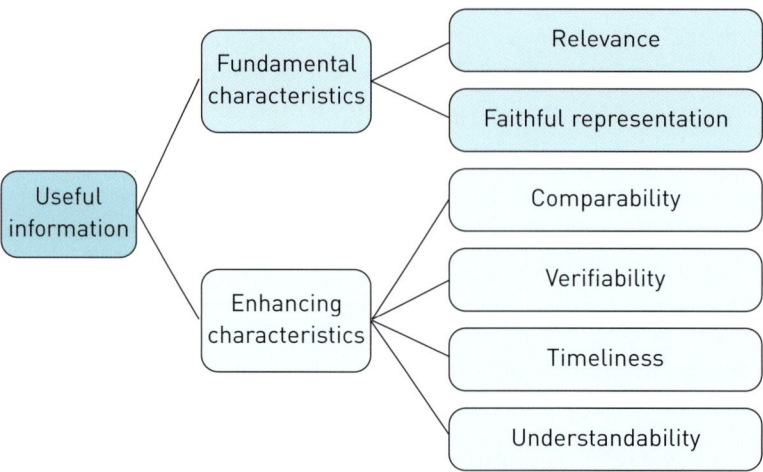

Although you may find some of the principles difficult to understand at this stage, the importance of the concepts will become clearer as you progress through the next few chapters. The following activity will help you think about some of the main qualitative characteristics that make financial information useful.

Activity

Think about your bank statements or credit card statement and answer the following questions:

	Yes	No
(a) Is any item insignificant or irrelevant?	❑	❑
(b) Does the information help you make spending or borrowing decisions?	❑	❑
(c) Is the information a faithful representation of your transactions?	❑	❑
(d) Is the information timely enough to make spending or borrowing decisions to stop you inadvertently incurring additional costs?	❑	❑
(e) Is the information prepared consistently so that you can compare it with corresponding information for previous periods?	❑	❑
(f) Assuming the information is relevant, is it easy to understand?	❑	❑

The Framework points out that cost is a key constraint on the information that can be provided by financial reporting and it is important that the costs are justified by the benefits. When applying the cost constraint in developing an IFRS, the IASB seeks qualitative and quantitative information from providers of financial information, users, auditors, academics and others about the expected nature and quantity of the benefits and costs of that standard in relation to financial reporting generally. That does not mean that assessments of costs and benefits always justify the same reporting requirements for all entities (QC35–39). As you will remember from the previous chapter, the *IFRS for SMEs* demonstrates that differences may be appropriate because of different sizes of entities, different ways of raising capital (publicly or privately), different users' needs or other factors.

5.5 Elements of financial statements

Chapter 4 of the Framework has not yet been revised and it is likely that there will be some changes to the definitions of the *elements of financial statements*. Therefore, you will need to keep up to date with any changes as they are published. The definitions of the element represent very important principles in the Framework as they form the foundation of IFRSs.

The chapter starts by confirming the *underlying assumption* that the financial statements are normally prepared on the basis that the business is a *going concern* and will continue in operation for the foreseeable future, unless it is known otherwise. If the entity intends or needs to liquidate or materially curtail the scale of its operations, the basis used must be disclosed (4.1). This important assumption underpins the accrual basis of accounting, which we discussed in the first chapter of this book.

For publicly accountable entities using IFRSs, guidance on the presentation of general purpose financial statements is contained in IAS 1, *Presentation of Financial Statements* (IASB, 2011). The presentation and general requirements are similar for non-publicly accountable entities under the *IFRS for SMEs* and only differ in terms of the minimum disclosure requirements. A complete set of financial statements under IAS 1 comprises a *statement of comprehensive income*, a *statement of financial position*, a *statement of changes in equity* and a *statement of cash flows*. An entity must present a complete set of financial statements at least annually with notes that provide a summary of accounting policies and other explanatory information relating to the items in the financial statements. Comparative information for the previous period must also be provided. Table 5.1 compares the IAS 1 titles for the financial statements with those traditionally used

Table 5.1 Set of financial statements under IAS 1

IAS 1 terminology	Traditional UK terminology
Statement of comprehensive income	Profit and loss account
Statement of financial position	Balance sheet
Statement of changes in equity	Statement of recognized gains and losses
Statement of cash flows	Cash flow statement

in the UK. You need to remember that reporting entities can use other titles for the financial statements and the illustrative formats are not mandatory.

The following items must be identified:

- the reporting enterprise
- whether the statements are for a single entity or a group
- the date or period covered
- the presentation currency and the level of precision (thousands, millions, etc).

Each material class of items must be presented separately in the financial statements and dissimilar items may be aggregated only if they are individually immaterial. For consistency, the presentation and classification of items in the financial statements should stay the same from one period to the next, unless a change is justified by a change in circumstances or a new IFRS (IAS 1, para 45).

We are now ready to consider the elements in the financial statements. The Framework explains that financial statements present the effects of economic transactions and other events in broad categories according to their economic characteristics, which form the elements of financial *statements*. The presentation of these elements in the statement of comprehensive income and the statement of financial position involves a process of sub-classification in order to present the information in a way that is useful to users (for example, by nature or by function). The statement of cash flows reflects elements in the statement of comprehensive income and some changes in the elements in the statement of financial position.

5.5.1   Financial performance

Financial performance is concerned with the profitability of the entity. Users need information on the entity's financial performance to assess potential changes in its economic resources and its capacity to generate cash from its resources. In addition, users need information to evaluate how effectively any additional resources might be used. The elements that relate to the measurement of financial performance are shown in the *statement of comprehensive income* and the *statement of changes in equity*. These are:

- income
- expenses.

Key definitions

- Income is increases in economic benefits during the accounting period in the form of inflows or enhancements of assets or decreases of liabilities that result in increases in equity, other than those relating to contributions from equity participants.
- Expenses are decreases in economic benefits during the accounting period in the form of outflows or depletions of assets or incurrences of liabilities that result in

> decreases in equity, other than those relating to distributions to equity
> participants.
>
> *Source*: IASB (2010, para 4.25).

Under IAS 1 (IASB, 2011) and the *IFRS for SMEs* (IASB, 2009), income and expenses must not be offset against each other, unless expressly required or permitted. The Framework explains that the definition of income encompasses both *revenue* and *gains*. Revenue arises in the course of the ordinary activities of the business. Gains represent other items that meet the definition of income and may, or may not, arise in the course of the ordinary activities of an entity. As gains represent increases in economic benefits, they are no different in nature from other revenue and are not treated as a separate element (4.29–30). The definition of expenses encompasses both *expenses* and *losses*. Expenses arise in the course of the ordinary activities of the business. Losses represent other items that meet the definition of expenses and may, or may not, arise in the course of the ordinary activities of an entity. As losses represent decreases in economic benefits, they are no different in nature from other expenses and are not treated as a separate element (4.33–34).

5.5.2   Financial position

Financial position is concerned with the economic resources the entity controls, its financial structure, its liquidity and solvency and its ability to adapt to changes in the business environment. Users need information on the entity's financial position to help them assess its ability to generate future cash flows and evaluate how those cash flows will be distributed among stakeholders. In addition, users need information to evaluate the entity's ability to raise any finance that might be needed and to meet financial commitments when they fall due. The elements that relate to the measurement of financial position are shown in the *statement of financial position*. These are:

- assets
- liabilities
- equity.

Key definitions

- An asset is a resource controlled by the entity as a result of past events and from which future economic benefits are expected to flow to the entity.
- A liability is a present obligation of the entity resulting from past events, the settlement of which is expected to result in an outflow from the entity of resources embodying economic benefits.
- Equity is the residual interest in the assets of the entity after deducting all its liabilities.

Source: IASB (2010, para 4.4).

Under IAS 1 (IASB, 2011) and the *IFRS for SMEs* (IASB, 2009), assets and liabilities must not be offset against each other, unless expressly required or permitted.

Activity

In the following scenarios decide whether you should classify the item as an asset or a liability.

	Asset	Liability
(a) Your taxi business, Parker Cars Ltd, provides a warranty to all contract customers that their chauffeur will arrive on time.	❑	❑
(b) Parker Cars Ltd has acquired a licence that cost £25,000 that allows you to operate your business close to the two main London airports. This will save you £5,000 in motoring costs over the next 4 years.	❑	❑
(c) Parker Cars Ltd has paid Autoshop Ltd £5,000 towards setting up a workshop that will give priority to any maintenance or repairs needed by your vehicles.	❑	❑

Answers: (a) Liability (b) Asset (c) Not an asset because the resource is not controlled by Parker Cars Ltd and argument that there are future economic benefits is weak.

5.6 Recognition and measurement of elements

The Framework defines *recognition* as the process of incorporating in the statement of financial position or statement of comprehensive income an item that meets the definition of an element and satisfies the following criteria for recognition:

- it is probable that any future economic benefit associated with the item will flow to or from the entity; and
- the item has a cost or value that can be measured with reliability (4.37–38).

Based on these general criteria:

- *Income* is recognized in the statement of comprehensive income when an increase in future economic benefits related to an increase in an asset or a decrease of a liability has arisen and can be measured reliably. Thus, the recognition of income occurs simultaneously with the recognition of an increase in an asset or a decrease of a liability.
- *Expenses* are recognized in the statement of comprehensive income when a decrease in future economic benefits related to a decrease in an asset or an increase of a liability has risen that can be measured reliably. Thus, the recognition of expenses occurs simultaneously with the recognition of an increase in a liability or a decrease in an asset.
- An *asset* is recognized in the statement of financial position when it is probable that the future economic benefits will flow to the entity and the asset has a cost or value that can be measured reliably.

- A *liability* is recognized in the statement of financial position when it is probable that an outflow of resources embodying economic benefits will result from the settlement of a present obligation and the amount at which the settlement will take place can be measured reliably.

The Framework defines measurement as the process of determining the monetary amounts at which the elements of the financial statements are to be recognized and carried in the statement of financial position and the statement of comprehensive income (4.54). It is important to note that the Framework does not include principles for selecting the basis of measurement for particular elements of financial statements or in particular circumstances, but mentions the following four bases:

- *Historical cost* We examined the fundamental accounting principles in Chapter 1 of this book. Under historical cost, assets are recorded at the amount paid or the fair value of the consideration given at the time they were acquired. Liabilities are recorded at the amount of proceeds received in exchange for the obligation or at the amounts expected to be paid to satisfy the liability in the normal course of business.
- *Current cost* Assets are carried at the amount of cash or cash equivalents that would have to be paid if the same or an equivalent asset was acquired currently. Liabilities are carried at the undiscounted amount of cash or cash equivalents that would be required to settle the obligation currently. From this you can see that current cost could be described as the replacement value or the entry value.
- *Realizable (settlement) value* Assets are carried at the amount of cash or cash equivalents that could currently be obtained by selling the asset in an orderly disposal. Liabilities are carried at their settlement values, which are the undiscounted amounts to be paid to satisfy the liabilities in the normal course of business. From this you can see that realizable value represents the exit value.
- *Present value* Assets are carried at the present discounted value of the future net cash inflows that the item is expected to generate in the normal course of business. Liabilities are carried at the present discounted value of the future net cash outflows that are expected to be required to settle the liabilities in the normal course of business.

Historical cost is the most commonly used measurement base, but is usually combined with others. We will look at specific examples when we examine specific IFRSs in subsequent chapters.

5.7   Concepts of capital and capital maintenance

The Framework provides two concepts of capital. An entity's choice should be based on user needs and most adopt a *financial concept* of capital when preparing their financial statements (4.47–58).

- Under a *financial concept of capital*, capital is synonymous with the net assets (assets minus liabilities) or equity.
- Under a *physical concept of capital*, capital is regarded as the productive capacity or operating capability of the entity (for example, as measured in units of output per day).

These concepts of capital give rise to the corresponding two concepts of *capital maintenance*, which provide the point of reference by which profit is measured. You may find it helpful to start with the notion that capital is maintained if the capital at the start of the accounting period is equal to the capital at the end of the period.

- Under the *financial capital maintenance concept*, the entity makes a profit if capital at the end of the accounting period is higher than capital at the start of the period, after excluding any distributions to and contributions from the owner during the period.
- Under the *physical capital maintenance concept*, the entity makes a profit if the productive capacity or operating capability is higher at the end of the accounting period than at the start of the period.

The following activity will help you understand the concepts of capital and capital maintenance.

Activity

Last year Joe Cash won £5 million in the national lottery, which he used to start up a business called Joe Cash Ltd. At the start of the year the business had £5 million capital and £5 million cash. During the year the business purchased inventory. By the end of the year all the inventory had been sold for £6.25 million. Assume there were no other transactions.

(a) Calculate the profit for the year under the financial capital maintenance concept.
(b) Joe finds out that it would cost £5.65 million to replace the inventory at the end of the year in terms of its operating capacity. Calculate the profit for the year under the physical capital maintenance concept.

Check your answer against the calculations below.

	Financial capital maintenance £m	Physical capital maintenance £m
Assets at the end of the year	6.25	6.25
Assets required at the end of the year to maintain capital		
(a) Financial capital maintenance	(5.00)	
(b) Physical capital maintenance		(5.65)
Profit for the period	1.25	0.60

This question is not as difficult as it might look. You just needed to remember the principles of the two capital maintenance concepts that explain how profit is earned. Under the financial capital maintenance concept, profit or loss is the difference between the capital at the end of the accounting period (£6.25 million) and capital at the start of the period (£5 million). In this simple exercise, there were no distributions to or contributions from the owner that need to be considered. Under the physical capital concept, the profit or loss is the difference between its operating capability at the end of the period (£6.25 million) and its operating capability at the start of the period (£5.65 million).

5.8　Conclusions

In this chapter we have examined the need for a conceptual framework for financial reporting and discussed the advantages and disadvantages in the context of dissatisfaction with the inductive and deductive approaches to standard setting. Because of the widespread use of IFRS around the world, we have focused on the latest issue of the *Conceptual Framework for Financial Reporting* (IASB, 2010). As this is in the process of being revised, you will need to be vigilant in finding out when the next update is available on the IASB's website.

The sections of the Framework that have been revised so far, and which we have discussed in this chapter, cover the principles relating to the objective of general purpose financial reporting, the identification of the primary user groups and the qualitative characteristics of useful financial information. The IASB has yet to issue the section on the reporting entity and to revise the final part of the Framework. Based on the original 1989 Framework, we have drawn your attention to the definitions of the elements of financial statements and the recognition and measurement criteria. We have also examined the concepts of capital and capital maintenance. A set of financial statements under IAS 1 comprises a statement of comprehensive income, a statement of financial position, a statement of changes in equity and a statement of cash flows. We will examine each of these statements in turn in the next chapters.

Practice questions

1　Explain what a conceptual framework is and the advantages of having such a framework.

2　Describe the objective of general purpose financial reporting and the information needs of the three primary user groups identified in the IASB Framework (2010).

3　Explain the fundamental and enhancing qualitative characteristics of usefulness in the latest issue of the IASB Framework.

4　Define the three elements of financial position and the two elements of financial performance in the IASB Framework (2010).

5 Explain the general recognition criteria relating to the elements of financial statements and outline the four measurement methods mentioned in the latest issue of the IASB Framework. In addition, explain the financial capital maintenance and physical capital maintenance concepts.

References

IASB (2009) *IFRS for SMEs*. London: International Accounting Standards Board.

IASB (2010) *The Conceptual Framework for Financial Reporting*, September. London: International Accounting Standards Board.

IASB (2011) IAS 1, *Presentation of Financial Statements*. London: International Accounting Standards Board.

IASC (1989) *Framework for the Preparation and Presentation of Financial Statements*. London: International Accounting Standards Committee.

Law, J. (ed.) (2010) *Dictionary of Accounting*, 4th edition. Oxford: Oxford University Press.

6 Statement of comprehensive income

Learning objectives

When you have studied this chapter, you should be able to:

- explain the purpose of the statement of comprehensive income
- differentiate between accruals and prepayments
- calculate depreciation using the straight-line method
- differentiate between bad debts and doubtful receivables
- prepare a statement of comprehensive income.

6.1 Introduction

In Chapters 4 and 5 we discussed the regulatory framework for financial reporting and the principles contained in the *Conceptual Framework for Financial Reporting* (IASB, 2010). The latter underpins the development and interpretation of International Financial Reporting Standards (IFRSs), which are one of the key elements of the regulatory framework in EU member states and many other jurisdictions around the world. The objective of general purpose financial reporting is to provide information about the reporting entity that is useful to existing and potential investors, lenders and other creditors in making decisions about providing resources to the entity. The annual report and accounts is the main source of financial information about a company or other reporting entity and it contains narrative reports as well as financial statements.

In Chapter 3 we explained that the accounting system used by most businesses is based on double-entry bookkeeping. This is an efficient and effective way of recording the economic transactions and events of the business. It also allows a trial balance to be prepared at the end of the accounting period, which forms the basis of the financial statements. In Chapter 5 we explained that under IFRS a full set of financial statements includes a *statement of comprehensive income*, which is the subject of this chapter.

6.2 Purpose of the statement of comprehensive income

The purpose of the *statement of comprehensive income* is to provide information to users on the financial performance of the business over the accounting period (usually one year) – in other words, the amount of the profit or loss the business has made during the period. Because it is retrospective, it is sometimes referred to as a financial history book. The elements that relate to the measurement of financial performance are income and expenses, which we defined in Chapter 5. The definition of *income* makes it clear that income includes both revenue and gains. The definition of *expenses* makes it clear that expenses include both costs and losses. A profit or loss is the difference between the income earned and expenses incurred over the accounting period.

Key definitions

- Income is increases in economic benefits during the accounting period in the form of inflows or enhancements of assets or decreases of liabilities that result in increases in equity, other than those relating to contributions from equity participants.
- Expenses are decreases in economic benefits during the accounting period in the form of outflows or depletions of assets or incurrences of liabilities that result in decreases in equity, other than those relating to distributions to equity participants.

Source: IASB (2010, 4.25).

One of the most important things to remember is that a profit or loss can be made whether the transactions of the business are for cash or on credit and is the difference between revenue and the expenses associated with achieving that income during the accounting. If this sounds familiar to you, it is because the statement of comprehensive income is prepared on an accrual basis. On the other hand, cash accounting is based on the principle that transactions and events are recognized when cash has been received or paid.

Key definition

Accrual accounting is based on the principle that revenue and costs are recognized as they are earned and incurred irrespective of when cash (or its equivalent) is received or paid (the realization principle), and they are matched with one another (the matching principle) and dealt with in the income statement of the period to which they relate (the period principle).

Activity

You may recall doing this activity in Chapter 2. Imagine you have £200 cash that you use to buy a computer from another student. You are a bit of an opportunist and see a chance to make some money. You decide to advertise the computer for sale, which costs £10, and you sell the computer for £300 cash. You have no other business transactions. Calculate your cash position at the end the month and your profit for the month.

It is likely that you have been able to work out the cash position and the profit in your head, but you may have decided to use the layout for a simple cash flow statement prepared for management that we illustrated in Chapter 2, where you deduct all the cash outflows from the total cash inflows to arrive at the net cash flow. To calculate the profit, you need to deduct all the costs you incurred in the month from the value of the sale. It does not matter at this stage how you calculated the figure, as long as you understand the principles involved. The layout of the following statement of comprehensive income is the one used by accountants:

Your business	
Cash flow statement for the month	
	£
Cash inflows	
Capital	200
Revenue	300
	500
Cash outflows	
Purchases	200
Advertising	10
	(210)
Net cash flow	290

Your business	
Statement of comprehensive income for the month	
	£
Revenue	300
Cost of sales	
Purchases	(200)
Gross profit	100
Expenses	
Advertising	(10)
Profit for the period	90

As you can see, the cash position is a cash surplus of £290 and you have made a profit of £90. You need to remember that the profit and loss account does not tell us anything about cash. For example, it does not tell us about the £200 capital or whether cash has been received for the sale of the computer; nor does it tell us whether the costs have actually been paid or merely incurred. To emphasize the difference between profit and cash we will make the example slightly more complex.

Activity

The information is the same as in the previous activity. You have £200 that you use to buy a computer. You advertise the computer, which costs £10, and sell it for £300. You have no other business transactions. This time, the buyer is not able to pay you straight away, so you give him one month's credit. Calculate your cash position and profit now:

Your business Cash flow statement for the month	
	£
Cash inflows	
Capital	200
Cash outflows	
Purchases	200
Advertising	10
	(210)
Net cash flow	(10)

Your business Statement of comprehensive income for the month	
	£
Revenue	300
Cost of sales	
Purchases	(200)
Gross profit	100
Expenses	
Advertising	(10)
Profit for the period	90

Looking at the terms we have used in this simple cash flow statement, you will remember from Chapter 2 that the term *capital* describes the money contributed by the owner to enable the business to function. *Purchases* is cash flowing out of the business to suppliers in respect of goods bought for resale, and advertising represents cash flowing out of the business when that expense is paid. However, in the statement of comprehensive income we have illustrated, *revenue* refers to all sales made to customers during the accounting period, irrespective of whether cash has changed hands.[1] In the statement of comprehensive income, the term *purchases* refers to the cost of goods that have been purchased from suppliers for resale, irrespective of whether cash has changed hands, and advertising refers to that expense irrespective of whether cash has changed hands.

If you have calculated the net cash flow correctly, the cash position is now a cash deficit of £10. This may have misled you into thinking that you have now made a loss of £10 (the cost you have incurred) or a loss of £300 (the amount owing to you). Neither figure is correct. The answer is still a profit of £90. It is very important to remember that profit is not the same as cash and that the profit and loss account is not a record of cash flows in and out of the business. When we calculate profit we are concerned with the intentions of the parties and the transactions they have entered into, regardless of whether any cash has changed hands. In other words, the figures for sales, cost of sales and expenses do not take into account whether you have paid the supplier for the computer, whether your customer has paid you for the computer or whether you have paid the newspaper for the advertisement. This is because you using the principles of accrual accounting when calculating the profit or loss for the period.

In Chapter 2 we constructed a simple cash flow statement for the first 6 months of trading of Candlewick Ltd, the company started by Sarah Wick on 1 January 2012. This showed that after Sarah had invested £10,000 capital in the business and the company had borrowed £650 from the bank, it had a cash surplus of £500 at 30 June 2012.

---

1. In some countries the terms 'sales' or 'turnover' have also been used to describe revenue.

Activity

Do you consider that the company's financial performance was satisfactory? Draw up a list of questions you would like to ask Sarah to find out whether she thinks the first 6 months were a financial success.

You may have thought of the following questions:

- Did Sarah think the cash surplus of £500 was a satisfactory cash position, considering the money, time and effort she put into the business?
- How much profit did she hope to achieve for the first 6 months?
- How much profit did she actually make?
- Did she think the profit she made was satisfactory, considering the money, time and effort she put into the business?
- Were her achievements typical for her type of business?
- Would she have been better off using her money, time and effort in some other enterprise?
- Has she built up a business that is worth something in terms of the assets it has acquired (such as cash or inventory) or its potential to generate profit?

This is a formidable list of questions and you may think that answering them will be very difficult. Although the simple cash flow statement we demonstrated in Chapter 2 provides some answers, we need to answer most of the questions by preparing a statement of comprehensive income.

6.3   Preparing a draft statement of comprehensive income

The first thing to determine when preparing a *statement of comprehensive income* is the accounting period over which the profit or loss will be calculated. As the financial statement will be prepared on an accrual basis, all sources of income for the period need to be included, irrespective of whether the transactions were for cash or on credit: in other words, irrespective of whether cash has been received yet. This revenue is then matched with the revenue expenditure, which are the costs and expenses incurred during the period in order to earn the income, irrespective of whether cash has been paid yet. The calculation of profit is based on the following equation:

$$\text{Income} - \text{Expenses} = \text{Profit or loss for the period}$$

Users of the financial statements of trading businesses need detailed information about profit made on buying and selling goods, which is known as the *gross profit*. This is calculated as the difference between revenue for the period and the *cost of sales*. The cost of sales is the cost of the goods that have been sold during the period:

$$\text{Revenue} - \text{Cost of sales} = \text{Gross profit}$$

Other income (such as interest received from investments) is added and *distribution costs* (such as packaging, postage, transport costs and insurance of goods in transit), *administrative expenses* (for example, general overheads relating to administrative activities such as office rent and the cost of office salaries, cleaning, telephone and stationery) and *other expenses* are deducted to provide the figure of *operating profit*. The distribution costs, administrative and other operating expenses are known collectively as *revenue expenditure*:

$$\text{Gross profit} - \text{Revenue expenditure} = \text{Operating profit}$$

Then any finance costs (for example, interest paid on loans) are deducted separately to give the *profit before tax*. Next, income tax expense is deducted to give the *profit for the year*. Finally, any holding gain made when an asset is sold is added to give the figure of *comprehensive income* that includes all profits and gains made over the accounting period.

Key definitions

- **Gross profit is the difference between the revenue and the cost of goods sold during the period.**
- **Operating profit is the difference between the operating income and revenue expenditure for the period.**
- **Comprehensive income is the total of all profits and gains made over the period.**

Under IAS 1, *Presentation of Financial Statements* (IASB, 2011) and the *IFRS for SMEs* (IASB, 2009), reporting entities have two main choices relating to the statement of comprehensive income:

1. Prepare a single *statement of comprehensive income* or the same information presented in two separate statements: an *income statement* showing components of profit or loss and a *statement of comprehensive income* that shows the components of other comprehensive income.
2. Analyse expenses by nature or by function, whichever provides information that is relevant and more reliable. If expenses are analysed by function, information by nature must be disclosed in the notes to the financial statements.

We are now ready to see whether Candlewick Ltd has made a profit over the first 6 months of trading. Here is a reminder of some of the facts:

- Office and other equipment was acquired on 1 January, but did not have to be paid for until February, as Sarah made use of the 1 month's interest-free credit period on the business credit card.
- Rent was payable every month.
- Advertising was payable 1 month in arrears.
- Telephone and Internet expenses were payable at the end of each quarter.

- Postage and packaging costs were incurred every month apart from February and were paid for in cash.
- Employees were paid monthly.

We need to look more closely at the actual sales and purchases for each month shown in the simple cash flow statement we constructed in Chapter 2. For ease of reference this is reproduced below.

Candlewick Ltd
Cash flow statement for January–June 2012

	January £	February £	March £	April £	May £	June £	Total £
Cash inflows							
Capital	10,000	0	0	0	0	0	10,000
Loan	6,500	0	0	0	0	0	6,500
Revenue (cash sales)	1,600	1,800	2,000	3,500	4,100	4,500	17,500
Revenue (credit sales)	0	0	4,800	5,400	6,000	7,800	24,000
	18,100	1,800	6,800	8,900	10,100	12,300	58,000
Cash outflows							
Purchases	0	6,000	6,000	7,500	8,400	9,000	36,900
Equipment	0	13,000	0	0	0	0	13,000
Rent	500	500	500	500	500	500	3,000
Advertising	50	50	50	50	50	50	300
Telephone and Internet	0	0	450	0	0	450	1,060
Printing, postage and stationery	0	100	100	100	100	100	500
Interest on loan	40	40	40	40	40	40	240
Salaries	0	500	500	500	500	660	2,500
	590	20,190	7,640	8,690	9,590	10,800	57,500
Net cash flow	17,510	(18,390)	(840)	210	510	1.500	500
Cumulative cash b/f	0	17,510	(880)	(1,720)	(1,510)	(1,000)	0
Cumulative cash c/f	17,510	(880)	(1,720)	(1,510)	(1,000)	500	500

When preparing a statement of comprehensive income, we are interested in the value of the economic transactions that took place over the accounting period. To calculate these figures, we need to focus on the months when the transactions took place, rather than when cash was received or paid. The cash flow statement shows the lag of one month between the purchase of candles and the payment of cash, and the lag of 2 months between credit sales and receipt of cash. The other point to note is that although Candlewick Ltd purchased the same number of boxes of candles as planned, the actual sales were lower than forecast. This means the company will have unsold goods at the end of the accounting period, which is known as *closing inventory*. A business needs to have a certain amount of goods in stock on the last day of the accounting period to be able to sell them on the first day of the next period, which means closing inventory at the end of the period is *opening inventory* at the start of the next period.

In order to value closing inventory, at the end of the accounting period (the maximum being one year), a physical count of goods is carried out to compare those quantities with the records. This is referred to as *stocktaking*. Once the total number of items in stock is known, the value is calculated by multiplying the number of items by the original cost of the item.

Activity

A garden centre purchased 100 plants at £2 each with a view to selling them at £2.40 each. At the end of the year 20 plants remained unsold. Because the plants are no longer in flower, the business will have to drop the price to £1.50 each. Calculate the value of the closing inventory.

You may have calculated the closing inventory as £40 (20 × £2), but the value the business must use is £30 (20 × £1.50) because these plants were worth less than the price that was paid for them. Apart from seasonal factors, other factors that may reduce demand for goods and services include changes in taste and fashion or advances in technology. IAS 2, *Inventories* (IASB, 2003) and the *IFRS for SMEs* (IASB, 2009) require inventory to be valued at the lower of cost or *net realizable value (NRV)*. Cost includes purchase cost, conversion cost (materials, labour and overheads) and other costs (excluding foreign exchange differences) to bring inventory to its present location and condition. We will be looking at the valuation methods permitted under IAS 2 in Part III.

Key definition

Net realizable value (NRV) is the sales value of the [inventory] less any additional costs likely to be incurred in getting the [inventories] into the hands of the customer.

Source: Law (2010, p. 294).

Returning to the example of Candlewick Ltd, the following table summarizes the quantities and values of the purchases and sales over the 6 months' period.

Date	Purchases		Cash sales		Credit sales	
	Quantity	£	Quantity	£	Quantity	£
January	400	6,000	80	1,600	240	4,800
February	400	6,000	90	1,800	270	5,400
March	500	7,500	100	2,000	300	6,000
April	560	8,400	175	3,500	390	7,800
May	600	9,000	205	4,100	410	8,200
June	600	9,000	225	4,500	425	8,500
Total	3,060	45,900	875	17,500	2,035	40,700

Activity

(a) **What was the revenue for the period?**

(b) **How many boxes of unsold candles did Candlewick Ltd have at the end of June and what was the total cost of that closing inventory?**

Taking the information from the preceding table, the first calculation is:

Working 1

	£
Cash sales	17,500
Credit sales	40,700
Revenue	58,200

There are several ways in which you can calculate the answer to the second question. The quantity of closing inventory is calculated as:

Quantity of opening inventory + Quantity purchased − Quantity sold

Candlewick Ltd had no opening inventory because this is the first 6 months of trading, so check your figures against the following calculations:

Working 2

	Quantity
Purchases	3,060
Cash sales	(875)
Credit sales	(2,035)
Closing inventory	150

The cost of sales is calculated as:

Value of opening inventory + Purchases − Closing inventory

For the reason already mentioned, Candlewick Ltd had no opening inventory, so we simply need to subtract the value of closing inventory from purchases:

Working 3

	£
Purchases (£15 × 3,060)	45,900
Closing inventory (£15 × 150)	(2,250)
Cost of sales	43,650

These workings allow us to draft the trading section of the statement of comprehensive income:

Candlewick Ltd
Draft statement of comprehensive income
for 6 months ending 30 June 2012

	£
Revenue (W1)	58,200
Cost of sales (W2 & W3)	(43,650)
Gross profit	14,550

As you can see, the company made a gross profit of £14,550 over the 6month period and we can cross-check this by doing a small calculation. We know that the business buys each box of candles for £15 and sells them for £20 per box, thus making a gross profit of £5 per box. As 2,910 candles have been sold in the period, the gross profit is £5 × 2,910 = £14,550. In a more complex business, you could not carry out these simple calculations.

Under the heading of *cost of sales* we have calculated the cost of the goods sold. In this case we have deducted the cost of the closing inventory from the cost of the goods purchased during the period. This is because we are preparing this financial statement on an *accrual* basis. Therefore, we are matching the revenue to the cost of purchasing the candles actually sold during the period and we are ignoring the movement of cash.

The term *gross* is used to describe the profit at this stage because this is the larger figure of profit before any of the expenses have been deducted. If the business had any other operating income, such as interest received on investments or rent received from lettings, it would be shown after the figure for gross profit.

The cost of sales is not the only expense incurred by the business and we need to deduct the operating expenses before we can calculate the operating profit. We then need to consider any other expenses, such as the income tax that Candlewick Ltd will have to pay. Sarah has decided to employ a part-time accountant, who estimates that this tax would be approximately £2,085. As Candlewick Ltd has no other income or gains, we now have everything we need to complete the draft statement of comprehensive income for the 6 months ended 30 June 2012 on the top of page 138.

The draft statement of comprehensive income shows that the business has made a profit of £4,865 over the first 6 months of trading. If the total expenses were greater than the total income the final figure would be negative and you would label it 'loss for the period'. Under the *IFRS for SMEs*, if an entity has no items of other comprehensive income in any of the periods for which financial statements are presented, it is allowed to present an income statement alone or it can present a statement of comprehensive income in which the 'bottom line' is labelled 'profit or loss'. That is what Sarah has done in this draft financial statement. We have called it a draft statement because later on in this chapter we will explain how to prepare the annual statement of comprehensive income with post trial balance adjustments.

```
                 Candlewick Ltd
      Draft statement of comprehensive income for
              6 months ended 30 June 2012
                                              £
Revenue (W1)                               58,200
Cost of sales (W2 & W3)                   (43,650)
Gross profit                               14,550
Expenses
Rent                                       (3,000)
Advertising                                  (300)
Telephone and Internet                       (900)
Printing, postage and stationery             (500)
Salaries                                    (2,660)
                                            (7,360)
Operating profit                            7,190
Finance costs                                (240)
Profit before tax                           6,950
Income tax expense (30%)                    (2,085)
Profit for the period                        4,865
```

6.4   Difference between cash and profit

To review the difference between cash and profit we need to look at the events that took place during the year. On 1 January 2012 Sarah invested £10,000 capital in Candlewick Ltd and borrowed £6,500 from the bank. After 6 months' trading, the simple cash flow statement prepared for management shows that the business has a cash surplus of £500 and the statement of comprehensive income for the same period shows a profit of £4,865. There seems to be a discrepancy of £4,365 (£4,865 – £500).

Activity

List the items that you think caused the difference between the cash and the profit by comparing the items in the cash flow statement with the items in the profit and loss account.

The items causing the apparent discrepancy are as follows:

- Sarah has allowed 2 months' credit to her credit customers. From the cash flow statement we can see that cash received from credit sales totalled £24,000, but that does not include the credit sales of £8,200 for May and £8,500 for June which, combined, represent £16,700 in trade receivables. This brings the value of credit sales to £40,700, to which we then add the cash sales of £17,500 to give us the total revenue figure shown in the statement of comprehensive income of £58,200.

Therefore, the difference in total revenue stated in the two financial statements is £16,700.

- On the other hand, Sarah has negotiated one month's credit from the supplier from whom she buys her candles. From the cash flow statement we can see that the cash paid for purchases totalled £36,900, but to calculate profit we need to include the purchases of £9,000 incurred in June, which represents £9,000 in trade payables. This brings the value of purchases to £45,900, which is the figure shown in the statement of comprehensive income.
- At 30 June the business had 150 boxes of candles in stock. These cost £15 each and this is how they have been valued in the trading section of the statement of comprehensive income: £15 × 150 = £225. This figure is not included in the cash flow statement.
- Sarah did not take up the offer of credit for the advertising expenses and none was available for the telephone and Internet expenses or the rent, so there is no discrepancy between cash and profit here.
- The cash flow statement shows all cash income and all cash expenditure. It includes cash inflows from the capital Sarah invested in the business and the loan made by the bank. It also shows the cash outflows on buying the equipment and Sarah's drawings. None of these items are shown in the statement of comprehensive income, so here is another difference between the two financial statements.
- The final difference is that because the income tax expense has not yet been paid, it is not shown in the cash flow statement, but it is included in the statement of comprehensive income.

In order to make the position clear, we will divide the information into good news and bad news. The good news is where Candlewick Ltd has assets and the bad news is where the business has incurred liabilities:

	£
Good news (assets)	
Equipment (at cost)	13,000
Cash owed by customers (trade receivables)	16,700
Closing inventory (at cost)	2,250
	31,950
Bad news (liabilities)	
Equity (owner's capital)	(10,000)
Loan owed to the bank	(6,500)
Cash owed to supplier (trade payables)	(9,000)
Cash owed to tax authorities	(2,085)
	(27,585)
Difference	4,365

As you can see, this analysis shows a difference between the assets and the liabilities of £4,365, which explains the apparent discrepancy between the profit of £4,865 for the period and the cash surplus of £500 (£4,865 – £500 = £4,365). There are a number of important lessons to be learned from the principle that cash is not the same as profit, and these can be used to run a business more efficiently:

1. Giving credit to customers may have the advantage of increasing sales and thus potential profit, but it results in a delay before the sales value is realized in the cash flow. In extreme cases this means that an organization can make a good profit, but at the same time risks failure due to lack of liquidity (insufficient cash for its activities).
2. Building up inventory to an unnecessarily high level can have an adverse effect on cash flow. Managers who take advantage of bargains, such as special discounts, often forget this – perhaps because they consider that cash flow is the concern of the accountant and not of the organization as a whole.
3. Taking credit from suppliers is one way of improving cash flow and is a form of free finance. However, if an organization takes more time than the agreed credit period, it runs the risk of losing this advantage: the supplier refusing to provide any more goods or services, and difficulty in obtaining credit in future.
4. Both the cash flow statement and the profit and loss account analyse financial information retrospectively over the accounting period. However, the past is not an accurate guide to the future. From a management point of view, planned or budgeted financial information should be compared frequently with actual information to ensure that the business is meeting its financial objectives.

So far we have only prepared a draft statement of comprehensive income using cash information. We will now explain how the statement of comprehensive income is prepared from a trial balance. Although the records in the accounting system may be fully up to date, there are always a number of *post trial balance adjustments*[2] that must be dealt with to ensure that the principles of the accruals concept are met. You will remember from Chapter 1 that the *accruals concept* is the principle that revenue and costs are recognized as they are earned and incurred, not as cash is received or paid, and they are matched with one another and dealt with in the income statement of the period to which they relate.

As we are interested in financial reporting, we will look at the trial balance at 31 December 2012, which marks the end of the first year of trading for Candlewick Ltd – see top of page 142.

In practice, all the post trial balance adjustments would be entered in the ledger accounts and a revised trial balance would be generated. However, we will show the post trial balance information as notes, as this is the way you are likely to encounter it in your assessments.

---

2. *Post* is Latin for 'after', so this phrase refers to adjustments that are made after the trial balance has been generated.

Candlewick Ltd
Trial balance at 31 December 2012

	Debit	Credit
	£	£
Revenue		173,200
Purchases	113,400	
Equipment (at cost)	13,000	
Trade receivables	27,500	
Trade payables		15,000
Cash	26,100	
Salaries	14,500	
Rent	6,000	
Advertising	600	
Telephone and Internet	1,960	
Printing, postage and stationery	1,100	
Interest on loan	540	
Loan		6,500
Share capital at 1 January 2012		10,000
	204,700	204,700

6.5   Inventory, accruals and prepayments

6.5.1   Inventory

In a trading business, *inventory* refers to unsold goods, but in a manufacturing business, it comprises raw materials, work in progress and finished goods. We introduced the adjustments for inventory earlier in this chapter when we explained that the valuation of closing inventory is guided by IAS 2, *Inventories* (IASB, 2003) and the *IFRS for SMEs* (IASB, 2009), which require inventory to be valued at the lower of cost or net realizable value (NRV). An important point to note is that the figure for inventory at the end of the period (closing inventory) is the figure for inventory at the start of the next period (opening inventory). In the statement of comprehensive income, the adjustments for opening and closing inventory are incorporated in the cost of sales calculation.

Activity

Total purchases during the year ending 31 December 2012 were £113,400, and at the end of the year the annual stocktake showed that Candlewick Ltd had 50 boxes of candles in stock which had cost £15 each. What are the figures for closing inventory at 31 December and cost of sales for the year ending 31 December 2012?

You should have found this straightforward. Closing inventory is cost (£15) × quantity (50) = £750. The cost of sales is purchases (£113,400) – Closing inventory (£750)

= £10,599 and this adjustment is shown in the statement of comprehensive income for the year ending 31 December 2012.

Activity

Imagine that £500 of inventory was stolen during the year, so that the figure for closing inventory is overstated in the statement of comprehensive income. What impact would it have if the true figure were substituted?

The greatest impact would be on the profit because the gross profit would decrease by £500. If a business has inventory stolen or it has deteriorated so that the value is less, it should be noticed during stocktaking. The loss is borne by the business and the reduced figure for closing inventory should then be shown in the financial statements. Because of the impact of closing inventory on profit, this is an area where fraud can be perpetrated if adjustments are not made to take account of lost or damaged goods. Therefore, inventory is one of the key checks made by the auditors. The following table illustrates the impact of overstated inventory on profit.

	Overstated inventory		Correct inventory	
	£	£	£	£
Revenue		173,200		173,200
Cost of sales				
Purchases	113,400		113,400	
Closing inventory	(750)	(112,650)	(250)	(113,150)
Gross profit		60,550		60,050

6.5.2 Accruals

When the ledger accounts are closed at the end of the accounting period, some expenses incurred for goods and services used during the period may not have been recorded because the business has not yet received an invoice from the supplier. For example, perhaps the business has had the use of telephone and Internet services during the final quarter of the year, but the provider has not yet sent the bill. The business needs to estimate the amount of any accrued expense or liability, and add the *accrual* to the trial balance figure for that expense because it belong to the accounting period for which the financial statements are being prepared.

Key definition

An accrual is an estimate of a liability that is not supported by an invoice or a request for payment at the time when the accounts are prepared.

Source: Law (2010, p. 11).

Candlewick Ltd has two accrued expenses:

1. The trial balance shows telephone and Internet expenses of £1,960, but these only cover the first 11 months and the accountant Sarah has employed estimates that a further £200 is owed for December. This means that the expense shown in the statement of comprehensive income should be £1,960 + £200 = £2,160.
2. The accountant knows from the invoices for advertising that the total amount paid was £600, but during December Sarah took out extra advertisements to promote sales over the festive season. The company will not be invoiced for these advertisements until January, but the accountant estimates the amount will be £100. This means that the expense shown in the statement of comprehensive income should be £600 + £100 = £700.

6.5.3 Prepayments

Another situation that commonly arises is where part of the amount paid for an expense in the current accounting period covers goods or services that will not be received until the next period. The amount of this payment in advance is known and the *prepayment* needs to be deducted from the trial balance figure for that expense.

Key definition

A prepayment is a payment made for goods or services before they are received.

Source: Law (2010, p. 328).

Candlewick Ltd has one prepayment. Sarah has recorded postage and packing expenses of £1,100 in the accounts, but at the end of December she realizes that she has accumulated a small surplus of these items that the business will not use until January. The cost of these items was £100. This means that the expense shown in the statement of comprehensive income should be £1,100 – £100 = £1,000.

6.6 Depreciation of property, plant and equipment

You will remember from the previous chapter that an asset is a resource controlled by the entity as a result of past events and from which future economic benefits are expected to flow to the entity (IASB, 2010, 4.4). IAS 16, *Property, Plant and Equipment* (IASB, 2008) and the *IFRS for SMEs* (IASB, 2009) give guidance on the accounting treatment of certain *tangible non-current assets* that include freehold and leasehold land, buildings, fixtures and fittings, machinery, equipment and delivery vehicles. As you can tell from these examples, tangible assets are non-monetary in nature and have a physical substance. They can be distinguished from *intangible non-current assets* that do not have a physical form, such as goodwill, patents and trademarks. IAS 16 defines property, plant and equipment (PPE) as tangible assets that:

- are held for use in the production or supply of goods or services, for rental to others, or for administrative purposes, and
- are expected to be used during more than one period.

Examples of tangible assets include freehold and leasehold land, buildings, fixtures and fittings, machinery, delivery vehicles and office equipment.

Key definitions

- Property, plant and equipment are tangible assets that are held for use in the production of supply of goods or services, for rental to others, or for administrative purposes, and are expected to be used during more than one period.

Source: IAS 16 (IASB, 2008, para 7).

Under IAS 16, all items of PPE with a finite life must be depreciated. *Depreciation*[3] is the systematic allocation of the cost or revalued amount of a tangible non-current asset, less any residual value, over its useful life. *Residual value* refers to the estimated amount that the entity would currently obtain from disposal of the asset, after deducting the estimated costs of disposal if the asset were already of the age and in the condition expected at the end of its useful life. The *depreciable amount* is the cost of an asset, or other amount substituted for cost (assets may be revalued in subsequent years), less its residual value.

The asset's *useful life* is an estimate of the number of years the asset is expected to be available for use by the entity or the number of production or similar units expected to be obtained from the asset by the entity. Some assets, such as fixtures and fittings or vehicles, will be worn out after a period of time; others, such as machinery or equipment, are likely to become obsolete through advances in technology. On the basis of materiality, some entities write off low-value items to expenses in the year of purchase (for example, equipment that cost £250 or less).

With large items of PPE, such as a ship or an aircraft, each significant component must be depreciated separately, but components can be grouped together if they have the same length of useful life and the same depreciation method is used. Although land and buildings are often acquired together, they must be accounted for separately. Buildings are always depreciated, but freehold land is not usually depreciated because it normally has an infinite life. An exception would be land held for coal mining or stone quarrying, where the useful life of the asset is depleted as the resources are extracted.

Key definitions

- Depreciation is the systematic allocation of the depreciable amount of an asset over its useful life.
- The depreciable amount is the cost of an asset, or other amount substituted for cost, less its residual value.
- Residual value is the estimated amount that an entity would currently obtain from disposal of the asset, after deducting the estimated costs of disposal, if the

---

3. Depreciation is sometimes referred to as 'amortization'.

> asset were already of the age and in the condition expected at the end of its useful life.
>
> - Useful life is the period over which an asset is expected to be available for use by an entity ... or the number of production or similar units expected to be obtained from the asset by the entity.
>
> *Source*: IAS 16 (IASB, 2008, para 6).

The cost of acquiring or producing the asset (for example, buying components and building a new computer system), or enhancing an existing asset (for example, extending or refurbishing a factory or office building) is classified as *capital expenditure*. An *allowance for depreciation* is made for each category of PPE in order to match the revenue the asset has helped generate during the accounting period to an estimate of the cost that has been consumed during the year.

The cost of an item of property, plant and equipment is recognized as an asset only if:

1. it is probable that future economic benefits associated with the item will flow to the entity, and
2. the cost of the item can be measured reliably.

Under the *IFRS for SMEs*, initial recognition is at cost. In subsequent years, recognition is at cost less any accumulated depreciation and any accumulated impairment losses. Under IAS 16, the initial measurement is also at cost, but in subsequent years two measurement models are offered:

- the *cost model*, where the asset is carried at cost less accumulated depreciation and accumulated impairment losses (the same as under the *IFRS for SMEs*), or
- the *revaluation model*, where the asset is carried at a revalued amount, being its fair value at the date of revaluation less subsequent accumulated depreciation and impairment, provided that fair value can be measured reliably (see Table 6.1 showing examples of fair value).

The model chosen must be applied consistently across the class of assets (e.g. all equipment).

Candlewick Ltd has one tangible fixed asset, which is the equipment that was bought on 1 January 2012 at a cost of £13,000. Sarah needs a method that will measure the proportion of the benefits that have been used up during the accounting period

Table 6.1   Examples of fair value

Example	Fair value based on
Buildings	Market-based evidence of fair value determined by professionally qualified valuer
Plant and equipment	Market-based evidence of fair value
Specialized items of PPE that are rarely sold	Fair value based on replacement cost since there is no market-based evidence

so that she can make an allowance for depreciation on equipment. Sarah estimates that the equipment has 4 years of useful life before technological advances mean it will become redundant. Nevertheless, at the end of 4 years she thinks the business will be able to sell it in the second-hand market for £1,000.

Activity

What do you consider it would be fair to charge as an expense in the statement of comprehensive income for the use of the equipment for the year ending 31 December 2012?

The clue to the correct figure is the word 'fair'. You might argue that the equipment has a historical cost of £13,000 and that this is the figure that should be used. Alternatively, you might think that the equipment has a residual value of £1,000 and therefore the answer should be £12,000. However, that cost covers 4 years' use and it would not be fair to charge the full amount against only one year's trading. Therefore, you may have rightly concluded that £3,000 is a fair figure since this takes all these factors into consideration. It would certainly not be fair to charge £1,000 as an expense for the year, as this is the estimated second-hand value of the asset at the end of 4 years.

The accountant has suggested that the company uses the *straight-line method* of depreciation, which spreads the cost (or revalued amount) evenly over the life of the asset. It is calculated using the following formula:

$$\frac{\text{Cost} - \text{Residual value}}{\text{Useful life}}$$

The first step is to deduct the estimated residual value from the cost and then divide the result by the estimated useful life:

$$\frac{£13,000 - £1,000}{4 \text{ years}} = \frac{£12,000}{4 \text{ years}} = £3,000 \text{ per annum}$$

Sarah can now add an allowance for depreciation on equipment of £3,000 to the other administrative expenses listed in the trial balance at 31 December 2012. We know that the cost of the asset was £13,000 and the equipment was bought on the first day of the accounting period (which for convenience we will call Year 0). At the end of the first year (Year 1), this figure will be reduced by the annual depreciation charge made in the statement of comprehensive income. This means that the cost of £13,000 will reduce by £3,000 each year for 4 years, and at the end of this time there will be a residual value of £1,000.

6.7   Bad debts and doubtful receivables

Candlewick Ltd has a combination of cash sales and credit sales and Sarah may not realize that some customers she has allowed to buy on credit may never pay for their candles. There are several reasons for this, such as the customer may have died without leaving enough money to pay for their debts, become bankrupt or moved away and cannot be traced. In such cases, as soon as Sarah found out the money was irrecoverable, she would have to consider the amount owed as a *bad debt*, which would be an expense the business has to bear. She would need to write it off as a charge against profit or against an existing allowance for doubtful receivables in the statement of comprehensive income. Occasionally news of a bad debt is not received until after the trial balance has been constructed, which means that the accountant will have to make a post trial balance adjustment.

Fortunately, Candlewick Ltd has not had any bad debts, but Sarah has been giving customers 2 months' credit and so far she has included all credit sales as part of revenue for the year. Her accountant advises her that she should be prudent and make some provision for the possibility that some customers may not pay by making an *allowance for doubtful receivables*.

> **Key definitions**
>
> - A bad debt is an amount owed to the entity that is considered to be irrecoverable. It is written off as a charge against profit or against an existing allowance for doubtful receivables.
> - An allowance for doubtful receivables is an amount charged against profit and deducted from receivables to allow for the estimated non-recovery of a proportion of debts.

The allowance for doubtful receivables can be based on specific debts where there is documentary evidence to suggests that the debts will not be paid, or it can be based on the general assumption that a certain percentage of receivables are doubtful.[4]

Activity

The trial balance at 31 December 2012 shows that revenue for the year was £173,200, which comprises cash sales of £63,750 and credit sales of £109,450. Trade receivables were £27,500. If Candlewick Ltd makes an allowance for doubtful receivables of 10%, which of the following figures is the correct amount?

1 £17,320
2 £6,375
3 £10,945
4 £2,750

The first amount is 10% of the total sales revenue, but as this includes cash sales this answer is wrong because these have been paid for. The figure of £6,375 is 10% of the

---

4. The latter method is not acceptable to the tax authorities in the UK.

cash sales and this is wrong because they too have been paid for. The amount of £10,945 is 10% of credit sales for the year, but the business has received payments for the first 10 months of the year and it is only the last 2 months' credit sales that are outstanding. This is the amount of £27,500 that is owed by customers at the year end and it is against this figure that Sarah should make the allowance for doubtful receivables. Sarah can now include an allowance for doubtful receivables amounting to £2,750 and this will be an additional expense to those listed in the trial balance. Consistency enhances comparability, so she will use the same method every year unless there is good reason to change it.

Supposing Sarah has trade receivables of £25,000 in Year 2 because she has improved the system of credit control, and she continues to make a 10% allowance for doubtful receivables. The calculation will be:

$$£25,000 \times 10\% = £2,500$$

This represents a *decrease* of £250 on Year 1 (£2,500 in Year 2 minus £2,750 in Year 1). Therefore, the allowance for doubtful receivables in Year 2 will decrease expenses by £250. If trade receivables in Year 3 are £26,000, the allowance for doubtful receivables will be:

$$£26,000 \times 10\% = £2,600$$

This is an *increase* of £100 on Year 2 (£2,600 in Year 3 minus £2,500 in Year 2). Therefore, the allowance for doubtful receivables in Year 3 will increase expenses by £100.

6.8 Finalizing the statement of comprehensive income

Sarah's accountant has explained that it would reduce disclosure of information about costs that may be useful to competitors if she classifies the company's expenses by function rather than by nature. This means that instead of listing the individual expenses, they are grouped into three categories: distribution costs, administrative expenses and finance costs. The guiding principle is that the classification should result in information that is relevant and reliable.

We now have all the information we need to prepare the statement of comprehensive income for Candlewick Ltd for the year ending 31 December 2012. Here is the trial balance and the notes that represent the post trial balance adjustments we have just examined – see top of page 150.

Additional information available at 31 December 2012:

- Closing inventory is valued at £750.
- Rent, advertising, telephone and Internet, printing, postage and packaging and salaries are allocated 50% to distribution costs and 50% to administrative expenses.

Candlewick Ltd		
Trial balance at 31 December 2012		
	Debit	Credit
	£	£
Revenue		173,200
Purchases	113,400	
Equipment (at cost)	13,000	
Trade receivables	27,500	
Trade payables		15,000
Cash	26,100	
Salaries	14,500	
Rent	6,000	
Telephone and Internet	1,960	
Printing, postage and stationery	1,100	
Advertising	600	
Interest on loan	540	
Loan		6,500
Share capital at 1 January 2012		10,000
	204,700	204,700

- There are accrued expenses of £100 for advertising and £200 for telephone and Internet.
- Printing, postage and packaging include a prepayment of £100.
- The equipment is expected to have a useful life of 4 years, and an estimated residual value of £1,000. Depreciation on equipment will be charged 50% to distribution costs and 50% to administrative expenses.
- An allowance for doubtful receivables will be based on 10% of trade receivables. This allowance will be charged 100% to administrative expenses.
- Income tax to be paid by 31 January 2013 will be £8,970.
- Sarah is the sole shareholder of the company and shareholders normally expect to receive a return from their investment. However, Sarah decides to leave all profits in the company to help it grow, rather than take some out in the form of a dividend.

Activity

Using the relevant items listed in the trial balance and taking account of every item of additional information provided for the post trial balance adjustments, prepare a statement of comprehensive income for Candlewick Ltd for the year ending 31 December 2012.

You may find it useful to start by drawing together all the calculations we have made in connection with the post trial balance adjustments at 31 December 2012. These can be summarized as follows:

Working 1

	£
Purchases	113,400
Closing inventory	(750)
Cost of sales	112,650

Working 2

$$\text{Depreciation on equipment} = \frac{£13,000 - £1,000}{4 \text{ years}} = £3,000$$

Working 3

$$\text{Doubtful receivables} = £27,500 \times 10\% = £2,750$$

Working 4

	Amount (£)	Distribution costs (£)	Administrative expenses (£)	Finance costs (£)
Rent	6,000	3,000	3,000	
Advertising (600 + 100)	700	700		
Telephone and Internet (1,960 + 200)	2,160		2,160	
Printing, postage and stationery (1,100 − 100)	1,000	500	500	
Interest paid on loan	540			540
Salaries	14,500	7,250	7,250	
Depreciation on equipment (W2)	3,000	1,500	1,500	
Doubtful receivables (W3)	2,750		2,750	
Total	30,650	12,950	17,160	540

Your completed financial statement should look like this:

Candlewick Ltd Statement of comprehensive income for the year ended 31 December 2012	
	£
Revenue	173,200
Cost of sales (W1)	(112,650)
Gross profit	60,550
Distribution costs (W2, W3, W4)	(12,950)
Administrative expenses (W2, W3, W4)	(17,160)
Operating profit	30,440
Finance costs (W4)	(540)
Profit before tax	29,900
Income tax expense	(8,970)
Profit for the period	20,930

This is a fairly simple statement of comprehensive income because Candlewick Ltd does not have any items to show under 'other comprehensive income'. As it is the company's first year of trading, it is not possible to provide comparative figures for the previous year. You will find it useful to learn the following layout for the statement of comprehensive income:

	This year	Last year
Name of entity		
Statement of comprehensive income for the year ended (day/month/year)		
	£	£
Revenue	X	X
Cost of sales	(X)	(X)
Gross profit	X	X
Other income	X	X
Distribution costs	(X)	(X)
Administrative expenses	(X)	(X)
Other expenses	(X)	(X)
Operating profit	X	X
Finance costs	(X)	(X)
Profit before tax	X	X
Income tax expense	(X)	(X)
Profit for the period	X	X
Other comprehensive income		
Gains on property revaluation	X	X
Available for sale financial assets	X	X
Income tax relating to other comprehensive income	(X)	(X)
Total comprehensive income for the period	X	X

6.9   Conclusions

The statement of comprehensive income is one of the four financial statements that are prepared by reporting entities at the end of the accounting period. Its purpose is to measure the financial performance of the business over the accounting period, which is usually one year. In this chapter we have described how to prepare a statement of comprehensive income for a simple trading business which shows all profits and gains made over the period.

If the business keeps cash records, after some adjustments these figures can be used as the basis for preparing the statement of comprehensive income, as we have demonstrated in this chapter. If the business uses a double-entry bookkeeping system, the figures are taken from the trial balance, which summarizes the economic transactions that have been identified, measured and recorded in the accounting system. We have examined some of the post trial balance adjustments that must be made before the statement of comprehensive income can be finalized. Common mistakes students make when preparing a statement of comprehensive income are:

- not showing the name of the business
- not stating the period covered by the financial statement
- forgetting to include the currency symbol
- confusing opening inventory with closing inventory
- not making all the post trial balance adjustments
- forgetting to show any workings
- forgetting that it is only the final figure that is double underlined.

Practice questions

1. Describe the general purpose of the statement of comprehensive income. In addition, explain the terms *income* and *expenses* as defined by the *Conceptual Framework for Financial Reporting* (IASB, 2010).

2. Explain the accrual basis of accounting by defining the principles involved. Illustrate your answer by taking the example of the cost of sales adjustment in the statement of comprehensive income.

3. Insert the missing figures in the following examples, remembering that some items will be added and others will be subtracted:

	(a) £	(b) £	(c) £	(d) £	(e) £
Opening inventory	100	?	1,020	?	14,960
Purchases	?	680	?	1,924	?
	500	730	?	2,156	?
Closing inventory	(50)	?	(1,550)	(150)	(18,815)
Cost of sales	?	520	9,680	?	159,715

	(f) £	(g) £	(h) £	(i) £	(j) £
Revenue	10,000	?	17,000	18,150	?
Cost of sales	(6,000)	(450)	?	?	(24,590)
Gross profit	?	150	3,500	17,470	3,160
Expenses	(3,500)	?	?	?	?
Profit for the period	?	50	250	2,100	740

4. Salma Ibrahim set up a company called Uplights Ltd and opened a lighting shop on 1 January 2012. Her brother is studying for his accountancy exams and helps her by doing the bookkeeping and managing the inventory. At the end of the first year of trading, he generates the following trial balance from the accounting records – see top of page 154.
   Additional information at 31 December 2012:

   - Inventory was valued at £8,000.
   - Estimated current tax payable is £2,000.
   - The company classifies expenses by nature.

Uplights Ltd
Trial balance at 31 December 2012

	Debit £	Credit £
Revenue		66,500
Purchases	20,000	
Fixtures and fittings (at cost)	20,000	
Trade receivables	2,000	
Trade payables		8,400
Cash	14,500	
Bank interest received		100
Rent and rates	24,000	
Salaries	21,500	
Insurance	2,000	
Lighting and heating	500	
Telephone and Internet	400	
Advertising	100	
Share capital at 1 January 2012		30,000
	105,000	105,000

Required

Use the relevant figures in the above information to prepare a draft statement of comprehensive income for Uplights Ltd for the year ending 31 December 2012. Show all your workings.

5 On 1 July 2011 Mark Farmer opened a shop called Miphone Ltd. The trial balance for the first year is shown below:

Miphone Ltd
Trial balance at 30 June 2012

	Debit £	Credit £
Revenue		75,200
Purchases	12,160	
Plant and equipment at cost	25,000	
Trade receivables	1,200	
Trade payables		1,600
Cash	3,260	
Other income		1,200
Salaries	24,000	
Rent and rates	18,000	
Insurance	7,200	
Advertising	860	
Lighting and heating	620	
Telephone and Internet	450	
General expenses	250	
Share capital at 1 July 2011		15,000
	93,000	93,000

Additional information at 30 June 2012:

- Inventory is valued at £890.
- Advertising paid in advance is £260.
- Accrued expenses are lighting and heating £540, telephone and Internet £290, and general expenses £160.
- Estimated current tax payable is £1,200.

Required

(a) Using a spreadsheet, prepare a draft statement of comprehensive income for Miphone Ltd for the year ended 30 June 2012, classifying expenses by nature.
(b) After taking advice from his accountant, Mark has decided to depreciate equipment using the straight-line method over 5 years, with no residual value. He has also decided to make an allowance for doubtful receivables and has decided to base it on 10% of opening trade receivables. Make these adjustments to your spreadsheet and generate a statement of comprehensive income for Miphone Ltd for the year ending 30 June 2013, classifying expenses by nature.
(c) The accountant's final suggestion is that Mark should reclassify the expenses by function: 50% to distribution costs and 50% to administrative expenses, with the exception of advertising which should be allocated 100% to distribution costs, and the allowance for doubtful receivables which should allocated 100% to administrative expenses. Revise your statement of comprehensive income to present the expenses classified by function.

6 Kavita Patel owns a business called Beauty Box Ltd, which started trading on 1 July 2010. At the end of the second year of trading, her accountant provides the following trial balance from the accounting system – see top of page 156.
Additional information at 30 June 2012:

- Inventory was valued at £12,000.
- Equipment has a useful life of 5 years and no residual value. They are depreciated using the straight-line method.
- The company makes an allowance for doubtful receivables based on 10% of opening trade receivables.
- Estimated current tax liability £4,500.
- The company classifies expenses by nature.

Required

Use the relevant figures in the above information to prepare a statement of comprehensive income for Beauty Box Ltd for the year ending 30 June 2012. Show all your workings.

Beauty Box Ltd
Trial balance at 30 June 2012

	Debit £	Credit £
Revenue		104,900
Purchases	39,700	
Inventory at 1 July 2011	10,000	
Equipment at cost	20,000	
Trade receivables	6,000	
Trade payables		8,000
Cash and cash equivalents	15,300	
Interest received		100
Salaries	30,000	
Rent and rates	15,000	
Insurance	3,000	
Lighting and heating	1,500	
Telephone and Internet	2,000	
Advertising	500	
Allowances at 1 July 2011:		
Depreciation on plant and equipment		4,000
Doubtful receivables		1,000
Share capital at 1 July 2011		20,000
Retained profit at 1 July 2011		5,000
	143,000	143,000

References

IASB (2003) IAS 2, *Inventories*. London: International Accounting Standards Board.

IASB (2008) IAS 16, *Property, Plant and Equipment*. London: International Accounting Standards Board.

IASB (2009) *IFRS for SMEs*. London: International Accounting Standards Board.

IASB (2010) *The Conceptual Framework for Financial Reporting*, September. London: International Accounting Standards Board.

Law, J. (ed.) (2010) *Dictionary of Accounting*, 4th edition. Oxford: Oxford University Press.

7 Statement of financial position

Learning objectives

When you have studied this chapter, you should be able to:

- explain the purpose of the statement of financial position
- differentiate between non-current assets and current assets
- differentiate between non-current liabilities and current liabilities
- calculate depreciation using the reducing balance method
- prepare a statement of financial position.

7.1 Introduction

In Chapter 6 we discussed the difference between cash and profit and explained how a statement of comprehensive income can be prepared from cash accounting information or from a trial balance generated from a double-entry bookkeeping system. We described the main post trial balance adjustments that need to be made and how they are shown in the statement of comprehensive income. This financial statement is prepared on an accruals basis and summarizes information about the entity's income and expenses. Users of the financial statements are interested in the statement of comprehensive income because it shows the financial performance of the business over the accounting period, but this is not the only aspect of the company's 'financial health' that is of interest to them.

Under IFRS, a full set of financial statements also includes a *statement of financial position*, which is the subject of this chapter. The statement of financial position summarizes what the business owns and what it owes on the last day of the accounting period. In this chapter we will explain how to prepare a statement of financial position.

7.2   Purpose of the statement of financial position

The purpose of the *statement of financial position* is to summarize the assets, equity and liabilities on the last day of the accounting period for which the statement of comprehensive income was prepared. Because it looks at what the business owns and owes at one particular point in time, it is sometimes referred to as a 'financial snapshot'.

All businesses need resources known as *assets* such as premises, machinery, vehicles, equipment, inventory and cash. Before the business can acquire any assets, it must have the necessary finance. In a new business the most likely source of finance is the capital invested by the owner(s), which become part of the *equity* of the business. As far as the business is concerned, equity is a liability because it is an amount that is owed to the owner(s). If this is the only source of finance, the assets of the business are equal to the capital. However, the business may have other *liabilities*; for example, it may owe money to lenders (such as the bank) or to suppliers who have not yet been paid).

Key definitions

- An asset is a resource controlled by the entity as a result of past events and from which future economic benefits are expected to flow to the entity.
- A liability is a present obligation of the entity resulting from past events, the settlement of which is expected to result in an outflow from the entity of resources embodying economic benefits.
- Equity is the residual interest in the assets of the entity after deducting all its liabilities.

Source: IASB (2010, para 4.4).

You need to remember that a business can have dealings with its owner(s) because it is a separate entity. The relationship between the assets, equity and liabilities forms what is known as the *accounting equation*:

$$\text{Assets} = \text{Equity} + \text{Liabilities}$$

The accounting equation reflects the dual nature of business transactions by stating that the assets of the entity are always equal to the claims against them: the equity and other liabilities. The point about any equation is that it balances; in other words, the total of the values on each side of the equation are equal. You may remember the following activity from Chapter 3.

Activity

A business has capital of £20,000 and assets of £20,000. It then borrows £10,000 from the bank to finance the purchase of some new office equipment. How does this affect the accounting equation?

In this case the business has assets of £20,000 which will increase by £10,000 (the new equipment), making total assets of £30,000. The equity of £20,000 remains the same, but the business has increased its liabilities by £10,000 (the bank loan); but the accounting equation still balances as shown below:

Assets	=	Equity	+	Liabilities
£		£		£
20,000		20,000		10,000
10,000				
30,000		20,000		10,000

This accounting equation underpins the statement of financial position.

7.3 Preparing a draft statement of financial position

The statement of financial position shows the assets, equity and liabilities on the last day of the accounting period and this financial statement is presented in two parts. Although IAS 1, *Presentation of Financial Statements* (IASB, 2011) and the *IFRS for SMEs* (IASB, 2009) suggest how the statement of financial position should be presented, they do not prescribe the format of the statement or the order in which the items listed should be shown. The format we are going to illustrate presents the assets of the business in the first part and the equity and liabilities in the second part.

Under IAS 1 (para 60) and the *IFRS for SMEs*, an entity must normally present a classified statement of financial position, separating non-current assets from current assets, and non-current liabilities from current liabilities. The current/non-current split can be omitted only if a presentation based on liquidity provides information that is reliable and more relevant.

Assets are separated into two groups:

- *Non-current assets* are assets that are intended for continuing use in the business. You may find it helpful to think of them as the long-term assets of the business. Non-current assets are subdivided into *tangible* non-current assets and *intangible* non-current assets. Tangible assets are non-monetary assets with physical substance such as property, plant and equipment, and intangible assets are identifiable non-monetary assets without physical substance, such as brands, patents, copyrights and licences. Other non-current assets include long-term investments.
- *Current assets* are not intended for continuing use. You may find it helpful to think of them as the short-term assets of the business. In a business that trades or manufactures goods, current assets will be constantly changing from cash to inventory to trade receivables, to cash and possibly to short-term investments. Trade receivables are amounts owed by customers who have received goods or services on credit and have not yet paid.

Equity is separated into three groups:

- *Share capital* is the finance received by the company from its owner(s) in exchange for shares.
- *Retained earnings* are reserves of profits that are retained in the business to help it grow.
- *Other reserves* include funds arising from the issue of share capital at more than its nominal value.

Liabilities are separated into two groups:

- *Non-current liabilities* are amounts that are due to be paid to lenders and creditors more than one year after the date of the statement of financial position. You may find it helpful to think of them as long-term liabilities. Examples include long-term finance lease obligations, borrowings and employee benefit liabilities such as pensions.
- *Current liabilities* are amounts due to be paid to lenders and creditors within one year of the date of the statement of financial position. You may find it helpful to think of them as short-term liabilities. Examples include trade and other payables, dividends payable, current tax liability and short-term provisions, borrowings and finance lease liabilities. Trade payables are amounts due to suppliers who have supplied goods or services on credit who have not yet been paid.

The classification of assets, equity and liabilities in the statement of financial position is summarized in Figure 7.1. The two halves of this financial statement should balance. In other words, the total assets calculated in the first part of the statement should be equal to the equity and liabilities calculated in the second part.

Figure 7.1 Classifying assets, equity and liabilities

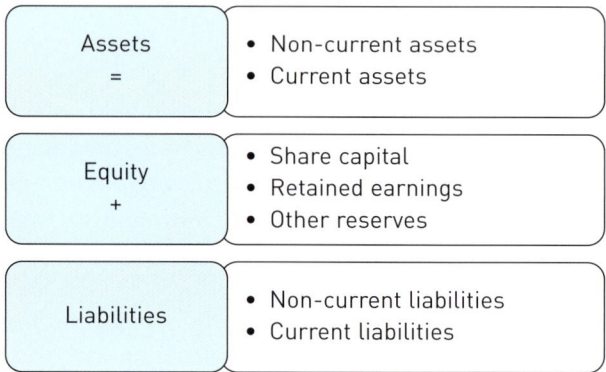

The last thing we need to mention is that accountants divide expenditure as follows:

- *Revenue expenditure* is the collective term for the costs and expenses that are written off in the statement of comprehensive income for the accounting period to which they relate.

- *Capital expenditure* is the collective term for the cost of non-current assets that are capitalized in the statement of financial position.

To illustrate the statement of financial position, we will continue to use the example of Candlewick Ltd, the company started by Sarah Wick on 1 January 2012. As you may remember from the previous chapter, on that day she opened a business bank account with her savings of £10,000 and took out a loan of £6,500, which was also put into the business account. On behalf of the business, she then bought equipment for £13,000 using the company credit card, which would not need to be paid until February.

It is important to remember that financial accounting and reporting is guided by the *business entity concept* (see Chapter 1). Therefore, Candlewick Ltd is considered to exist separately from its owner, Sarah Wick. This separation is crucial because the statement of financial position shows the financial position of the business and not that of its owner. On 1 January 2012 the draft statement of financial position for Candlewick Ltd looked like this:

Candlewick Ltd
Draft statement of financial position at
1 January 2012

	£
ASSETS	
Non-current assets	
Equipment (at cost)	13,000
Current assets	
Cash and cash equivalents	16,500
Total assets	**29,500**
EQUITY AND LIABILITIES	
Equity	
Share capital	(10,000)
Non-current liabilities	
Loan	(6,500)
Current liabilities	
Trade and other payables	(13,000)
Total equity and liabilities	**(29,500)**

As you can see, the name of the business and the date at which the statement of financial position has been prepared is given at the top of the statement. The assets on that date are listed in the first part of the statement and the equity and liabilities in the second part. Moreover, the total assets are equal to the total equity and liabilities. The order in which the assets are shown is based on liquidity, starting with those that would take the longest to turn into cash and ending with the most liquid. The order in which the liabilities are shown is based on immediacy, starting with long-term liabilities and ending with those that must be paid the soonest.

A statement of financial position can be prepared at any moment in time, so we will move forward to 2 January, by which time Sarah has started trading by buying 100 boxes of candles at £15 each, which the business will not need to pay for until February:

Candlewick Ltd Draft statement of financial position at 2 January 2012	
	£
ASSETS	
Non-current assets	
Equipment (at cost)	13,000
Current assets	
Inventory	1,500
Cash and cash equivalents	16,500
	18,000
Total assets	**31,000**
EQUITY AND LIABILITIES	
Equity	
Share capital	(10,000)
Non-current liabilities	
Loan	(6,500)
Current liabilities	
Trade and other payables	(14,500)
Total equity and liabilities	**(31,000)**

As you can see, although the figures have changed, the statement of financial position still balances. This is significant. The business has £31,000 in assets, which have been financed by a combination of Sarah's capital and creditors. Current liabilities are £13,000 owing on the business credit card for the equipment and £1,500 owed to the supplier for the boxes of candles bought in January, giving a total of £1,450. Credit cards and credit agreed with suppliers are useful sources of interest-free credit as long as the debt is paid off within the agreed credit period.

Activity

We will now move on to 7 January, which is the end of the first week of trading. The business has made cash sales of 10 boxes of candles at £20 each and credit sales of 20 boxes of candles at £20 each. Using the following pro forma, prepare a draft statement of financial position at 7 January. Any profit the business has made should be shown beneath the figure for share capital as retained earnings. Like the share capital, profit is a liability because it is owed by the business to the owner. At this stage in trading you can ignore the fact that a proportion of operating expenses should be deducted from the profit and simply calculate the gross profit:

Candlewick Ltd
Draft statement of financial position at 7 January 2012

	£
ASSETS	
Non-current assets	
Equipment (at cost)	_____
Current assets	
Inventory	
Trade and other receivables	
Cash and cash equivalents	_____
	_____
Total assets	_____
EQUITY AND LIABILITIES	
Equity	
Share capital	
Retained earnings	_____
	_____
Non-current liabilities	
Loan	
Current liabilities	
Trade and other payables	_____
	_____
Total equity and liabilities	_____

There are a number of computations you need to make before you can complete the statement of financial position. One of these calculations is to find out what profit the business has made over the period. For this reason it is usual to prepare the statement of comprehensive income for the period before drawing up the statement of financial position. We will now review the computations needed to calculate the gross profit. The first working calculates the revenue:

Working 1

	£
Cash sales (£20 × 10)	200
Credit sales (£20 × 20)	400
Revenue	600

Working 2 calculates the quantity of closing inventory. There is no opening inventory because this is a new business, so we only need to subtract the quantity sold from the quantity purchased:

Working 2

	Quantity
Purchases	100
Cash sales	(10)
Credit sales	(20)
Closing inventory	70

This allows us to calculate the cost of sales in Working 3 by subtracting the value of closing inventory from the cost of purchases:

Working 3

	£
Purchases (£15 × 100)	1,500
Closing inventory (£15 × 70)	(1,050)
Cost of sales	450

We can now draft the trading section of the statement of comprehensive income, which shows that the gross profit made by Candlewick Ltd during the first week was £150:

Candlewick Ltd
Draft statement of comprehensive income
for the week ending 7 January 2012

	£
Revenue (W1)	600
Cost of sales (W2 & W3)	(450)
Gross profit	150

Strictly speaking, we should deduct a proportion of the expenses for the period and calculate the profit for the period, but since trading has barely commenced we are going to use the gross profit figure.

We can now turn our attention to the draft statement of financial position. On 7 January the company still has non-current assets (the equipment), which cost £13,000, but the current assets have changed since the statement of financial position on 2 January. The trading account for the week ending 7 January shows that value of closing inventory was £1,050, but since Candlewick Ltd has begun trading we need to consider the effect on the other current assets. The company has customers who have not yet paid for 20 boxes of candles sold on credit at £20 each (£400), and cash from the sale of 10 boxes of candles at £20 each (£200). Current liabilities are still £13,000 owing on the business credit card for the equipment and £1,500 owed to the supplier for the boxes of candles bought in January:

Working 4

	£
Trade payables	1,500
Other payables	13,000
Trade and other payables	14,500

Check your figures against the following draft statement of financial position at 7 January:

```
                    Candlewick Ltd
        Draft statement of financial position at
                    7 January 2012
                                              £
ASSETS
Non-current assets
Equipment (at cost)                        13,000
Current assets
Inventory                                   1,050
Trade and other receivables                   400
Cash and cash equivalents                  16,700
                                           18,150
Total assets                               31,150
EQUITY AND LIABILITIES
Equity
Share capital                             (10,000)
Retained earnings                            (150)
                                          (10,150)

Non-current liabilities
Loan                                       (6,500)
Current liabilities
Trade and other payables (W4)             (14,500)
Total equity and liabilities              (31,150)
```

We could continue to construct a series of statements of financial position covering Sarah's business on a day-to-day basis, but this would be somewhat tedious. So we will move on to the end of the first 6 months and prepare a draft statement of financial position at 30 June 2012 based on the following information from Chapter 6:

- Candlewick Ltd bought equipment on the company's credit card for £13,000, which was paid off in full in February. The equipment is for long-term use in the business.
- Closing inventory at 30 June was valued at £2,250 (150 boxes of candles at £15).
- Since the company allows credit customers 2 months to pay, customers buying in May and June have not yet paid. Therefore trade receivables are £16,700 (total credit sales for the period of £40,700 minus £24,000 cash received from credit sales).
- We know from the cash flow statement prepared for Sarah that the company had a cash surplus of £500 at 30 June.
- Sarah has invested £10,000 of her own money as capital in the business and the company is also financed by a medium-term bank loan of £6,500.
- We know from the draft statement of comprehensive income for the 6 months ending 30 June 2012 that we prepared in Chapter 6 that the profit for the period was £4,865.
- Sarah has not taken any of the profits as dividends.
- Trade suppliers give one month's credit, which means that inventory purchased in June has not yet been paid for. Therefore, trade payables are £9,000 (total

purchases of £45,900 minus £36,900 cash paid to suppliers).
The estimated current tax liability is £2,085.

Activity

Using the following pro forma, prepare a draft statement of financial position for Candlewick Ltd at 30 June 2012:

Candlewick Ltd
Draft statement of financial position at 30 June 2012

	£
ASSETS	
Non-current assets	
Equipment (at cost)	_____
Current assets	
Inventory	
Trade and other receivables	
Cash and cash equivalents	_____
	_____
Total assets	_____
EQUITY AND LIABILITIES	
Equity	
Share capital	
Retained earnings	_____
	_____
Non-current liabilities	
Loan	
Current liabilities	
Trade and other payables	
Current tax liability	_____
	_____
Total equity and liabilities	_____

Your completed statement of financial position should look like the top of page 167.

An important point to note is that if Sarah takes boxes of candles from the business for her own use or to give to her friends and family, she must pay for them. If she takes cash out of the business, this transaction is treated as dividends, which reduces the amount of retained earnings. By keeping Sarah's personal transactions separate from the economic transactions of the business in this way, the statement of financial position demonstrates compliance with the business entity concept. Therefore, it presents the financial position of the business and not that of its owner.

You may have noticed that when you were preparing the draft statement of financial position, you needed some of the figures from the statement of comprehensive income. The closing inventory shown in the statement of comprehensive income also

```
                    Candlewick Ltd
         Draft statement of financial position at
                    30 June 2012
                                                    £
ASSETS
Non-current assets
Equipment (at cost)                               13,000
Current assets
Inventory                                          2,250
Trade and other receivables                       16,700
Cash and cash equivalents                            500
                                                  19,450
Total assets                                      32,450

EQUITY AND LIABILITIES
Equity
Share capital                                    (10,000)
Retained earnings                                 (4,865)
                                                 (14,865)

Non-current liabilities
Loan                                              (6,500)
Current liabilities
Trade and other payables                          (9,000)
Current tax liability                             (2,085)
                                                 (17,585)
Total equity and liabilities                     (32,450)
```

appeared in the statement of financial position. In addition, you will recall that the difference between the figure for revenue in the cash flow statement (cash received from cash and credit sales during the period) and the figure for revenue in the statement of comprehensive income (total revenue for the period irrespective of whether cash has been received) is shown as trade receivables in the statement of financial position. Similarly, the difference between the figure for purchases in the cash flow statement (cash paid for purchases of inventory) and the figure for purchases in the statement of comprehensive income (total purchases for the period irrespective of whether cash has been paid) is shown as trade payables in the statement of financial position. You are now beginning to see the relationship between the two main financial statements.

So far we have only prepared a draft statement of financial position using cash information. We will now explain how the statement of financial position is prepared from a trial balance and other information available at the end of the accounting period. First we will explain how the *post trial balance adjustments* affect the statement of financial position. Here is the trial balance at 31 December 2012, which marks the end of the first year of trading for Candlewick Ltd:

Candlewick Ltd Trial balance at 31 December 2012		
	Debit £	Credit £
Revenue		173,200
Purchases	113,400	
Equipment (at cost)	13,000	
Trade receivables	27,500	
Trade payables		15,000
Cash	26,100	
Salaries	14,500	
Rent	6,000	
Telephone and Internet	1,960	
Postage and packing	1,100	
Advertising	600	
Interest on loan	540	
Loan		6,500
Share capital at 1 January 2012		10,000
	204,700	204,700

As mentioned in the previous chapter, all the post trial balance adjustments would normally be entered in the ledger accounts and a revised trial balance would be generated. However, we will show the post trial balance items of information as notes since this is the way you are likely to encounter them in your assessments.

7.4 Inventory, accruals and prepayments

7.4.1 Inventory

As you will remember, the valuation of closing inventory is guided by IAS 2, *Inventories* (IASB, 2003) and the *IFRS for SMEs* (IASB, 2009), which require inventory to be valued at the lower of cost or net realizable value (NRV). Sarah carried out a stocktaking exercise on 31 December 2012 and found that Candlewick Ltd had 50 boxes of candles in stock which had cost £15 each. Therefore the value of closing inventory is £15 × 50 = £750. In Chapter 6 you made an adjustment in the statement of comprehensive income for the first year of trading ending 31 December 2012, by deducting £750 from the cost of purchases. Since inventory is one of the assets of the business that it hopes to sell in the next accounting period, you need to make a corresponding adjustment in the statement of financial position by showing £750 of closing inventory under current assets.

7.4.2 Accruals

You will remember from Chapter 6 that an *accrual* is an estimate of a liability that is not supported by an invoice or a request for payment at the time when the accounts are prepared. Candlewick Ltd has two accrued expenses:

- The trial balance shows that telephone and Internet expenses were £1,960, but there is an accrual of £200. This means that the expense shown in the statement of comprehensive income should be £1,960 + £200 = £2,160.
- The trial balance shows that advertising expenses were £3,000, but there is an accrual of £100. Therefore, the expense shown in the statement of comprehensive income should be £3,000 + £100 = £3,100.

You need to make a corresponding adjustment in the statement of financial position by adding together the accruals (£200 + £100 = £300) and including this aggregated amount in the calculation of trade and other payables. Trade and other payables are shown under current liabilities because they will be paid during the next accounting period.

7.4.3 Prepayments

A *prepayment* is a payment made for goods or services before they are received. The amount that belongs to the next accounting period needs to be deducted from the trial balance figure for that expense. Candlewick Ltd has one prepayment:

- The trial balance shows postage and packing expenses were £1,100 in the accounts, but there is a prepayment of £100. This means that the expense shown in the statement of comprehensive income should be £1,100 – £100 = £1,000.

As you are now beginning to realize, you now need to make a corresponding adjustment in the statement of financial position. The general rule is to include the aggregated prepaid amounts in the calculation of trade and other receivables which are shown under current assets.

7.5 Depreciation of property, plant and equipment

Under IAS 16, *Property, Plant and Equipment* (IASB, 2008) and the *IFRS for SMEs* (IASB, 2009), items of property, plant and equipment (PPE) with a finite life must be depreciated. In Chapter 6 we explained that *depreciation* is the systematic allocation of the depreciable amount of an asset over its useful life, and the *depreciable amount* is the cost of the asset, or other amount substituted for cost, less its residual value. *Residual value* is the estimated amount that an entity would currently obtain from disposal of the asset, after deducting the estimated costs of disposal, if the asset were already of the age and in the condition expected at the end of its useful life. As you will recall, *useful life* is the period over which an asset is expected to be available for use by an entity, or the number of production or similar units expected to be obtained from the asset by the entity.

Candlewick Ltd has one tangible non-current asset, which is the equipment that was bought on 1 January at a cost of £13,000. The equipment has a residual value of £1,000 at the end of its useful life of 4 years. The accountant has advised Sarah to use the *straight-line method* of depreciation, which spreads the cost (or revalued amount) evenly over the life of the asset.

Activity

Using the following formula, calculate the allowance for depreciation for the year ending 31 December 2012:

$$\frac{\text{Cost} - \text{Residual value}}{\text{Useful life}}$$

You should have found this exercise easy, since we explained it in the previous chapter. Check your answer against the calculations below:

$$\frac{£13,000 - £1,000}{4 \text{ years}} = \frac{£12,000}{4 \text{ years}} = £3,000$$

The allowance for depreciation on equipment of £3,000 is included in the calculation of administrative expenses in the statement of comprehensive income for the year ending 31 December 2012. Since part of the cost of the asset has been apportioned as an expense for the period, an adjustment is needed to the value of the asset in the statement of financial position. Instead of showing the asset at cost, as Sarah did when preparing the draft statement of financial position, the accountant tells her that it will be shown at the *carrying amount*.[1] The carrying amount is the amount at which an asset is recognized after deducting any accumulated depreciation and accumulated impairment losses. Each significant part of an item of PPE is depreciated separately and its residual value and useful life must be reviewed annually. If an asset is revalued, the valuation is substituted for the carrying amount and this will result in a revaluation gain or loss. An impairment loss is a reduction in the recoverable amount of the asset due to obsolescence, damage or a fall in the market value of such assets.

We now need to calculate the carrying amount of the equipment that will be shown under non-current assets in the statement of financial position. We know that the cost of the equipment was £13,000 and it was bought on the first day of the financial period. At the end of the first year, the closing carrying amount is the cost minus the allowance for depreciation charged to the statement of comprehensive income. The closing carrying amount at the end of one year becomes the opening carrying amount at the start of the next, and each year the opening carrying amount will be reduced by

---

1. The carrying amount is sometimes referred to as the *net book value* or the *written down value* of the asset.

£3,000 until at the end of the fourth year only the residual value of £1,000 remains. The following table illustrates a convenient way of setting out your workings.

Year	Opening carrying amount	Allowance for depreciation	Closing carrying amount
	£	£	£
1	13,000	(3,000)	10,000
2	10,000	(3,000)	7,000
3	7,000	(3,000)	4,000
4	4,000	(3,000)	1,000

Sarah's accountant tells her about a second method that is used to depreciate some types of tangible assets. It is known as the *diminishing balance method* of depreciation because the cost reduces over the life of the asset. The method involves applying a depreciation rate to the opening carrying amount each year. In the first year, the opening carrying amount is the cost of the asset and the formula is:

$$(\text{Cost} - \text{Residual value}) \times \text{Depreciation rate (\%)}$$

In subsequent years the formula is:

$$\text{Opening carrying amount} \times \text{Depreciation rate (\%)}$$

The following table shows how the diminishing balance method would be applied to the equipment. As a very rough rule of thumb, the percentage is nearly double that required for the straight-line method. Since the annual allowance for depreciation under the straight-line method was 25% (£3,000 ÷ £12,000), we will use a rate of 48% in this illustration of the diminishing balance method. The first step is to calculate the allowance for depreciation for the first year:

$$(£13,000 - £1,000) \times 48\% = £5,760$$

We can now use this to work out the closing carrying amount at the end of Year 1 (£7,240), which becomes the opening carrying amount for Year 2. The depreciation rate of 48% is then applied to find the depreciation charge for Year 2 (£7,240 × 48% = £3,475). This is then deducted from the opening carrying amount to arrive at the closing carrying amount. This continues until the end of Year 4, when the following table shows that we are left with the residual value of just over £1,000.

Year	Opening carrying amount	Depreciation 48%	Closing carrying amount
	£	£	£
1	13,000	(5,760)	7,240
2	7,240	(3,475)	3,765
3	3,765	(1,807)	1,958
4	1,958	(940)	1,018

Sarah's accountant also mentions that methods based on usage, such as the units of production method, are also permitted. These would be relevant to businesses in the manufacturing sector. The depreciation method chosen should reflect the pattern in which the asset's economic benefits are consumed by the entity. If there has been a significant change since the last annual reporting date in the pattern by which the entity expects to consume an asset's future economic benefits, management must review the present depreciation method and, if current expectations differ, change the method to reflect the new pattern.

The straight-line method is widely used as it is simple and easy to use and apportions the cost of the asset evenly over its useful life to the business. If the pattern in which the economic benefits are consumed is uncertain, the straight-line method is usually adopted. Although the diminishing balance method is more complex, the lower depreciation charge in later years helps to offset higher maintenance costs that are likely when assets such as plant, machinery and vehicles age. Thus the overall cost of such assets is spread evenly. To aid comparison, the same depreciation method is used for all assets that are classified as belonging to the same group, and consistently from one period to the next.

7.6   Bad debts and doubtful receivables

As discussed in Chapter 6, Candlewick Ltd did not have any bad debts during the first year of trading. A bad debt is an amount owed by customers that is considered to be irrecoverable and it must be written off as a charge against profit or against an existing allowance for doubtful receivables in the statement of comprehensive income. Since customers who cannot pay are no longer assets of the business, such amounts should not be included in the figure for trade receivables. Sarah's accountant has advised her that she should make an *allowance for doubtful receivables* to allow for the estimated non-recovery of receivables. This is an amount charged against profit in the statement of comprehensive income (in this case, another item to be included with distribution costs) and deducted from trade receivables, which are shown under current assets in the statement of financial position.

In the previous chapter we mentioned that the allowance for doubtful receivables can be based on specific debts where there is documentary evidence that suggests that the debts will not be paid, or on the general assumption that a certain percentage of receivables are doubtful. Sarah has decided to base the allowance on 10% of trade receivables: £27,500 × 10% = £2,750. Therefore, this is the amount that will be added to the distribution costs in the statement of comprehensive income and deducted from trade receivables in the statement of financial position. Before deciding, Sarah's accountant showed her an alternative method. The following table analyses the company's trade receivables by the age of the debt. As you can see, most debts are 2 months old or less because the business gives customers 2 months to pay. However, some are more than 3 months old, which means that some customers are taking longer than the agreed 2 months. If Sarah does not improve her credit control, there is a strong risk that some customers will not pay for their candles and this is reflected in the higher percentages the accountant has applied to older debts when calculating the allowance for doubtful receivables.

Age of debt (months)	Trade receivables £	Estimated bad receivables	Allowance for doubtful receivables £
1	12,500	1%	125
2	10,500	10%	1,050
3	3,000	50%	1,500
4 or more	1,500	75%	1,125
Total	27,500		3,800

It is important to remember that methods based on arbitrary percentages are estimates of the proportion of receivables that will not be paid. For financial reporting purposes, the entity should choose the method that gives the most realistic allowance and then use it consistently to aid comparability.

7.7 Finalizing the statement of financial position

We now have all the information we need to prepare the statement of comprehensive income for Candlewick Ltd for the year ending 31 December 2012 and also the statement of financial position. Here is the trial balance and the notes that represent the post trial balance adjustments:

Candlewick Ltd
Trial balance at 31 December 2012

	Debit £	Credit £
Revenue		173,200
Purchases	113,400	
Equipment (at cost)	13,000	
Trade receivables	27,500	
Trade payables		15,000
Cash	26,100	
Salaries	14,500	
Rent	6,000	
Telephone and Internet	1,960	
Printing, postage and stationery	1,100	
Advertising	600	
Interest on loan	540	
Loan		6,500
Share capital at 1 January 2012		10,000
	204,700	204,700

Additional information available at 31 December 2012:

- Closing inventory is valued at £750.
- Rent, advertising, telephone and Internet, printing, postage and packaging and salaries are allocated 50% to distribution costs and 50% to administrative expenses.
- There are accrued expenses of £100 for advertising and £200 for telephone and Internet.
- Printing, postage and packaging include a prepayment of £100.
- The equipment is expected to have a useful life of 4 years, and an estimated residual value of £1,000. Depreciation on equipment will be charged 50% to distribution costs and 50% to administrative expenses.
- An allowance for doubtful receivables will be made based on 10% of trade receivables and will be charged 100% to distribution costs.
- The estimated current tax liability is £8,970.
- Sarah has decided that this year she will leave all profits in the company to help it grow rather than take some for herself in the form of a dividend.

Activity

Prepare a statement of comprehensive income for Candlewick Ltd for the year ending 31 December 2012 and a statement of financial position at 31 December 2012 using all the items listed in the trial balance and taking account of every item of additional information provided for the post trial balance adjustments. You will find it helpful to tick each item as you use it. When you have finished, all the items in the trial balance will have one tick because they are either shown in the statement of comprehensive income or the statement of financial position. On the other hand, since every item in the notes represents a post trial balance adjustment it will have two ticks: one for when you show the adjustment in the statement of comprehensive income and the other for when you show the adjustment in the statement of financial position.

You need to start by drawing together all the calculations we have made in connection with the post trial balance adjustments at 31 December 2012. These can be summarized as follows:

Working 1

	£
Purchases	113,400
Closing inventory	(750)
Cost of sales	112,650

One tick against the information about closing inventory when you use it to calculate cost of sales in the statement of comprehensive income, and another when you include it under current assets in the statement of financial position.

Working 2

$$\text{Depreciation on equipment} = \frac{£13,000 - £1,000}{4 \text{ years}} = £3,000$$

Closing carrying amount = £13,000 − £3,000 = £10,000

One tick against the information about the allowance for depreciation on equipment when you use it to calculate distribution costs and administrative expenses in the statement of comprehensive income, and another when you show the carrying amount of equipment under non-current assets in the statement of financial position.

Working 3

Allowance for doubtful receivables = £27,500 × 10% = £2,750

One tick against the information about the allowance for doubtful receivables when you use it to calculate distribution costs and administrative expenses in the statement of comprehensive income, and another when you include it in the calculation of trade and other receivables under current assets in the statement of financial position.

Working 4

	Amount (£)	Distribution costs (£)	Administrative expenses (£)	Finance costs (£)
Rent	6,000	3,000	3,000	
Advertising (600 + 100)	700	700		
Telephone and Internet (1,960 + 200)	2,160		2,160	
Printing, postage and stationery (1,100 − 100)	1,000	500	500	
Interest paid on loan	540			540
Salaries	14,500	7,250	7,250	
Depreciation (W2)	3,000	1,500	1,500	
Doubtful receivables (W3)	2,750		2,750	
Total	30,650	12,950	17,160	540

Working 5

	£
Trade receivables in trial balance	27,500
Doubtful receivables (10%)	(2,750)
Trade receivables	24,750
Prepayments	100
Trade and other receivables	24,850

Working 6

	£
Trade payables in trial balance	15,000
Accruals	300
Trade and other payables	15,300

Your completed financial statements should look like this.

Candlewick Ltd
Statement of comprehensive income for the year ending
31 December 2012

	£
Revenue	173,200
Cost of sales (W1)	(112,650)
Gross profit	**60,550**
Distribution costs (W2, W3, W4)	(15,700)
Administrative expenses (W2, W3, W4)	(14,410)
Operating profit	**30,440**
Finance costs (W4)	(540)
Profit before tax	**29,900**
Income tax expense	(8,970)
Profit for the period	**20,930**

Candlewick Ltd
Statement of financial position at 31 December 2012

	£
ASSETS	
Non-current assets	
Equipment (W2)	10,000
Current assets	
Inventory	750
Trade and other receivables (W5)	24,850
Cash and cash equivalents	26,100
	51,700
Total assets	**61,700**
EQUITY AND LIABILITIES	
Equity	
Share capital	(10,000)
Retained earnings	(20,930)
	(30,930)
Non-current liabilities	
Loan	(6,500)
Current liabilities	
Trade and other payables (W6)	(15,300)
Current tax liability	(8,970)
	(30,770)
Total equity and liabilities	**(61,700)**

These are fairly simple financial statements and because it is the company's first year of trading, it is not possible to provide comparative figures for the previous year. You will find it useful to learn the following more detailed layout for the statement of financial position, which is consistent with the minimum requirements of IAS 1.

Name of entity		
Statement of financial position at (day/month/year)		
	This year	Last year
	£	£
ASSETS		
Non-current assets		
Property, plant and equipment	X	X
Intangible assets	X	X
Investments	X	X
	X	X
Current assets		
Inventories	X	X
Trade and other receivables	X	X
Investments	X	X
Cash and cash equivalents	X	X
	X	X
Total assets	**X**	**X**
EQUITY AND LIABILITIES		
Equity		
Share capital	X	X
Retained earnings	X	X
Other reserves	X	X
	X	X
Non-current liabilities		
Finance lease liabilities	X	X
Borrowings	X	X
	X	X
Current liabilities		
Trade and other payables	X	X
Dividends payable	X	X
Current tax liability	X	X
Provisions	X	X
Borrowings	X	X
Finance lease liabilities	X	X
	X	X
Total equity and liabilities	**X**	**X**

7.8 Conclusions

We have now explained two of the four financial statements that are prepared by reporting entities at the end of the accounting period. The purpose of the statement of comprehensive income is to measure the financial performance of the business over the accounting period, which is usually one year. This financial statement gives users important information about all profits and gains made by the entity over the period. In this chapter we have explained that the purpose of the statement of financial position is to measure the financial position of the business on the last day of the accounting period for which the statement of comprehensive income has been prepared. This second financial statement gives users important information about the assets, equity and other liabilities of the business. We have shown you how a business that uses cash records can prepare these two financial statements after making some adjustments. We have also demonstrated how the statements can be prepared from a trial balance generated by a business that uses a double-entry bookkeeping system. The knowledge you gained in Chapter 6 should have been reinforced if you have studied this chapter because we have shown you how to reflect the post trial balance adjustments in the statement of comprehensive income and in the statement of financial position.

In the exercises in this book, these adjustments are shown as additional information below the trial balance. If you adopt a ticking system when using the information to prepare the statement of comprehensive income and the statement of financial position, you should find that you have one tick against every item in the trial balance and two ticks against every adjustment. You tick every adjustment twice because you make one adjustment to an item in the statement of comprehensive income and a corresponding adjustment in the statement of financial position. After the first year, previous year figures must be disclosed in these two annual financial statements to enhance the comparability of the information. Common mistakes students make when drawing up the statement of financial position are:

- not showing the name of the business
- not stating the date at which the statement of financial position is prepared
- forgetting to include the currency symbol
- confusing opening inventory with closing inventory
- not making all the post trial balance adjustments
- forgetting to show any workings
- not classifying assets and liabilities correctly
- forgetting that it is only the two balancing figures that are underlined (total assets in the first part and total equity and liabilities in the second part).

Practice questions

1 Describe the general purpose of the statement of financial position. In addition, explain the terms *asset, liability* and *equity* as defined by the *Conceptual Framework for Financial Reporting* (IASB, 2010).

2 Explain the going concern basis of accounting by defining the principles involved. Illustrate your answer by taking the example of the valuation of tangible assets in the statement of financial position.

3 Insert the missing figures in the following examples, remembering that some items will be added and others will be subtracted.

	(a)	(b)	(c)	(d)	(e)
	£	£	£	£	£
ASSETS					
Non-current assets	12,400	22,800	?	42,200	?
Current assets	?	3,700	4,200	?	11,800
Total assets	15,800	?	36,200	52,800	66,000
EQUITY AND LIABILITIES					
Equity					
Capital	?	(6,000)	(10,000)	?	(10,000)
Retained earnings	(4,800)	(13,300)	?	(25,800)	?
	(9,800)	?	(32,700)	(40,800)	(47,700)
Liabilities					
Non-current liabilities	?	(6,000)	(2,000)	(10,000)	?
Current liabilities	(1,000)	(1,200)	?	(2,000)	(3,300)
	(6,000)	?	(3,500)	?	(18,300)
Total equity and liabilities	?	?	?	?	?

4 Salma Ibrahim set up a company called Uplights Ltd and opened a lighting shop on 1 January 2012. Her brother is studying for his accountancy exams and helps her by doing the bookkeeping and managing the inventory. At the end of the first year of trading, he generates the following trial balance from the accounting records.

Uplights Ltd		
Trial balance at 31 December 2012		
	Debit	Credit
	£	£
Revenue		66,500
Purchases	20,000	
Fixtures and fittings (at cost)	20,000	
Trade receivables	2,000	
Trade payables		8,400
Cash	14,500	
Bank interest received		100
Rent and rates	24,000	
Salaries	21,500	
Insurance	2,000	
Lighting and heating	500	
Telephone and Internet	400	
Advertising	100	
Share capital at 1 January 2012		30,000
	105,000	105,000

Additional information at 30 June 2012:

- Inventory was valued at £8,000.
- Estimated current tax payable is £2,000.
- The company classifies expenses by nature.

Required

Prepare a draft statement of comprehensive income for Uplights Ltd for the year ending 31 December 2012 and a draft statement of financial position at that date. Show all your workings.

5 On 1 July 2011 Mark Farmer opened a shop called Miphone Ltd. The trial balance for the first year is shown below.

Miphone Ltd
Trial balance at 30 June 2012

	Debit £	Credit £
Revenue		75,200
Purchases	12,160	
Plant and equipment at cost	25,000	
Trade receivables	1,200	
Trade payables		1,600
Cash	3,260	
Other income		1,200
Salaries	24,000	
Rent and rates	18,000	
Insurance	7,200	
Advertising	860	
Lighting and heating	620	
Telephone and Internet	450	
General expenses	250	
Share capital at 1 July 2011		15,000
	93,000	93,000

Additional information at 30 June 2012:

- Inventory is valued at £890.
- Advertising paid in advance is £260.
- Accrued expenses are lighting and heating £540, telephone and Internet £290 and general expenses £160.
- Estimated current tax payable is £1,200.

Required

(a) Using a spreadsheet, prepare a draft statement of comprehensive income for Miphone Ltd for the year ended 30 June 2012, classifying expenses by nature. In addition, prepare a draft statement of financial position at that date.

(b) After taking advice from his accountant, Mark has decided to depreciate equipment using the straight-line method over 5 years, with no residual value. He has also decided to make an allowance for doubtful receivables and has decided to base it on 10% of opening trade receivables. Make these adjustments to your spreadsheet and prepare a statement of comprehensive income for Miphone Ltd for the year ending 30 June 2013, classifying expenses by nature. In addition, prepare a statement of financial position at that date.

6 Kavita Patel owns a business called Beauty Box Ltd, which started trading on 1 July 2010. At the end of the second year of trading, her accountant provides the following trial balance from the accounting system:

Beauty Box Ltd
Trial balance at 30 June 2012

	Debit £	Credit £
Revenue		104,900
Purchases	39,700	
Inventory at 1 July 2011	10,000	
Equipment at cost	20,000	
Trade receivables	6,000	
Trade payables		8,000
Cash and cash equivalents	15,300	
Interest received		100
Salaries	30,000	
Rent and rates	15,000	
Insurance	3,000	
Lighting and heating	1,500	
Telephone and Internet	2,000	
Advertising	500	
Allowances at 1 July 2011:		
Depreciation on plant and equipment		4,000
Doubtful receivables		1,000
Share capital at 1 July 2011		20,000
Retained profit at 1 July 2011		5,000
	143,000	143,000

Additional information at 30 June 2012:

- Inventory was valued at £12,000.
- Equipment has a useful life of 5 years and no residual value. They are depreciated using the straight-line method.
- The company makes an allowance for doubtful receivables based on 10% of opening trade receivables.
- Estimated current tax liability £4,500.
- The company classifies expenses by nature.

Required

Use the relevant figures in the above information to prepare a statement of comprehensive income for Beauty Box Ltd for the year ending 30 June 2012. In addition, prepare a statement of financial position at that date. Show all your workings.

References

IASB (2008) IAS 16, *Property, Plant and Equipment*. London: International Accounting Standards Board.

IASB (2009) *IFRS for SMEs*. London: International Accounting Standards Board.

IASB (2010) *The Conceptual Framework for Financial Reporting*, September. London: International Accounting Standards Board.

8 Consolidated financial statements

Learning objectives

When you have studied this chapter, you should be able to:

- Explain the importance of control
- Prepare a consolidated statement of financial position
- Prepare a consolidated statement of comprehensive income and a consolidated statement of changes in equity
- Account for an investment in an associate
- Account for an investment in a joint arrangement.

8.1 Introduction

The main focus of this chapter is on *group* accounting. A group is a *parent* company and one or more *subsidiaries* that are controlled by the parent. Control is achieved if the parent holds more than 50% of the shares of the subsidiary. Most major companies in the UK use a group structure and the financial statements of a group are known as *consolidated financial statements*. These are obtained by combining the information contained in the individual financial statements of the parent and subsidiaries. Although a subsidiary could be a partnership or a trust, most are companies. Therefore, this chapter examines accounting for groups of companies.

We start by looking at the importance of control in a group structure of companies and the need for consolidated financial statements. We then explain a step-by-step approach to the preparation of a consolidated financial statement of financial position at the date of acquisition of a subsidiary and at the end of subsequent years. This is followed by an explanation of how the consolidated statement of comprehensive income and the consolidated statement of changes in equity are prepared. In the final sections of the chapter we describe the different accounting treatments used when the investment is not in a subsidiary but in an *associate* or *a joint arrangement*.

8.2   Financial statements of a group

A *group* comprises a parent company and one or more subsidiaries. A subsidiary is an entity (a company or an unincorporated entity such as a partnership) that is controlled by another entity (known as the parent entity). The subsidiary can be created or acquired. As the parent company is investing in the subsidiary, the parent can be referred to as the investor and the subsidiary as the investee.

The advantages of a group structure include the following:

- The parent can assign accountability and responsibility to the manager of each subsidiary as they control the activities of their respective business.
- Each subsidiary has its own separately audited financial statements, giving them an ability to borrow without the need for parental involvement.
- The assets of the subsidiary can be offered as security against its borrowings without restricting the activities of other group entities.
- It allows for the easier acquisition and disposal of individual businesses.

Under IFRS 10, *Consolidated Financial Statements* (IASB, 2011a), a parent entity is required to prepare *consolidated financial statements*. These are financial statements in which the assets, liabilities, equity, income, expenses and cash flows of the parent and its subsidiaries are combined as if they were a single economic entity. Consolidated financial statements are provided in addition to the parent entity's financial statements. As the requirements of IAS 1, *Presentation of Financial Statements* (IASB 2011b) apply to entities that present consolidated financial statements, a complete set of financial statements includes:

- a consolidated statement of financial position
- a consolidated statement of comprehensive income
- a consolidated statement of changes in equity
- a consolidated statement of cash flows
- notes to the consolidated accounts that explain accounting policies and other disclosures.

Key definitions

A parent is an entity that controls one or more entities.

Consolidated financial statements are the financial statements of a group in which the assets, liabilities, equity, income, expenses and cash flows of the parent and its subsidiaries are presented as those of a single economic entity.

Source: IFRS 10 (IASB, 2011a, Appendix A)

Activity

Why do parent companies need to prepare consolidated financial statements?

Without the requirement to consolidate the activities of the parent and its subsidiaries, the shareholders of the parent company would only receive the financial statements of the parent. These would not include the assets, liabilities and profits of the subsidiaries and the parent could exploit its group structure to manipulate the financial and business performance it reports in its own accounts. For example, a parent could disguise its gearing by using its subsidiaries to secure off-balance sheet financing. The key principle is that the consolidated financial statements present a faithful representation (see Chapter 5) of the economic activities of the group as a single economic entity.

Irrespective of the general requirement of IFRS 10 to present group accounts, a parent need not present consolidated financial statements where all of the following conditions are met:

- The parent company is either a wholly owned subsidiary or a partially owned subsidiary of another company, and its owners do not object to the parent not presenting consolidated financial statements.
- The parent's shares or securities are not publicly traded.
- The parent's own parent company presents consolidated financial statements that comply with international accounting standards.

8.2.1 Control

The concept of *control* provides the threshold test for determining whether the financial statements of an entity should be included in the consolidated financial statements of the group. Establishing an appropriate definition of control is more difficult than it first appears. For example, control can often be achieved without an investor possessing any direct legal ownership in the investee company.

Activity

What are the main issues that need to be considered when deciding whether a parent controls another entity?

When an investor acquires an ownership interest in the ordinary share capital of another company this normally grants ownership over an equal proportion over the company's voting rights. Control is achieved if the investor acquires more than 50% of the investee's voting rights. A parent may exercise indirect control over a subsidiary through intermediate companies that are themselves controlled by the parent. Control does not always require possession of the majority of an investee's voting rights due to the size of the investor's voting rights relative to the size and dispersion of other vote holders. For example, an investor may hold 40% of the voting rights in an investee and the remaining shares are held by thousands of individual shareholders who have not participated in voting in the past. In such circumstances, the 40% shareholder is deemed to have *de facto* control.

Under IFRS 10, *control of an investee* is achieved when the investor is exposed, or has rights, to variable returns from its involvement with the investee and has the ability to affect those returns through its power over the investee. As a result, control is only achieved if the investor possesses all three of the following elements of control:

- power over the investee by having rights that give the ability to direct the relevant activities
- exposure, or rights, to variable returns from its involvement with the investee
- ability to use its power over the investee to affect the amount of these returns.

The concept of control focuses on power and returns, rather than on voting rights. Power rests with the party that has the ability to direct decisions about the *relevant activities* that significantly affect the investee's returns. Relevant activities are activities of the investee that significantly affect the investee's returns. Examples include:

- product development
- purchases and sales of goods or services
- acquiring and disposing of assets
- obtaining finance.

Key decisions about relevant activities include:

- devising and establishing operating policies
- controlling capital expenditure decisions
- appointing key management personnel.

Key definitions

Control of an investee is achieved when the investor is exposed, or has rights, to variable returns from its involvement with the investee and has the ability to affect those returns through its power over the investee.

Power refers to existing rights [of the investor] that give the current ability to direct the relevant activities [of the investee].

Protective rights are rights designed to protect the interest of the party holding those rights without giving that party power over the entity to which those rights relate.

Relevant activities are the activities of the investee that significantly affect the investee's returns.

Source: IFRS 10 (IASB, 2011a, Appendix A)

8.2.2 Voting rights

While the power to direct relevant activities normally arises through voting rights obtained from owning equity shares, it can also arise through contractual arrangements.

Therefore, when assessing whether an investor has power over an investee, the following sources of power must be considered:

- voting rights
- potential voting rights that the holder could exercise (for example those obtained from a share option or convertible financial instrument)
- an investor's contractual and non-contractual rights (for example the ability to appoint an investee's key personnel or veto significant transactions)
- special relationships between an investor and investor (for example the investee's operations may be dependent on the investor or its key personnel may also be employed by the investor).

Only *substantive rights* are capable of providing power. A right is substantive if it grants the holder the practical ability to exercise the right when decisions about the relevant activities of the investee need to be made. For example, the right of a lender to seize assets in the event of an investee defaulting on its debt is not substantive, as it does not give the lender power over the investee's relevant activities.

While power to direct decision making over relevant activities is an important determinate of control, it also requires that an investor benefit from that power in the form of a variable return from its involvement with the investee. The returns must vary as a result of the investee's performance and can be positive, negative or both. Examples of investor returns include:

- changes in the value of the investor's investment
- dividends
- returns that are unavailable to other interest holders (e.g. cost savings or synergies obtained from interactions between the investor and investee).

As well as obtaining this variable return, control also requires that an investor has the ability to affect those returns through its power over the investee's decision making. This relationship between power and returns is an essential component of control under IFRS 10. In each of the following cases, the investor does not control the investee:

- Investor A has the power to direct the relevant activities of an investee, but has no right to a variable return from its involvement with the investee.
- Investor B receives a return from an investee but cannot use its power to direct the relevant activities of the investee.

Although there is often a correlation between voting rights and the power to direct decision making over the relevant activities of an investee, it should not be assumed. When voting rights control decision making and those rights entitle an investor to a return (for example voting shares that are entitled to dividends), whoever holds a majority of those rights controls the investee. In other cases, an investor might have power and secure *de facto* control over an investee by virtue of:

- the size of its voting rights relative to the size and dispersion of other vote holders
- voting patterns and lack of attendance at the investee's previous shareholders' meetings

Activity

Using the definition of control provided by IFRS 10 and the following information, assess whether Giant Ltd has control over Tiny Ltd.

Giant Ltd acquires 48% of the voting rights of Tiny Ltd by purchasing 48% of its ordinary share capital. The remaining voting rights are held by 50,000 other shareholders, none of whom individually hold more than 1% of the voting rights. None of the shareholders has any arrangement to consult any of the others or make collective decisions. Furthermore, these small shareholders have never voted at previous shareholders' meetings of Tiny Ltd.

For control to be achieved by Giant Ltd, the three elements of control must be present:

- Although Giant Ltd does not control the majority of the voting rights in Tiny Ltd, it does have power over the relevant activities of Tiny Ltd. This power is obtained from the size of Giant Ltd's voting rights relative to the size and dispersion of the other vote holders. This power over Tiny Ltd's voting rights is reinforced by the fact that the 50,000 other shareholders have never voted at a shareholders' meeting.
- Giant Ltd obtains variable returns from its investment, as its ownership of Tiny Ltd's ordinary shares provides dividends and a 48% share of any change in the value of Tiny Ltd.
- Giant Ltd has the power to affect the returns of Tiny Ltd by directing its relevant activities. As all three elements of control exist, Giant Ltd has control over Tiny Ltd and must include it within the consolidated financial statements.

8.3   Consolidated statement of financial position at acquisition

We will start by explaining the process for preparing consolidated financial statements for a parent and its subsidiary on the date the parent acquires its subsidiary. Under IFRS 3, *Business Combinations* (IASB, 2010a), a business combination occurs when an economic transaction gives an acquirer control of a business. Where control is achieved, the financial statements of the subsidiary must be combined with those of the parent to form consolidated financial statements using the *acquisition method* of accounting. This requires:

- identifying the acquirer (i.e. the entity that controls the acquiree)
- determining the acquisition date
- recognising and measuring the identifiable assets acquired, the liabilities assumed and any *non-controlling interest* in the acquiree
- recognising and measuring goodwill or a gain from a bargain purchase.

8.3.1 Main steps in the acquisition method

Constructing a consolidated statement of financial position at the date of acquisition of a subsidiary involves the following five steps:

1. Identify whether control exists and establish the parent's proportionate share of the subsidiary at the date of acquisition. We explained how to apply the IFRS 10 concept of control in the previous section. In the activities that follow, we will assume that the parent's share of a subsidiary equals the percentage of its ordinary shares being acquired.

2. Calculate the *fair value* of the consideration transferred by the parent. A parent's investment in a subsidiary is called the consideration transferred. An investor does not always use cash to finance its investment in a subsidiary, so the consideration transferred includes the fair value of any assets given, liabilities incurred or assumed and the equity instruments (shares) issued by the parent.

3. Calculate the fair value of the subsidiary's identifiable assets and liabilities recognised at the date of acquisition. IFRS 3 requires that a subsidiary's identifiable assets and liabilities should be recognised at fair value rather than current book value (carrying value) at the date of acquisition.

   IFRS 3 requires measurement of a subsidiary's assets and liabilities at fair value as it provides a faithful representation of their economic value at the date of acquisition. To qualify for recognition, the assets and liabilities of the subsidiary must be part of the business acquired and meet the definitions of an asset and liability in the IASB Framework (IASB, 2010b). The term *net assets* refers to the difference between total assets and total liabilities and is equal to equity in the accounting equation.

4. Calculate the non-controlling interest's proportionate share of the subsidiary's identifiable net assets at the date of acquisition. A parent does not need to acquire 100% of a subsidiary's ordinary shares to obtain control. The holders of any remaining shares are referred to as the *non-controlling interest* (NCI) and represent the subsidiary's equity that is not attributable to the parent. As the purpose of consolidated accounts is to show the effectiveness of the parent's control, all of the assets and liabilities of the subsidiary are included within the consolidated statement of financial position and a NCI should be shown as partly financing those net assets. Under IFRS 3, the NCI is typically measured at the NCI's proportionate share of the subsidiary's identifiable net assets. This is the method used to compute NCI throughout this chapter, but IFRS 3 does provide an alternative option for measuring NCI at fair value.

5. Calculate the *goodwill* at the date of acquisition. Goodwill is an asset that represents the future economic benefits arising from assets acquired in a business combination that cannot be individually separately identified and recognised, such as the company's reputation and loyalty of its workforce and customer base. IFRS 3 states that goodwill can only recognised in the group accounts as a result of a business

combination. Goodwill at the date of acquisition is the excess of the fair value of the consideration transferred plus the value of any NCI less the fair value of the identifiable net assets acquired, as shown below:

	£
Working 2 Fair value of the consideration transferred	X
Working 4 Non-controlling interest at the acquisition date	X
Working 3 Fair value of subsidiary's net assets at date of acquisition	(X)
Goodwill	X)

Goodwill is normally positive, although negative goodwill may occur when the subsidiary is purchased at a bargain price. Once recognised, positive goodwill is carried in the consolidated statement of financial position at cost and tested for impairment at least annually in accordance with IAS 36, *Impairment of Assets* (IASB, 2009). An impairment review is a procedure undertaken by an appropriately qualified person to assess whether goodwill has suffered from a diminution in value, and if it has, the impairment loss is deducted from the group's retained earnings.

Key definition

Fair value is the price that would be received to sell an asset or paid to transfer a liability in an orderly transaction between market participants at the measurement date

Source: IFRS 13 (IASB, 2011c, Appendix A)

Key definitions

A non-controlling interest is the equity in a subsidiary not attributable, directly or indirectly, to a parent.

Goodwill is an asset representing the future economic benefits arising from other assets acquired in a business combination that are not individually identified and separately recognised.

Source: IFRS 3 (IASB, 2010a, Appendix A)

We will now work through these five steps using an example. On 31 January 2011 Global Ltd paid £3.50 per share in order to acquire 100% of the £1 ordinary shares of Local Ltd. At this date all Local Ltd's assets and liabilities were valued at fair value. The statements of financial position of the two companies at the date of acquisition were as follows.

Statements of financial position at 31 January 2011	Global Ltd	Local Ltd
	£'000	£'000
ASSETS		
Non-current assets		
Property, plant and equipment	1,500	3,000
Investment in Local Ltd	3,500	–
	5,000	**3,000**
Current assets	1,000	1,000
Total assets	**6,000**	**4,000**
EQUITY AND LIABILITIES		
Equity		
Ordinary share capital	2,000	1,000
Retained earnings	2,000	2,000
	4,000	**3,000**
Current liabilities	2,000	1,000
Total equity and liabilities	**6,000**	**4,000**

1. Global Ltd has taken control of Local Ltd by purchasing 100% of its ordinary share capital for £3.50 per share, so Local Ltd becomes a wholly owned subsidiary of Global Ltd.

2. The ordinary share capital of Local Ltd has a nominal value of £1 per share, so it has 1m ordinary shares (£1m ordinary share capital ÷ £1 per share). At a purchase price of £3.50 per share, the fair value of the consideration transferred by Global Ltd was £3.5m (1m shares × £3.50 per share).

3. The assets and liabilities of Local Ltd were already valued at their fair value at the date of acquisition. In exchange for the consideration transferred, Global Ltd obtains control over Local Ltd's identifiable net assets that had a fair value of £3m at the date of acquisition (£4m assets – £1m current liabilities).

4. As Global Ltd has acquired 100% of Local Ltd's ordinary share capital there is no NCI. The accounting entries for dealing with a NCI will be explained within the Giga Ltd and Mega Ltd activity later in this section.

5. The consideration transferred by Global Ltd was £0.5m more than the fair value of Local Ltd's net assets at the acquisition date (£3.5m consideration transferred by Global Ltd – £3m Local Ltd's identifiable net assets). As there is no NCI, this excess represents the goodwill on consolidation as shown below.

	£'000
Fair value of the consideration transferred	3,500
Non-controlling interest at the acquisition date	–
Fair value of subsidiary's identifiable net assets at the date of acquisition	(3,000)
Goodwill	500

The figure for goodwill will be shown in the consolidated statement of financial position at cost and will be tested for impairment at least annually.

8.3.2 Preparing the consolidated statement of financial position at acquisition

Because it is prepared for the shareholders of the parent company, only the parent's share capital is included. If a transaction is shown as an asset in the statement of financial position of one entity and as equity (or a liability) in another entity's financial statement, all such items must be eliminated (offset) during the consolidation process as follows:

- The carrying amount of the parent's investment (the consideration transferred) is eliminated against its share of the subsidiary's equity at the date of acquisition. Any excess is show as goodwill. As a result, the investment in the subsidiary is replaced by the net assets that the parent has acquired.
- Any intra-group balances or debts resulting from intra-group trading are eliminated (there are no such amounts in this example).

Working 1 in the following consolidated statement of financial position for Global Ltd provides details of the elimination process. The £3.5m investment in Local Ltd is eliminated against Global Ltd's 100% share of Local Ltd's £3m equity at the acquisition date (£1m ordinary share capital + £2m retained earnings). After these amounts are eliminated, £0.5m of the investment remains. This is shown as goodwill under intangible non-current assets. The remaining assets and liabilities of Global Ltd and Local Ltd (the property, plant and equipment, current assets and current liabilities are aggregated item by item to provide the relevant figures for the consolidated statement of financial position.

Global Ltd
Consolidated statement of financial position at 31 January 2011

	Global Ltd £'000	Local Ltd £'000	W1 £'000	Group £'000
ASSETS				
Non-current assets				
Property, plant and equipment	1,500	3,000	–	4,500
Investment in Local Ltd	3,500	–	(3,500)	
Intangible assets (goodwill)	–	–	500	500
	5,000	**3,000**	**(3,000)**	**5,000**
Current assets	1,000	1,000	–	2,000
Total assets	**6,000**	**4,000**	**(3,000)**	**7,000**
EQUITY AND LIABILITIES				
Equity				
Ordinary share capital	2,000	1,000	(1,000)	2,000
Retained earnings	2,000	2,000	(2,000)	2,000
	4,000	**3,000**	**(3,000)**	**4,000**
Current liabilities	2,000	1,000	–	3,000
Total equity and liabilities	**6,000**	**4,000**	**(3,000)**	**7,000**

Many business combinations involve situations where a parent purchases less than 100% of a subsidiary as in the next example. On 30 April 2011, Giga Ltd paid £7.50 per share in order to acquire 90% of the 25p ordinary shares of Mega Ltd. The statements of financial position for each company at the date of acquisition are shown below.

Statements of financial position at 30 April 2011		
	Giga Ltd	Mega Ltd
	£'000	£'000
ASSETS		
Non-current assets		
Property, plant and equipment	2,600	3,000
Investment in Mega Ltd	5,400	–
	8,000	**3,000**
Current assets	1,500	1,200
Total assets	**9,500**	**4,200**
EQUITY AND LIABILITIES		
Ordinary share capital	2,500	200
Retained earnings	2,000	3,300
	4,500	**3,500**
Current liabilities	5,000	700
Total equity and liabilities	**9,500**	**4,200**

The following information is available about the Mega Ltd's net assets at the date of acquisition:

- Freehold property with a carrying value of £1.8m had a market value of £2.9m.
- Current assets include £0.5m inventory with a net realizable value of only £250,000.

Activity

Work through the five steps to calculate the figures you need for the consolidated statement of financial position for Giga Ltd.

Check your calculations against the following solution.

1. Giga Ltd acquired 90% of Mega Ltd. As Mega Ltd's £200,000 of ordinary share capital has a nominal value of 25p per share, the subsidiary has a total of 800,000 shares available for purchase. Giga Ltd purchased 720,000 of these shares.
2. Giga Ltd purchased 90% of Mega Ltd's ordinary shares for £7.50 per share. The consideration transferred was £5.4m (720,000 shares × £7.50 per share).
3. Mega Ltd's identifiable net assets must be restated to their fair value at the date of acquisition. Before these adjustments, Mega Ltd's nets assets had a carrying value of £3.5m (total assets £4.2m – current liabilities £0.7m). At this date, its net assets could also be measured using the £3.5m of total equity. The fair value adjustments to Mega Ltd's assets are calculated as follows:
   - The value of freehold property is increased by £1m and a balancing revaluation reserve is created in Mega Ltd's statement of financial position.

- Current assets must be reduced by £250,000 to reflect lower value of the inventory. This write down reduces the retained earnings of Mega Ltd by £250,000.

Fair value adjustments for Mega Ltd at 30 April 2011:

	Original £'000	Adjustment £'000	Fair value £'000
ASSETS			
Non-current assets			
Property, plant and equipment	3,000	1,100	4,100
Current assets	1,200	(250)	950
Total assets	4,200	850	5,050
EQUITY AND LIABILITIES			
Equity			
Ordinary share capital	200	–	200
Retained earnings	3,300	(250)	3,050
Revaluation reserve	–	1,100	1,100
	3,500	850	4,350
Current liabilities	700	–	700
Total equity and liabilities	4,200	850	5,050

4. In this case the NCI is financing 10% of the subsidiary's equity. As we mentioned earlier, we measure the NCI at its proportionate share (10% in this case) of Mega Ltd's identifiable net assets. This is calculated as 10% × £4,350,000 = £435,000, and will be included in the group statement of financial position under equity.
5. Goodwill on the acquisition of Mega Ltd:

	£'000
Fair value of the consideration transferred	5,400
NCI at the acquisition date	435
Fair value of subsidiary's net assets at the acquisition date	(4,350)
Goodwill	1,485

Activity

Use your five workings to prepare a consolidated statement of financial position for Giga Ltd.

As Mega Ltd's statement of financial position required fair value adjustments, you must use these when preparing the consolidated statement of financial position. You need to start by eliminating Giga Ltd's investment of £5.4m against the 90% share (£3.915m) of the equity of Mega Ltd at the date of acquisition. The balancing figure represents goodwill (£1.485m) which must be recognised as an intangible non-current asset in the group accounts. You should show the elimination process in the column headed W1 where the total amount eliminated is £3.915m. This represents the 90% share of the equity in Mega Ltd at the date of acquisition.

Giga Ltd's share of Mega Ltd's equity at the acquisition date:

		£'000
Ordinary share capital	90% × £200,000	180
Retained earnings	90% × £3,050,000	2,745
Revaluation reserve	90% × £1,100,000	990
Total equity (= net assets acquired)		3,915

After the elimination process, 10% of Mega Ltd's equity and reserves at the date of acquisition remains. This represents the NCI's ownership of Mega Ltd and should also be eliminated and shown in the group accounts as a NCI of £435,000. This adjustment is shown under column W2 of the solution.

10% NCI share of Mega Ltd's equity at the date of acquisition:

		£'000
Ordinary share capital	10% × £200,000	20
Retained earnings	10% × £3,050,000	305
Revaluation reserve	10% × £1,100,000	110
Total equity (= net assets acquired)		435

After these two elimination processes have been completed, the individual figures for property plant and equipment, current assets and current liabilities for each entity can be combined. Remember that you should only include the equity of the parent and the NCI in the consolidated statement of financial position. Now check your answer against the following solution.

Giga Ltd
Consolidated statement of financial position at 30 April 2011

	Giga Ltd	Mega Ltd at fair value	W1	W2	Group
	£'000	£'000	£'000	£'000	£'000
ASSETS					
Non-current assets					
Property, plant and equipment	2,600	4,100	–	–	6,700
Investment in Mega Ltd	5,400	–	(5,400)	–	
Intangible assets (goodwill)	–	–	1,485	–	1,485
	8,000	4,100	(3,915)	–	8,185
Current assets	1,500	950	–	–	2,450
	9,500	5,050	(3,915)	–	10,635
EQUITY AND LIABILITIES					
Equity					
Ordinary share capital	2,500	200	(180)	(20)	2,500
Retained earnings	2,000	3,050	(2,745)	(305)	2,000
Revaluation reserve		1,100	(990)	(110)	–
Non controlling interest (NCI)				435	435
	4,500	4,350	(3,915)	–	4,935
Current liabilities	5,000	700			5,700
Total equity and liabilities	9,500	5,050	(3,915)	–	10,635

8.4 Consolidated statement of financial position after acquisition

We will now move on to consider what happens after acquisition when the subsidiary continues to trade and earns *post acquisition* profits (or losses). The parent's share of the profit is the return on its investment and must be added to the group's retained earnings in the consolidated statement of financial position. If a NCI exists, its proportionate share of the subsidiary's post-acquisition profits should be added to the carrying amount of the NCI in the group accounts. If a subsidiary makes a post-acquisition loss, the same process applies but in reserve. While a subsidiary's retained earnings are the most likely of its reserves to have changed since it was first acquired by its parent, it is that possible that other reserves, such as the revaluation reserve, have changed. In such situations, any changes should be accounted for in the same way as movements in a subsidiary's post-acquisition retained earnings.

Another issue to consider is whether the goodwill recognised in the group accounts has experienced an impairment loss. Goodwill should be shown on the group statement of financial position at its cost less accumulated impairment losses. Any impairment must be recognised in the accounts and written off against the retained earnings of the group.

8.4.1 Preparing a consolidated statement of financial position after acquisition

One year has passed since Giga Ltd acquired 90% of the subsidiary, Mega Ltd and the statements of financial position for Giga Ltd and Mega Ltd are shown below.

Statements of financial position at 30 April 2012	Giga Ltd £'000	Mega Ltd £'000
ASSETS		
Non-current assets		
Property, plant and equipment	2,900	4,400
Investment in Mega Ltd	5,400	–
	8,300	4,400
Current assets	1,500	1,050
Total assets	9,800	5,450
EQUITY AND LIABILITIES		
Equity		
Ordinary share capital	2,500	200
Retained earnings	2,500	3,550
Revaluation reserve	–	1,100
	5,000	4,850
Current liabilities	4,800	600
Total assets and liabilities	9,800	5,450

The statement of financial position for Mega Ltd at 30 April 2012 incorporates the fair value adjustments made on 30 April 2011. The following post-acquisition events took place during the year ending 30 April 2012:

- Giga Ltd and Mega Ltd both generated a profit of £500,000.
- Following an impairment review, it was found that the £1.485m goodwill arising on consolidation had suffered an impairment loss of 40% due to increased market competition.

Activity

Prepare a consolidated statement of financial position for Giga Ltd that reflects the post-acquisition events or transactions.

Check your answer against the following solution, which provides four columns for workings that relate to the steps needed to prepare the consolidated statement of financial position at 30 April 2012. Workings 1 and 2 are identical to the calculations for the consolidated statement of financial position at 30 April 2011.

- W1 shows the eliminations needed to recognise goodwill by eliminating Giga Ltd's investment against its share of Mega Ltd's equity at the date of acquisition.
- W2 shows the adjustments needed to recognise 10% of the NCI in Mega Ltd.
- W3 shows the adjustments needed to apportion £500,000 post acquisition profits of Mega Ltd between the group and the NCI. The total equity of Mega Ltd has increased by £500,000 since being acquired by Giga Ltd on 30 April 2011. Of this amount, 90% or £450,000 should be allocated to the retained earnings of the group. The remaining 10% or £50,000 must be added to the carrying value of the NCI in the consolidation statement of financial position. As a result, the carrying value of the NCI in the group increases to £485,000 (£435,000 at acquisition date + £50,000 share of Mega Ltd's post acquisition profits).
- W4 accounts for the 40% impairment of goodwill. The carrying value of goodwill must be reduced by £594,000 (£1,485,000 × 40%). This amount is written off against the retained earnings of the group.

	Giga Ltd	Mega Ltd	W1	W2	W3	W4	Group
Giga Ltd **Consolidated statement of financial position at 30 April 2012**							
	£'000	£'000	£'000	£'000	£'000	£'000	£'000
ASSETS							
Non-current assets							
Property, plant and equipment	2,900	4,400	–	–	–	–	7,300
Investment in Mega Ltd	5,400	–	(5,400)	–	–	–	–
Intangible assets (goodwill)	–	–	1,485	–	–	(594)	891
	8,300	–	–	–	–	(594)	8,191
Current assets	1,500	1,050	–	–	–		2,550
Total assets	**9,800**	**5,450**	**(3915)**	**–**	**–**	**(594)**	**10,741**
EQUITY AND LIABILITIES							
Equity							
Ordinary share capital	2,500	200	(180)	(20)	–	–	2,500
Retained earnings:							
Mega Ltd pre–acquisition	–	3,050	(2,745)	(305)	–	–	–
Giga Ltd's earnings and	2,500	500	–	–	(50)	(594)	2,356
Mega Ltd's post-acquisition							
earnings							
Revaluation reserve	–	1,100	(990)	(110)			–
Non controlling interest (NCI)	–	–	–	435	50		485
	5,000	4,850	(3,915)	–	–	(594)	5,341
Current liabilities	4,800	600	–	–	–		5,400
Total equity and liabilities	**9,800**	**5,450**	**(3,915)**	**–**	**–**	**(594)**	**10,741**

The group statement of financial position for Giga Ltd at 30 April 2012 reflects the impact of the combined business transactions for the post-acquisition period.

8.5　Consolidated statements of comprehensive income and changes in equity

We will start by looking at the *consolidated statement of comprehensive income*. A consolidated statement of comprehensive income presents a calculation of the profit or loss of the group as if it was a single economic entity. It is constructed by aggregating the individual statements of comprehensive income for each entity and cancelling any intra-group items, such as:

- Intra-group sales and trading between the parent and its subsidiaries
- Unrealised profits on inventory sold by one group company to another
- Intra-group interest payable by one group entity to another
- Dividends that a subsidiary pays to its parent company.

In addition to these adjustments, the consolidated statement of comprehensive income includes any adjustment for the impairment of goodwill.

8.5.1   Preparing a consolidated statement of comprehensive income

The statements of comprehensive income for Giga Ltd and Mega Ltd for the year ending 30 April 2012 are shown below.

Statements of comprehensive income for year ended 30 April 2012		
	Giga Ltd	Mega Ltd
	£'000	£'000
Revenue	2,200	2,000
Cost of sales	(700)	(800)
Gross profit	**1,500**	**1,200**
Administrative expenses	(400)	(300)
Distribution costs	(350)	150)
Operating profit	**750**	**750**
Income tax expense	(250)	(250)
Profit for the period	**500**	**500**

The following events took place during the year ending 30 April 2012:

* Giga Ltd sold Mega Ltd inventories at cost for £200,000 plus a mark-up of 50%. By the end of the year, this inventory had been sold by Mega Ltd
* The group's goodwill of £1,485,000 suffered an impairment loss of 40%.

Many items in the individual statements of comprehensive income statement for the parent and subsidiary can be aggregated to provide the figures for the consolidated financial statement. However, there are three adjustments to be made in this example:

* W1 should eliminate the intra-group sales. The cost of these inventory items was £200,000 but Giga Ltd added a 50% mark up before selling them to Mega Ltd. As a result, revenue must be reduced by £300,000 (£200,000 cost + £100,000 mark up) to remove the intra-group revenue. An offsetting amount of £300,000 is deducted from group's cost of sales.
* W2 should account for the 40% impairment to the £1,485,000 of goodwill on the acquisition of Mega Ltd acquisition. The £594,000 impairment loss (40% × £1,485,000) is included as an expense in the group statement of comprehensive income.
* W3 needs to show the division of the group's £406,000 profit for the year amongst the parent's shareholders and the NCI. As the NCI owns 10% of the ordinary shares of Mega Ltd, it is entitled to receive 10% or £50,000 of the subsidiary's £500,000 profit for the year.

Activity

Prepare the consolidated statement of comprehensive income for the year ending 30 April 2012 for Giga Ltd.

Check your answer against the following solution.

	Giga Ltd	Mega Ltd	W1	Group
Giga Ltd **Consolidated statement of comprehensive income** **for the year ending 30 April 2012**				
	£'000	£'000	£'000	£'000
Revenue	2,200	2,000	(300)	3,900
Cost of sales	(700)	(800)	300	(1,200)
Gross profit	**1,500**	**1,200**	–	**2,700**
Administrative expenses	(400)	(300)	–	(700)
Distribution costs	(350)	(150)	–	(500)
Impairment of goodwill (W2)			–	(594)
Profit before tax	750	750	–	906
Income tax expense	(250)	(250)	–	(500)
Profit for the period	**500**	**500**	**–**	**406**
Profit attributable to:				
NCI (10% of Mega Ltd's profit for the year) (W3)				50
Giga Ltd's shareholders (balancing figure)				356
Profit for the period				**406**

8.5.2 Preparing a consolidated statement of changes in equity

Although the parent, Giga Ltd and the subsidiary, Mega Ltd, both achieved profits of £500,000 in the year following acquisition, the group profit was only £406,000 due to the impairment of goodwill. We can check whether the calculation of group profit is correct by preparing a *consolidated statement of changes in equity*. This shows the changes in equity and reserves during the period and provides a link between the consolidated statement of comprehensive income and the amount of equity shown in the consolidated statement of financial position.

The consolidated statement of changes in equity for the year ended 30 April 2012 is shown below. The columns for share capital and retained earnings show the amounts attributable to the owners of the parent, Giga Ltd, together with the equity supplied by the NCI. The figures for the individual balances at 30 April 2011 and 30 April 2012 are obtained from the two consolidated statements of financial position that you prepared in the activities in the previous section. The calculation of £406,000 consolidated comprehensive income for the year is correct as it equals the change in the group's total equity for the same period (£5.341m equity at 20 April 2012 – £4.935m equity at 30 April 2011).

Giga Ltd					
Consolidated statement of changes in equity for year ended 30 April 2012					
	Share capital	Retained earnings	Total	NCI	Group
	£'000	£'000	£'000	£'000	£'000
Balance at 30 April 2011	**2,500**	**2,000**	**4,500**	**435**	**4,935**
Comprehensive income for the period		356	356	50	406
Balance at 30 April 2012	**2,500**	**2,356**	**4,856**	**485**	**5,341**

8.6 Associates

In addition to investments that result in an investor (the parent company) having control over the investee (a subsidiary entity), other types of investment result in different levels of influence over the investee. An *associate* is an entity over which an investor has significant influence rather than control. Significant influence only provides the power to participate in the financial and operating policy decisions of the investee.

8.6.1 Significant influence

An investment that grants *significant influence* is presumed to exist where an investor holds 20% or more of the voting power (directly or indirectly) of an investee and can also be shown when one or more of the following exists:

- an investor has representation on the investee's board of directors
- an investor participates in policy making decisions at the investee
- there are material transactions between the investor and investee
- there is an interchange of managerial personnel between the entities
- there is provision of essential technical information between the entities

> **Key definitions**
>
> An associate is an entity over which the investor has significant influence.
>
> Significant influence is the power to participate in the financial and operating policy decisions of the investee but is not control or joint control of those policies.
>
> *Source*: IAS 28 (IASB, 2011d, para 3)

8.6.2 Accounting for an associate using the equity method

IAS 28, *Investments in Associates and Joint Ventures* (IASB, 2011d) requires that an investment in an associate should be accounted for using the *equity method*. This is a method of accounting whereby the investment is initially recognised at cost. This represents the investor's share of the fair value of the net assets acquired plus goodwill.

Goodwill is not disclosed separately, but is included in the carrying amount of the investment. In subsequent accounting periods, the carrying amount of the investment is adjusted for the investor's share of the post-acquisition changes in the associate's net assets. In addition, the investor's profit or loss for the period includes its share of the investee's profit or loss, and the investor's other comprehensive income includes its share of the investee's other comprehensive income. In the consolidated statement of financial position, the investment in the associate is shown as a single non-current asset. Similarly, only the investor's share of the associate's profit or loss is shown in the consolidated statement of comprehensive income.

We will now look at an example. On 1 April 2011 Invest Plc acquired 20% of the ordinary shares of Assist Ltd at a cost of £20,000. Assist Ltd had retained earnings of £40,000 at that date and its assets and liabilities were carried at fair value. Assist Ltd has issued no shares since Invest Plc acquired its 20% shareholding. The draft consolidated financial statements for Invest Plc for the year ending 31 March 2012 and the financial statements of Assist Ltd for the same period are shown below. Invest Plc is the parent of several wholly-owned subsidiaries.

Statement of financial position at 31 March 2012		
	Invest Plc and its subsidiaries £'000	Assist Ltd £'000
ASSETS		
Non-current assets		
Property, plant and equipment	550	130
Investment in Assist Ltd	20	–
	570	**130**
Current assets	230	30
Total assets	**800**	**160**
EQUITY AND LIABILITIES		
Equity		
Ordinary share capital	200	60
Retained earnings	500	60
	700	**120**
Current liabilities	100	40
Total assets and liabilities	**800**	**160**

Statement of comprehensive income at 31 March 2012		
	Invest Plc and its subsidiaries	Assist Ltd
	£'000	£'000
Revenue	900	300
Cost of sales	(300)	150
Gross profit	600	150
Administrative expenses	(125)	(55)
Distribution costs	(100)	(50)
Profit before tax	375	45
Income tax expense	(75)	(25)
Profit for the period	300	20

Activity

Use the equity method to integrate Assist Ltd in the consolidated statements of comprehensive income and financial position of Invest Plc for the year ended 31 March 2012.

Because of its 20% ownership of Assist Ltd, we will assume that Invest Plc has significant influence over the company and should include it as an associate in consolidated financial statements. On 1 April 2011 Invest Plc acquired 20% of the equity or net assets of Assist Ltd at a cost of £20,000.

Fair value of Assist Ltd's equity at 1 April 2011:

	£'000	Invest Plc's 20% share of associate £'000
Ordinary share capital	60	12
Retained earnings	40	8
Total	100	20

As Invest plc paid £20,000 to acquire net assets worth £20,000, there was no goodwill. On 1 April 2011 the initial cost of the investment in the associate was £20,000, and this is the amount shown in the draft consolidated accounts for Invest Plc. We must now use the equity method to update the carrying value of the investment for the associate's trading activities during the year ended 31 March 2012. We start by adding Invest Plc's share of Assist Ltd's £20,000 profit for the period to the consolidated statement of comprehensive income. As Invest Plc holds 20% of Assist Ltd's shares, it is entitled to £4,000 of the associate's profit for 2012 (20% × £20,000). This is added to group operating profit in the consolidated statement of comprehensive income.

Invest Plc	
Consolidated statement of comprehensive income	
for the year ending 31 March 2012	
	£'000
Revenue	900
Cost of sales	(300)
Gross profit	**600**
Administrative expenses	(125)
Distribution costs	(100)
Operating profit	**375**
Share of profit of associate	4
Profit before tax	**379**
Income tax expense	(75)
Profit for the period	**304**

As the group profit for the year is increased by £4,000, the carrying value of the investment in the associate in the consolidated statement of financial position must also be increased by £4,000 and will now be shown at £24,000. The retained earnings of the group must also be increased by £4,000 to give a total of £504,000 as 31 March 2012. After these adjustments, the results of the associate are included within the consolidated financial statements of Invest Plc.

Invest Plc	
Consolidated statement of financial position at	
31 March 2012	
	£'000
ASSETS	
Non-current assets	
Property, plant and equipment	550
Investment in associates	24
	574
Current assets	230
Total assets	**804**
EQUITY AND LIABILITIES	
Equity	
Ordinary share capital	(200)
Retained earnings	(504)
	(704)
Current liabilities	(100)
Total equity and liabilities	**(804)**

8.7 Joint arrangements

A *joint arrangement* describes an investment that results in the investor entity having *joint control* with one or more other parties over an economic activity or entity. There are two types of joint arrangement:

- A *joint operation* is where the parties that have joint control of the arrangement have rights to the assets, and obligations for the liabilities, relating to the arrangement. In a joint operation the parties usually share revenues, purchase jointly controlled assets, incur their own expenses and are responsible for raising their own finance. A joint agreement that is not structured through a separate legal entity (such as a corporation) is always classified as a joint operation.
- A *joint venture* is where the parties that have joint control of the arrangement have rights to the net assets of the arrangement. In a joint venture, the parties do not have individual rights to assets and obligations for the liabilities of the joint venture.

You may have noticed that joint control is mentioned as a characteristic of both types of joint arrangement. An investment that offers *joint control* provides a contractually agreed sharing of control where strategic decisions about the relevant activities, such as capital expenditure and approving a business plan, require the unanimous consent of the parties sharing control. The key aspects of joint control are:

- Collective control – the parties must collectively control the arrangement in accordance with the definition of control in IFRS 10 (see above).
- Contractually agreed – written contractual agreements are usually established that provide the terms of the arrangement
- Unanimous consent – any party can prevent any of the other parties from making unilateral decisions (about the relevant activities) without its consent.

Key definitions

A joint operation is a joint arrangement whereby the parties that have joint control of the arrangement have rights to the assets, and obligations for the liabilities, relating to the arrangement.

A joint venture is a joint arrangement whereby the parties that have joint control of the arrangement have rights to the net assets of the arrangement.

Joint control is the contractually agreed sharing of control of an arrangement, which exists only when decisions about the relevant activities over an economic activity require the unanimous consent of the parties sharing control.

Source: IFRS 11 (IASB, 2011e, Appendix A)

You will recall that accounting for subsidiaries is guided by IFRS 3, *Business Combinations* and IFRS 10, *Consolidated Financial Statements*, which require the investor to use the acquisition method. However, accounting for joint operations is guided by IFRS 11, *Joint Arrangements* (IASB, 2011d) and IAS 28, *Investments in*

Table 8.1   Accounting methods for different types of investee

Level of control/ influence	Classification	Accounting method
Control	Subsidiary	Consolidation under IFRS 3 and IFRS 10
Significant influence	Associate	Equity method under IAS 28
Joint control	Joint venture	Equity method under IAS 28
Joint control	Joint operation	Each party to recognize the assets, liabilities, income and expenses from their involvement in the operation under IFRS 11

Associates and Joint Ventures (IASB, 2011c), which require the equity method to be used. Determining whether an investee is a subsidiary, associate or joint arrangement is a matter of judgement. Therefore, IFRS 12, *Disclosure of Interests in Other Entities* (IASB, 2011c) requires disclosure of the significant assumptions made when determining whether the investor has control, significant influence or joint control over each investee in the consolidated financial statements. Table 8.1 summarises this information.

8.7.1   Joint operations

For an investment classified as a joint operation, the joint operator must recognise the following in relation to its interest in a joint operation:

- Its assets and liabilities, including its share of any jointly held assets or liabilities;
- Its share of the income and expenses from the joint operation.

The required accounting entries are recorded in the investor's own individual financial statements, and are included within the consolidated financial statements if the investor is part of a group. To illustrate this, we will look at an example.

On 1 January 2012, Air Plc and Jet Plc agreed to contribute £2.5m each towards the purchase and installation of baggage handling equipment that cost £5m and has a useful life of ten years with no residual value. A separate legal entity was not created for the arrangement, but the directors of the companies signed an agreement which stated that all operational decisions would require the unanimous consent of both parties. The agreement specified that annual income and expenses would be shared equally. Air Plc employs the baggage handling operatives. The following cash flow information is available.

Cash flows for the year ending 31 December 2012		
	Air Plc	Jet Plc
	£'000	£'000
Cash inflows		
Revenue	850	–
Cash outflows		
Equipment costs	(2,000)	(2,000)
Installation costs	(1,000)	–
Operatives' wages	(200)	–
Net cash flow	**(2,350)**	**(2,000)**

Air Plc financed its involvement in the joint operation through a £2.5m interest-free EU loan.

Activity

Decide whether the above joint arrangement should be accounted for as a joint venture or a joint operation.

You would be right in thinking that joint control exists for this arrangement because:

- the parties have collective control over the arrangement
- a contractual agreement exists
- decisions regarding the relevant activities of the baggage operation require the unanimous consent of both airlines.

This joint arrangement should be accounted for as a joint operation because it is not structured as a separate legal entity and each party jointly owns the baggage equipment.

The accountant of Air Plc has prepared the following draft of the revenue, expenses, assets and liabilities of the company working on the joint operation (JO) during 2012.

Air Plc Draft income statement for the JO for the year ending 31 December 2012	
	£'000
Revenue	850
Depreciation	(250)
Operatives' wages	(200)
Profit for the period	**400**

Air Plc Draft statement of financial position for the JO at 31 December 2012	
	£'000
ASSETS	
Non-current assets	
Property, plant and equipment	2,500
Accumulated depreciation	(250)
	2,250
Current assets	
Recoverable from Jet Plc	500
Cash	150
Total assets	**2,900**
EQUITY AND LIABILITIES	
Equity	
Retained earnings (operating profit from the JO)	400
Non-current liabilities	
EU loan	(2,500)
Total equity and liabilities	**2,900**

Although the draft figures provide a record of Air Plc's transactions with regard to the joint operation for 2012, they must be adjusted to reflect the terms of the agreement:

• Annual expenses and revenues must be shared equally.
• Air Plc and Jet Plc agreed to contribute £2.5m each towards the cost of the equipment.

The draft income statement for Air plc has the following issues:

• It includes all of the £850,000 revenue collected by Air plc, even though £425,000 (50%) belongs to Jet plc under the terms of the agreement.
• Air Plc has incurred £200,000 of the operatives' wages, even though Jet Plc should bear 50% of this expense.

The first step is to calculate the income and expenditure of the joint operation for the year ending 31 December 2012 so that 50% can be shared between the parties. The income and expenditure of the joint operation for the year ending 31 December 2012 is shown below.

Air Plc JO income statement for the year ending 31 December 2012		
	100% of JO	50% of JO
	£'000	£'000
Revenue	850	425
Depreciation	(500)	(250)
Operatives' wages	(200)	(100)
Profit for the period	**150**	**75**

The £850,000 revenue relates to income that Air Plc received from other airlines. As the baggage equipment has a total cost of £5m (£2m × 2 = £4m + £m installation cost) and a ten year useful life, annual depreciation using the straight-line method is £500,000 (£5m ÷ 10 years). The operatives' wages of £200,000 were paid by Air Plc. Combining these joint revenues and expenses, the annual profit from the joint operation for 2012 was £150,000. According to this calculation, Air Plc's statement of comprehensive income should reflect 50% of this and show a profit for the period of £75,000. As Air Plc's draft accounts reported a profit for the year of £400,000, this amount must be restated to the company's 50% share of the income and expenses of the joint operation.

As a result of the requirement to show the contractually agreed amounts of expenses and revenues, the two entities must transfer various amounts to each other in order to balance the accounts. For example, Air Plc's draft statement of financial position already includes £500,000 received from Jet Plc for its unpaid 50% share of the £1m installation costs. This amount must be updated to reflect each entity's 50% share of the income and expenses of the joint operation. Once all the contractual obligations are accounted for, Air Plc should receive £175,000 from Jet Plc to cover the unpaid share of the joint costs of the arrangement as shown below.

	Air Plc	Jet Plc's share	Due to/from Jet Plc
	£'000	£'000	£'000
Installation costs	(1,000)	(500)	500
Operatives' wages	(200)	(100)	100
Income	850	425	(425)
Receivable at 31 January 2012			175

The amount receivable from Jet plc at 31 December 2012 is £175,000 and this must be shown as a current asset in Air Plc's individual financial statements at this date. This completes the adjustments needed to account for the joint operation in the financial statements of Air Plc.

Activity

Prepare the financial statements of Air Plc to show its share of the income, expenses, assets and liabilities from the joint operation for the year ended 31 January 2012.

If you have worked through all the activities in this chapter, you should not have had too much difficulty with this. Check your answer against the following solution.

Air Plc
Income statement for the joint operation for the year ending 31 December 2012

	Draft	50% of JO	W1	Adjusted
	£'000	£'000	£'000	£'000
Revenue	850	425	(425)	425
Depreciation	(250)	(250)	–	(250)
Operatives' wages	(200)	(100)	(100)	(100)
Profit/(loss) for the period	**400**	**75**	**(325)**	**75**

Statement of financial position for the joint operation at 31 December 2012

	Draft	50% of JO	Adjusted
	£'000	£'000	£'000
ASSETS			
Non-current assets			
Property, plant and equipment	2,500	–	2,500
Depreciation	(250)	–	(250)
	2,250	–	2,250
Current assets			
Receivables	500	(325)	175
Cash (W2)	150	–	150
Total assets	**2,900**	**(325)**	**2,575**
EQUITY AND LIABILITIES			
Equity			
Retained earnings	400	(325)	75
Non-current liabilities			
EU loan	2,500	–	2,500
Total equity and liabilities	**2,900**	**(325)**	**2,575**

Working 1 shows the adjustments that must be made to reflect Air Plc's 50% share of the income and expenses from the joint operation: Air Plc must allocate 50% of the revenue (£425,000) to Jet Plc and recoup 50% or £100,000 of the operatives' wages from Jet Plc. This results in profit being reduced by £325,000 to £75,000. Air Plc's profit is now 50% of the operation's £150,000 profit for the year. In the draft statement of financial position the current assets showed that Jet Plc owed Air Plc £500,000 for its share of the installation expenses. That is now is reduced by £325,000 to £175,000 in order to reflect the income and expenses Air Plc has shared with Jet Plc.

Working W2 shows that Air Plc used £3.2m cash (£2m towards the cost of equipment, £1m for installation costs and £200,000 in operatives' wages) and received £3.35 cash during the period (£850,000 revenue from the joint operation and £2,500,000 cash inflow from the EU loan), leaving a balance of £150,000.

We have presented the workings for the joint operation in the form of a draft income statement and statement of financial position to help you understand the process. IFRS 11 does not require entities to prepare separate financial statements for a joint operation, but merely that the investor recognises the assets, liabilities, income and expenses from the joint operation in its financial statements. As Air Plc controls other subsidiaries, the assets, liabilities, income and expenses from the joint operation as shown in the adjusted column of the solution will be combined with those of the group in the company's consolidated financial statements.

8.8 Conclusions

In this chapter we have examined the situation where a company has made an investment in a subsidiary, associate, joint operation or joint venture. The classification of the investee as one of these is determined by the level of control or influence the investor has over it. This classification determines the accounting treatment for the investment in the consolidated financial statements of the investor. Whatever the type of investment, the purpose of consolidated financial statements is to show a faithful representation of the investment and the investor's control over the investee.

Building on the knowledge you gained from studying Chapter 7, we have described the five main steps in the preparation of a consolidation statement of financial position at the date of acquisition of a subsidiary and subsequently. As part of these explanations we have considered the calculation of goodwill, the importance of recognising the fair value of a subsidiary's assets and how to account for a non-controlling interest (NCI). We have extended what you learned in Chapter 6 by explaining how to prepare a consolidated statement of comprehensive income by eliminating intra-group items and recognising the impairment of goodwill. We have also introduced you to a simple consolidated statement of changes in equity. In the final sections of the chapter we looked at how the equity method is used to account for associate companies and joint ventures under the equity method of accounting, and explained how a joint operation should be accounted for within the consolidated financial statements.

Practice questions

1 Briefly explain the difference between 'control' and 'joint control'.

2 Explain why goodwill is only shown within consolidated financial statements.

3 Explain why the net assets of a subsidiary should be adjusted to their fair value at the date of acquisition.

4 Agro Ltd acquired 80% of Seeds Ltd for £500,000 on 1 July 2012. Seed Ltd's net assets include property, plant and equipment, inventory and trade receivables with a total book value of £200,000 at the date of acquisition. Following independent appraisal of the PPE at the acquisition date, it was discovered that these assets had a fair value £100,000 greater than their book value.

Required

Calculate the following figures that will be shown in the consolidated statement of financial position at the acquisition date:

(a) goodwill

(b) the non-controlling interest

5 On 1 August 2011 Major Ltd paid £1.50 per share to acquire 40,000 of the £1 ordinary shares of Minor Ltd. At this date, the share capital and reserves of Minor Ltd were:

	£
£1 ordinary share capital	50,000
Retained earnings	16,250
Total	66,250

The statements of financial position for each company at 31 July 2012 were as follows:

	Major Ltd	Minor Ltd
	£	£
ASSETS		
Non-current assets		
Property, plant and equipment	150,000	82,000
Investment in Minor Ltd	60,000	
	210,000	
Current assets	195,000	92,250
Total assets	**405,000**	**174,250**
EQUITY AND LIABILITIES		
Equity		
Ordinary share capital	250,000	50,000
Retained earnings	32,000	36,250
Revaluation reserve		10,000
	282,000	96,250
Current liabilities	123,000	78,000
Total equity and liabilities	**405,000**	**174,250**

Following an impairment review on 31 July 2012, it was found that the goodwill arising on the business combination with Minor Ltd had suffered an impairment loss of 50%.

Required

(a) Calculate the goodwill that will be paid by Major Ltd on the acquisition of Minor Ltd.

(b) Prepare the consolidated statement of financial position for Major Ltd at 31 July 2012.

References

IASB (2009) IAS 36, *Impairment of Assets*, London: International Accounting Standards Board.

IASB (2010a) IFRS 3, *Business Combinations*, London: International Accounting Standards Board.

IASB (2010b) *The Conceptual Framework for Financial Reporting*, London: International Accounting Standards Board.

IASB (2011a) IFRS 10, *Consolidated Financial Statements*, London: International Accounting Standards Board.

IASB (2011b) IAS 1, *Presentation of Financial Statements*, London: International Accounting Standards Board.

IASB (2011c) IFRS 13, *Fair Value Measurement*, London: International Accounting Standards Board.

IASB (2011d) IAS 28, *Investments in Associates and Joint Ventures*, London: International Accounting Standards Board.

IASB (2011e) IFRS 11, *Joint Arrangements*, London: International Accounting Standards Board.

IASB (2011f) IFRS 12, *Disclosure of Interests in Other Entities*, London: International Accounting Standards Board.

9 Financial statement analysis

Learning objectives

When you have studied this chapter, you should be able to:

- explain the purpose of ratio analysis
- calculate the main investment and profitability ratios
- calculate the main liquidity, efficiency and gearing ratios
- interpret the meaning of these ratios and recognize their limitations.

9.1 Introduction

Regardless of the size and type of organization you work in now or in the future, being able to read and understand the financial statements of different entities is an achievement worth striving for. This skill becomes even more valuable if you can also analyse financial statements, because you can then identify the financial strengths and weaknesses of the business and compare your results with previous periods, similar businesses or industry benchmarks. In this chapter we introduce a technique known as *ratio analysis* that is used by management, existing and potential investors, existing and potential lenders and creditors analysing financial statements. We should add that it is also used by major customers, investment analysts and financial journalists.

We will start by showing you how different types of ratio can be calculated and then used to assess the operating performance, liquidity and efficiency in the management of the working capital of a business. We then look at the ratios used to examine the financial structure of the business, assess financial risk and evaluate the shareholders' return. Although we will be illustrating the analysis by applying ratios to the annual financial statements of a public limited company, you should bear in mind that ratio analysis can be conducted on the financial statements of smaller entities and also on financial statements prepared for interim reporting or for management purposes.

9.2 Ratio analysis

Ratio analysis is a technique for evaluating the financial performance and stability of an entity. It helps internal and external users to analyse financial statements by examining ratios that describe the quantitative relationship between two data items. A ratio is usually presented as x:1 or x%. In some cases it is presented in monetary terms, such as x pence per share. Once a ratio has been calculated, it is compared with:

- the predetermined budget or target (internal users only)
- previous periods for the same business
- other businesses in the same sector (known as inter-firm comparison)
- industry benchmarks (published averages for the industrial sector).

Key definition

Ratio analysis is the use of accounting ratios to evaluate a company's operating performance and financial stability ... In conducting an analysis comparisons will be made with other companies and with industry averages over a period of time. The analysis of ratios can indicate how well a company is run, the risks of financial insolvency, and the financial returns provided.

Source: Law (2010, p. 345).

It is important to note that there are no standard definitions of the terms used in ratios. Therefore, if you are using ratios published in the annual report and accounts, the financial press or those provided in financial databases, you will need to find out what formulae were used and how the terms were defined before you can understand fully what is being referred to and whether comparisons are appropriate. Obviously, you cannot compare ratios from different sources if they have not been calculated on the same basis. When calculating ratios yourself, you need to state the formulae and meaning of any general terms you are using. You will see examples of this in this chapter.

There are four main types of ratio and each has a different purpose:

- *Investment ratios* are used for evaluating shareholders' return.
- *Profitability ratios* are used for assessing the operating performance of the business.
- *Liquidity and efficiency ratios* are used for evaluating the solvency, financial stability and management of working capital of the business.
- *Gearing ratios* are used for examining the financial structure of the business and assessing financial risk.

We will examine a selection of the main ratios in each of the above categories, but in any financial analysis, the choice of ratios depends on the needs of the user and the availability of relevant data. Figure 9.1 summarizes the main types of ratios and those we will describe in this chapter.

Figure 9.1   Examples of main types of ratio

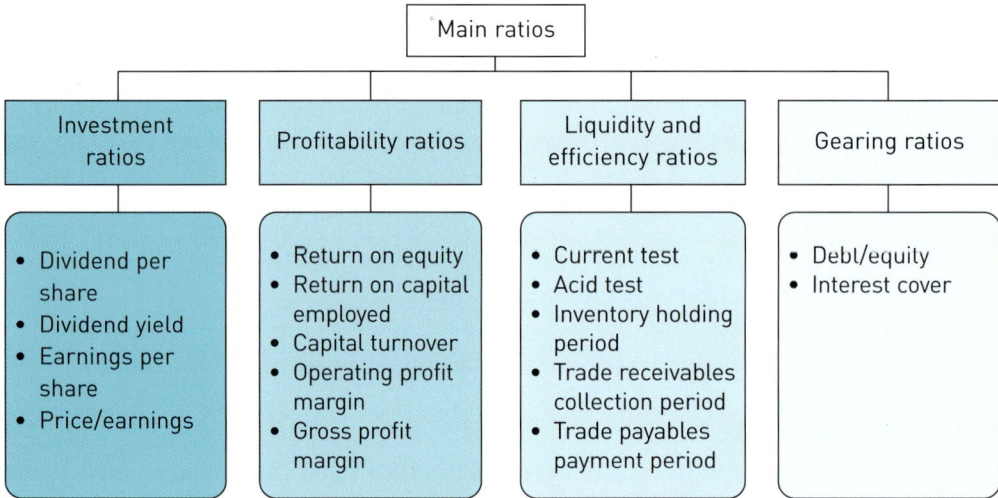

Ratios can be applied to the financial statements of any size and type of business. We are going to apply them to the financial statements of Ted Baker PLC, whose annual report and accounts we discussed in Chapter 4. Extracts from the financial statements that relate to the Group are reproduced in Figure 9.2. You will see that Ted Baker has adopted the two-statement approach and has prepared a separate statement of income and statement of comprehensive income. In addition, the Group refers to the statement of financial position as the balance sheet, which reflects the traditional UK GAAP terminology.

9.3   Investment ratios

We are starting our analysis from an investor perspective since existing and potential investors are the first of the three primary user groups. We are going to look at four *investment ratios* that are widely used by personal and institutional investors, investment analysts and financial journalists to evaluate shareholders' return and aid investment decisions:

- dividend per share
- dividend yield
- earnings per share
- price/earnings.

Figure 9.2   Ted Baker Report and Accounts 2010/11 (abridged extracts) (*continued overleaf*)

Group Income Statement For the 52 weeks ended 29 January 2011	Note	52 weeks ended 29 January 2011	52 weeks ended 30 January 2010
		£'000	£'000
Revenue	2	187,700	163,586
Cost of sales		(71,923)	(63,659)
Gross profit		**115,777**	**99,927**
Distribution costs		(73,690)	(64,573)
Administrative expenses			
– Other administrative expenses		(24,259)	(20,395)
– Impairment losses		–	(750)
Licence income		6,227	5,493
Other operating income		77	80
Operating profit		24,132	19,782
Finance income	4	42	10
Finance expenses	4	(120)	(374)
Share of profit of jointly controlled entity, net of tax	12	174	86
Profit before tax	3,6	**24,228**	**19,504**
Income tax expense	6	(6,948)	(5,977)
Profit for the period		**17,280**	**13,527**
Attributable to:			
– Equity shareholders of the parent company		17,280	13,576
– Non-controlling interest		–	(49)
Profit for the period		**17,280**	**13,527**

Group Statement of Comprehensive Income For the 52 weeks ended 29 January 2011	Note	52 weeks ended 29 January 2011	52 weeks ended 30 January 2010
		£'000	£'000
Profit for the period		**17,280**	**13,527**
Other comprehensive income			
Net effective portion of changes in fair value of cash flow hedges		143	(1,334)
Net change in fair value of cash flow hedges transferred to profit or loss		(279)	(391)
Exchange rate movement		112	(1,058)
Other comprehensive income for the period		(24)	(2,783)
Total comprehensive income for the period		**17,256**	**10,744**
Attributable to:			
– Equity shareholders of the parent company		17,256	10,793
– Non-controlling interest		–	(49)
Total comprehensive income for the period		**17,256**	**10,744**

Figure 9.2 *continued*

Group Balance Sheet At 29 January 2011	Note	29 January 2011	30 January 2010
		£'000	£'000
Non-current assets			
Intangible assets	10	997	634
Property, plant and equipment	11	28,368	25,508
Investment in equity accounted investee	12	345	171
Deferred tax assets	13	2,470	1,598
Prepayments		777	842
		32,957	**28,753**
Current assets			
Inventories	14	42,492	33,450
Trade and other receivables	15	27,384	19,698
Amount due from equity accounted investee	12	286	261
Derivative financial assets	16	102	280
Cash and cash equivalents	17	13,536	13,698
		83,800	**67,387**
Current liabilities			
Trade and other payables	18	(34,970)	(24,779)
Income tax payable		(3,761)	(3,511)
Derivative financial liabilities	16	(455)	(304)
		(39,186)	**(28,594)**
Non-current liabilities			
Deferred tax liabilities	13	(1,547)	(1,316)
		(1,547)	**(1,316)**
Net assets		**76,024**	**66,230**
Equity			
Share capital	19	2,160	2,160
Share premium account	19	9,137	9,137
Other reserves	19	(148)	(12)
Translation reserve	19	236	124
Retained earnings	19	64,639	54,906
Total equity attributable to the equity shareholders of the parent company		**76,024**	**66,315**
Non-controlling interest			(85)
Total equity		**76,024**	**66,230**

Extracts from notes to the financial statements		29 January 2011	30 January 2010
4	Of which, interest payable	(65)	(148)
8	Total dividends for the period (£'000)	8,574	7,138
9	Weighted number of ordinary shares ('000)	41,786	41,623
15	Of which, trade receivables	18,182	14,436
18	Of which, trade payables	18,888	10,392
20	Weighted average share price (pence)	441.4	439.1
20	Maximum risk free interest rate	5.29%	5.29%

9.3.1   Dividend per share

The first investment ratio we are going to calculate is the *dividend per share*. The dividend per share measures the amount of dividend paid on one ordinary share during the year. You will remember that dividends are a distribution of part of the earnings of the entity to its ordinary shareholders. Therefore, dividends represent a portion of the return to shareholders on their investment that is paid in cash. At the end of the year, the directors make a decision about how much of the current year's earnings will be kept in the business to help it grow and how much will be distributed as dividends. The directors will want to increase the dividend or at least keep it stable in order to satisfy existing shareholders and attract new investors. Therefore, during times of economic recession when profits may be relatively low, the directors may decide to use some of the retained profits to maintain dividend levels. Dividend per share is expressed in pence and is calculated using the following formula:

$$\text{Dividend per share} = \frac{\text{Dividends}}{\text{Number of ordinary shares}} \quad [\times 100 \text{ for pence}]$$

Activity

Calculate Ted Baker's dividend per share for ordinary shareholders for 2010/11 and 2009/10.

You will find that the data you need for this ratio are given in the extracts from Notes 8 and 9 below the financial statements in Figure 9.2. Full details appear on page 58 in Ted Baker's Report and Accounts 2010/11. The first step is to calculate the dividends for the period. Check your answer against the following workings:[1]

Working 1

	2010/11	2009/10
	£'000	£'000
Interim dividend	2,622	2,185
Second interim dividend		4,745
Final dividend	5,952	208
Total dividends	8,574	7,138

	2010/11	2009/10

$$\text{Dividend per share} = \frac{£8{,}574\text{k}}{41{,}786\text{k}} \times 100 = 20.52\text{p} \qquad \frac{£7{,}138\text{k}}{41{,}623\text{k}} \times 100 = 17.15\text{p}$$

The good news for shareholders is that, despite the recession, the dividend per share increased by just over 3p per share in 2010/11 compared to the previous year. This reflects the increased proportion of total dividends to the number of ordinary shares.

---

1. The letter 'k' against a figure indicates thousands.

9.3.2 Dividend yield

Dividend yield builds on the above ratio and measures the dividend yielded on one ordinary share in relation to the average share price over the year. The ratio is shown as a percentage and is calculated using the following formula:

$$\text{Dividend yield} = \frac{\text{Dividend per share}}{\text{Average share price}} \ [\times \ 100 \text{ for } \%]$$

Activity

Calculate Ted Baker's dividend yield for 2010/11 and 2009/10.

You have just calculated the dividend per share and you can obtain the average share price from Note 20 in Figure 9.2 which is taken from page 66 of Ted Baker's Report and Accounts 2010/11. Check your calculations against the following solutions:

| 2010/11 | 2009/10 |

$$\text{Dividend yield} = \frac{20.52\text{p}}{441.40\text{p}} \times 100 = 4.65\% \qquad \frac{17.15\text{p}}{439.10\text{p}} \times 100 = 3.91\%$$

These results show that the slightly higher dividend per share and increased average share price for 2010/11 gave a better yield than the previous year. This is good news for existing investors and will help attract new investors.

9.3.3 Earnings per share

The next ratio we are going to illustrate is *earnings per share (EPS)*. So far we have only looked at ratios that focus on profit distributed to shareholders as dividends. However, the directors need to retain some of the profit earned during the year to invest in new assets to help the business earn more profits in the future. Nevertheless, the profit retained still belongs to the shareholders. By focusing on total profit, EPS measures the shareholders' total return and calculates the amount of profit earned by one ordinary share. It is shown in pence and is calculated using the following formula:

$$\text{Earnings per share} = \frac{\text{Profit for ordinary shareholders}}{\text{Number of ordinary shares}} \ [\times \ 100 \text{ for pence}]$$

Activity

Calculate Ted Baker's earnings per share for ordinary shareholders for 2010/11 and 2009/10.

You may have wondered which figure of profit to use. The figure you need is the profit for the period. This is the profit after interest and tax. Do not be distracted by the fact that the income statement shows the breakdown of profit attributable to the shareholders of the parent company and the company in which the parent has a minority interest. You looked up the average number of ordinary shares in Note 9 for one of the ratios you calculated earlier, so all you have to do now is insert the figures into the formula:

2010/11 **2009/10**

$$\text{Earnings per share} = \frac{£17{,}280\text{k}}{41{,}786\text{k}} \times 100 = 41.35\text{p} \qquad \frac{£13{,}527\text{k}}{41{,}623\text{k}} \times 100 = 32.50\text{p}$$

EPS is a measure on which many shareholders place considerable weight. In the case of the Ted Baker, there was an increase of nearly 9p in 2010/11, which indicates the higher profit performance for shareholders in that year. It is important to remember that EPS is a measure of the entity's performance and not an amount of money distributed to shareholders. You will remember that the ratio that shows the amount of money paid on one share is the dividend per share. That figure is always lower than EPS because it is based on the dividends, which are only part of the profit for the year. EPS is based on the total profit for the year: dividends plus retained profit.

In order to improve performance comparisons between different entities in the same reporting period and between periods for the same entity, IAS 33, *Earnings Per Share* (IASB, 2003) sets out the principles for determining and presenting EPS. If you look at page 41 in Ted Baker's Report and Accounts 2010/11, you will see the figures for the basic and diluted EPS are given below the income statement. Basic EPS is calculated by dividing profit or loss attributable to ordinary shareholders by the weighted average number of ordinary shares outstanding during the period, as we have done. For your information, diluted EPS is based on adjusting the earnings and number of shares for the effects of dilutive options and other dilutive potential ordinary shares, but further discussion is beyond the scope of this book.

9.3.4 Price/earnings ratio

The final investment ratio we are going to examine is the *price/earnings (P/E)* ratio, which is based on EPS. This compares the amount invested in one share with the EPS and reflects the stock market's view on how long the current level of earnings per share will be sustained. It is measured in years and is calculated using the following formula:

$$\text{P/E} = \frac{\text{Share price}}{\text{Earnings per share}}$$

Activity

Calculate Ted Baker's P/E ratio for 2010/11 and 2009/10.

Calculating the ratios should be straightforward. Check your answer against the following solution:

2010/11   **2009/10**

$$P/E = \frac{441.40p}{41.35p} = 10.67 \text{ years} \qquad \frac{439.10p}{32.50p} = 13.51 \text{ years}$$

The lower P/E ratio in 2010/11 indicates that the stock market is less confident about how long the current level of EPS will be sustained than it was in 2009/10 and probably reflects the general pessimism in the stock market due to the economic recession. As you can see, the length of time is reduced by nearly 3 years. This indicates that shareholders are less optimistic about the future and might therefore be unwilling to pay more for the Group's shares than the current level of earnings would justify.

If we had the data, it would be useful to analyse all the investment ratios for Ted Baker over a longer period of time to identify the trend. We could also compare them with similar businesses and with industry benchmarks.

9.4 Profitability ratios

Profitability ratios are used by internal and external users to assess how effective the directors have been in managing the business in terms of generating income and controlling costs. Not only are investors, lenders and creditors interested in the profitability of the business, but also employees, major suppliers and customers. We are going to look at the following widely used ratios in this category:

- return on equity
- return on capital employed
- capital turnover
- operating profit margin
- gross profit margin.

9.4.1 Return on equity

The first profitability ratio we are going to look at is the *return on equity (ROE)*. This is of particular interest to investors because it focuses on the profit generated on the investment of shareholders' funds. This helps them assess the stewardship of management. The ratio focuses solely on shareholders' equity and ignores any long-term finance shown under non-current liabilities. For this ratio we will define *return* as profit for ordinary shareholders. It is calculated using the following formula:

$$ROE = \frac{\text{Profit for ordinary shareholders}}{\text{Equity}} \; [\times 100 \text{ for } \%]$$

Calculate Ted Baker's ROE for 2010/11 and 2009/10.

The figure of profit you need is the profit for the period. This represents the profit after interest and tax. The figure for equity is the total equity. Do not be distracted by the fact that Ted Baker's balance sheet (statement of financial position) shows the breakdown of equity attributable to the shareholders of the parent company and the company in which the parent has a non-controlling interest. Check your results against the following solution:

2010/11   **2009/10**

$$\text{ROE} = \frac{£17,280k}{£76,024k} \times 100 = 22.73\% \qquad \frac{£13,527k}{£66,230k} \times 100 = 20.42\%$$

The results provide good news for investors as ROE improved in 2010/11 when it represented £22.73 for every £100 of equity, compared to £20.42 the previous year. In both years the return is considerably higher than the maximum risk-free interest rate of 5.29%.

9.4.2   Return on capital employed

The *return on capital employed (ROCE)* measures the percentage return on the total funds used to finance the business. This provides useful information about management's effectiveness in generating income from all the resources and controlling costs. For this ratio we will define *return* as the operating profit, which is the profit before interest and tax, and *capital employed* as equity plus non-current liabilities. This means we will include the shareholders' funds and all sources of long-term finance. The ratio is calculated using the following formula:

$$\text{ROCE} = \frac{\text{Operating profit}}{\text{Equity} + \text{Non-current liabilities}} \; [\times 100 \text{ for } \%]$$

Calculate Ted Baker's ROCE for 2010/11 and 2009/10.

Finding the operating profit should be straightforward, but you need to calculate the capital employed by adding total equity to the total for non-current liabilities, ignoring the negative sign on the total non-current liabilities. Check your answer against the following workings:

Working 1

	2010/11	2009/10
	£'000	£'000
Equity	76,024	66,230
Non-current liabilities	1,547	1,316
Capital employed	77,571	67,546

2010/11   **2009/10**

$$\text{ROCE} = \frac{£24,132k}{£77,571k} \times 100 = 31.11\% \qquad \frac{£19,782k}{£67,546k} \times 100 = 29.29\%$$

The increased capital in 2010/11 gave proportionately higher profits and the results show an improvement of nearly 2% in ROCE compared with the previous year. This suggests the directors and other managers have been using the entity's resources effectively to generate income and that they have also been able to control costs. ROCE should reflect the element of risk in the investment and can be compared with interest rates for other investments where there is barely any risk, such as bank deposit rates. In this case, the return in both years is well above the maximum risk-free interest rate of 5.29% shown in Note 20.

If you compare the ratios you calculated for ROCE with those you calculated for ROE, you will see that ROE shows a more modest return. This is because ROCE does not take account of the obligation the business has to service and repay long-term debt. The definition of capital employed was equity plus non-current assets, which is the same as total assets minus current liabilities. Compare the two ratios:

$$\text{ROCE} = \frac{\text{Operating profit}}{\text{Equity} + \text{Non-current liabilities}} \qquad \begin{array}{l}\text{(Profit before finance expenses)}\\ \text{(Total assets – Current liabilities)}\end{array}$$

$$\text{ROE} = \frac{\text{Profit for ordinary shareholders}}{\text{Equity}} \qquad \begin{array}{l}\text{(Profit after finance expenses)}\\ \text{(Total assets – Total liabilities)}\end{array}$$

ROCE is referred to as the prime ratio because it is related to two subsidiary ratios: capital turnover and operating profit margin, which show how this profitability has been achieved and how it can be improved. We will look at capital turnover next.

9.4.3 Capital turnover

Capital turnover measures the number of times capital employed was used during the year to achieve the revenue. It is usually expressed as the number of times during the period and the formula is:

$$\text{Capital turnover} = \frac{\text{Revenue}}{\text{Equity} + \text{Non-current liabilities}}$$

Activity

Calculate Ted Baker's capital turnover for 2010/11 and 2009/10.

Finding the figure for revenue should be straightforward and you have already calculated the figure for capital employed, so all you need to do is insert them in the formula as follows:

2010/11	2009/10
Capital turnover $= \dfrac{£187,700k}{£77,571k} = 2.42$ times	$\dfrac{£163,586k}{£67,546k} = 2.42$ times

The level of activity should be as high as possible for the lowest level of investment. In this case, the capital employed in the business was turned over nearly $2\frac{1}{2}$ times in both years to achieve the revenue.

9.4.4 Operating profit margin

The *operating profit margin* measures the percentage return on revenue based on the operating profit. The ratio is calculated using the following formula:

$$\text{Operating profit margin} = \frac{\text{Operating profit}}{\text{Revenue}} \; [\times 100 \text{ for \%}]$$

Activity

Calculate Ted Baker's operating profit margin for 2010/11 and 2009/10.

All you need to do is to identify the figures in the income statement. Check your calculations against the following answer:

2010/11	2009/10
Operating profit margin $= \dfrac{£24,132k}{£187,700k} \times 100 = 12.86\%$	$\dfrac{£19,782k}{£163,586k} \times 100 = 12.09\%$

The results show that the operating profit margin was similar in both years, with the business making a slightly larger operating profit of £12.86 on every £100 of revenue in 2010/11. The operating profit margin can be improved by increasing selling prices (if the market permits), which would increase revenue, or finding ways of cutting costs. The small improvement in 2010/11 suggests higher selling prices and/or better control of operating costs.

The last three ratios we have looked at are interrelated:

$$\text{Capital turnover} \times \text{Operating profit margin} = \text{ROCE}$$

We can test this by inserting the ratios we have calculated for Ted Baker. The slight difference in the calculation of ROCE in the solution below is due to having rounded the original ratios to two decimal places:

2010/11
$2.42 \times 12.86 = 31.12\%$

2009/10
$2.42 \times 12.09 \times = 29.26\%$

A business can improve ROCE (the prime ratio) by reducing costs and/or raising selling prices if that is feasible, and this will improve its operating profit margin. Alternatively, it can increase its sales volume and/or reduce its capital employed, which will improve its capital turnover.

Activity

Which of the following methods would you suggest Ted Baker's directors should use to try to improve the capital turnover?

(a) Decrease the sales volume.
(b) Increase the sales volume.
(c) Reduce the capital invested in the business.
(d) Keep the capital invested in the business at the same level.

What the directors need to do is to increase the sales volume and at the same time keep the capital invested at the same level or lower if that is possible. Therefore, all the answers are correct except (a). Publicly accountable companies must provide a statement of comprehensive income (or a separate income statement and statement of comprehensive income, as Ted Baker has done), that discloses the gross profit. For businesses in the retail sector in particular, the gross profit is considered to be an essential feature of management control and a guide to pricing and purchasing policies. Therefore we will look at this next.

9.4.5 Gross profit margin

The *gross profit margin* measures the percentage on revenue based on the operating profit. The ratio is calculated using the following formula:

$$\text{Gross profit margin} = \frac{\text{Gross profit}}{\text{Revenue}} \, [\times 100 \text{ for } \%]$$

Activity

Calculate Ted Baker's gross profit margin for 2010/11 and 2009/10.

Both these figures are given in the income statement, so all you need to do is insert them into the formula. Check your calculations against the following solution:

2010/11	2009/10

$$\text{Gross profit margin} = \frac{£115,777k}{£187,700k} \times 100 = 61.68\% \qquad \frac{£99,927k}{£163,586k} \times 100 = 61.09\%$$

As you can see, the gross profit margin was similar in both years, with the business making a slightly larger gross profit of £61.68 on every £100 of revenue in 2010/11. The small improvement suggests higher selling prices and/or better control of the cost of sales. The gross profit margin is much higher than the operating profit margin because the gross profit only takes account of revenue and the cost of sales, whereas the operating profit takes account of revenue and other operating income, and all the operating costs (cost of sales, distribution costs and administrative expenses).

Further interpretation of the profitability ratios for Ted Baker that we have calculated in this section would be possible if we analysed over a longer period of time to identify the trend. We could also compare them with similar businesses and with industry benchmarks.

9.5 Liquidity and efficiency ratios

Liquidity ratios are used to evaluate the solvency and financial stability of a business and are therefore of interest to all users who have an interest in whether the business is a going concern. The liquidity of the business is of particular importance to lenders and creditors who need to assess whether the business is able to service loans and pay for goods and services bought on credit. *Efficiency ratios*, which are also known as *funds management ratios*, are used to assess how effectively the directors have managed the *working capital* of the business (the current assets and current liabilities). We will examine the following widely used ratios in these categories:

- current test
- acid test
- inventory holding period
- trade receivables collection period
- trade payables payment period.

9.5.1 Current ratio and the acid test

We will start by looking at the *current ratio*. This is a liquidity ratio that measures the relationship between current assets and short-term liabilities and is expressed as x:1. The formula is:

$$\text{Current ratio} = \frac{\text{Current assets}}{\text{Current liabilities}}$$

The *acid test* is more stringent and measures the relationship between the liquid assets and short-term liabilities. We will define liquid assets as current assets minus inventories, which cannot be converted into cash at short notice. The formula is:

$$\text{Acid test} = \frac{\text{Current assets} - \text{Inventories}}{\text{Current liabilities}}$$

Activity

Calculate Ted Baker's current ratio and acid test for 2010/11 and 2009/10.

The figures you need are disclosed in Ted Baker's balance sheet (statement of financial position), so all you need to do is insert them into each formula. Check your answers against the solutions below:

	2010/11	2009/10
Current ratio =	$\dfrac{£83,800k}{£39,186k} = 2.14:1$	$\dfrac{£67,387k}{£28,594k} = 2.36:1$
Acid test =	$\dfrac{£83,800k - £42,492k}{£39,186k} = 1.05:1$	$\dfrac{£67,387k - £33,450k}{£28,594k} = 1.19:1$

The results demonstrate that the ratios are stable. In 2010/11 the Group had £2.14 of current assets for every £1 of current liabilities and £1.05 of liquid assets for every £1 of current liabilities. Although both ratios are lower than in the previous year, the Group would have no difficulty in paying all current creditors in the unlikely event that they all demanded immediate payment.

A ratio of less than 1:1 is not always cause for concern. You need to remember that the accounts are prepared on a prudent basis, which means that all possible costs and losses are accrued even if the amounts are based on estimates. In addition, the trade payables at the end of the year will be due at different times in the next financial year. It is also good funds management to give a shorter credit period to customers than agreed with suppliers. For example, some businesses give their customers 30 days' credit, but negotiate 90 days' credit from their suppliers. Such a trading policy would result in lower trade receivables (which are part of current assets) than trade payables (which are part of current liabilities) at the end of the year. It is difficult to generalize about ideal levels of liquidity, but in many industries there are benchmarks of what is considered to be a good acid test ratio.

9.5.2   Inventory holding period

The *inventory holding period* is an efficiency ratio that measures the average period between purchase and sale (or use) of inventory over the year. We will use a formula that calculates the ratio in months:

$$\text{Inventory holding period} = \frac{\text{Inventory}}{\text{Cost of sales}} \; [\times 12 \text{ for months}]$$

Ideally we should use the average inventory:

$$\frac{\text{Opening inventory} + \text{Closing inventory}}{2}$$

Since closing inventory for one year is opening inventory for the next, we would be able to calculate the average inventory for 2010/11. However, because we do not have the opening inventory for the previous year, we will define inventory as closing inventory to allow us to compare the ratios for the two years.

Activity

Calculate Ted Baker's inventory holding period for 2010/11 and 2009/10.

You need to identify the figures for inventories in the Group's balance sheet (statement of financial position) and the cost of sales figures from the income statement. Check your results against the following workings:

2010/11	2009/10

$$\text{Inventory holding period} = \frac{£42,492k}{£71,923k} \times 12 = 7.09 \text{ months} \qquad \frac{£33,450k}{£63,659k} \times 12 = 6.31 \text{ months}$$

In general, the shorter the period inventories are held the better as this reduces storage costs and the risk of damage, wastage and obsolescence. The results show a slight deterioration in 2010/11 because management has moved inventory less quickly than last year. In both years, you can see that on average it took more than 6 months (one fashion season) to sell (or use) the inventories. However, this is no major cause for concern as sales of some products may straddle the seasons.

9.5.3 Trade receivables collection period

The *trade receivables collection period* is an efficiency ratio that measures the average time customers took to pay for goods and services bought on credit over the year. We will use a formula that calculates the ratio in months:

$$\text{Trade receivables collection period} = \frac{\text{Trade receivables}}{\text{Revenue}} \times 12$$

Activity

Calculate Ted Baker's trade receivables collection period for 2010/11 and 2009/10.

You will find the data you need for trade receivables in the extract from Note 15 below the financial statements in Figure 9.2. Full details appear on page 63 in Ted Baker's Report and Accounts 2010/11. You identified the figure for revenue in an earlier activity and will remember that it is disclosed in the Group's income statement. Check your answer against the following solution:

$$2010/11$$

$$\text{Trade receivables collection period} = \frac{£18,182k}{£187,700k} \times 12 = 1.16 \text{ months}$$

$$2009/10$$

$$\frac{£14,436k}{£163,586k} \times 12 = 1.06 \text{ months}$$

The results demonstrate that the ratios are stable and the average period customers took to settle their debts was approximately one month. If the Group's policy is to give customers one month's credit, then this suggests management has an efficient system of credit control. However, we would want to confirm this assumption before drawing firm conclusions.

9.5.4 Trade payables payment period

The *trade payables payment period* is an efficiency ratio that measures the average time the business took to pay for goods and services purchased on credit from trade suppliers over the year. We use a formula that calculates the ratio in months:

$$\text{Trade payables payment period} = \frac{\text{Trade payables}}{\text{Cost of sales}} \times 12$$

Ideally we should use purchases, but as this is not disclosed we will use cost of sales. This is an inferior proxy for purchases as it is affected by fluctuations in inventory levels, but as long as we are consistent, it is possible to draw conclusions from it.

Activity

Calculate Ted Baker's trade payables payment period for 2010/11 and 2009/10.

You will find the data you need for trade payables receivables in the extract from Note 18 below the financial statements in Figure 9.2. Full details appear on page 64 in Ted Baker's Report and Accounts 2010/11. You identified the figure for cost of sales in the Group's income statement in an earlier activity. Check your results against the following answer:

2010/11

$$\text{Trade payables payment period} = \frac{\text{£18,888k}}{\text{£71,923k}} \times 12 = 3.15 \text{ months}$$

2009/10

$$\frac{\text{£10,392k}}{\text{£63,659k}} \times 12 = 1.96 \text{ months}$$

The interpretation of the results depends on the length of credit period agreed with trade suppliers. If the Group had a credit period of 2 months in 2009/10, then the results for that year show good funds management because the Group is making maximum use of the credit period. However, in 2010/11 the average period taken increased to just over 3 months. This may indicate bad financial management, because suppliers are likely to charge interest on late payment and/or reduce the period granted. On the other hand, the result may indicate that Ted Baker has negotiated a longer credit period with suppliers. Therefore, it is difficult to interpret the results without details of the average length of time agreed with suppliers.

Some people do not like getting into debt and prefer to pay invoices straight away rather than wait until they are due. However, this is not a good way of managing cash since receiving goods and services on credit is equivalent to being given an interest-free loan. In a business context, if suppliers do not give credit, the business may have to go into overdraft to pay cash for the goods and services. This does not mean that a business should wait until it receives a solicitor's letter or risk supplies being cut off, but management should take the maximum time allowed to pay suppliers. In addition, the credit controller should collect money from customers as quickly as possible. This is what Ted Baker appears to be doing and this shows efficient financial management.

If we had the data, it would be useful to analyse all the liquidity and efficiency ratios for Ted Baker over a longer period of time to identify the trend. We could also compare them with similar businesses and with industry benchmarks.

9.6   Gearing ratios

Gearing (or *leverage*) refers to the relationship between equity and long-term debt finance in the business. The financial structure of a business can have an impact on its financial performance and gearing ratios are used by investors and lenders to assess financial risk when a business has an obligation to service and repay long-term debt(s). The following are the two main ratios used:

- debt/equity ratio
- interest cover.

9.6.1 Debt/equity ratio

The *debt/equity ratio* focuses on the statement of financial position and describes the financial structure of the business in terms of the proportion of long-term debt to shareholders' funds. There are a number of ways in which *debt* can be defined, but we will define it as non-current liabilities. The ratio is shown as a percentage and can be calculated using the following formula:

$$\text{Debt/equity ratio} = \frac{\text{Non-current liabilities}}{\text{Equity}} \, [\times \, 100 \text{ for } \%]$$

Activity

Calculate Ted Baker's debt/equity ratio for 2010/11 and 2009/10.

You should have had little difficulty with this, as both figures are shown in the Group's balance sheet (statement of financial position). Check your answer against the following solution:

	2010/11	2009/10

$$\text{Debt/equity ratio} = \frac{£1,547\text{k}}{£76,024\text{k}} \times 100 = 2.03\% \qquad \frac{£1,316\text{k}}{£66,230\text{k}} \times 100 = 1.99\%$$

The results show that the business was slightly more highly geared in 2010/11 than in the previous year. The general interpretation is that the higher the gearing, the higher the risk that the business will be unable to pay the interest on its loans or make repayments when profits are low. On the other hand, the higher the gearing, the higher the returns to shareholders in strong economic conditions. In this case the results show that in 2010/11 the Group had low gearing with only £2.03 of long-term debt for every £100 of equity. Therefore, the financial structure does not increase the risk to lenders or investors.

9.6.2 Interest cover

Interest cover is a gearing ratio that focuses on the income statement (or statement of comprehensive income if the entity adopts a single-statement approach). It assesses the relative safety of interest payments by measuring the number of times interest payable on long-term debt is covered by the available profits. This avoids problems relating to the different ways in which debt can be defined. The ratio can be calculated using the following formulae:

$$\text{Interest cover} = \frac{\text{Operating profit}}{\text{Interest payable}}$$

Activity

Calculate Ted Baker's interest cover for 2010/11 and 2009/10.

Interest payable is one of the finance expenses and you will find the data you need in the extract from Note 4 below the financial statements in Figure 9.2. Full details appear on page 56 in Ted Baker's Report and Accounts 2010/11.

2010/11	**2009/10**

$$\text{Interest cover} = \frac{£24,132k}{£65k} = 371.26 \text{ times} \qquad \frac{£19,782k}{£148k} = 133.66 \text{ times}$$

There is good news that the interest cover was even more generous in 2010/11 than it was the previous year because operating profit was higher and long-term liabilities were lower. In other words, the Group's gearing was even lower in 2010/11 than it was the previous year. As you can see, interest payable was covered by operating profit more than 100 times in both years, which seems very safe. This means there is low risk to lenders and/or long-term creditors that the Group would be unable to service its long-term debts.

If we had the data, it would be useful to analyse the gearing ratios for Ted Baker over a longer period of time to identify the trend. We could also compare them with similar businesses and with industry benchmarks.

9.7   Trend analysis

We have mentioned several times how useful it would be if we had the data to calculate the ratios for Ted Baker over a longer period. This is known as trend analysis. Figure 9.3 shows an example of a trend analysis that traces the performance of the Group in terms of its operating profit margin.

Figure 9.3   Five-year analysis of Ted Baker's operating profit margin

Formula	2006/07	2007/08	2008/09	2009/10	2010/11
$\dfrac{\text{Operating profit}}{\text{Revenue}} \times 100$	$\dfrac{£18,334k}{£117,832k} \times 100$	$\dfrac{£22,142k}{£142,231k} \times 100$	$\dfrac{£17,161k}{£152,661k} \times 100$	$\dfrac{£19,782k}{£163,586k} \times 100$	$\dfrac{£24,132k}{£187,700k} \times 100$
Operating profit margin:	15.56%	15.57%	11.24%	12.09%	12.86%

The trend was stable until 2008/09, when the economic recession began to hit Ted Baker's net profit margin. There was a small improvement in 2009/10 and again in 2010/11 led by increased revenue, but costs have risen throughout the period. The ratios for the last three years suggest that the Group's selling prices have been constrained by lower consumer spending and have not kept pace with rising costs.

Although the table is useful because we can see the underlying figures used to calculate the ratio, the line graph shown in Figure 9.4 allows us to see the trend at a glance.

Figure 9.4 Five-year trend in Ted Baker's operating profit margin

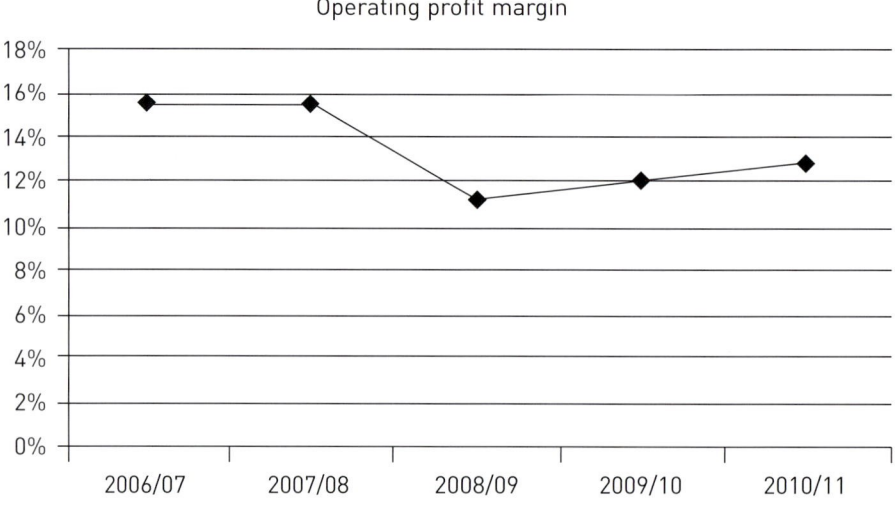

You may find it interesting to look at the key statistics shown on page 77 of Ted Baker's Report and Accounts 2010/11 (the final block of data in the Five Year Summary) and compare the ratios for 2010/11 with those you have calculated in the activities in this chapter. There should be no difference in respect of EPS, because this is guided by IAS 33, *Earnings Per Share* (IASB, 2003). Any differences in the other ratios will be due to the fact that accounting standards do not specify how the terms should be defined and Ted Baker's definitions may not be the same as those we have used.

9.8 Limitations of ratio analysis

The ratios calculated for a financial statement analysis depend on the needs of the user and the availability of the data. The possibility that the data required for trend analysis might not be available and the reminder about differences due to different definitions being used leads us to consider the *limitations* of ratio analysis. Like all accounting techniques, there are weaknesses that need to be considered. We can summarize the general limitations of ratio analysis as follows:

- There are no agreed definitions of the terms used, so ratios based on different definitions will not be comparable.
- The figures needed to calculate the ratios may not be disclosed and less precise alternatives may have to be used.

- Comparative data may not be available for previous periods (for example, trend analysis is not possible for a new business).
- Comparative data may not be available for competitors (for example, industry benchmarks may not be available or the business may occupy a niche market).
- Figures in financial statements can be misleading if there is high inflation or unscrupulous manipulation. However, if an unusual accounting treatment has been used, the figures for earlier years are adjusted in published trends.

Any discussion of the limitations of ratio analysis would be incomplete without linking them to the limitations of financial statements. The main limitations of general purpose financial statements are as follows:

- Financial statements only contain quantitative data. Therefore, ratio analysis does not take account of non-financial factors such as whether the business has sound plans for the future, a good reputation, a strong customer base, reliable suppliers, loyal employees, obsolete assets, strong competitors, poor industrial relations or activities in a high-risk industry.
- Financial statements do not focus on any non-financial effects of transactions or events.
- They do not reflect future transactions or events that may enhance or impair the entity's operations.
- They do not anticipate the impact of potential changes in the economic environment.
- There is a substantial degree of classification and aggregation in the financial statements and the effect of allocating continuous operations to the reporting period (ASB, 1999).

Despite these drawbacks, ratio analysis is an invaluable tool for appraising general purpose financial statements. Nevertheless, users should not treat ratios as absolute answers, but as an indication of where further investigation might be directed to better understand the present and future financial performance and position.

9.9 Conclusions

In this chapter we have examined a technique for analysing the financial statements of a business known as ratio analysis. This type of analysis is widely used by management, investors, lenders and creditors, as well as major customers, investment analysts and financial journalists. We have described a number of the main investment, profitability, liquidity, efficiency and gearing ratios.

In order to interpret ratios effectively, there needs to be some basis of comparison. This can be between businesses in the same industrial sector or a particular business and the industry benchmark. Comparison of ratios between the current period and the preceding period for a particular business and trend analysis is also useful. Ultimately the choice of analysis depends on the needs of the user and the availability of the data.

In this chapter we have considered the main limitations of ratio analysis, but despite some drawbacks, you need to remember that this method of interpreting financial statements is one of the most useful and commonly used techniques in the financial world.

Practice questions

1 Explain the purpose of ratio analysis and describe its limitations as a tool for evaluating the financial statements of a business.

2 The following extracts are taken from the financial statements of Adams Ltd and Eve Ltd.

	Adams Ltd £	Eve Ltd £
Capital employed	281,000	596,000
Operating profit	29,500	41,500
Gross profit	71,400	156,200
Revenue	354,900	706,260

Required
(a) Calculate the main profitability ratios for both companies.
(b) Suggest reasons for any differences you find.

3 The following information is taken from Ted Baker's Report and Accounts 2005/06 about 18 months before the recession began.

Group income statement for the year ended 28 January 2006	Note	*52 weeks ended 29 January 2006*	*52 weeks ended 30 January 2005*
		£'000	£'000
Revenue		117,832	105,753
Cost of sales		(48,979)	(43,357)
Gross profit		**68,853**	**62,396**
Distribution costs		(39,007)	(34,417)
Administration expenses		(15,339)	(15,089)
Other operating income		3,827	3,515
Operating profit		**18,334**	**16,405**
Finance income		129	68
Finance expenses	4	(109)	(221)
Profit before tax		**18,354**	**16,252**
Income tax expense		(5,435)	(4,884)
Profit for the period		**12,919**	**11,368**
Attributable to:			
Equity shareholders of the parent company		12,931	11,347
Non-controlling interests		(12)	21
Profit for the period		**12,919**	**11,368**

Group balance sheet at 28 January 2006	Note	52 weeks ended 29 January 2006	52 weeks ended 30 January 2005
		£'000	£'000
Non-current assets			
Intangible assets		501	506
Property, plant and equipment		18,667	17,346
Deferred tax assets		1,543	567
Available-for-sale financial assets		176	
		20,887	**18,419**
Current assets			
Inventories		23,475	22,725
Trade and other receivables	16	11,764	8,762
Derivative financial assets		155	
Cash and cash equivalents		11,381	9,603
		46,775	**41,090**
Current liabilities			
Trade and other payables	19	(17,507)	(15,806)
Borrowings		(563)	
Current tax payable		(6,544)	(6,123)
Derivative financial liabilities		(126)	
		(24,740)	**(21,929)**
Non-current liabilities			
Deferred tax liabilities		(750)	(750)
		(750)	**(750)**
Total liabilities		**(25,490)**	**(22,679)**
Net assets		**42,172**	**36,830**
Equity			
Share capital		2,149	2,149
Share premium account		6,983	6,983
Other reserves		169	
Retained profits	8	32,923	27,738
Total equity attributable to equity shareholders of parent		**42,224**	36,870
Non-controlling interests		(52)	(40)
Total equity		**42,172**	**36,830**

Selected notes to the financial statements	29 January 2006	30 January 2005
4 Of which, interest payable	**(109)**	(221)
8 Total dividends for the period (£'000)	**5,079**	4,556
9 Weighted number of ordinary shares ('000)	**42,237**	42,375
16 Of which, trade receivables (£'000)	**7,943**	6,367
19 Of which, trade payables (£'000)	**(10,803)**	(9,434)
20 Weighted average share price (pence)	**519.0**	507.5

Required

Analyse the financial statements by calculating the following ratios for 2005/06 and 2004/05. In each case, include the formula in words, your workings and append brief comments that explain the purpose of the ratio and interpret your results:

(a) Earnings per share

(b) Return on equity

(c) Return on capital employed

(d) Operating profit margin

(e) Acid test

(f) Inventory holding period

(g) Debt/equity

(h) Interest cover.

4 The following abridged information is taken from Ted Baker's Report and Accounts 2007/08 around the time the recession began.

Group Income Statement *for 52 weeks ended 26 January 2008*	*Note*	*52 weeks ended* *26 January* *2008*	*52 weeks ended* *27 January* *2007*
		£'000	£'000
Revenue		142,231	125,648
Cost of sales		(59,560)	(51,986)
Gross profit		**82,671**	**73,662**
Distribution costs		(48,320)	(41,404)
Administration expenses		(17,844)	(16,645)
Other operating income		5,635	4,436
Operating profit		**22,142**	**20,049**
Finance income		292	192
Finance expenses	4	(387)	(191)
Share of profit of jointly controlled entity		10	0
Profit before tax		**22,057**	**20,050**
Income tax expense		(6,815)	(5,634)
Profit for the period		**15,242**	**14,416**
Attributable to:			
Equity shareholders of the parent		15,196	14,421
Minority interests		46	(5)
Profit for the period		**15,242**	**14,416**

Group Balance Sheet *at 26 January 2008*	Note	*52 weeks ended* *26 January* *2008* £'000	*52 weeks ended* *27 January* *2007* £'000
Non-current assets			
Intangible assets		543	482
Property, plant and equipment		23,061	19,209
Investments in equity accounted investee		10	
Deferred tax assets		336	525
Prepayments		849	
		24,799	**20,216**
Current assets			
Inventories		29,315	27,825
Trade and other receivables	15	14,128	11,843
Amount due from equity accounted investee		178	
Derivative financial assets		603	216
Cash and cash equivalents		13,105	13,513
		57,329	**53,397**
Current liabilities			
Trade and other payables	18	(21,777)	(20,274)
Income tax payable		(3,418)	(1,708)
Derivative financial liabilities		(378)	(307)
		(25,573)	**(22,289)**
Non-current liabilities			
Deferred tax liabilities		(843)	(43)
		(843)	**(43)**
Net assets		**55,712**	**51,281**
Equity			
Share capital	9 & 20	2,160	2,160
Share premium account		9,137	9,052
Other reserves		251	(90)
Translation reserve		(520)	(493)
Retained profits	8	44,695	40,709
Total equity attributable to equity shareholders of parent		55,723	51,338
Non-controlling interests		(11)	(57)
Total equity		**55,712**	**51,281**

Selected notes to the financial statements		*26 January* *2008*	*27 January* *2007*
4	Of which interest payable	(387)	(67)
8	Total dividends paid on ordinary shares (£'000)	5,079	4,556
9	Weighted number of ordinary shares ('000s)	42,321	42,915
15	Of which trade receivables	10,217	8,543
18	Of which trade payables	(13,361)	(11,770)
20	Average share price (pence)	480.0	641.5
20	Risk-free interest rate (%)	5.29	4.77

Required

Imagine that you work for a firm of investment analysts. Your manager asks you to conduct a financial analysis to help clients with shares in Ted Baker PLC monitor their investments. Calculate the following ratios for 2007/08 and 2006/07 showing all your workings. In each case, explain the purpose of the ratio and interpret your results. Include brief comments on any change in the risks and rewards to investors over the period:

(a) Dividend per share
(b) Dividend yield
(c) Earnings per share
(d) Price earnings
(e) Return on equity
(f) Return on capital employed
(g) Operating profit margin
(h) Capital turnover.

5 Now imagine that you work for the bank that provides short-term finance to Ted Baker PLC. Your manager asks you to conduct a financial analysis to help the bank monitor the lending risks and returns.

Required

Calculate the following ratios for 2007/08 and 2006/07 showing all your workings. In each case, explain the purpose of the ratio and interpret your results. Include brief comments on any change in the lending risk over the period.

(a) Current ratio
(b) Acid test
(c) Inventory holding period
(d) Trade receivables collection period
(e) Trade payables payment period
(f) Debt/equity
(g) Interest cover

In addition, describe the limitations of the analysis you have conducted.

References

ASB (1999) *Statement of Principles for Financial Reporting*, December. London: Accounting Standards Board.

IASB (2003) IAS 33, *Earnings Per Share*. London: International Accounting Standards Board.

Law, J. (ed.) (2010) *Dictionary of Accounting*, 4th edition. Oxford: Oxford University Press.

10 Ethics, governance and corporate social responsibility

Learning objectives

When you have studied this chapter, you should be able to:

- explain the advantages and disadvantages of a code of ethics for accountants
- explain the disclosure requirements of the UK Corporate Governance Code
- explain what is meant by corporate social responsibility
- describe the incentives for environmental and corporate social responsibility.

10.1 Introduction

In previous chapters we have explained that financial reporting refers to the statutory disclosure of general purpose financial information by limited liability entities via the annual report and accounts. We also discussed the need for a regulatory framework to guide this important activity. The regulatory framework for financial reporting in the UK is rooted in *accounting principles* based on best practice, but is now strengthened by company law, accounting standards and, for listed companies, stock exchange rules. High-quality financial reporting also requires some means of ensuring that accountants act with integrity, reporting entities follow governance standards, and the information needs of users are considered.

This chapter focuses on three mechanisms that have been developed to meet these needs: the *code of ethics for professional accountants*, the *corporate governance code* and *corporate social reporting* practices respectively. Corporate governance and corporate social reporting are often considered together because they both relate to how well the entity is managed and how successful management is in communicating this. Corporate governance is primarily concerned with the way in which the directors are managing the resources for the benefit of the investors, whereas *environmental and corporate social responsibility* focuses on the expectations that investors, consumers and other stakeholders have that the company is being managed in a sustainable and socially responsible manner.

10.2   Ethics and the professional accountant

The preparation of the statutory financial statements is the responsibility of the directors of the company. In all but the smallest private companies, it is likely that an internal or external professional accountant will be employed to prepare these important financial statements. In addition, an independent professional accountant will have played a role in auditing the financial statements, unless the company qualifies for audit exemption. In all these activities, the work of professional accountants is guided by a code of ethics.

As you will remember from previous chapters, the regulatory framework for financial reporting ensures that the financial statements are prepared in a standard way and provide high-quality, reliable information for users. A code of ethics for professional accountants ensures that the financial information is unbiased and objective. At the corporate level, the interests of investors and other users of the annual report and accounts are protected by a number of statutory and voluntary mechanisms that ensure that the entity both recognizes and reports on its obligations to each of its stakeholders. Figure 10.1 summarizes these influences on the quality and content of disclosures made in the annual report and accounts in the UK.

Companies are guided by the *UK Corporate Governance Code* issued by the Financial Reporting Council (FRC, 2010a). You will remember from Chapter 4 that the FRC is the independent regulator responsible for promoting confidence in financial reporting and corporate governance. Companies must also meet the corporate social reporting (CSR) obligations contained in CA2006. The actions and behaviour of professional accountants are guided by the *Code of Ethics for Professional Accountants* published in 2009 by the *International Federation of Accountants (IFAC)*. This requires professional accountants to observe the highest standards of conduct and integrity, uphold the good standing and reputation of the profession and refrain from any conduct which might discredit the profession.

IFAC is an association of professional bodies of accountants throughout the world. It was founded in 1977 and now has 164 professional accountancy bodies as members and associates in 125 jurisdictions. It has three main boards, which issue high-quality professional standards:

- International Auditing and Assurance Standards Board (IAASB)
- International Accounting Education Standards Board (IAESB)
- International Ethics Standards Board for Accountants (IESBA).

Figure 10.1 Factors influencing disclosures in the annual report and accounts of UK companies

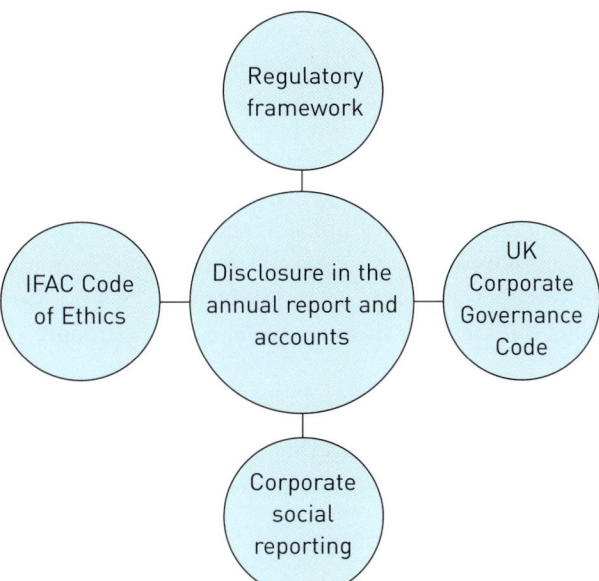

IESBA develops and issues ethical standards and other pronouncements for use by professional accountants around the world. The *Code of Ethics for Professional Accountants* (IFAC Code of Ethics) establishes ethical requirements for professional accountants. 'A distinguishing mark of the accounting profession is its acceptance of the responsibility to act in the public interest. Therefore, a professional accountant's responsibility is not exclusively to satisfy the needs of an individual client or employer' (IESBA, 2009, para 100.1). In acting in the public interest, a professional accountant must comply with the requirements of the IFAC Code of Ethics, but if prohibited from doing so by law or regulation, he or she should comply with all other parts of the Code.

The IFAC Code of Ethics requires a professional accountant to comply with the following five fundamental principles (IESBA, 2009, para 100.5):

(a) Integrity – to be straightforward and honest in all professional and business relationships.
(b) Objectivity – to not allow bias, conflict of interest or undue influence of others to override professional judgments.
(c) Professional Competence and Due Care – to maintain professional knowledge and skill at the level required to ensure that a client or employer receives competent professional services based on current developments in practice, legislation and techniques, and act diligently and in accordance with applicable technical and professional standards.
(d) Confidentiality – to respect the confidentiality of information acquired as a result of professional and business relationships, and, therefore, not disclose any such

information to third parties without proper and specific authority, unless there is a legal or professional right or duty to disclose, nor use the information for the personal advantage of the professional accountant or third parties.

(e) Professional Behaviour – to comply with relevant laws and regulations and to avoid any action that discredits the profession.

These principles illustrate the need for accountants to act in a neutral, unbiased and professional manner, and for them to achieve their work outputs in a way that best serves the public interest and upholds the reputation of the profession. As a result, an accountant employed by an organization should not allow the influence of other people to override their professional judgement or be associated with any information that contains a materially false or misleading statement.

Activity

What are the advantages and disadvantages of the IFAC Code of Ethics for Professional Accountants?

You may have thought of some of the following specific *advantages*:

- It provides explicit guidance to accountants and aids their understanding of the expectations placed upon them in terms of their ethical behaviour.
- It lets clients know what they can expect from their professional accountants.
- It provides a standard for disciplining professional accountants who adopt poor accounting practices.
- It enhances the reputation of professional accountants.
- It promotes a commitment to best practice within the profession.
- Abiding by a code may decrease the legal liability of professional accountants from inappropriate actions.
- It provides users of the accounts with a standard against which they can compare the ethical behaviour of their professional accountants and complain about poor accounting practice.

The potential *disadvantages* are:

- The publication of a code may be seen as a publicity exercise rather than offering any meaningful change in the ethical behaviour of professional accountants.
- Without proper guidance and enforcement, different accountants may interpret the code differently.
- The code may raise public expectations to a level that some professional accountants may be unable to achieve.

While the principles of the IFAC Code of Ethics are clear, how should a professional accountant or auditor respond if they discover, for example, fraudulent activity within the organization where they work? In such circumstances, a professional accountant should firstly consult with those charged with governance of the organization, such as the board of directors. If the conflict cannot be resolved following this consultation, an accountant may wish to obtain professional advice from his/her professional body or legal advisers to obtain guidance on the ethical issue without breaching confidentiality. The reporting of this fraudulent activity to the relevant authorities may breach the professional accountant's responsibility to respect confidentiality, so legal advice is essential for determining whether there is a requirement to report. If, after exhausting all relevant possibilities, the ethical conflict remains unresolved, a professional accountant should, where possible, refuse to remain associated with the matter creating the conflict. The professional accountant may determine that, in the circumstances, it is appropriate to resign altogether from the employing organization.

Activity

You are a qualified accountant and a member of one of the UK accountancy bodies. You are employed by a firm of accountants in the town where you live and expect to be a partner in this accountancy practice soon.

Five years ago you introduced an important client to your firm, with whom you regularly play golf. After your most recent game, the client asks if you will 'modify' the revenue estimate in the pro forma income statement recently prepared by you (and others) as part of a forthcoming initial public offering (IPO) when your client's business will be floated on the stock exchange. Your client makes it clear that he believes that the revenue estimate is too low.

Discuss the following questions:

1. Is there is an ethical issue for you in this scenario?
2. The IFAC Code of Ethics states that 'a professional accountant shall not knowingly be associated with reports, returns, communications or other information where the professional accountant believes that the information … contains a materially false or misleading statement' (IESBA, 2009, para 110.2). If you agree to increase the revenue estimate, would the income statement contain a materially false or misleading statement?
3. How likely is it that you will associate yourself with this client's income statement if he insists on increasing the revenue? (*Circle the number closest to your view*)

	Likely				Unlikely
I would associate myself with the income statement	5	4	3	2	1

When discussing this scenario you should apply the principles of the IFAC Code of Ethics, as you are acting as a professional accountant working for this client. It is clear that there is an ethical dilemma to resolve, because the client is asking you to override your professional judgement to subjectively increase the revenue reported in the income statement. As an accountant, you are required to act with integrity, be objective and avoid actions that discredit your profession. Agreeing to your client's request would be unethical since it would result in a misleading and subjective statement of revenue, which serves to discredit both you and your profession. In terms of part (c), ethical accountants would indicate that they would be unlikely to knowingly associate themselves with this misleading income statement by circling the lowest number on the scale.

In this section we have highlighted the role that the ethical codes of professional accountants play within the financial reporting process, and how abiding by the principles of these codes has the potential to cause ethical conflict with the board of directors at a reporting entity. As a result, it is important that reporting entities possess appropriate governance procedures that ensure good management practices at a corporate level in order to eliminate demands for the use of unethical accounting and business practices.

10.3   Corporate governance

Financial reporting focuses on providing financial information that allows users to assess the financial performance, financial position and changes in financial position of the entity. It also allows investors to assess the stewardship of management, which means they are interested in how effectively and efficiently the directors have discharged their responsibilities. *Corporate governance* refers to the manner in which organizations are managed and the nature of accountability of the managers to the owners.

Corporate governance has been of increased importance since the publication of the *Cadbury Report* in 1992, which set out a code of practice for UK companies that was subsequently incorporated in the *UK Corporate Governance Code* (the UK Code). Cadbury (1992, p. 15) defines corporate governance as: 'the system by which companies are directed and controlled. Boards of directors are responsible for the governance of their companies. The shareholders' role in governance is to appoint the directors and the auditors and to satisfy themselves that an appropriate governance structure is in place. The responsibilities of the board include setting the company's strategic aims, providing the leadership to put them into effect, supervising the management of the business and reporting to shareholders on their stewardship. The board's actions are subject to laws, regulations and the shareholders in general meeting'.

> **Key definition**
>
> Corporate governance is the manner in which organizations, particularly limited companies, are managed and the nature of accountability of the managers to the owners.
>
> *Source*: Law (2010, p. 113).

The UK Code sets out principles of good practice in relation to board leadership and effectiveness, remuneration, accountability and relations with shareholders.

Developments and revisions to the UK Code are overseen by the Committee on Corporate Governance, which is appointed by the FRC. The Committee on Corporate Governance is responsible for:

- reviewing developments in corporate governance and considering whether any actions by the FRC would be desirable, and to put proposals to the Board where appropriate
- monitoring the operation of the UK Code and its implementation by listed companies and by shareholders
- clarifying problems with the interpretation of the UK Code.

In relation to our discussion on ethics and the professional accountant in the previous section, it is important to note that the FRC also oversees the regulatory activities of the professional accountancy bodies and provides independent disciplinary arrangements for public interest cases involving accountants and actuaries. It does this through the activities of its Professional Oversight Board (POB), Accountancy and Actuarial Discipline Board (AADB) and Auditing Practices Board (APB). The POB provides oversight of the regulation of the auditing and accountancy professions by the recognized supervisory, qualifying and professional accountancy bodies. The AADB is the independent, investigative and disciplinary body for accountants and actuaries in the UK and is responsible for operating and administering an independent disciplinary scheme (the Accountancy Scheme) covering members of accountants' professional bodies in the UK. The AADB's role is the investigation, and, where appropriate, hearing by a disciplinary tribunal of public interest cases; other cases will continue to be dealt with by the individual accountancy body of the member concerned. The APB helps to develop auditing practice in the UK in order to establish high standards and ensure public confidence in the auditing process.

Ensuring that companies comply with UK GAAP is a key part of corporate governance and it is clear that the internal rules, systems and processes by which authority is exercised and controlled are also the mechanisms by which management is held to account. However, it should not be forgotten that corporate governance in non-publicly accountable smaller entities is equally important. Although the operations of such entities may be less complex, the business environment is not, and so good corporate governance is still useful to ensure that that they comply with the operational and financial reporting regulations. If the business is expanding its activities into unfamiliar operations or geographical sectors, it needs to have appropriate procedures in place to ensure that it is not penalized for non-compliance.

Activity

What are the problems with incorporating the UK Code in company law?

It may occur to you that the main problem lies with the difference between principles and rules, a debate we have discussed in connection with international differences in the development of accounting standards. The UK Code is based upon a set of general principles that allows companies a flexible 'comply or explain' approach on how to apply them. Although the UK Code is voluntary, the fact that it is endorsed by the UK Listing Authority, which is overseen by the Financial Services Authority (FSA), means that all companies with a premium listing of equity shares in the UK must report on how they have applied the main principles of the UK Code in their annual report and accounts; if they have not applied them, they must explain their reasons. A premium listing is only available for the equity shares of trading companies and certain investment entities. To obtain such a listing a company is expected to comply with all UK regulations and as a direct consequence may enjoy a lower cost of capital through enhanced investor confidence. Private limited companies and public limited companies that do not have a premium listing of equity shares do not have to comply with the UK Code, but may comply with certain aspects on a voluntary basis.

Activity

What are the advantages of allowing a premium-listed company to select which parts of the UK Code to apply?

You may not have thought that the flexibility this offers is an advantage because you may feel that a premium-listed company should not be allowed to decide which of the UK Code's requirements to follow. However, consider the following case. At present the FRC only requires companies in the FTSE 350 to comply with the annual director re-election provision, but management may consider this is not appropriate if they are engaged in a takeover. Therefore, it would be acceptable for the company to explain rather than comply. Enforcement can be made by the FSA, but the UK Code will continue to be enforced primarily by the shareholders, through engagement and the use of legal rights, such as their voting rights. To this end, the FRC published *The UK Stewardship Code* (FRC, 2010b) with the aim of enhancing the quality of engagement between companies and their institutional investors. The UK Stewardship Code is complementary to the UK Code and should lend greater emphasis to the concept of 'comply or explain' by providing a stronger link between governance and the investment process.

10.4 Development of the corporate governance code in the UK

The development of corporate governance guidance in the UK was a response to the financial scandals of the late 1980s and early 1990s, such as the collapse of companies like Polly Peck International and Coloroll (Mallin, 2009). There was also a general lack of confidence in financial reporting, which led to the FRC, the London Stock Exchange and the accountancy profession establishing the Committee on the Financial Aspects of Corporate Governance in 1991. A subsequent financial scandal at the Bank of Credit and Commerce International, together with the collapse of the Maxwell Group, led the Committee to widen its remit to look at corporate governance as a whole. The resulting Cadbury Report in 1992 established a set of principles for good corporate governance. These principles were then enshrined in a code of best practice, compliance with which was required as they were then incorporated into the Listing Rules of the London Stock Exchange. The Cadbury Report introduced the principle of 'comply or explain', whereby listed companies had to produce a narrative statement detailing the extent of their compliance with the code and an explanation if they had not complied with any of its principles. These requirements are incorporated in the current UK Code. In addition, the Listing Rules have been given statutory authority under the *Financial Services and Markets Act 2000*.

A number of subsequent reports developed the recommendations of the Cadbury Report. In 1995 the *Greenbury Report* responded to concerns about the size of directors' remuneration packages and the lack of full disclosure of these in company accounts (Solomon, 2007). In 1998 the *Hampel Report* reviewed the extent to which the objectives of the Cadbury and Greenbury Reports were being achieved; it led to the publication of *The Combined Code on Corporate Governance* in 1998 (the Combined Code), which applied to all listed companies. The collapse of the investment bank, Barings, in 1995 focused attention on corporate governance again and on issues relating to risk management and internal control. This led to the *Turnbull Report* in 1999, which provided guidance on the internal control requirements of the Combined Code.

The failure of the Enron Corporation in 2001 and the associated demise of Arthur Andersen, one of the five largest accountancy firms, resulted in further pressure for reform. Enron had been one of the USA's most innovative companies and at its peak had a market value of $70 billion. However, following the publication of its financial results for 2001, Enron showed a $638 million loss on its income statement and disclosed debts of $1.2 billion which had been excluded from its previous balance sheets. These revelations shocked the stock market, and had been hidden through Enron's use of creative accounting techniques that inflated earnings and reduced liabilities in its published financial statements. In the United States, this accounting scandal resulted in the Sarbanes–Oxley Act of 2002. The Act requires all US public companies to submit an annual assessment of the effectiveness of their internal control systems to the *Securities and Exchange Commission (SEC)*. It also requires the company's auditors to audit and report on the internal control reports produced by management, in the same way as they audit financial statements (Soloman, 2007). The UK government's response was to commission the *Higgs Review* on the role and effectiveness of non-executive directors, which was published in 2003, with the aim of improving the existing Combined Code. The same year, the FRC published the *Smith Report* on audit committees. The recommendations from both reports led to amendments to the Combined Code, a revised version of which was published in July 2003. Since then the FRC has kept the Combined Code under review, with updates in 2006 and 2008. The *Tyson Report* in 2003 considered how to improve the recruitment and development of non-executive directors.

Given the apparent link between corporate governance and business scandals, it was inevitable that further investigations into corporate governance would follow the global financial crisis which started in 2007. The initial move was the government-commissioned review of corporate governance of the banking industry, which resulted in the *Walker Report* (2009). However, the FRC responded in March 2009 by bringing forward its review of the Combined Code to ensure consistency with the banking sector work.

The outcome of the FRC's review was a revised version of the Combined Code entitled *The UK Corporate Governance Code* (the UK Code) (FRC, 2010a), which sets out what is considered current best practice for corporate governance. Its main principles cover:

- the leadership role of the chairman and the need for constructive challenge from non-executive directors
- a requirement for the chairman to hold regular development meetings with each director, and to have the board evaluated by an external facilitator at least once every three years
- the right composition of the board and how selection should encourage diversity
- the board's responsibilities to set a company's risk profile along with a requirement to describe their business model in the annual report
- alignment of performance-related pay with the long-term interests of the company
- improved board accountability, with directors in FTSE 350 listed companies facing annual re-election.

Following a consultation in 2011 it is likely that further amendments to the UK Code will come into effect from October 2012. At the time of writing these changes have not been announced, but you will be able to keep up to date via the FRC's website (www.frc.org.uk/).

10.5   The UK Corporate Governance Code (2010)

We will now take a closer look at principles and specific provisions of the Corporate Governance Code (FRC, 2010) (the UK Code). As already discussed, listed companies are required to report on how they have applied the main principles of the UK Code, and either confirm that they have complied with its provisions or, where they have not, provide an explanation. The increased importance placed on corporate governance is evident in the number of pages devoted to this topic in a company's annual report and accounts.

There are 18 disclosure requirements in the UK Code and the statutory annual report and accounts of a listed entity must include the following:

1. A statement of how the board of directors operates, including a high-level statement of which types of decisions are to be taken by the board and which are to be delegated to management.

2. The names of the chairman, the deputy chairman, the chief executive, the senior independent director, the chairmen and members of the board committees.
3. The individual attendance record for directors at board and committee meetings.
4. Where a chief executive is appointed chairman, the reasons for their appointment (this only needs to be done in the annual report following the appointment).
5. The names of the independent non-executive directors, with reasons where necessary to justify independence.
6. A separate section describing the work of the nomination committee, including the process it has used in relation to board appointments and in particular in relation to the appointment of a chairman or a non-executive director.
7. Any significant external commitments of the chairman and any changes during the year.
8. An explanation of how performance evaluation of the board, its committees and its directors has been conducted.
9. An explanation from the directors of their responsibility for preparing the accounts and a statement by the auditors about their reporting responsibilities.
10. An explanation from the directors of the basis on which the company generates or preserves value over the longer term (the business model) and the strategy for delivering the objectives of the company.
11. A statement from the directors that the business is a going concern, with supporting assumptions or qualifications as necessary.
12. A report that the board has conducted a review of the effectiveness of the company's risk management and internal controls systems.
13. A section describing the work of the audit committee.
14. Where there is no internal audit function, an explanation for its absence.
15. Where the board does not accept the audit committee's recommendation on the appointment, reappointment or removal of an external auditor, a statement from the audit committee explaining the recommendation and the reasons why the board has taken a different position.
16. An explanation of how, if the auditor provides non-audit services, auditor objectivity and independence is safeguarded.
17. A description of the work of the remuneration committee including, where an executive director serves as a non-executive director elsewhere, whether or not the director will retain such earnings and, if so, what this is.
18. The steps taken to ensure that members of the board, in particular the non-executive directors, develop an understanding of the views of major shareholders about their company.

A majority of these disclosure requirements can be clearly seen in the annual report and accounts of Ted Baker PLC for 2010/11 (Ted Baker, 2011a). As the company has a premium listing on the London Stock Exchange, it must report on how it has applied the main principles of the UK Code, and the corporate governance extracts from its latest annual report are shown in Figures 10.2 to 10.6. As Ted Baker's latest annual report and accounts cover a financial year that commenced before 29 June 2010, the company only needed to comply with the disclosure requirements of the Combined Code rather than the new UK Code. Early adoption of the UK Code was possible but since Ted Baker did not make this choice, examples of corporate governance disclosures from the annual report and accounts of Marks and Spencer PLC (M&S) for 2010/11 are also provided.

Disclosure by both companies about non-executive directors and their independence is shown in Figure 10.3. While M&S include a similar statement to Ted Baker, its extract highlights the 'comply or explain' part of the UK Code and the fact that most companies tend to want to comply with its provisions. Previously M&S had not divided the roles of Chairman and Chief Executive, but it has now fallen into line with best practice and formally acknowledges this change in its corporate governance structure.

As Figure 10.4 illustrates, Ted Baker also takes its responsibility to communicate with its shareholders very seriously. The company provides shareholders with a copy

Figure 10.2 Examples of statements of compliance with the UK Code

Statement of compliance with the Combined Code [Ted Baker]

The Company has complied throughout the year with all of the provisions of the Combined Code on Corporate Governance issued in June 2008 (the "Combined Code"). The Board has noted and is aware of the recently introduced UK Corporate Governance Code (which will apply to the financial period of the Group ending 28 January 2012). The Board will seek to comply with the new code where it determines that to do so would be beneficial to the Company and its stakeholders.

Corporate Governance Statement [M&S]

We welcomed the publication in June 2010 of the UK Corporate Governance Code and have used both the 2008 and 2010 Governance Codes as the standard against which we have measured ourselves in 2010/11. The two significant amendments to the 2008 Code: the annual re-election of directors and the external evaluation of the Board at least every three years, will both be achieved this year. With the exception of Louise Patten, all of the Board are seeking election at the 2011 AGM, marking a departure from the previous one-third of directors seeking election on a rotation basis. We have also completed the Company's first fully independent Board evaluation. This was conducted in a spirit of openness and collaboration and supported by the whole Board.

Sources: Ted Baker (2011a, p. 17) and Marks and Spencer (2011, p. 38).

Figure 10.3 Examples of disclosures about non-executive directors and their independence

The Board [Ted Baker]

The Board currently comprises a non-executive chairman, a chief executive, one other executive director and three non-executive directors. Biographies of these directors appear on page 25.

David Bernstein has held the position of non-executive director since 2003 and has been confirmed by the Board as the Company's senior independent director. All the non-executive directors are considered by the Board to be independent of management and free of any relationship that could materially interfere with the exercise of their independent judgement.

The Board [M&S]

Throughout the year ended 2 April 2011, the Company complied with all provisions of the 2008 Code with the exception that for part of the year, the role of Chairman and Chief Executive was exercised by the same individual, Sir Stuart Rose. Stuart stepped down as Executive Chairman on 31 July 2010 but remained as Chairman until the appointment of Robert Swannell as Non-Executive Chairman on 4 January 2011. We recognise that Stuart's role as Chairman and Chief Executive was out of line with best practice as were his independence criteria on appointment as Chairman. We understand the concerns that shareholders had, but maintain that robust governance structures were in place, while benefiting from retaining Stuart at the helm. With the separation of the roles of Chairman and Chief Executive we have now returned to best practice.

Sources: Ted Baker (2011a, p. 17) and Marks and Spencer (2011, p. 41).

Figure 10.4   Example of disclosure on communications with shareholders

Communications with Shareholders [Ted Baker]

The Group attaches considerable importance to the effectiveness of its communication with its shareholders. The full report and accounts are sent to all shareholders and further copies are distributed to others with potential interest in the Group's performance.

The directors seek to build on a mutual understanding of objectives between the Company and its institutional shareholders by making general presentations after the interim and preliminary results; meeting shareholders to discuss long-term issues and gather feedback; and communicating regularly throughout the year. All shareholders have access to these presentations, as well as to the annual report and accounts and to other information about the Company, through the website at www.tedbaker.com. They may also attend the Company's Annual General Meeting at which they have the opportunity to ask questions.

Non-executive directors are kept informed of the views of shareholders by the executive directors and are provided with independent feedback from investor meetings.

Source: Ted Baker (2011a, p. 18).

of the annual report and accounts and welcomes their attendance at the AGM. Institutional investors are given half-yearly presentations and the chance to discuss issues with the directors. The disclosure is as outlined below.

Figures 10.5 and 10.6 on page 254 highlight the disclosures made by Ted Baker in relation to requirements for the establishment of separate committees covering audit and remuneration. In summary, Ted Baker's corporate governance disclosures attempt to provide a coherent commentary on the company's management structure and operational controls.

10.6   Overview of international corporate governance codes

At an international level, the Organization for Economic Cooperation and Development (OECD) developed a series of principles covering best practice in corporate governance in 1999, which were last updated in 2004 and are currently under review. These have become a benchmark for policy makers, investors, corporations and other stakeholders worldwide. The principles, which include board responsibilities, disclosure and transparency requirements and the rights of shareholders, have contributed to legislative and regulatory initiatives in OECD and non-OECD countries.

While the USA has legislated on corporate governance with the 2002 Sarbanes–Oxley Act, the European model has been to follow the 'comply or explain'

Figure 10.5 Example of disclosure on the audit committee

Audit Committee [Ted Baker]

The Audit Committee (the "Committee") is chaired by Ronald Stewart and its other members are Robert Breare and David Bernstein, all of whom are independent non-executive Directors and served throughout the course of the year. The Committee met three times during the year with full attendance.

The Committee meets to review and approve the interim and annual financial statements, before submission for approval by the Board and considers any matters raised by the auditors. The committee will consider significant financial reporting judgements contained in the financial statements, including accounting policies and compliance, areas of management judgements and estimates and the effectiveness of financial reporting and controls. The Board considers all members to have relevant financial experience.

The Committee oversees the Company's relationship with the external auditors and makes recommendations to the Board in relation to their appointment, re-appointment and removal and approves their remuneration and terms of engagement. The Committee also reviews the independence of the external auditors and the Company's policy on the supply of non-audit services by the external auditors.

Source: Ted Baker (2011a, p. 18).

Figure 10.6 Example of disclosure on the remuneration committee

Remuneration Committee [Ted Baker]

The Remuneration Committee (the "Committee") is chaired by David Bernstein and its other members are Robert Breare and Ronald Stewart, all of whom are independent non-executive Directors and served throughout the course of the year. The Committee met once during the year with full attendance.

The Committee consulted Ernst & Young LLP (which also provided tax, legal and accounting services to the Group in the year) on executive remuneration issues.

The Committee is responsible for setting the remuneration packages of the executive directors of the Board and other senior executives who fall within the scope of the Committee. It approves all service contracts or other contracts between the Company and its executive directors and senior executives and considers and, if thought fit, approves any outside interests and other directorships of the executive directors. The Committee also reviews and approves the design of the Company's share based incentive schemes and determines the level of awards to be made and approves the performance targets.

Source: Ted Baker (2011a, p. 26).

approach first defined in the 1992 Cadbury Report. To date, there has been no systematic attempt to create a pan-European code on corporate governance.

Activity

Why do you think there is no EU code on corporate governance?

A comparative study of the corporate governance codes used in each Member State (EC, 2002) concluded that greater coordination of these various corporate governance codes would encourage convergence that would directly reduce barriers to cross-border voting by shareholders and assist the transfer of governance information. A subsequent study (EC, 2011a) assessed the effectiveness of monitoring and enforcement of corporate governance codes in Member States and noted that nearly 20 years after the publication of the Cadbury Report, all but two had a 'comply or explain' based code.

Currently there exists a body of corporate governance principles and rules, which consist of a number of recommendations on the independence of non-executive directors, on board committees, and on remuneration, while listed companies have an obligation to issue a corporate governance statement. The directives on takeovers (2004/25/EC), transparency of listed companies (2004/109/EC), shareholders' rights

(2007/36/EC), market abuse (2003/6/EC) and audit (2006/43/EC) have helped shape corporate governance in EU Member States.

The European Commission's Green Paper on the EU corporate governance framework addressed ways in which the corporate governance of European companies might be improved (EC, 2011b). The paper consulted on three key areas that were considered to lie at the heart of good corporate governance:

- the roles and responsibilities of the board of directors
- the engagement and involvement by shareholders
- the monitoring and enforcement of existing national corporate governance codes (the 'comply or explain' approach).

The outcome of this consultation may have implications for the operation of the UK Code.

10.7 Environmental and corporate social responsibility

While corporate governance is primarily concerned with the way in which the directors are managing the resources for the benefit of the investors, *environmental and corporate social responsibility* focuses on the concerns of investors, consumers and other stakeholders about whether the company is being managed in a sustainable and socially responsible manner. The term *stakeholder* refers to investors and all other parties with interests in the company who could be affected by the environmental or social consequences of the company's activities. Although there are many definitions of corporate social responsibility (CSR), there is general agreement that a socially responsible entity adopts an approach to business that 'embodies transparency and ethical behaviour, respect for stakeholder groups and a commitment to add economic, social and environmental value' (Sustainability, 2004, p. 4).

Key definition

Stakeholders are all those with interests in an organization; for example, as shareholders, employees, suppliers, customers, or members of the wider community (who could be affected by the social or environmental consequences of an organization's activities).

Source: Law (2010, p. 390).

Activity

Identify two UK companies that you consider follow and abide by CSR principles.

You may have thought of examples such as the Body Shop or the Co-operative Bank, both of which fully embrace the notion of CSR and actively manage their relationship with all stakeholder groups through *environmental and social reporting*. The former considers the environment and ethics in relation to its beauty products range, while the latter looks to conduct its business operations in an environmentally and socially responsible manner. According to the founder of The Body Shop, Dame Anita Roddick, 'the business of business should not just be about money, it should be about responsibility. It should be about public good, not private greed' (The Body Shop, 2011). As these brief examples show, many UK companies now take their CSR responsibilities seriously, and even publish substantial voluntary information about their social and environmental impacts on their websites and as additional reports. By way of contrast, other UK companies choose to discharge their obligations by producing a few brief paragraphs about CSR within their annual report and accounts. Whatever approach is adopted, it must be noted that enhanced CSR disclosure does not necessarily imply that a company is acting in a socially and environmentally responsible manner.

With the apparent variation in the level of UK CSR transparency and disclosure, what are the legal requirements for CSR information provision in the UK? The UK legal requirements for CSR disclosures are set out in Section 417 of the Companies Act 2006. This covers the business review, which is part of the directors' report, and it requires the standard type of business performance data (for example, a description of the principal risks and uncertainties facing the company) but, for quoted companies, there are additional CSR-related requirements. The rules in 417 (5b) require that details about environmental matters (including the impact of the company's business on the environment), the company's employees, and social and community issues should be disclosed. Figure 10.7 shows the CSR disclosures included within Ted Baker's *Ted Baker Report and Accounts 2010/2011* (Ted Baker, 2011a). The information reveals what this company views as important to show in terms of its statutory obligation to report on CSR issues.

As you can see, Ted Baker's latest CSR disclosures provide detailed information about sustainability and the environment, ethical sourcing of products, community involvement, diversity in the workplace, health and safety and the corporate policy on recruitment of disabled employees.

The volume and detail of the CSR information disclosed by Ted Baker in 2010/11 is considerably greater than in 2009/2010, which may be a response to criticisms about the company's employment and manufacturing practices in the Third World. For example, the employment rights groups, Labour behind the Label and War on Want, identified Ted Baker as one of the clothing brands that failed to disclose transparent information about the employment and ethical treatment of overseas workers: 'These brands make no meaningful information available to suggest that they have engaged with the living wage or other labour rights issues, and continue not to respond to our inquiries about their policies and practices' (Hearson and Morser, 2007, p. 14). Thus, from the perspective of certain pressure groups, Ted Baker, like many other UK clothing retailers, fails to provide the detailed CSR disclosures that stakeholders demand: 'Retailers cannot continue to pay lip service to corporate social responsibility whilst engaging in buying practices that systematically undermine the principles of decent work' (War on Want, 2010, p. 1).

Activity

What additional voluntary CSR information do *you* think Ted Baker might disclose?

Figure 10.7   Example of corporate social reporting (*continued overleaf*)

SUSTAINABILITY AND THE ENVIRONMENT

We believe in being open and honest in the way we do business and doing the right thing by all of our stakeholders; by operating in a responsible and sustainable manner.

How we work

Mr L D Page has been given specific responsibility for overseeing the formulation of the Group's policies and procedures for managing risks arising from social, environmental and ethical matters ("SEE"). In addition, the Board has tasked four members of the Executive Committee to oversee specific areas of our SEE agenda for the Group. These Executive Committee members participate because of the relevance of their departments to our ongoing commitment in these areas, Brand Communication, Product Design, Production and Special Projects (Interior Design). We employed a full time Green Guardian in April 2010 to manage the Group's cross-functional team (the "Green Team") which is responsible for addressing SEE concerns of the Group.

Key Issues

Ethical and Sustainable Sourcing

Ethical and sustainable sourcing is an area of great importance to the Group. We believe that our products should be produced in factories that are committed to providing a fair and safe environment for their workers. Our trusted partners within the supply chain are one of our most valuable assets. The Group is committed to reducing our impact on the environment, reducing our use of resources and increasing efficiencies wherever possible to ensure our business is sustainable.

- All Ted Baker suppliers are governed by our Company Code of Conduct, which is based on the Social Accountability International Code, an internationally recognised benchmark for ethical excellence, and can be found at www.tedbaker.com

- We announced our partnership with not-for-profit organisation, MADE-BY in May 2010. MADE-BY is a non-profit multi-stakeholder initiative set up to improve sustainability within the fashion industry. We are working with it to set realistic and achievable internal targets to improve the social and environmental standards in line with its internationally accredited benchmarks. Our first scorecard, detailing our current performance against these benchmarks, will be issued on MADE-BY's website during 2011

- Our partnership with MADE-BY has enabled us to access its expertise on sustainable fibres. We have set long term internal targets for the quantity of sustainable fibres used within our collections, and will be showing our progress yearly on our MADE-BY scorecards

Environmental Impacts

- As a Green 500 Member, we are committed to reducing our carbon footprint and were rewarded in June 2010 with a Platinum Award. This reflects the extent of our carbon reductions and acknowledges the successful implementation of our carbon saving initiatives

- We are working on both a baseline measurement for our carbon footprint as well as on projects that will help reduce it such as installing energy efficient LED lights within our showrooms and SMART meters within our stores to monitor energy consumption

- All of our business travel is CarbonNeutral®. This means that the unavoidable emissions generated by the air, road and rail journeys, required to visit our stores and suppliers, have been reduced to net zero through purchasing carbon credits from Voluntary Carbon Standard ("VCS") validated projects

- We continue to participate in The Carbon Disclosure Project to measure and disclose our greenhouse gas emissions and climate change strategies

- We participate in the Wastepak Compliance Scheme as part of the Producer Responsibility Obligation (Packaging Waste) Regulations 1997, and continue to reduce unnecessary packaging

- Our employees are our greatest asset, and we have Green Team members in every department and store encouraging colleagues to be more environmentally aware

- We are constantly looking at the waste our business creates, and working towards our overall aim to ensure no waste goes to landfill. We participate in recycling schemes in all properties

- We have installed two buckfast bee colonies on the roof of our London head office, to help give the bees a haven in which to recuperate their local population

Community

Our Charity Partner for 2009/2010 was Everyman, a prostate and testicular cancer charity. We used our underwear boxes as a vehicle to further raise awareness of their charity and funds for research into prostate and testicular cancer. We have also worked with them business wise to support a number of their initiatives.

We have also made other one-off in-kind donations throughout the year. Donations paid during the year can be found on page 33.

Source: Ted Baker (2011a, pp. 20–1).

Figure 10.7 *continued*

PEOPLE

The talent, commitment and passion of the Ted Baker team are key factors in the success of our business and brand. The value we place on our team is shown in the way we motivate them, encourage learning and development, nurture their growth and potential, and recognise and reward their contributions.

Culture

The spirit in which we conduct our business and interact with our team always takes into consideration 'Would Ted do it that way?' We regularly host internal events, including sessions with the chief executive, telling the story behind the brand and also Family Days where we open our doors to friends and family. During the period we invited investors and analysts to a series of presentations led by the Ted Baker management team to demonstrate the culture of our business and the strength of the team behind the brand.

Reward and Recognition

Remuneration is reviewed annually and a benchmarking review is undertaken to ensure we remain competitive and fair across all areas of the business. Our rewards include bonus schemes linked to sales targets and individual and corporate performance. We encourage our team members to join our Save As You Earn ("SAYE") schemes. This year we saw the launch of our Wisdom Awards; recognition for the longer serving members of the team and a chance for them to celebrate and share their stories with the rest of the team.

Learning and Development

Performance is reviewed bi-annually with each team member to discuss personal and career development. Within this process, goals and objectives are set and linked to personal growth and business development. We allow our team members to broaden their abilities and knowledge by exposing them to new experiences. We invest in training which ranges from specialist and technical skills training, to in-house developed courses focusing on management skills, leadership skills, brand awareness and self awareness. Firm career paths exist across the Group and inter-departmental and international moves play a large part in maintaining and growing talent.

Diversity

The Group believes in respecting individuals and their rights in the workplace. With this in mind, specific policies are in place covering harassment and bullying, whistle blowing, equal opportunities and data protection. Our team represents a wide and diverse workforce from all backgrounds, sexual orientation, nationality, ethnic and religious groups. We support sponsorship of visa applications, where appropriate, to retain specific talent within the business. With continued overseas expansion our workforce is becoming more diverse and we respect cultural differences and actively seek to learn about them in each territory we operate.

Health, Safety and Welfare

Our duty and commitment to the well being of our team is supported by activity such as healthcare, occupational health, health seminars and funding for flu jabs. During the period, we introduced a Cycle to Work Scheme, with a Childcare Voucher Scheme introduced in previous years. During 2011, we will introduce an Employee Assistance Programme which will further support our genuine concern for the well-being of our team. The prevention and identification of risks and accidents is supported by an external Health and Safety service provider and ongoing training of management teams. A dedicated Health & Safety Officer will be recruited to strengthen our knowledge and commitment in this area of our business.

Disabled Employees

Applications for employment by disabled persons are always fully and fairly considered, bearing in mind the aptitudes of the applicant concerned. In the event of team members becoming disabled every effort is made to ensure that their employment with the Group continues and that appropriate training is arranged. It is the policy of the Group that the training, career development and promotion of disabled persons should, as far as possible, be identical with that of other employees.

Employee Engagement

The Group places considerable value on the involvement of its team members and continues to keep them informed on matters affecting them and on the significant factors affecting the performance of the Group. This is achieved through formal and informal meetings and employee representatives are consulted regularly on a wide range of matters affecting employees current and future interests. Team members are regularly informed of the Group's performance and the factors affecting its performance during the year.

Ted Baker supplements the statutory CSR disclosures contained within its annual report with additional voluntary CSR information on its website. Ted Baker's website publishes documents entitled *Ted's Ethical statement* (Ted Baker, 2011b) and the *Ted Baker Ethical Code of Conduct* (Ted Baker, 2011c) which together describe the company's ethical position and approach. The main document is the Ethical Statement, which formally defines the values, standards and policy that the company has on the ethical treatment of its employees, environmental and sustainability issues, animal testing and charitable donations. This is reproduced in Figure 10.8.

Ted Baker's *Ethical Code of Conduct* (Ted Baker, 2011c) is not reproduced here but is a supplementary document that contains additional information about the

Figure 10.8 Example of website CSR

Ted's Ethical Statement

At our head office, stores and warehouses we are working tirelessly to reduce the amount of waste we send to landfill, and we would love you to help us by thinking about your waste too. After all, one man's trash is another man's treasure.

We especially want to make sure that all electrical products are taken care of properly; things like batteries can be extremely harmful to the environment if not disposed of correctly. Within the UK, we have grouped together with other retailers and joined the 'Distributor Take Back Scheme', helping the UK's local councils with the provision of improved recycling facilities for you as part of our commitment to the UK and European WEEE Directive (Waste Electrical and Electronic Equipment).

This is why on these products we display the crossed-out wheelie bin symbol. Please do not dispose of these with your household waste. For our UK customers, please take them to your local recycling centre run by your local council. You can find your closest centre at **www.recycle-more.co.uk**. Here you can also find out where to recycle things as diverse as fridges, milk cartons and even your old Ted clothes.

We also believe in playing fair. It's not just about being honest and open in the way we do business. We encourage our suppliers to do the same. Important as those points are, it's bigger than that, Global in fact.

You see we also have a responsibility to do right by the environment in terms of reducing our waste and consumption of resources. In other words, keeping our carbon footprint as dainty as possible.

We have joined forces with MADE-BY, a not for profit association who are helping Ted to look at our garments a bit more closely, from the fibres we use to make the products to the conditions for the people who work within our factories. They have helped us to set targets to continuously improve the overall sustainability of our collections, and you will soon be able see our progress measured against MADE-BY's internationally accredited and recognised benchmarks on their website**www.made-by.org/**

Environment
Ted knows two heads are better than one. With this in mind, he's become a member of the Green 500 organisation. The leading companies in London that make up the Green 500 have been working together to collectively cut their carbon emissions by 1.5 million tonnes over the last 2 ½ years, in line with the London Mayor's Energy Strategy. In summer 2010 Ted became a proud Platinum award holder for the Green 500. For more information click here **www.green500.co.uk/**

Ethical Conduct
Ted likes to know his employees are taken care of. The factories and overseas organisations we work with are reputable firms and we've built trustworthy relationships with them over many years, and in 2010 Ted made another friend and partner in MADE-BY. We are committed to working with MADE-BY on a step-by-step action plan that we have created to help improve the overall sustainability of our collections, across the whole supply chain.

Ted likes to know his employees are taken care of. We have an ethical **Code of Conduct** for those who work directly with Ted Baker - click **here** to read it.

Sustainability
Ted Baker wares are built to last – we do not deal in disposable clothing. Our quality fabrics are sourced from highly regarded mills, and Ted's classic styles can be worn for many seasons. Many of our garments are also made more sustainable fibres such as Organic Cotton and Tencel, and as part of our work with MADE-BY we are aiming to improve the quantities of these fibres within our collections over time. Read our fabrics guide for more information on the materials we use and where they come from.

Beauty
Our policy is that we do not test on animals, nor do we use animal derived ingredients in our products. The only exception to this (and this is only really relevant to Vegans) is that we do use beeswax in some of our hair waxes.

Charity
We donate thousands of pounds to charity each year, but being a modest fellow, Ted doesn't like to shout about it. By donating gifts, funds and getting involved with events, we've worked with a variety of groups, ranging from individual fundraisers to large research organisations.

Source: Ted Baker (2011b).

company's ethical employment practices, including details of its policies of supply a safe and healthy working environment, to pay a living wage to workers and to outlaw the use of child labour (see Ted Baker, 2011c). These additional web-based CSR disclosures are voluntary and supply much-needed extra contextual information about Ted Baker's CSR responsibilities. However, Ted Baker's disclosures must not be seen as an exemplar of CSR practice, as many worldwide companies, including Royal Dutch Shell, McDonalds, Nokia, Bayer and Puma, produce far greater levels of detailed voluntary CSR information. Royal Dutch Shell, for example, produces a voluntary sustainability report that includes annual environmental and social performance data about its generation of greenhouse gas emissions, worker injury levels and total expenditure on community development projects (Royal Dutch Shell, 2010).

The importance of CSR is growing and stakeholder groups within society are increasingly demanding disclosure of information about the social and environmental impact of business operations. While legal changes have underlined the importance of CSR disclosure, there is still room for improvement. For example, during 2010 60% of FTSE 100 companies failed to link CSR to their overall business strategy in their annual reports, and only 38% provided a specific CSR governance discussion in their management statements (Black Sun, 2010).

10.8   Conclusions

The regulatory framework provided by UK GAAP ensures that the statutory annual report and accounts communicate high-quality, reliable information and allow users to assess the stewardship of management. The additional guidance provided by the IFAC Code of Ethics, the UK Corporate Governance Code and those relating to CSR aid this objective. In this chapter we have examined the main principles of the international code of ethics and reviewed the development of the UK Code. We have also examined how these codes and notions of corporate social responsibility (CSR) are integrated into UK financial reporting practice. We have also looked at examples of the application of the UK Code and CSR disclosures in a premium listed company on the London Stock Exchange and compared them with disclosure requirements of other types and sizes of business.

Professional accountants must abide by a code of ethics which gives them guidance on how to do their work with integrity, objectivity and competence, even if this gives rise to conflict with the directors and managers of the reporting entity. Corporate governance is an important aspect of management and the aim of the UK Code is to promote best practice. Companies should comply with the spirit of the UK Code rather than devise mechanisms that create the illusion of compliance. The same is true in terms of CSR. A business must accept that it has a responsibility to all stakeholders and disclose meaningful information about the social and environmental impact of its operations.

Practice questions

1 Explain why professional accountancy bodies issue codes of ethics for their members.

2 Define the term 'corporate governance' and explain its importance to investors.

3 Define the term 'corporate social responsibility' and explain why a company has a responsibility to society.

4 Obtain a copy of the annual report and accounts for two public limited companies and compare the information they disclose on corporate governance. Write a summary analysing the differences in the wording used and noting any non-compliance with the UK Code of Corporate Governance.

5 Select one public limited company and analyse the data provided on corporate governance and on corporate social responsibility. Interpret your findings from the perspective of:
(a) a present or potential investor
(b) a supplier
(c) a customer
(d) a member of the general public.

References

Black Sun (2010) 'Talking the talk or walking the walk: A comprehensive analysis of FTSE 100 corporate responsibility reporting trends, benchmarks and best practice in Annual Reports'. Available from: http://www.blacksunplc.com/corporate/ideas_insight/index.jsp (accessed 6 December 2011).

Cadbury (1992) *The Report of the Committee on the Financial Aspects of Corporate Governance*, December. London: Gee Professional Publishing.

EC (2002) *Comparative Study of Corporate Governance Codes Relevant to the European Union and Its Member States*. Available at: http://ec.europa.eu/internal_market/company/docs/corpgov/corp-gov-codes-rpt-part1_en.pdf (accessed 6 December 2011).

EC (2011a) European Corporate Governance Forum page. Available at: http://ec.europa.eu/internal_market/company/ecgforum/studies_en.htm (accessed 6 December 2011).

EC (2011b) *Green Paper: The EU Corporate Governance Framework*. Available at: http://ec.europa.eu/internal_market/company/docs/modern/com2011-164_en.pdf (accessed 6 December 2011).

FRC (2009) FRC to review the Combined Code, Press release, 18 March. Available at: http://www.frc.org.uk/press/pub2024.html (accessed 6 December 2011).

FRC (2010a) *The UK Corporate Governance Code*. London: Financial Reporting Council. Available at: http://www.frc.org.uk/documents/pagemanager/Corporate_Governance/UK%20Corp%20Gov%20Code%20June%202010.pdf (accessed 6 December 2011).

FRC (2010b) *The UK Stewardship Code*. London: Financial Reporting Council. Available at: http://www.frc.org.uk/images/uploaded/documents/UK%20Stewardship%20Code%20July%2020103.pdf (accessed 6 December 2011).

Greenbury, R. (1995) *Directors Remuneration: Report of a Study Group*. London: Gee Publishing.

Hampel, R. (1998) *Committee on Corporate Governance Final Report*. London: Gee Publishing.

Hearson, M. and Morser, A. (2007) *Let's Clean up Fashion: 2007 Update*. Available at: http://www.waronwant.org/attachments/Lets%20Clean%20up%20Fashion%20-%20Update%202007.pdf (accessed 6 December 2011).

Higgs, D. (2003) *Review of the Role and Effectiveness of Non-Executive Directors*. London: DTI.

IESBA (2009) *Code of Ethics for Professional Accountants*. New York: International Ethics Standards Board for Accountants. Available at: http://www.ifac.org/sites/default/files/publications/files/2010-handbook-of-the-code-o.pdf (accessed 6 December 2011).

Law, J. (ed.) (2010) *Dictionary of Accounting*, 4th edition. Oxford: Oxford University Press.

Mallin, C. (2009) *Corporate Governance*, 3rd edition. Oxford: Oxford University Press.

Marks and Spencer (2011) *Marks and Spencer Group Plc Annual Report and Financial Statements 2011*. Available at: http://corporate.marksandspencer.com/documents/publications/2011/annual%20report%202011 (accessed 6 December 2011).

Royal Dutch Shell (2010) *Sustainability Report 2010*. Available at: http://sustainabilityreport.shell.com/2010/servicepages/downloads/files/all_shell_sr10.pdf (accessed 6 December 2011).

Smith Committee (2003) Audit Committees Combined Code Guidance. London: FRC.

Solomon, J. (2007) *Corporate Governance and Accountability*, 2nd edition. Chichester: John Wiley.

Sustainability (2004) *Gearing Up: From Corporate Responsibility to Good Governance and Scaleable Solutions*. London: Sustainability.

Ted Baker (2011a) *Ted Baker Report and Accounts 2010/2011*. London: Ted Baker PLC. Available at: http://www.tedbakerplc.com/ted/uploads/results/TedBakerAnnualReport2011.pdf (accessed 6 December 2011).

Ted Baker (2011b) *Ted's Ethical Statement*. Available at: http://www.tedbaker.com/about_us/our_policies/content.aspx#ethical_statement (accessed 6 December 2011).

Ted Baker (2011c) *Ted's Ethical Code of Conduct*. Available at: http://externalresources.tedbaker.com/legaldocs/codes_of_conduct.pdf (accessed 6 December 2011).

The Body Shop (2011) *About Us*. Available at: http://www.thebodyshop.co.uk/_en/_gb/services/aboutus_company.aspx (accessed 6 December 2011).

Tyson, L. (2003) *The Tyson Report on the Recruitment and Development of Non-Executive Directors*. London: London Business School. Available at:

http://www.thecapability.uk.com/postboylbs/templates/non-personalised/documents/Tyson_Report_June_2003.pdf (accessed 6 December 2011).

Turnbull, N. (1999) *Internal control: Guidance for Directors on the Combined Code*. London: ICAEW.

War on Want (2010) *Fashion Victims II: How UK Clothing Retailers Are Keeping Workers in Poverty*. Available at: http://www.waronwant.org/attachments/Fashion%20Victims%20II.pdf (accessed 6 December 2011).

Management accounting

11 Importance of cost information

Learning objectives

When you have studied this chapter, you should be able to:

- explain why it is important to know the cost of making a product or providing a service
- distinguish between direct costs and indirect costs
- construct a simple statement to calculate the total cost per unit
- calculate the selling price based on the total cost per unit.

11.1 Introduction

As you will remember from earlier chapters, financial accounting is the branch of accounting concerned with classifying, measuring and recording the economic transactions of an entity in accordance with established principles, legal requirements and accounting standards. It is primarily concerned with communicating a true and fair view of the financial performance and financial position of an entity to external parties at the end of the accounting period. Financial reporting is a key part of financial accounting and refers to the statutory disclosure of general purpose financial information by limited liability entities via the annual report and accounts. This means that the format and content of the financial statements are guided by a regulatory framework for financial reporting. In this third part of the book we focus on management accounting, which has evolved from financial accounting and is concerned with techniques that provide information to internal users.

In this chapter we are going to start looking at a particular aspect of management accounting known as *cost accounting*. Cost accounting is concerned with providing timely and detailed information to management about the cost of manufacturing goods or providing services. In this chapter we will explain why management needs systems for supplying detailed information about costs and clarifying what we mean by *cost*. We also explain what is meant by a *cost unit* and a *cost centre* and look at the various ways in which cost can be classified. We then demonstrate how the elements of cost are built up to calculate the total cost per unit and how this cost information can be used to establish the selling price per unit.

11.2   Management's need for information

Research suggests that accounting systems and the information they provide develop according to management's needs – in other words, on a contingency basis (Gordon and Miller, 1976; Chapman, 1997). During the early stages of the development of the business the owner-manager obtains information using informal methods and relies on tacit knowledge. As the number of business transactions increases, this informal personal control by the owner-manager becomes stretched and is replaced by formal delegated methods. This does not mean that formerly information and control had been poor, but that they are no longer appropriate to the size and complexity of the business (Perren, Berry and Partridge, 1999).

Table 11.1 summarizes the key characteristics of small firms and compares them with those of their larger counterparts, where it is likely that the need for more detailed and timely information will have led to the development of formal systems of control.

Table 11.1   Typical characteristics of small and large firms

Small firms	Large firms
Typically 1–2 owners	Many owners
Likely to be owner-managed	Managed by managers/directors
Little delegation of control	Control is delegated
Operations are relatively simple	Operations are complex and divided into functional areas
Multitasking is common	Need for functional specialists
Systems tend to be informal	Systems tend to be formal
Reliance on tacit knowledge	Reliance on explicit information

In order to run a business successfully, those responsible for management need to know the *cost* of running the business. Costs include:

- the cost of sales, such as the cost of goods sold in a trading business, the cost of goods manufactured in a manufacturing business or the cost of services sold in a business in the service sector
- the overhead expenses and other expenditure.

There are a number of different ways of defining cost, but we will start with a general definition.

Key definition

Cost is the expenditure on goods and services required to carry out the operations of an organization.

Source: Law (2010, p. 115).

The calculation of the cost of sales for a sole trader is:

Opening inventory + Purchases – Closing inventory

You will remember from Chapter 1 that the accounting principles guide the accountant to value opening inventory and purchases at the *historical cost*, and to value closing inventory prudently at the lower of cost or net realizable value. Therefore, calculating the cost of goods sold for a trading business is relatively straightforward. However, calculating of the cost of goods manufactured (for an entity in the manufacturing sector) or calculating the cost of services (for an entity in the service sector) is more complex. This is made even more difficult if more than one type of product or service is produced, because the cost of each one must be built up from the individual elements of cost that can be identified.

Activity

To understand the importance of cost information it is useful to consider why managers need such information. Why do you think managers of a business in the manufacturing sector need to know the cost of making a product or supplying a service?

Business is about making money and those managing the business are responsible for ensuring that it makes a profit. Therefore, the main reasons why managers need to have cost information are:

- To value inventory – In a manufacturing business, managers need cost information to help them value inventories of raw materials, work in progress and unsold finished goods.
- To plan production – It would be very difficult to determine the best way to plan production without knowing the relevant costs. It is necessary to know the cost of all the elements making up the production process and the funds required to support them. Such costs are not confined to materials and labour, but also include machinery, buildings, transport, administration, maintenance and many other items.
- To maintain control – Managers have no control if they do not know the costs incurred and are unable to compare them with the original plan. This would lead to the organization's resources being employed inefficiently, resulting in waste and, in the worst circumstances, the complete failure of the organization.
- To aid decision making – It is imperative that managers have knowledge of costs for the correct decisions to be taken. For example, managers need information about

costs to decide whether it would be worthwhile investing in new manufacturing machinery, to evaluate alternative ways of carrying out activities and to determine the selling prices of products and services.

Although we have used an example of a manufacturing business, many of the above reasons apply to businesses in other industrial sectors.

Activity

Despite having stressed the importance of knowing the costs involved in making a product or providing a service, they are not always easy to identify. Imagine that you buy a box of 10 computer disks for £15 on Friday. On Sunday a friend asks you to sell him one for some urgent work he is doing. You know that if you were to replace that single disk on Monday it would cost you £2.00. What is the cost of the disk?

(a) £1.50
(b) £2.00
(c) Both these figures
(d) Neither of these figures

You may have answered this by taking the original cost of 10 disks (£15) and dividing it by the number of disks to reach the answer of £1.50, or you may have decided that the cost is Monday's price of £2.00. You may be surprised to know that in some senses all the answers are correct. However, to decide the most appropriate answer, we need to define what we mean by *cost* precisely and put it in a context. As you can see, one difficulty we have is that our view of cost is determined by:

- whether we are buyers or sellers
- the context in which we are making our calculations
- our reasons for wanting the information.

11.3   Cost accounting

To meet managers' needs for precise information about costs, a branch of management accounting known as *cost accounting* has developed, which is based on analysing the costs relating to *cost units* and *cost centres*.

Key definition

Cost accounting refers to the techniques used in collecting, processing and presenting financial and quantitative data within an organization to ascertain the cost of the cost centres, cost units and the various operations.

Source: Law (2010, p. 115).

All organizations provide an identifiable output, which may be in the form of a service, a product or both. The output of a business can be measured by devising some form of *cost unit*. A cost unit is a quantitative unit of the product or service to which costs are allocated. The type of cost unit depends on the type of industry. In a manufacturing industry there may be a large number of identical products. For example, a brick manufacturer may have a cost unit of 1,000 bricks, because the cost of one brick is so small that it would be difficult to measure. In the service sector the cost unit may be of a more abstract nature. For example, in a hotel the cost unit may be a room occupied.

Activity

Suggest appropriate cost units for the following businesses:

- **a car manufacturer**
- **a carrier bag manufacturer**
- **a transport business**
- **a plumber**
- **a sports and leisure centre**
- **a hairdresser.**

Some of these businesses may have been more difficult than others to find suitable cost units for, particularly if you are not familiar with the industries. However, you may have identified some of the following types of cost unit:

- A car manufacturer producing a range of different models could use each model as a cost unit. If the same organization manufactures the engine, gearbox, body and electrical system, these could also be treated as separate cost units.
- A carrier bag manufacturer has the same problems as a brick manufacturer: the costs identified with manufacturing one carrier bag are so small that they cannot be measured. Therefore, a suitable cost unit might be 1,000 bags of each type produced.
- A transport business is a bit more difficult. You need to consider what information management would find useful. This might be the costs associated with moving 1 tonne of goods over 1 mile. Therefore, the cost unit will be 1 tonne/mile.
- Plumbers often work on a number of small jobs, which may vary from fitting a bathroom suite to replacing a tap washer. The plumber needs to know the cost of each job and so a suitable cost unit would be each job.
- In the case of a sports and leisure centre the management needs to know the separate costs of supplying badminton, squash, swimming, table tennis, keep fit, etc. for a period of time. Therefore, a suitable cost unit would be each activity for an hour.
- A hairdresser is likely to offer a number of standard services, such as cut and blow dry, restyling, colouring, etc. Therefore, a suitable cost unit would be each standard service.

As you can see from these examples, many businesses offer a range of different products or services. Before the cost of each product or service can be calculated, a quantitative unit must be identified to which costs can be allocated.

Key definition

A cost unit is a unit of production for which the management of an organization wishes to collect the costs incurred.

Source: Law (2010, p. 119).

The cost unit can be:

- the final product (for example, a chair or a table in a furniture factory)
- a sub-assembly of a more complex product (for example, a car chassis in the motor industry)
- a batch of products where the unit cost of an individual product is very small (for example, a batch of 120 light bulbs in a light bulb factory).

In a manufacturing business it should be fairly easy to identify the cost units as being the products made. In a service organization there may not be any identifiable cost units. In a hotel the cost unit used might be the room occupancy; in a distribution company a cost unit might be a tonne/mile (the cost involved in moving 1 tonne of goods 1 mile); in a dating agency it may be the cost of matching one couple.

As well as calculating the costs for each cost unit, management will also probably need to know the costs for particular *cost centres*. A cost centre is an identifiable part of the organization for which costs can be collected, such as a location, function, activity or item of equipment.

Activity

Indicate which of the following could be cost centres in the following two businesses:

Toy manufacturer	*Hotel*
Assembly department	Kitchen
Stores department	Cost of drinks sold
Sales team	Reception area
Specialized moulding machine	Laundry
Clerical salaries	Restaurant

You may not know anything about the manufacture of toys, but the definition of a cost centre given above should have helped you to identify the first four of these as possible cost centres. Clerical salaries are usually an expense, not a cost centre. The specialized moulding machine may be a cost centre if it is sufficiently important and complex to allow a number of costs to be identified with that particular activity. Of course, not all toy manufacturers would use the above cost centres, but they are all areas of activity where managers may need to know the costs. As far as the hotel is concerned, the cost of drinks sold is an item of expense, but all the others are potential cost centres.

Key definition

A cost centre is the area of an organization for which costs are collected for the purpose of cost ascertainment, planning, decision making and control.

Source: Law (2010, p. 116).

Cost centres are of two main types:

- *production cost centres* are those concerned with making a product
- *service cost centres* provide a service to other parts of the organization.

Identifying cost centres is relatively easy as they are usually clearly defined. One example is that of a factory canteen or a college refectory. In a manufacturing business, departments may be referred to as shops (for example, the machine shop). The sort of financial information that would be available for a canteen include employees' wages, the cost of electricity used for cooking, lighting and heating, the cost of food and beverages, etc., and the meals may be used as the cost units. Figure 11.1 shows typical cost centres in a light bulb factory where costs are collected for a cost unit consisting of a batch of 120 light bulbs.

Some businesses do not formally identify their cost centres or cost units, but answering the following questions should help you to identify them:

- What can be regarded as the cost centres and cost units in the organization?
- What financial information is generated in respect of potential cost centres and cost units?
- Is someone directly responsible for any of them or able to influence them?

Figure 11.1   Typical cost centres in a factory

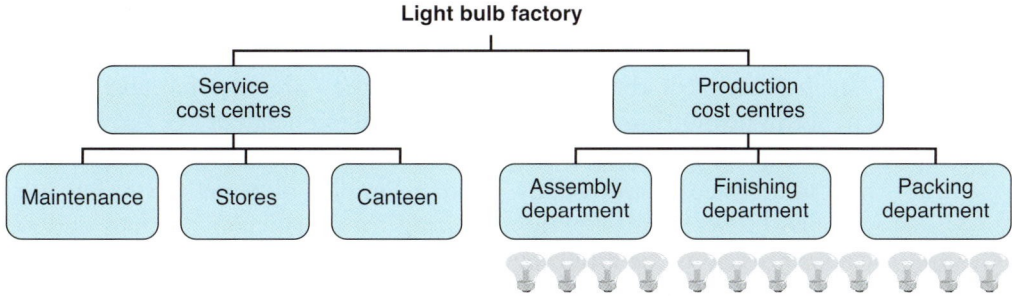

11.4   Classifying costs and expenses

In Chapter 7 we explained that expenditure can be divided into revenue expenditure and capital expenditure:

- *Revenue expenditure* is the collective term for the costs and expenses that are written off in the statement of comprehensive income for the accounting period to which they relate.
- *Capital expenditure* is the collective term for the cost of non-current assets that are capitalized in the statement of financial position.

Although it is useful to know the total revenue expenditure for an accounting period, it is even more useful if revenue expenditure is broken down into individual costs and expenses. By classifying costs, we can obtain more detailed information and use it in a variety of ways for planning, controlling and decision making. In addition, classifying costs helps us to understand better what is meant by the term cost.

Costs can be classified by:

- The *nature* of the cost, such as those that can be identified for materials, labour and expenses, and those for materials that can be divided into the different types of raw materials, maintenance materials, cleaning materials, etc.
- The *function* of costs, such as production costs, administration costs, selling and distribution costs.
- Whether they are *product costs*, which can be identified with the cost unit and are part of the value of inventory, or *period costs*, such as selling costs and administrative expenses, which are deducted as expenses in the current period.
- Whether they are *direct costs*, which can be identified with a specific cost unit, or *indirect costs*, which cannot be identified with a specific cost unit, although they may be traced directly to a particular cost centre. Indirect costs must be shared by the cost units. Examples of direct costs are the cost of materials used to make a product; the cost of labour if employees are paid according to the number of products made or services provided; the cost of expenses, such as subcontract work. Examples of indirect costs are expenses such as rent and managers' salaries.
- The *behaviour* of the cost and whether they are *variable costs*, which in total change in proportion with the level of production activity or *fixed costs*, which are not changed by fluctuations in production levels. Direct costs are usually variable and indirect costs are usually fixed. Examples of direct costs that are fixed are patents, licences and copyright relating to a particular product and some direct expenses such as the hire of a particular piece of equipment to produce a specific order.

Figure 11.2 summarizes this typology.

Activity

Classify the following costs into direct costs, indirect costs, variable costs and fixed costs:

- materials used in the product
- cost of renting the factory

- **insurance of the factory**
- **depreciation**
- **maintenance of machinery**
- **canteen**
- **supervisors' salaries**
- **production workers' wages**
- **accountants' salaries.**

Figure 11.2 Classifying expenditure

Product direct costs (always variable costs)	Indirect costs (usually fixed costs)
• Direct materials (e.g. components) • Direct labour (e.g. piecework wages) • Direct expenses (e.g. subcontractor)	• Production overheads • Non-production overheads (e.g. administrative expenses, distribution costs, research & development costs)

Even if you do not have any experience of working in a manufacturing environment, you should have been able to work out the answers from the definitions of direct and indirect costs. Materials can be identified with the product and are therefore direct costs; so too are the production workers' wages if they are paid according to the number of units produced rather than a flat rate irrespective of the level of production. Rent, insurance, maintenance of machinery, canteen and the salaries cannot be identified with a single product, but must be shared over a number of products; therefore these are indirect costs. In a service industry, the same principles apply.

You may have had more difficulty in distinguishing between fixed and variable costs. One thing you may have noticed is that direct costs in our example are also variable costs and the indirect costs are also fixed costs. For example, the materials used in the product can be identified directly with the product, and the more items produced, the higher the total cost of materials used. Therefore, these product direct costs are variable costs. On the other hand, rent and insurance for the period remain the same, regardless of the quantity of products produced, and therefore these are classified as fixed costs.

We will now look more closely at the difference between fixed and variable costs using an example. Sam Reeves has a taxi business. The average mileage by a taxi for 3 months is 15,000 miles and the following table shows the quarterly costs, analysed by nature:

Expense	Cost per quarter £
Driver's salary	2,670
Petrol and oil	1,050
Maintenance and repairs	450
Tax and insurance	1,110
Depreciation	870

We can use the details of Sam's business expenses as the basis for calculating further cost information. For example, we can add up the costs so that Sam can find out that the total costs per quarter for one taxi are £6,150. From this we can calculate the total cost per mile:

$$\frac{\text{Total costs}}{\text{Total mileage}} = \frac{£6{,}150}{15{,}000 \text{ miles}} = 41\text{p per mile}$$

We can now calculate the cost per mile for each of the expenses:

Expense	Cost per quarter £	Cost per mile Pence
Driver's salary	2,670	17.8
Petrol and oil	1,050	7.0
Maintenance and repairs	450	3.0
Tax and insurance	1,110	7.4
Depreciation	870	5.8
Total	6,150	41.0

Sam now has a considerable amount of information, including the total cost per mile, which is further analysed by the nature of the expense. However, there are some problems if Sam tries to use this cost information without understanding the difference between fixed and variable costs. For example, he may want to know what the cost is per mile if the taxi travelled 30,000 miles in one quarter. Your immediate response may be to say that the cost per mile would remain at 41p. However, on consideration, you may have seen that the cost per mile is likely to be lower. This is because the total fixed costs (the cost of the driver's salary, taxation, insurance and depreciation) will remain the same, even though the mileage has doubled. On the other hand, the total variable costs (the cost of petrol and oil) will change in direct proportion to the change in the level of activity. This means that if activity doubles (in our example, if mileage doubles), the variable costs will double. We shall be looking at the importance of fixed and variable costs again in Chapter 15, but for the moment you need to remember that calculating the average total cost per unit can be misleading if there are significant changes in the activity level of the business.

11.5 Elements of total cost

The *total cost* of a product or cost unit is built up from a number of different elements. In order to identify these elements, costs are classified according to their nature, function, whether they are product or period costs and whether they are direct costs or indirect costs, as we described in the previous section. The following cost statement shows the *elements of total cost* in a typical manufacturing business:

Total cost statement	
	£
Product direct costs	
Direct materials	X
Direct labour	X
Direct expenses	X
Prime cost	X
Production overheads	X
Production cost	X
Indirect costs	
Administration costs	X
Distribution costs	X
Research and development costs	X
	X
Total cost	X

The *direct costs*, which are costs that can be traced directly to the product or cost unit, are added together to give what is known as the *prime cost*. Then the production overheads are added to give the *production cost*. Production overheads are the indirect production costs that cannot be traced directly to the product or cost unit. Finally, the non-production overheads are added to arrive at the total cost.

Direct costs can be classified as:

- *direct materials*, which are the cost of materials and components used to make the product
- *direct labour*, which are the costs of employing the workforce that converts the direct materials into the finished product
- *direct expenses*, which are not always incurred but include such costs as subcontract work or special tools and equipment bought for a particular order.

Indirect costs can be classified as:

- *administration costs*, which are the non-production costs of operating the business
- *distribution costs*, which are the costs of promoting, selling and delivering the products (and any after-sales services)
- *research and development costs*, which are not always present but are the costs associated with developing or improving products and production processes.

Key definitions

- Direct costs are product costs that can be traced directly to a product or cost unit.
- Indirect costs are expenses that cannot be traced directly to a product or cost unit and are therefore overheads.

Source: Law (2010, pp. 145 and 230).

Activity

Jon Hazel is the owner-manager of Hazelwood Products Ltd that makes 10 traditionally crafted bookcases per week. The costs for week ending 7 January are as follows:

Direct materials	£440
Direct labour	£660
Production overheads	£200
Administration costs	£80
Distribution costs	£60

The business has no direct expenses or research and development costs. Using the following pro forma, calculate the total cost for the week.

Hazelwood Products Ltd Total cost w/e 7 January (10 bookcases)	
	£
Direct costs	
Direct materials	
Direct labour	_____
Prime cost	
Production overheads	_____
Production cost	_____
Indirect costs	
Administration costs	
Distribution costs	_____
	_____
Total cost	=====

Your answer should look like this:

```
            Hazelwood Products Ltd
    Total cost w/e 7 January (10 bookcases)
                                            £
Direct costs
Direct materials                           440
Direct labour                              660
Prime cost                               1,100
Production overheads                       200
Production cost                          1,300
Indirect costs
Administration costs                        80
Distribution costs                          60
                                           140
Total cost                               1,440
```

Now he knows the total cost per week, Jon can ensure that the business has sufficient funds to support these costs. The most important source of funds will be the sales revenue generated from selling the bookcases and further analysis of the above cost information will help Jon decide on an appropriate selling price for the bookcases.

Activity

Using the same layout as before, construct a statement showing the total cost per unit (in this case, one bookcase). As this is a very simple business, you can apportion the overheads by dividing them by the number of units produced. In addition, calculate the selling price if Hazelwood Products Ltd wants to make a profit that represents a mark-up of 40% on the production cost.

You should have found this fairly straightforward and the answer is given below:

```
            Hazelwood Products Ltd
                Total cost (1 unit)
                                            £
Direct costs
Direct materials                            44
Direct labour                               66
Prime cost                                 110
Production overheads                        20
Production cost                            130
Indirect costs
Administration costs                         8
Distribution costs                           6
                                            14
Total cost                                 144
Profit (£130 × 40%)                         52
Selling price                              196
```

The total cost per unit is £144 and all you need to do is add the profit element based on 40% of the production cost (£130 × 40% = £52) to arrive at a selling price of £196. In other words, if each bookcase is sold for £196, the total cost per unit of £144 will be covered and the business will make a profit of £52.

11.6   Conclusions

In this chapter we have looked the importance of cost information to those responsible for the management of a business, particularly those in the manufacturing and service sectors. Cost accounting techniques require costs to be classified so that the cost of all the designated cost centres and cost units can be ascertained. Production cost centres are those concerned with making a product, while service costs centres provide a service to other parts of the organization. A cost unit can be the final product, a sub-assembly or a batch of products.

The classification of costs involves distinguishing between direct and indirect costs, variable and fixed costs, the nature of costs and the function of costs. The cost per unit is calculated by identifying the different elements of cost: the direct costs plus a fair share of the indirect costs. A percentage mark-up representing profit can be added to the cost per unit to establish the selling price per unit.

Practice questions

1 Explain the purpose of cost accounting and why it is important for managers to have cost information.

2 Describe the main classifications of cost.

3 Classify the following costs incurred in a manufacturing business into production costs, selling costs, distribution costs and administration costs:
   (a) factory rent
   (b) insurance of office buildings
   (c) electricity for powering machinery
   (d) electricity for office lighting and heating
   (e) tax and insurance of delivery vehicles
   (f) depreciation of factory machinery
   (g) depreciation of office equipment
   (h) commission paid to sales team
   (i) salaries paid to accounts office staff
   (j) factory manager's salary
   (k) delivery drivers' salaries
   (l) factory security guards' salaries
   (m) piecework wages paid to factory operatives
   (n) salary paid to managing director's secretary
   (o) salaries paid to factory canteen staff

(p) fees paid to advertising agency
(q) maintenance of machinery
(r) accounting software
(s) bonuses for factory staff
(t) training course for clerical staff.

4 Petra Petrova is the owner-manager of Petra Pots Ltd, which makes plant pots. The business plans to produce 2,000 units over the next month and each unit requires the same amount of materials and takes the same time to produce. The expected costs for next month are as follows:

	£
Rent:	
Factory	1,000
Office	400
Lighting and heating:	
Factory	2,000
Office	800
Power	700
Factory wages:	
Operators (piecework)	10,000
Maintenance staff (fixed)	1,500
Canteen staff (fixed)	2,500
Sand, cement and clay	6,000
Depreciation:	
Moulds	2,200
Factory fixtures and fittings	800
Office equipment	200
Office salaries	1,800
Sales team's salaries and commission	2,200
Sales team's car expenses	1,600
Delivery expenses	500
Cement mixer repairs	900
Finishing paint	200
Packing	800

Required

(a) Prepare a costing statement for Petra Pots Ltd that shows the elements of cost and calculates the total cost of producing 2,000 pots.
(b) Interpret your statement by explaining the following terms:
- direct costs
- prime cost
- production cost
- indirect costs
- total cost.

5 Using the information for Petra Pots Ltd in question 4, construct a statement that shows the elements of total cost for one unit (as this is a very simple business, you can apportion the overheads by dividing them by the number of units produced). In addition, calculate the selling price of one unit if the business requires a profit margin based on 50% of the production cost.

References

Chapman, C. S. (1997) Reflections on a contingent view of accounting. *Accounting Organizations and Society* 22, 189–205.

Gordon, L. A. and Miller, D. (1976) A contingency framework for the design of accounting information systems. *Accounting Organizations and Society* 1(1), 59–69.

Law, J. (ed.) (2010) *Dictionary of Accounting*, 4th edition. Oxford: Oxford University Press.

Perren, L., Berry, A. and Partridge, M. (1999) The evolution of management information, control and decision-making processes in small growth-orientated service sector businesses: exploratory lessons from four cases of success. *Journal of Small Business and Enterprise Development* 5(4), 351–61.

12 Costing for product direct costs

Learning objectives

When you have studied this chapter, you should be able to:

- describe the main stages in controlling direct materials
- calculate the cost of direct materials and closing inventory using different costing methods
- describe the advantages and disadvantages of different costing methods
- describe and apply methods for costing direct labour and direct expenses.

12.1 Introduction

In Chapter 11 we identified the *prime cost* as one of the key components of the total cost of a cost unit. In this chapter we are going to examine the individual elements of the *prime cost*, which are the product direct costs relating to *direct materials*, *direct labour* and *direct expenses*.

Even in the smallest business, the minimum information required is the total for each of these different elements of cost that are incurred in producing the cost units. However, management usually needs more detailed information and a breakdown of the cost of each product or service helps them in their responsibility for planning, controlling and decision making. For example, managers need to know the cost of all the different materials used in making a product, the cost of the different types of labour in the factory, maintenance department, stores and canteen, and any direct expenses. Once systems have been established to collect this detailed information, the total cost of direct materials, the total cost of direct labour and the total cost of any direct expenses can be calculated for each product or service. For example, a car manufacturer can establish the prime cost of making a particular model; a civil engineering company can establish the prime cost of constructing a particular building; and a plumber can establish the prime cost for a particular job.

In this chapter we start by describing the procedures and documents used to record and control the purchase and receipt of materials used to produce a product or cost unit. We go on to examine two methods that are used for pricing issues of direct materials from stores and valuing the remaining inventory. We also describe the procedures and documents used to record the direct labour costs associated with each cost unit, which are related to the methods of remuneration for employees involved in production process. Finally, we discuss the difficulty of identifying direct expenses.

12.2 Material control

In a manufacturing business the control of materials used in the production process is essential. *Material control* is necessary to ensure that production is not delayed due to shortages of materials and it is equally important that the business does not tie up capital by storing excess quantities of inventory. In a well-managed business, materials are available in the right place, at the right time and in the right quantities, and all materials are properly accounted for.

> **Key definition**
>
> **Material is the production supplies of an organization that feature as revenue expenditure purchased from a third party ... Materials are not necessarily raw materials, but can include components and sub-assemblies used in the finished product.**
>
> *Source*: Law (2010, p. 278).

The cost of materials purchased from a supplier is classified as revenue expenditure. Materials can be divided into direct materials, which feature in the final product produced (such as wood and metal in furniture), or indirect materials, which are necessary to carry out production but do not feature in the final product (such as maintenance and cleaning materials). Initially, deliveries of materials are taken to the place where they will be stored (the stores) and records are kept of quantities received and prices paid. Depending on the amount of space needed to house the materials, the stores may consist of anything from a small stockroom to a large warehouse or secure yard from which they can be issued conveniently to production when they are required.

Some businesses have *just-in-time (JIT)* manufacturing systems in which products are produced in time to meet demand, rather than producing products in case they are needed. This greatly reduces or eliminates the need for large inventories of materials. In some cases the value of materials in stores is very high (for example, precious metals or other scarce resources used in the production process). Records should be maintained of the quantity of goods in store and it is essential that a physical count is made because of the possibility of errors and theft. This is known as *stocktaking* and should be done at least annually. It requires a substantial amount of work and can be very disruptive. Some organizations use continuous stocktaking, where employees check a few items every day so that all inventories are checked at least once a year.

The stores often carry many hundreds of different types of materials. Therefore the business requires an efficient and accurate system for recording and controlling the cost of materials. This can be either a manual or a computerized system. Although managers devise material control systems and procedures to suit their particular needs, there are a number of different prime documents used at each stage and each of these forms must be properly completed and authorized. The main stages in material control are as follows:

- The stores or production department sends a *purchase requisition* to the purchasing department, giving details of the quantity and type of materials required.
- The buyer in the purchasing department sends a *purchase order* to the supplier.
- The supplier sends the materials with a *goods received note*, which is checked against the materials received and the purchase order.
- The materials are added to the existing inventory in the stores and the quantity is added to the inventory level shown on the *bin card*.
- When materials are required, the production department sends a *materials requisition* to the stores and the stores issues the materials and deducts the quantity from the inventory level shown on the *bin card*. Periodic stocktaking ensures that a physical count of all inventories is made to confirm that the actual quantities support the levels shown on the bin cards.

Copies of all prime documents are sent to the accountant so that he or she can check that materials have been properly ordered and received before paying the supplier's invoice. The accountant also records all inventory movements (the quantity and value of receipts and issues of materials), and the quantity and value of inventory balances for each type of material are recorded in an *inventory account*. This allows the cost of materials used in each cost unit to be calculated.

Activity

Draw a diagram showing the flow of documents used to control the movement of materials.

The design of your diagram will depend on your creative abilities and the assumptions you have made, but you should have shown a logical flow of information that relates to the main stages in material control we have outlined in this section.

12.3   Costing direct materials

The purchase of direct materials used in the production process represents a substantial cost and managers require information to establish what these costs are. Having looked at the procedures for purchasing, storing and issuing materials, we now need to consider the methods used for *costing direct materials* issued to production. These focus on the price at which materials are issued from stores to production and an effective system ensures that:

- the correct materials are delivered
- materials are stored and issued only with proper authorization
- production is charged with the cost of materials used
- the inventory of materials in the stores is correctly valued.

Calculating the cost of direct materials can be a problem. For example, it may not be possible to identify each issue of materials with the corresponding receipt into stores or it may be complicated by the fact that materials have been received on different dates and at a number of different purchase prices. Fluctuating prices may be due to a number of reasons, such as the following:

- a general rise in the price of goods or services due to inflation or a general lowering of prices due to deflation
- variations in exchange rates if materials are purchased overseas
- shortages in the supply of materials
- temporary discounts, such as special offers.

There are a number of methods for costing materials issued to production. The method chosen not only has implications for the cost of the units produced, but also for the value of closing inventory remaining in the stores. Although some valuation methods might be satisfactory for management purposes, they are not suitable for valuing inventory for financial reporting purposes. You will remember from earlier chapters that IAS 2, *Inventories* requires that inventory is valued at the lower of cost or net realizable value. In a manufacturing business, cost refers to the total cost incurred in bringing the product to its present location and condition, including an appropriate proportion of production overhead costs. Therefore, to avoid having to use one method for management accounting purposes and another for financial accounting purposes, most businesses choose a method that is suitable for both. There are four main methods:

- The *standard cost* method uses predetermined planned costs known as standard costs. The standard cost is derived from a standard quantity of materials allowed for the production of a specific cost unit at standard direct materials price. This method of standard costing is closely associated with a system of budgetary control and we will be looking at these topics in subsequent chapters.
- The *unit cost* method is the simplest method as far as actual costs are concerned, but it can only be used in a relatively small business where the cost of purchasing

the specific direct materials used to produce the cost unit can be identified. As a business grows in terms of production volume and range of products, this is clearly no longer possible.

- The *first in, first out (FIFO) cost* method uses the price of the earliest consignment of materials for all issues to production until the quantity received at that price has been issued, then the price of the next consignment.
- The *continuous weighted average (CWA) cost* method uses the weighted average price of materials received, which is recalculated every time a new consignment of that item is received. The weighted average price is calculated as:

$$\frac{\text{Total value of inventory}}{\text{Total quantity of inventory}}$$

We will look at the last two methods in some detail.

Activity

Hazelwood Products Ltd started making bookshelves on 1 January. The goods received notes and the materials requisitions show the following receipts and issues of wood during the first 3 days. As you can see, Jon Hazel, the owner-manager, was able to negotiate a lower introductory price for the first delivery and then paid the regular price for the second delivery.

1 January	Received 50 units at £3.00 per unit
2 January	Received a further 50 units at £4.00 per unit
3 January	Issued 50 units to production

Complete the following record in the inventory account and calculate the cost of the 50 units issued to production on 3 January and 50 units remaining in inventory using FIFO cost and CWA cost.

FIFO	Receipts			Issues			Inventory balance	
January	Quantity	Price	Value	Quantity	Price	Value	Quantity	Value
		£	£		£	£		£
1								
2								
3						_____		
Total								

CWA	Receipts			Issues			Inventory balance	
January	Quantity	Price	Value	Quantity	Price	Value	Quantity	Value
		£	£		£	£		£
1								
2								
3						_____		
Total								

Check your answer against the solution below:

FIFO	Receipts			Issues			Inventory balance	
January	Quantity	Price	Value	Quantity	Price	Value	Quantity	Value
		£	£		£	£		£
1	50	3.00	150.00			50	150.00	
2	50	4.00	200.00			100	350.00	
3				50	3.00	150.00	50	200.00
Total						150.00		

CWA	Receipts			Issues			Inventory balance	
January	Quantity	Price	Value	Quantity	Price	Value	Quantity	Value
		£	£		£	£		£
1	50	3.00	150.00				50	150.00
2	50	4.00	200.00				100	350.00
3				50	3.50	175.00	50	175.00
Total						175.00		

If you compare the results, you can see that the total cost of materials issued to production (and hence the cost of direct materials used in the product) and the value of the inventory remaining in stores vary according to the method used.

Key definitions

First in, first out (FIFO) cost is a method of valuing units of raw materials or finished goods issued from [inventory] based on using the earliest unit value for pricing the issues until all the [inventory] received at that price has been used up. The next latest price is then used for pricing the issues, and so on. Because the issues are based on a FIFO cost, the valuation of closing [inventory] is described as being on the same FIFO basis.

Source: Law (2010, p. 192).

Continuous weighted average (CWA) cost is a method of valuing units of raw materials or finished goods issued from inventory based on the weighted-average price, which is recalculated every time a new consignment is received.

To make certain you fully understand the two methods, we will extend the illustration by adding further information. As the number of receipts and issues increase, Jon Hazel may find it is more efficient to use a spreadsheet to record the movement of inventory and calculate a continuous inventory balance, and you may wish to do so for the next activity.

Activity

Unfortunately, the wood Jon wanted was not available on 4 January and he had to purchase a more expensive type. However, he kept his order as small as possible and his supplier was able to meet his next order on 6 January. Using the following information, calculate the quantity and value of materials issued to production during the first week and the quantity and value of closing inventory at 7 January using FIFO cost and CWA cost.

1 January	Received 50 units at £3.00 per unit
2 January	Received 50 units at £4.00 per unit
3 January	Issued 50 units to production
4 January	Received 10 units at £5.00 per unit
5 January	Issued 40 units to production
6 January	Received 40 units at £4.00 per unit
7 January	Issued 30 units to production

Check your answer against the following tables.

FIFO	Receipts			Issues			Inventory balance	
January	Quantity	Price	Value	Quantity	Price	Value	Quantity	Value
		£	£		£	£		£
1	50	3.00	150.00				50	150.00
2	50	4.00	200.00				100	350.00
3				50	3.00	150.00	50	200.00
4	10	5.00	50.00				60	250.00
5				40	4.00	160.00	20	90.00
6	40	4.00	160.00				60	250.00
7				10	4.00	40.00	50	210.00
7				10	5.00	50.00	40	160.00
7				10	4.00	40.00	30	120.00
Total						440.00		

CWA	Receipts			Issues			Inventory balance	
January	Quantity	Price	Value	Quantity	Price	Value	Quantity	Value
		£	£		£	£		£
1	50	3.00	150.00				50	150.00
2	50	4.00	200.00				100	350.00
3				50	3.50	175.00	50	175.00
4	10	5.00	50.00				60	225.00
5				40	3.75	150.00	20	75.00
6	40	4.00	160.00				60	235.00
7				30	3.92	117.50	30	117.50
Total						442.50		

If you have used a spreadsheet to create the two different inventory accounts, you may find it useful to look at the illustrations showing the formulae in Figure 12.1. To reveal the formulae in an Excel Workbook (a file with the suffix .xlsx), click on Formulas in the main menu and select Show Formulas in the Formula Auditing tab. Deselect Show Formulas when you want to return to data view.

The main thing to remember about using CWA is that you need to recalculate the

Figure 12.1 Illustration of formulae in an Excel Workbook

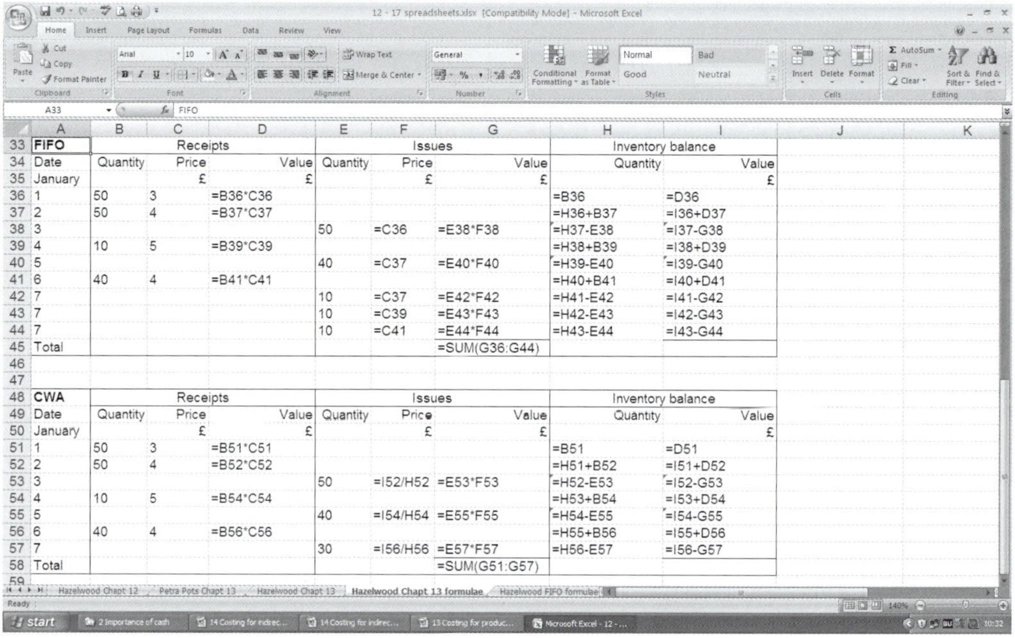

	A	B	C	D	E	F	G	H	I
33	FIFO		Receipts			Issues		Inventory balance	
34	Date	Quantity	Price	Value	Quantity	Price	Value	Quantity	Value
35	January		£	£		£	£		£
36	1	50	3	=B36*C36				=B36	=D36
37	2	50	4	=B37*C37				=H36+B37	=I36+D37
38	3				50	=C36	=E38*F38	=H37-E38	=I37-G38
39	4	10	5	=B39*C39				=H38+B39	=I38+D39
40	5				40	=C37	=E40*F40	=H39-E40	=I39-G40
41	6	40	4	=B41*C41				=H40+B41	=I40+D41
42	7				10	=C37	=E42*F42	=H41-E42	=I41-G42
43	7				10	=C39	=E43*F43	=H42-E43	=I42-G43
44	7				10	=C41	=E44*F44	=H43-E44	=I43-G44
45	Total						=SUM(G36:G44)		
46									
47									
48	CWA		Receipts			Issues		Inventory balance	
49	Date	Quantity	Price	Value	Quantity	Price	Value	Quantity	Value
50	January		£	£		£	£		£
51	1	50	3	=B51*C51				=B51	=D51
52	2	50	4	=B52*C52				=H51+B52	=I51+D52
53	3				50	=I52/H52	=E53*F53	=H52-E53	=I52-G53
54	4	10	5	=B54*C54				=H53+B54	=I53+D54
55	5				40	=I54/H54	=E55*F55	=H54-E55	=I54-G55
56	6	40	4	=B56*C56				=H55+B56	=I55+D56
57	7				30	=I56/H56	=E57*F57	=H56-E57	=I56-G57
58	Total						=SUM(G51:G57)		

average price at which inventory will be issued if a new consignment of that particular item has been received. This means calculating the new total value of inventory and dividing it by the new total quantity of inventory at that date. To find the cost of materials issued on 3 January you should have divided the inventory value of £350 by the quantity of inventory (100 units) to arrive at £3.50 per unit. Another consignment is received on 4 January, so the cost of materials issued on 5 January is the new inventory value of £225 divided by the new quantity of inventory (60 units), which is £3.75 per unit. Since further inventory is delivered on 6 January, you need to divide the new inventory value of £235 by the new quantity of inventory (60 units), which is £3.92 per unit (rounded to the nearest 1p). This is the new weighted average price used for the materials issued on 7 January.

In Chapter 11 we looked at the total costs for Hazelwood Products Ltd for week ending 7 January, when 10 bookcases were produced, in the context of describing the different elements of cost. In the above activity we have been focusing on how the cost of direct materials is calculated. You can see from the total cost statement, which we have reproduced on page 291, that Jon used a figure of £440 as the cost of the direct materials issued to production during week ending 7 January.

If you look at the same figure in the two sets of inventory accounts you have drawn up for the above activity, you will see that Jon must have been using the FIFO method, as the CWA method results in the higher figure of £442.50. Both figures are correct and this is another example of why business owners and managers need to have some

Hazelwood Products Ltd	
Total cost w/e 7 January (10 bookcases)	
	£
Direct costs	
Direct materials	440
Direct labour	660
Prime cost	1,100
Production overheads	200
Production cost	1,300
Indirect costs	
Administration costs	80
Distribution costs	60
Total cost	1,440

understanding of the techniques used by accountants in order to make informed decisions about their accounting policies.

12.4 Advantages and disadvantages of different costing methods

There are a number of advantages and disadvantages associated with the different methods for costing direct materials. Since this information is likely to be used for financial reporting purposes, it is important that the business chooses the most appropriate method and uses it consistently, unless there is a good reason for changing it. You will remember that consistency helps achieve comparability, which is a quality that enhances the usefulness of financial information in general purpose financial statements.

Activity

Compare the FIFO cost and CWA cost methods by drawing up lists of the advantages and disadvantages of each.

Your list may include some of the following:

Advantages of FIFO cost

- It is acceptable to financial accountants in the UK and also to HM Revenue and Customs. This means that in addition to being used for management accounting purposes, it can be used for financial reporting and computing profits for taxation purposes.
- It is a logical choice if it coincides with the order in which inventory is physically issued to production. For example, if the inventory consists of perishable materials or materials that have a finite life for some other reason, it makes sense to issue those that have been stored the longest first. This avoids the possibility of deterioration, obsolescence and waste.

- It charges the cost of direct materials against profits in the same order as costs are incurred.
- The value of inventory at end of period is close to current prices.

Disadvantages of FIFO cost

- It is complex and an arithmetical burden, even when a spreadsheet is used.
- The cost of direct materials issued to production is based on historical prices.

Advantages of CWA cost

- It is acceptable to financial accountants in the UK and also to HM Revenue and Customs. This means that in addition to being used for management accounting purposes, it can be used for financial reporting and for computing profits for taxation purposes.
- It is a logical choice if it coincides with the way in which inventory is physically issued to production. For example, if inventory consists of volume and liquid materials (for example, building materials or chemicals), an averaging method makes sense as it may not be possible to differentiate between old and new inventory held in bulk storage containers.
- It smoothes out the impact of price changes in the statement of comprehensive income.
- It takes account of quantities purchased and changing prices.
- It takes account of prices relating to previous periods.
- It can be relatively simple to calculate by entering the quantity and pricing information from the goods received notes and purchase orders (or stores requisitions) into a spreadsheet or specialist software package.

Disadvantages of CWA cost

- Prices of materials issued to production must be recalculated every time a new consignment is received.
- Prices of materials issued may not match any of the prices actually paid.
- Value of closing inventory lags behind current prices if prices are rising.

12.5   Costing direct labour

Apart from materials, a second element of direct costs is expenditure on the wages paid to the workforce who are directly employed in producing the products or cost units. The methods for *costing direct labour* are closely related to the different methods of remuneration. The main types of pay schemes are:

- *piecework schemes*, which are used when workers are paid an agreed amount for each unit produced or piecework time is paid for each unit produced
- *time-based schemes*, which are used when workers are paid a basic rate per time period

- *incentive schemes*, which are used when a time allowance is given for each job and a bonus is paid for any time saved.

The documents used in labour costing depend largely on the method of payment used. The main documents used in a manual system are as follows, but many businesses now use computerized *direct data entry* from individual department terminals:

- *piecework tickets*, which refer to each stage of manufacture
- *clock cards*, which record attendance time
- daily or weekly *time sheets*, which record how workers have spent their time, and are usually required to be countersigned by a supervisor or manager
- *job cards*, which refer to a single job or a batch of small jobs, and record how long each activity takes to pass through the production process.

You should not be misled into thinking that costing for labour is used only in manufacturing businesses. For example, professionals such as solicitors and accountants usually complete *time sheets* so that individual clients can be properly billed for the services they receive. In all organizations it is necessary to have a system to ensure that employees are properly remunerated for their contribution. In many service organizations, some form of bonus or profit-sharing scheme is likely to exist and this requires more detailed information to be kept.

In *piecework schemes* wages can be calculated using the following formula:

$$\text{Units produced} \times \text{Rate of pay per cost unit}$$

For example, if an employee is paid £1.50 per cost unit and produces 240 units in a week, his or her weekly pay will be £360. This method works only where all units are identical, and if the employee produces a number of units a conversion factor must be applied. As a piecework system is based on time spent on production, a standard time allowance is given for each unit in order to arrive at a total of piecework hours. Perhaps the same employee is allowed 15 minutes to produce 1 unit of product A (a simple electronic circuit board) and 30 minutes to produce 1 unit of product B (a more complex electronic circuit board). If the employee produces 40 units of product A and 60 units of product B and is paid £7.50 per hour, his or her pay can be calculated as follows:

Product	Number of units	Time allowance per unit	Total hours
A	40	0.25 hours	10
B	60	0.50 hours	30
			40
		Pay (40 × £7.50)	£300

Calculating pay for *time-based schemes* is straightforward. A system is required to ensure that the employee is properly appointed and, if necessary, a procedure is in place to record the employee's attendance at the workplace. In many jobs it is assumed that the employee is present unless absence is specifically reported. The records from the clock cards and/or time sheets are then used as the basis for calculating pay.

Incentive schemes are usually introduced where workers are paid under a time-based scheme. There are various types of scheme in operation, but most are based on setting a target for output and actual performance is compared with the target. If actual performance exceeds the target, employees receive a payment for their efficiency. This payment is a proportion of the savings made by the business because of the increased efficiency and therefore the labour cost per unit should be lower. It is important to remember that a performance-based scheme cannot be used if the output cannot be measured reliably. Even though output might be easy to measure, it would be preferable to adopt a time-based method of remuneration where the quality of output is important. This would avoid the danger of quality deteriorating as workers strive to achieve higher levels of output that bring them increased monetary rewards.

Activity

Jon Hazel employs Chris, Mike and Adam in the workshop of Hazelwood Products Ltd. As Chris and Mike are apprentices, they are paid £5 per hour, but Adam has qualifications and experience and is paid £10 per hour. Their time sheets for week ending 7 January show that Chris spent 35 hours, Mike spent 35 hours and Adam spent 25 hours on making the 10 bookcases they produced. Jon's accountant, who handles the payroll, estimates that the additional costs incurred in terms of employer's national insurance, pension contributions and holiday pay amount to an additional 10% of the wages they are paid. Calculate the direct labour cost for the 10 bookcases produced.

Check your answer against the following workings:

	Hours	Rate per hour	Total
	£		£
Chris	35	5.00	175
Mike	35	5.00	175
Adam	25	10.00	250
			600
Employer's costs (600 × 10%)			60
Total direct labour costs			660

If you look at the total cost statement for Hazelwood Products Ltd, which is reproduced below, the direct labour costs are the most significant element of the direct costs for this business and therefore a key part of the prime costs for the week. One way in which Jon Hazel controls the direct labour costs in his business is by ensuring that employees complete their time sheets accurately and differentiate between time spent on making bookshelves and time spent on general tasks, such as clearing up and maintenance. Indeed, both Chris and Adam spent half an hour each day on general tasks and Adam spent two and a half hours each day supervising the apprentices and helping Jon plan the production process. Since this time cannot be identified directly with the products, the wages bill for this part of their jobs (£50) is included with the production overheads in the costing statement.

Hazelwood Products Ltd	
Total cost w/e 7 January (10 bookcases)	
	£
Direct costs	
Direct materials	440
Direct labour	660
Prime cost	1,100
Production overheads	200
Production cost	1,300
Indirect costs	
Administration costs	80
Distribution costs	60
Total cost	1,440

Sometimes students find it difficult to decide which costs are direct labour costs and which are indirect costs when classifying the elements of cost. The guide to remember is that direct labour costs are those which can conveniently be identified with a cost unit. To do this, a documentation system, as described in this chapter, is needed. Indirect labour costs are the wages of indirect workers, such as supervisors and maintenance staff, plus the wages of direct workers when working on indirect tasks, such as cleaning machinery and setting up production lines.

12.6 Costing direct expenses

Apart from direct materials and direct labour, a business may have some *direct expenses*. Examples of direct expenses include subcontract work or hiring special equipment for a particular job. For instance, Jon Hazel might decide to continue to produce bookcases with a simple wax finish, but also to make some with a paint finish as chosen by the customer. He may decide to subcontract the finishing of the painted bookcases ordered by customers to an expert. The cost of this extra work is not a direct material, as the paint is never owned by Hazelwood Products Ltd, nor is it direct labour, as the painter is not on the payroll, but the cost can be directly traced to a product. Therefore it is classified as a direct expense.

The main method for *costing direct expenses* to a product or cost unit is very simple and the accountant bases the cost on the amount shown in the relevant invoice. If it is not possible to do this because it is too difficult to trace the expense to a particular cost unit, the amount is simply added to the production overheads. We will be looking at these in more detail in the next chapter.

12.7 Conclusions

In this chapter we have described the key documents and procedures involved in costing for product direct costs. These are the costs that can be directly traced to a cost unit. When aggregated, these make up the prime cost. They can be divided into three elements: direct materials, direct labour and direct expenses.

Goods received notes give details of the direct materials received into the stores and materials requisitions give details of the inventory issued for use in the production process. If the materials are stored for a period of time before they are used, records are maintained that will ensure an adequate level of inventory, and periodic stocktaking ensures proper inventory control. In the accounts department, the inventory account records the quantity and cost of materials to be charged to the cost unit. We have examined two methods for pricing direct materials and valuing closing inventory and discussed the main reasons why different methods for costing direct materials might be adopted.

Direct labour converts the direct materials into the finished goods. The time employees spend on cost units can be calculated from clock cards, time sheets, job cards, piecework tickets or direct data entry systems, and the method used for costing direct labour is related to the method of remuneration. We have also examined the reasons why direct expenses are not always identifiable, but should be included if they can be traced directly to the appropriate cost unit. For example, subcontract costs can be charged by means of an invoice from the subcontractor.

In many businesses the systems for recording and controlling direct costs are computerized and part of a management information system that is capable of providing a wide range of information for different purposes. Typically, this includes accounting information that is used for both financial and management accounting purposes.

Practice questions

1 Describe the main stages in controlling direct materials.

2 Compare and contrast the advantages and disadvantages of the FIFO and CWA methods.

3 Janet's wages are based on piecework and she is paid £5 per piecework hour. Calculate her pay for a 36-hour week in which she produces the following units:

Product	Number of units	Time allowance per unit
A	12	0.8 hours
B	30	0.6 hours
C	24	0.5 hours

4 Perfect Pans Ltd manufactures cooking pans. On 1 December the inventory records show 500 kg of metal alloy, which is valued at £2.00 per kg. The goods received notes and materials requisitions show the following receipts and issues during the month:

2 December	Issued 450 kg to production
7 December	Received 550 kg at £2.10 per kg
8 December	Issued 500 kg to production
14 December	Received 600 kg at £2.20 per kg
15 December	Issued 600 kg to production
30 December	Received 500 kg at £2.30 per kg
31 December	Issued 100 kg to production

Required

(a) Prepare the inventory account for Perfect Pans Ltd and calculate the cost of metal alloy used in the production process during December and the inventory balance in terms of quantity and value at the end of the month using:
   (i) FIFO cost
   (ii) CWA cost

(b) Assuming that the business needs to choose between the two methods, recommend which method management should adopt, giving at least five reasons.

5 The following records show the movement of inventory for beans, the main ingredient used by Baked Bean PLC in its canned products, for the month of September:

September	Receipts		Issues
	Quantity (tonnes)	Price per tonne £	Quantity (tonnes)
1	1,000	5.00	
2	1,000	5.50	
3			750
14			750
15	1,000	6.00	
16			750
29	1,000	6.50	
30			750

Required

(a) Prepare the inventory account for Baked Bean PLC and calculate the cost of beans used in the product during September and the inventory balance in terms of quantity and value at the end of the month using:
   (i) FIFO cost
   (ii) CWA cost

(b) Identify which of the two methods would give the higher profit for the month in this particular case, giving your reasons.

Reference

Law, J. (ed.) (2010) *Dictionary of Accounting*, 4th edition. Oxford: Oxford University Press.

13 Costing for indirect costs

Learning objectives

When you have studied this chapter, you should be able to:

- describe the main purposes of absorption costing
- explain the main stages in costing indirect costs
- construct a production overhead analysis
- calculate the total cost of a cost unit using absorption costing methods
- describe the problems associated with apportioning and absorbing indirect costs.

13.1 Introduction

In Chapter 12 we looked at the methods that allow us to calculate the product direct costs (direct materials, direct labour and direct expenses) for each cost unit. However, the direct costs are only part of the total cost of producing a product or service; there are also the *indirect costs* of the business that need to be considered when making management decisions. The indirect costs are the *overheads* incurred by the business, which can be classified as production overheads, administration overheads, distribution overheads or research and development overheads. In many businesses these indirect costs are very high and it is essential to find a suitable method for charging them to the cost units. *Absorption costing* is the traditional costing technique used to meet this need.

In this chapter we are going to focus on how to allocate and apportion the indirect costs to the cost centres and cost units so that the total cost of a single cost unit can be calculated. To do this, we will be working out the total costs of the business. This information will be similar to that found in the financial accounts, but there are differences. In management accounting the total costs are required on a monthly basis and in some cases they may be based on forecast figures. Therefore, the figures may be less accurate than those prepared for financial accounting purposes, but because they are calculated more frequently than once a year, they are timelier. In addition, more detailed information is required in a management accounting system than is needed for financial accounting. However, at the end of the financial year, we would expect the total costs for the business shown in the annual financial statements to be very similar to the aggregated costs in the management accounts.

13.2 Absorption costing

Absorption costing is a technique that analyses *revenue expenditure* in order to arrive at a total cost for each cost unit. You will remember from Chapter 11 that revenue expenditure refers to the costs that are written off to the profit and loss account in the period in which they incurred. Since the focus of absorption costing is on calculating the total cost per unit, it is also known as *total costing*. The production cost of a product or other cost unit is primarily needed for valuing inventory and for planning and controlling production costs, whereas the total cost is needed to determine the selling price.

Key definitions

Absorption costing is the cost accounting system in which the overheads of an organization are charged to the production by means of the process of absorption. Costs are first allocated or apportioned to the cost centres, where they are absorbed into the cost unit using absorption rates.

An overhead absorption rate (OAR) is the rate or rates calculated in an absorption costing system in advance of an accounting period for the purpose of charging the overheads to the production of that period.

Source: Law (2010, p. 2).

In Chapter 11 we looked at the ways in which costs can be classified and one way is to divide them into *direct costs* and *indirect costs*. The total of the product direct costs is the *prime cost* and if we then add the indirect costs of production (the production overheads) we arrive at the *production cost*. The following activity allows us to examine this in more detail.

Activity

Hazelwood Products Ltd, the business we looked at in previous chapters, is thriving. During the first year, the workshop made 1,000 bookcases with the same design and size specifications. Production overheads for the year were £20,000; direct materials for each bookcase were £50 and direct labour costs for each bookcase were £80.

What is the production cost of one bookcase?

You should have had no problem in deciding that the total direct costs are £130, made up of £50 for materials and £80 for labour. However, the total cost must include a fair share of the production overheads – but what is a 'fair share'? As the business is making only one product and they are all the same, a fair method would be to divide the production overheads by the total number of units produced:

$$\frac{£20,000}{1,000} = £20$$

The following costing statement draws these calculations together:

Hazelwood Products Ltd Production cost (1 bookcase)	
	£
Direct costs	
Direct materials	50
Direct labour	80
Prime cost	130
Production overheads	20
Production cost	150

As a business grows, it is likely to become more complex than Hazelwood Products Ltd was in its first year and when this happens a business may decide to organize itself into a number of functional departments. In a manufacturing business, some of these will be production departments, whilst others will be service departments providing services, such as maintenance, storage or canteen facilities, administration, selling and distribution functions, etc. In addition, the business may have a range of different products or other cost units, with each spending a different amount of time in the

Figure 13.1 Main stages in absorption costing

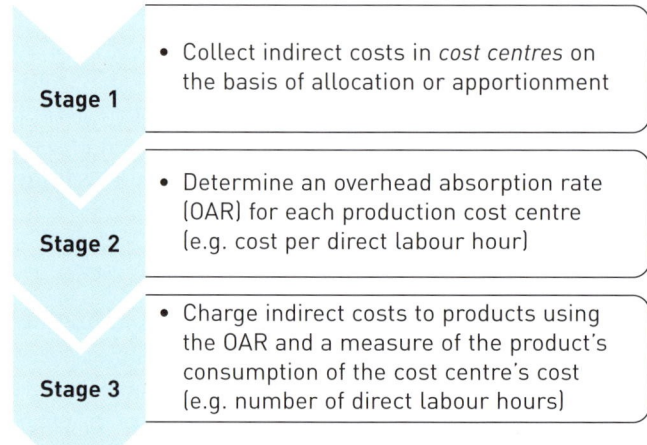

Stage 1
- Collect indirect costs in *cost centres* on the basis of allocation or apportionment

Stage 2
- Determine an overhead absorption rate (OAR) for each production cost centre (e.g. cost per direct labour hour)

Stage 3
- Charge indirect costs to products using the OAR and a measure of the product's consumption of the cost centre's cost (e.g. number of direct labour hours)

production department and therefore making different demands on resources. In such cases, the method we have used for Hazelwood Products Ltd is not a fair way of sharing the production overheads over the cost units. However, absorption costing helps overcome this difficulty, by apportioning these indirect (overhead) costs to the cost units using rates that are calculated for each cost centre, as shown in Figure 13.1.

13.3 Allocating and apportioning production overheads

Absorption costing seeks to provide answers to two practical problems:

- how to share the total overheads of the organization over the various production cost centres
- how to share the overheads for a particular production cost centre over the various products passing through it.

Activity

In the previous example of Hazelwood Products Ltd, was the method used a solution to the first or the second of these problems?

The method used was a solution to the second problem because we were looking at a small organization with only one production department or workshop. By dividing the total overheads by the number of bookcases produced, we shared the production overheads over the products passing through the production department. Usually we have to solve the first problem before we can tackle the second.

You will remember from Chapter 11 that we can classify overheads by *nature*, such as rent, wages and depreciation. When overheads are classified in this way, they fall into two main groups. The first group is those that can be wholly identified with one particular cost centre, for example all the depreciation charge on machinery may be due to only one particular production department. This process of charging to one particular cost centre is called *cost allocation*. The second group of overheads is those which cannot be identified with a single cost centre, but must be shared or apportioned over all the cost centres benefiting from them. This process is known as *cost apportionment*; for example, factory rent might be apportioned over the production cost centres on the basis of the proportion of space each department occupies in the factory. In order to charge the production overheads to cost centres by allocation and apportionment a *production overhead analysis* is prepared. This classifies the total overheads by nature and then shows how they are apportioned across the production cost centres. We will use an activity to illustrate this.

Activity

Jarvis Jackets Ltd makes leather jackets. It has two cost centres: the cutting department where the jackets are cut out by machine, and the stitching department where they are sewn and finished. Some of the production overheads have been allocated to the two cost centres from information available within the business, but the remainder must be apportioned in some way. The following information should help you decide a fair way of sharing them between the two departments.

	Total	Cutting department	Stitching department
Production area	400 sq metres	250 sq metres	150 sq metres
Number of employees	20	5	15
Value of machinery	£120,000	£100,000	£20,0000
Value of inventory	£120,000	£40,000	£80,0000

Before you can complete the following pro forma, you need to decide on the basis on which the production overheads will be apportioned and then calculate the portion that will be borne by each cost centre. The indirect materials and indirect labour used in production have already been allocated and entered in the analysis. The rent has also been apportioned to show you the method. Rent is best apportioned on the basis of the area occupied. The total area is 250 + 150 = 400 sq metres and the rent is £12,000. Therefore, the rent can be apportioned as follows:

$$\text{Cutting department: } \frac{250}{400} \text{ sq metres} \times £12,000 = £7,500$$

$$\text{Stitching department: } \frac{150}{400} \text{ sq metres} \times £12,000 = £4,500$$

Jarvis Jackets Ltd
Production overhead analysis

Overhead	Total	Basis of Apportionment	Cutting department	Stitching department
	£		£	£
Indirect materials	40,000	Allocated	17,500	22,500
Indirect labour	17,100	Allocated	4,200	12,900
Rent and rates	12,000	Area	7,500	4,500
Lighting and heating	4,000			
Depreciation on machinery	9,000			
Supervisors' salaries	22,000			
Insurance	900			
Total	105,000			

After deciding a fair way of apportioning the production overheads, the calculations should not have presented any great problems. Check your completed analysis against the following solution.

Overhead	Total	Basis of Apportionment	Cutting department	Stitching department
	£		£	£
Indirect materials	40,000	Allocated	17,500	22,500
Indirect labour	17,100	Allocated	4,200	12,900
Rent and rates	12,000	Area	7,500	4,500
Lighting and heating	4,000	Area	2,500	1,500
Depreciation on machinery	9,000	Value of machinery	7,500	1,500
Supervisors' salaries	22,000	No. of employees	5,500	16,500
Insurance	900	Value of inventory	300	600
Total	105,000		45,000	60,000

Jarvis Jackets Ltd
Production overhead analysis

If your answer differs from the above, it may be because you decided to use different bases of apportionment, so we will look at the reasons for the choices we made. Both rent and electricity would seem to be best shared on the basis of the area occupied by each cost centre. Depreciation is clearly related to the value of the machinery used in each cost centre. Deciding on the best way to apportion the supervisors' salaries is more difficult. In the absence of any other information, we have assumed that their salaries are related to the number of employees. You might argue that they could be related to floor space and in some circumstances you would be right. Finally, the insurance of inventory is based on its value and therefore has been allocated accordingly.

Agreeing on a fair way to apportion overheads is a major problem in many organizations and it is important to remember that the methods of apportionment are arbitrary. Nevertheless, the method chosen should be reasonable. It should be relatively easy to obtain from the records of the business and relate to the manner in which the cost is incurred by the cost centre benefiting from its use. Finally, it should reflect the use by the cost centre of the resources represented by the overhead. Later in this chapter we will be looking at the problem of service cost centres, but at this stage we will concentrate on how to allocate or apportion production overheads to our two production departments. Table 13.1 shows some commonly used bases of apportionment.

Table 13.1   Main bases for apportioning production overheads

Production overhead	Basis of apportionment
Rent and rates	Area or volume
Lighting and heating	Area or volume
Buildings insurance	Area
Insurance of machinery	Value of machinery
Depreciation of machinery	Value of machinery
Power for machinery	Machine hours, horsepower or horsepower per hour
Supervisors' salaries	Number of employees
Canteen	Number of employees

13.4 Calculating the production overhead absorption rate

We now know that the total production overheads are £45,000 for the cutting department and £60,000 for the finishing department. Next we must decide on an appropriate *overhead absorption rate* to share the production overheads between all the jackets passing through the two production cost centres. The choice of absorption rate depends on the basis of apportionment and the resources used. We will examine the following methods:

- the cost unit overhead absorption rate
- the direct labour hour overhead absorption rate
- the machine hour overhead absorption rate.

The *cost unit overhead absorption rate* is the simplest method and involves dividing the production overheads for each production cost centre by the number of cost units passing through them. We applied this in the Hazelwood Products Ltd example. In a more complex business there may be more than one production cost centre and a different overhead absorption rate will be needed for each. For example, Jarvis Jackets Ltd makes two styles of jacket: the classic jacket and the designer jacket. In one year, 4,000 classic jackets are made and 1,000 designer jackets, making a total of 5,000 cost units. Using the cost unit overhead absorption rate, we will now calculate the amount of the overheads that will be borne by each jacket. This requires some care, as we need to remember that each jacket must pass through both the cutting department and the stitching department. Therefore, a separate overhead absorption rate per jacket must be calculated for each cost centre and then aggregated.

	Cutting department	Stitching department
Cost unit overhead absorption rate:		
$\dfrac{\text{Cost centre overheads}}{\text{Total cost units}}$	$\dfrac{£45,000}{5,000} = £9.00$	$\dfrac{£60,000}{5,000} = £12.00$

The absorption rate will be £21.00 (£9.00 + £12.00). This means that every jacket will absorb £21.00 of the production overheads incurred in running these two production cost centres.

Although using cost unit overhead absorption rate is the easiest method, it would be unfair to charge the same overhead to the different styles of jackets, since the more expensive designer jackets use up more of the resources. It would be fairer if the product that uses up more of the resources bears more of the overhead. For example, if you took your car to the garage merely to have the brakes adjusted and you were charged the same overhead charge as someone who had had a full service, you would be very upset. It would not help if the garage owner told you that he had worked out his overhead charge by dividing his total overheads by the number of cars repaired. So what other basis might he use for charging overheads on the work done?

You may consider that the overheads should be charged on a time basis. Garages usually charge an hourly rate for repairs, as do many other businesses, such as plumbers and electricians. The hourly rate can be calculated on the basis of the time an employee spends working on the product, the *direct labour hour rate*, or on how long the product is on a machine, the *machine hour rate*.

Activity

Returning to our example of Jarvis Jackets Ltd, now calculate the hourly overhead absorption rate for each department. You can choose to base the rate on direct labour hours or on machine hours. The following table gives details of the direct labour hours and machine hours required in each department to make 5,000 jackets.

	Cutting department	Stitching department
Direct labour hours	10,000	30,000
Machine hours	40,000	5,000

You may have found this difficult. To calculate the direct labour hours overhead absorption rate for each cost centre, you need to divide the overhead by the total direct labour hours and add them together. If you decided to calculate the machine hours overhead absorption rate for each cost centre, you should have divided the overhead by the total number of machine hours and added them together. Check your answer against the following workings.

	Cutting department	Stitching department
Direct labour hour overhead absorption rate:		
$\dfrac{\text{Cost centre overheads}}{\text{Total direct labour hours}}$	$\dfrac{£45,000}{10,000} = £4.50$	$\dfrac{£60,000}{30,000} = £2.00$
Machine hour overhead absorption rate:		
$\dfrac{\text{Cost centre overheads}}{\text{Total machine hours}}$	$\dfrac{£45,000}{40,000} = £1.13$	$\dfrac{£60,000}{5,000} = £12.00$

Other types of overhead absorption rates in use are often based on a percentage calculation, but we will concentrate on these three widely used methods as they illustrate the main principles. The following table summarizes the information we have so far:

	Cutting department	Stitching department
Total overheads	£45,000	£60,000
Number of cost units	5,000	5,000
Direct labour hours	10,000	30,000
Machine hours	40,000	5,000
Cost units overhead absorption rate	£9.00	£12.00
Direct labour hours overhead absorption rate	£4.50	£2.00
Machine hours overhead absorption rate	£1.13	£12.00

Although we have calculated three different types of overhead rate for Jarvis Jackets Ltd, only one rate will be used in each department – but you can see that since each produces a different absorption rate, it is important that the management accountant uses the fairest rate for each cost centre, bearing in mind that the same rate need not be used in both departments. We have already pointed out that it would be unfair to use the cost unit absorption rate because the two types of jacket use unequal amounts of resources. With the other two rates, we need to consider the main sources of expenditure in each department by examining the overhead costs. In the cutting department, you can see that the overheads have been incurred mainly in terms of machine hours. Therefore this is the most appropriate basis for calculating the overhead absorption rate for that cost centre. However, in the finishing department, the work is mainly manual; therefore, the direct labour hour rate is the most appropriate overhead absorption rate to use for this cost centre.

13.5   Calculating the production cost per unit

We have now reached the final and most important stage of our calculations. Although we have spent some time learning how the overheads are calculated, we must not forget to charge for the product direct costs (the direct materials and direct labour used in making the jackets). The following information is available:

	Classic jacket	Designer jacket
Direct materials	£50	£80
Direct labour	£20	£40
Cutting department machine hours	7	12
Stitching department direct labour hours	5	10

We can now calculate the production cost incurred in making each type of jacket.

Production cost per unit		
	Classic jacket	Designer jacket
	£	£
Direct costs		
Direct materials	50.00	80.00
Direct labour	20.00	40.00
Prime cost	70.00	120.00
Production overheads		
Cutting department (7 hours × £1.13 per machine hour)	7.91	13.56
Stitching department (5 hours × £2.00 per direct labour hour)	10.00	20.00
	17.91	33.56
Production cost	87.91	153.56

You may consider that calculating a different overhead absorption rate for each production department is a complex activity: it would be far simpler to calculate a factory-wide absorption rate. Thus, if a factory had total overheads of £1m and there were 250,000 direct labour hours worked during the period, the overhead absorption rate would be £4.00 per labour hour in all the separate departments. Although this method is simple and inexpensive to apply, it is likely to generate incorrect data, except in the most straightforward production systems. If there are a number of departments and products do not spend an equal time in each department, separate departmental overhead absorption rates must be calculated. If this is not done, some products will receive a higher overhead charge than they should fairly bear and others a lower charge. This will make it difficult for management to control costs and make decisions on pricing and alternative production systems.

13.6 Apportioning service cost centre overheads

So far, we have considered only production cost centres. However, most businesses also have cost centres that provide services to other cost centres. Examples of *service cost centres* include departments associated with the production areas, such as maintenance, stores and canteen, and others which are not, such as administration and distribution. The first stage is to calculate the total production cost as before, but this time we will include the service cost centres associated with the production area. We will deal with other overheads later. The same procedure is used: the different types of production overheads are allocated and apportioned, and subtotalled. Then the subtotal of the service cost centres is apportioned to the production cost centres on a fair basis.

Activity

Jon Hazel's business, Hazelwood Products Ltd, has expanded and now makes bookcases of different sizes. Instead of a single production department, Jon has found it more efficient to divide the work into separate stages and there are now three departments, each of which is a separate cost centre. The following information is available.

	Joinery department	Finishing department	Maintenance department
Area	200 sq metres	200 sq metres	100 sq metres
Number of employees	12	16	4
Value of machinery	£250,000	£100,000	£50,000

Complete the following production overhead analysis by showing the basis of apportionment and the overhead to be borne by each of the three production cost centres. The allocated overheads have been entered for you. Once you have arrived at a subtotal for all three cost centres, you must apportion the service costs for the maintenance department over the two production departments on whatever basis you consider appropriate.

Overhead	Total	Basis of apportionment	Joinery department	Finishing department	Maintenance Department
	£		£	£	£
Indirect materials	10,000	Allocated	6,000	3,000	1,000
Indirect labour	31,500	Allocated	4,000	8,000	19,500
Rent and rates	20,000				
Electricity	5,000				
Depreciation on machinery	40,000				
Supervisors' salaries	36,000				
	142,500				
Apportioned service costs	–				
Total	142,500				–

Hazelwood Products Ltd
Production overhead analysis

Your completed production overhead analysis should look like this:

Hazelwood Products Ltd
Production overhead analysis

Overhead	Total	Basis of apportionment	Joinery department	Finishing department	Maintenance Department
	£		£	£	£
Indirect materials	10,000	Allocated	6,000	3,000	1,000
Indirect labour	31,500	Allocated	4,000	8,000	19,500
Rent and rates	20,000	Area	8,000	8,000	4,000
Electricity	5,000	Area	2,000	2,000	1,000
Depreciation on machinery	40,000	Value of machinery	25,000	10,000	5,000
Supervisors' salaries	36,000	No. of employees	13,500	18,000	4,500
	142,500		58,500	49,000	35,000
Apportioned service costs	–	Value of machinery	25,000	10,000	(35,000)
Total	142,500		83,500	59,000	–

The overhead costs of £35,000, which represent the cost of running the maintenance department, have been apportioned to the two production departments on the basis of the value of the machinery in these two departments (the value of the machinery in the maintenance department itself is excluded from the calculations). The total cost of machinery is £250,000 + £100,000 = £350,000. Therefore, the maintenance department overheads can be apportioned as follows:

$$\text{Joinery department:} \frac{£250,000}{£350,000} \times £35,000 = £25,000$$

$$\text{Finishing department: } \frac{£100{,}000}{£350{,}000} \times £35{,}000 = £10{,}000$$

Continuing this example, the overhead absorption rate in the joinery department is based on 10,000 machine hours and in the finishing department on 30,000 direct labour hours. We can now calculate the two overhead absorption rates in the joinery and finishing departments. This is done by dividing the total cost centre overhead for the period by the number of units of the basis of absorption; in this case, the machine hours in the joinery department and the direct labour hours in the finishing department:

$$\text{Joinery department: } \frac{£83{,}500}{10{,}000} = £8.35 \text{ per machine hour}$$

$$\text{Finishing department: } \frac{£59{,}000}{30{,}000} = £1.97 \text{ per direct labour hour}$$

Supposing a customer puts in an order for a bookcase for which the direct costs are direct materials £80.00 and direct labour £50.00. It is estimated that the bookcase will require 8 machine hours in the joinery department and 10 labour hours in the finishing department. We can calculate the total production cost as follows:

Hazelwood Products Ltd Production cost (1 bookcase)	£
Direct costs	
Direct materials	80.00
Direct labour	50.00
Prime cost	130.00
Production overheads	
Joinery department (8 hours × £8.35)	66.80
Finishing department (10 hours × £1.97)	19.70
	86.70
Production cost	216.50

What we have just calculated is the production cost for the bookcase, but you will remember from Chapter 11 that in order to find out the total cost per unit, we need to add a proportion of the non-production overheads. In this example, these consist of the administration overheads and distribution overheads. The data for the period are as follows:

	£		£
Direct costs	87,500	Administration overheads	18,250
Production overheads	142,500	Distribution overheads	27,750
Total production cost	230,000	Total non-production overheads	46,000

A simple method for apportioning non-production overheads to a cost unit is to add a percentage representing the proportion of non-production costs to production costs. This is an arbitrary measure, as there is no theoretical justification for a relationship between these two costs. The formula is:

$$\frac{\text{Non-production overheads}}{\text{Production cost}} \times 100$$

Substituting the figures in the formula:

$$\frac{£46,000}{£230,000} \times 100 = 20\% \text{ of the production cost } (£216.50 \times 20\%) = £43.30$$

Now we have all the figures we need to calculate the total cost of the bookcase. This is primarily of use to management for determining the selling price, since inventory valuation and controlling production costs do not require the inclusion of the non-production costs.

Production cost (1 bookcase)	
	£
Direct costs	
Direct materials	80.00
Direct labour	50.00
Prime cost	130.00
Production overheads	
Joinery department (8 hours @ £8.35)	66.80
Finishing department (10 hours @ £1.97)	19.70
	86.50
Production cost	216.50
Non-production overheads (Production cost × 20%)	43.30
Total cost	259.80

13.7 Predetermined overhead absorption rates

So far, we have implied that the absorption rates are based on actual costs, but in practice these costs are usually estimated, which means that the overhead absorption rates are based on predicted figures. The actual costs are not used because the collection, analysis and absorption of overheads to cost units takes a considerable time, and the actual figures may not be available until after the end of the financial period. Naturally it would be impossible to wait until then to invoice customers, submit estimates, make decisions on production methods or carry out any other management task.

Before the start of a financial period, which may be as short as a month or as long as a year, decisions will be made on the likely level of activity and the estimated costs that will be incurred during the period. In Chapter 16 we will be looking at budgetary control, which is the process of establishing detailed financial plans for a forthcoming period, comparing them with the actual figures during the period and taking action to remedy any adverse variances. As far as absorption costing is concerned, the planned level of activity will need to be decided, the number of machine hours and labour hours estimated and forecasts made of the likely overhead costs. This will allow a *predetermined overhead absorption rate* to be calculated at the beginning of the financial period and applied throughout the period.

Activity

What problems do you think might arise from using a predetermined overhead rate instead of an actual rate?

You may have thought of the following main problems:

- actual overheads are likely to differ from those budgeted
- the actual absorption rate may differ from that used in the budget
- a combination of the above factors.

These problems can have serious consequences. If an organization has been invoicing customers on a predetermined overhead rate that is wrong, it could have a significant impact on profits. Where the overheads charged to production are higher than the actual overheads for the period, the variance is known as *overabsorption*. In other words, too much overhead has been charged to production. Where the overheads charged to production are lower than the actual overheads, the variance is known as *underabsorption*. The underabsorption or overabsorption of overheads is written off as an expense in the statement of comprehensive income for the period in which it is incurred.

13.8 Conclusions

Revenue expenditure can be classified into product direct costs, which can be traced directly to a cost unit, and indirect costs, which cannot. We looked at the methods for costing product direct costs (direct materials, direct labour and direct expenses) in Chapter 12. In this chapter we have looked at absorption costing, which is a cost accounting system that charges each cost unit with a fair share of the indirect costs or overheads. This enables the total cost (the direct and the indirect costs) of a cost unit to be calculated. The main steps in absorption costing are:

1. Using a production overhead analysis, allocate or apportion indirect costs to each cost centre on a fair basis using an appropriate method of apportionment.
2. Allocate or apportion indirect costs from service cost centres to the production cost centres.

3. Then absorb the resulting overheads from each production cost centre into the cost unit using a suitable overhead absorption rate.
4. Construct a costing statement showing the different elements of direct and indirect costs for the cost unit.

Absorption costing can be based on either predetermined or actual costs. The information thus provided can be used to aid the planning and control of costs and for establishing the selling price of products. Although we have used the manufacture of furniture and jackets in this chapter as examples, the same principles of allocating, apportioning and absorbing overheads apply in all organizations where management wants to know the total cost of a cost unit. However, it is important to remember that absorption costing has some limitations, since it is based on a series of simple assumptions and rudimentary arithmetical apportioning. We will explain an alternative technique for charging overheads in the next chapter, which examines activity-based costing.

Practice questions

1 Describe the main stages for calculating the total cost per unit under an absorption costing system.

2 Explain what it means to allocate, apportion and absorb indirect costs.

3 Discuss the advantages and disadvantages of using an absorption costing system for calculating the total cost of a product.

4 The monthly production overheads for Toy Craft Ltd are as follows:

Production overheads	£
Indirect materials	24,500
Indirect labour	54,500
Rent and rates	26,000
Electricity	4,000
Depreciation on machinery	36,000
Supervisors' salaries	42,000

The business has two production cost centres and one service cost centre, details of which are given below.

	Machine department	Assembly department	Maintenance department
Allocation of indirect materials	£12,000	£10,000	£2,500
Allocation of indirect labour costs	£14,000	£18,000	£22,500
Area (sq metres)	500	400	100
Value of machinery (£)	£300,000	£100,000	£50,000
Number of employees	7	21	2
Number of machine hours	42,500	–	–
Number of direct labour hours	–	15,000	–

Required

(a) Decide on a suitable basis of apportionment for each of the indirect costs that are not going to be allocated and construct a production overhead analysis for Toy Craft Ltd.

(b) Calculate the machine hour overhead absorption rate for the machine department.

(c) Calculate the direct labour hour overhead absorption rate for the assembly department.

5 West Wales Windsurfers Ltd makes two models of windsurfer: the Fun Wave and the Hot Racer. The company has two production departments. It also has a canteen, which serves all employees. The predicted sales and costs for next year are as follows:

	Fun Wave	Hot Racer
Selling price per unit	£600	£700
Sales/production volume	2,000 units	2,500 units
Material costs per unit	£80	£50
Direct labour:		
Body workshop (£3 per hour)	50 hours per unit	60 hours per unit
Finishing workshop (£2 per hour)	40 hours per unit	40 hours per unit
Machine hours:		
Body workshop	30 hours per unit	80 hours per unit
Finishing workshop	10 hours per unit	

The production overheads for the cost centres are shown below, together with other relevant data.

Production overheads	Total	Body workshop	Finishing workshop	Canteen
	£	£	£	£
Variable costs	350,000	260,000	90,000	0
Fixed costs	880,000	420,000	300,000	160,000
Total	1,230,000	680,000	390,000	160,000
Number of employees	150	90	10	
Floor area (sq metres)	40,000	10,000	10,000	

Required

(a) Advise West Wales Windsurfers Ltd on the method of overhead absorption that should be used for each cost centre, giving reasons for your choice.

(b) Calculate an appropriate overhead absorption rate for each production department.

(c) Calculate the predicted production cost per unit for each model.

14 Activity-based costing

Learning objectives

When you have studied this chapter, you should be able to:

- explain how activity-based costing can add value to the business
- calculate product costs using activity-based costing
- apply activity-based costing to marketing and administration functions
- describe the advantages and disadvantages of activity-based costing.

14.1 Introduction

You will remember from previous chapters that revenue expenditure can be classified into product direct costs, which can be traced directly to a cost unit, and indirect costs, which cannot. We looked at the methods for costing product direct costs (direct materials, direct labour and direct expenses) in Chapter 12 and then examined *absorption costing* in Chapter 13. Absorption costing is based on the allocation and apportionment of indirect costs or overheads to production cost centres and their absorption into the cost of products using predetermined rates. *Activity-based costing (ABC)* is an alternative cost accounting system for indirect costs that has been developed. Its name is derived from the fact that costs are assigned first to activities and then to the cost units on the basis of the use they make of these activities.

In this chapter we start by examining the need for an alternative approach and explain how ABC developed as a reaction to perceived deficiencies in absorption costing, the traditional approach. We describe the main stages in ABC and define the terms used. We then go on to provide a worked example in order to demonstrate how the product costs are calculated before considering the advantages and disadvantages of this alternative method.

14.2   Need for an alternative to absorption costing

In *absorption costing* (see Chapter 13), each product or cost unit is charged with a fair share of the indirect costs or overheads, thus enabling the total cost (the direct costs plus the indirect costs) of the firm's products to be calculated. Under this system, any overheads that cannot be allocated to a particular production cost centre must be apportioned on whatever is judged to be a fair basis. The resulting total production cost centre overhead is then absorbed into the cost of the product using a predetermined overhead absorption rate. In a simple business with only one product, this rate can be based on the number of cost units passing through the production cost centre. In a more complex business, it is commonly based on time, such as direct labour hours or machine hours.

Although accountants try to be as rigorous as possible in the application of absorption costing, this costing system is based on arbitrary decisions about the basis for apportionment and absorption of overheads. In addition, general overheads are spread across the product range with little regard for how the costs are actually generated. Therefore, there is always some concern that the total cost of each product is not being calculated in the most precise manner. If the business is miscalculating the cost of its products and basing its selling prices on this inaccurate information, it could have a dramatic impact on financial performance. For example, if the inaccuracies result in selling prices that are too high, the business could lose market share to competitors; if they result in selling prices that are too low, the business will not achieve its planned profit. To overcome these potential problems, some firms now use *activity-based costing (ABC)*.

ABC was proposed by Johnson and Kaplan (1987), who questioned the relevance of traditional management accounting practices to modern business. Management accounting has its roots in the Industrial Revolution of the nineteenth century, when manufacturing was the major industry. However, as the century progressed, a need for financial accounting began to evolve, and Johnson and Kaplan suggest that this split was one of the main causes of what they describe as the fall in the relevance of management accounting. A second reason they give is that modern business is no longer dominated by the manufacturing industry and therefore management accounting techniques based on the needs of manufacturers are not relevant to businesses in non-manufacturing sectors.

Activity

Due to the increased complexity of production operations, many manufacturing businesses now use computer-controlled operations and robotic methods of production (car manufacturers, for example). Why do you think this might encourage firms to consider activity-based costing as an alternative to absorption costing?

You may have thought of several reasons, but one key reason is that advances in technology have increased overhead costs, such as power, maintenance and depreciation of machinery. Therefore, it is critical that these costs are charged to the products as accurately as possible. The increased use of technology has also been associated with a decline in the importance of direct labour and a change in its characteristics. Employees who provide direct labour are often paid on a monthly basis rather than an hourly basis as in the past. In addition, their remuneration is less closely related to the level of production and they are likely to receive additional benefits, such as pensions and sick pay, which were formerly only given to managers and administrators.

A further factor that is important in some firms is the amount of inventory they hold. You will recall from previous chapters that the correct value placed on *closing inventory* is critical for calculating the profit or loss for a financial period. This stock value normally includes a share of indirect overheads. Increasingly companies have moved to JIT (just-in-time) techniques, where a low level of inventory is held and receipts of raw materials and delivery of finished goods to customers are phased in with the production process. With low inventory levels, the value of closing inventory has declined in importance.

In addition to these internal developments, competition has been increasing and firms are using a variety of techniques to improve the efficiency of their manufacturing operations. These include *value-added analysis*, where operations that do not add value in converting the raw materials into the final product are examined and eliminated if possible. One of the claims made for ABC is that it enhances the value added to production for a business that has complex manufacturing processes and several different products, because it recognizes that costs are incurred by every activity in the organization and is based on the principle that the cost units should bear costs according to the activities they use.

Key definitions

Activity-based costing (ABC) is a system of costing ... that recognizes that costs are incurred by each activity that takes place within an organization and that products (or customers) should bear costs according to the activities they use. Cost drivers are identified, together with the appropriate activity cost pools, which are used to charge cost to products.

An activity cost pool is a collection of indirect costs grouped according to the activity involved.

A cost driver is any factor such as number of units, number of transactions, or duration of transactions that drives the costs arising from a particular activity. When such factors can be clearly identified and measured, they will be used as a basis for allocating costs to cost objects.

Source: Law (2010, pp. 15 and 117).

14.3 Main stages in activity-based costing

The two main stages in ABC are shown in Figure 14.1. First, the overhead costs are assigned to the different activities in the business, and then cost drivers are used to attach activity costs to the cost units.

Figure 14.1 Main stages in ABC

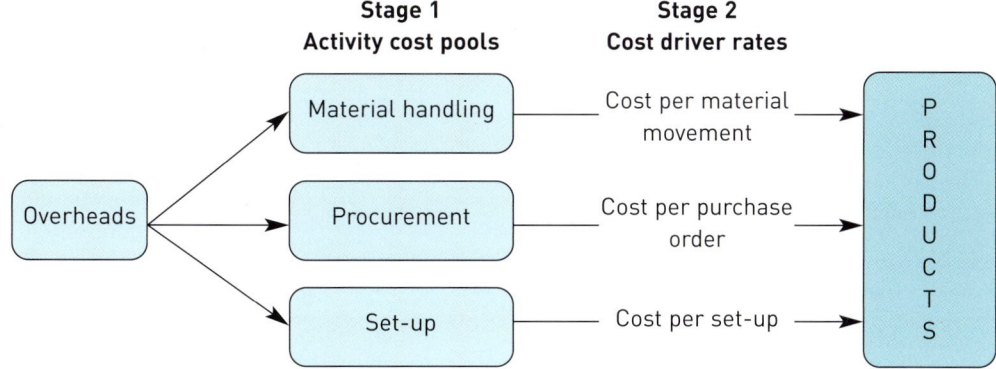

Source: Adapted from CIMA (2005, p. 3).

This makes ABC look misleadingly simple, but each stage involves a substantial amount of research into the firm's operations and costing procedures. This can be highly beneficial, but can cause disruption to normal production. The *implementation* of an activity-based costing system involves four main steps:

1. Identify the main *activities* in the organization and classify them into activity centres if there are a large number of different activities. An activity centre is an identifiable unit of the organization that performs an operation that uses resources. For most organizations the first activity will be the purchase of materials. This will involve several sub-activities, such as drawing up material specifications, selecting suppliers, placing the order, receiving and inspecting the materials that have been delivered.
2. Identify the *cost drivers* associated with each activity centre. A cost driver is any factor that causes a change in the cost of an activity or series of activities that takes place in the business. For example, with the purchase of materials, it would be the number of orders placed. If we were looking at the costs of operating a customer support hotline, it might be the number of calls answered; for a quality control activity, it might be the number of hours of inspection conducted. Some activities have multiple cost drivers and it is important to note that cost drivers are not confined to a specific department.
3. Calculate the *cost driver rate*. This is the cost per unit of activity. For example, in purchasing it would be the cost per order placed.
4. Assign costs to the products by multiplying the cost driver rate by the volume of the cost driver units consumed by the product. With purchasing, the cost driver rate

will be calculated on the basis of orders placed. If Product A requires 15 orders to be placed in January, the cost of purchasing activity for Product A will be 15 times the cost driver rate.

Figure 14.2 contrasts the main stages in absorption costing with those involved in ABC.

Figure 14.2 Comparison of the main stages in absorption costing and ABC

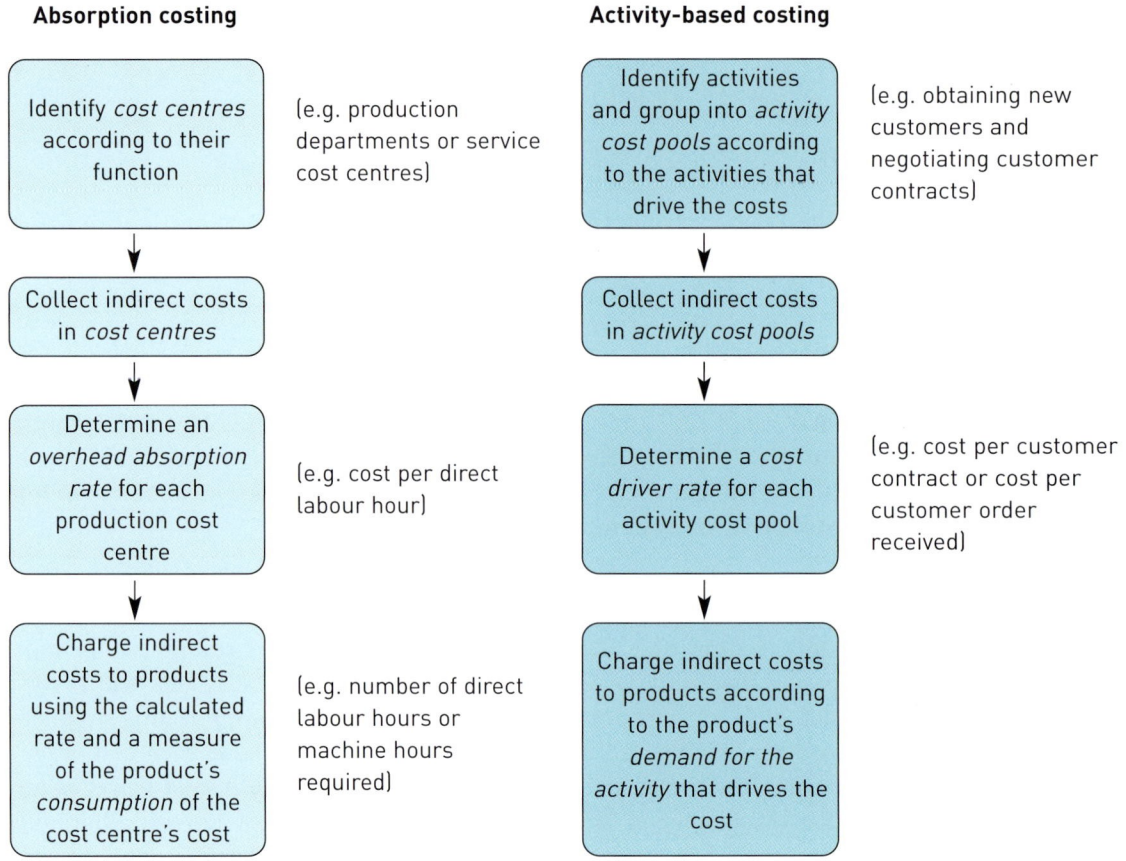

Source: Adapted from Weetman (1999, p. 751).

14.4 Activities and cost drivers

As a general rule, the more complex the production process is, the greater the number of different activities and cost drivers. A business making a simple product is likely to find that any differences have little impact on overhead costs.

Activity

List the various activities that the owner of a takeaway pizza business has to undertake in order to make and deliver pizzas to customers.

You may be surprised at the number of activities you have been able to list, even if you omit all the administration and advertising. You will probably have identified some of the following activities or more, depending on the assumptions you made about the size of the business:

- ordering raw materials, such as flour, meat and vegetables (usually referred to as procurement)
- preparation of raw materials and disposal of waste
- cooking
- cleaning and maintenance of kitchen equipment
- employment of delivery staff
- receiving orders from customers
- dealing with complaints.

With complex productions and a wide range of products, there are likely to be a great many activities, but companies usually restrict their analysis to the key activities. Any major activity is likely to have several overhead costs associated with it, which are grouped together to form a *cost pool*. Then the cost pool is charged to the product using a common *cost driver*. The following table gives examples of activities and cost drivers and shows how the predetermined cost driver rate is calculated by dividing the predetermined overhead by the predetermined cost driver volume.

Activity	Cost driver	Predetermined annual overhead £	Predetermined cost driver volume	Predetermined cost driver rate
Purchasing	Number of orders placed	400,000	100,000 orders	£4 per order
Machine setups	Number of machine setups	300,000	300 setups	£1,000 per setup
Quality control	Number of inspection hours	500,000	5,000 hours	£100 per hour
Power	Number of machine hours	250,000	100,000 hours	£2.50 per hour
Total		1,450,000		

As you can see, the business anticipates the annual production overheads will be £1,450,000. You need to remember that this is in addition to the direct costs (direct materials, direct labour and direct expenses). The predetermined cost driver volume has been calculated for the year and the last column shows the calculation of the predetermined cost driver rate.

Activity

A business makes two products (Product A and Product B). Using the following information for the month of January, calculate the total production cost of the two products for the period.

	Product A	Product B
Direct labour costs	£95,000	£120,000
Direct material costs	£116,000	£145,000
Number of purchase orders placed	3,000	8,000
Number of machine setups	12	18
Total of inspection hours	350	180
Total machine hours	6,000	5,500

At this stage in your studies, you should have had little difficulty in activity-based costing procedures. Check your calculations against the following model answer.

	Product A £	Product B £
Direct labour costs	95,000	120,000
Direct material costs	116,000	145,000
Purchasing	12,000	32,000
Machine setups	12,000	18,000
Quality control	35,000	18,000
Power	15,000	13,750
Total	285,000	346,750

14.5 The decision to adopt activity-based costing

Managers considering whether to adopt ABC will need to make a number of decisions. The example in the previous section simplifies the process greatly; in real life there are likely to be many problems that must be resolved.

Activity

What do you consider are the main benefits and drawbacks to adopting an activity-based costing system?

There are several benefits and drawbacks, most of which relate to the benefit of having more accurate cost information and the drawback of incurring costs in order to acquire it. You may have identified the following:

- The different basis for assigning costs to products is likely to result in a different total cost per unit. This can have important consequences for decision making and strategy in the company.
- The cost information should be more accurate and could lead to some products being eliminated and changes in the market price of other products.
- More record keeping will be involved and this may require more trained staff and new computer systems.
- Installing the system will require teamwork between accounting, production, marketing and other functions in the company.

Management must conduct a cost/benefit analysis before implementing ABC. Unless the expected benefits are greater than the costs, the firm should not go ahead with changing from absorption costing to ABC.

14.6 Costing for marketing and administration overheads

Many firms that use traditional absorption costing to calculate the total cost of a product tend to concentrate on production costs. *Marketing overheads* and *administration overheads* are often added to the total production cost using a *blanket rate* for the factory as a whole, which replaces the need to calculate a separate rate for each production cost centre.

Activity

What are the advantages and disadvantages in using a blanket rate?

A key advantage is that it is simple to calculate and apply. The accountant only needs to collect all the overheads together and then select one allocation base. The allocation base is normally related to volume, so it could be number of products, direct hour rate or machine hour rate. A blanket rate may be acceptable in a very simple organization with very few products, but there are disadvantages. One main disadvantage is that if there is more than one activity, the blanket rate may distort the total cost. For example, if there are two products and the marketing department is spending most of its time in promoting one of them, it would not be equitable to charge the other product the same overhead rate. Firms using absorption costing will attempt to achieve a better allocation of costs by identifying separate departments and different rates. It will take more time and effort to collect the information and make the calculations, but the resulting costing data will be more informative for management decision making.

In complex organizations, management may decide it is worth the additional costs to implement ABC. In such cases, this cost accounting system can be used to break down the costs involved in marketing and administration by applying the same principles as used for production costs. This enables management to make decisions about the operation of marketing and administration and determine whether it is possible to add value.

We will demonstrate this by applying the principles to Photoprint Ltd, a small company that designs and prints high-quality calendars. One of the products is a wildlife calendar, which features photographs and information on endangered species. Each calendar costs £20 to print and it has been the firm's practice to add 15% to cover the cost of advertising, postage and packaging (£20 × 15% = £3.00). Advertising has been by sending leaflets to a large customer mailing list that the company has built up over the years.

However, management is concerned that the price it charges for the calendar to make a profit is not sufficiently competitive and that its existing customer database contains a substantial amount of out-of-date information. In addition, the accountant has looked at the marketing side of the operation and has identified the following activities that give rise to costs:

- sending out leaflets to potential customers
- taking orders by post, telephone or through the Internet
- sending calendars to customers who have ordered them
- dealing with customer queries (for example, non-deliveries and complaints about damaged goods).

These activities are shown in the first column of the following table and the second column identifies the cost driver. The third column shows an estimate of the annual costs for each activity and the fourth column gives details of the estimated annual driver volume. The final column calculates the cost driver rate by dividing the estimated annual cost of each activity by its estimated driver volume.

Activities	Cost drivers	Estimated annual costs £	Estimated driver volume	Cost driver rate £
Leaflet design and printing	Customer mailing list	80,000	100,000	0.80
Leaflet dispatch	Customer mailing list	23,000	100,000	0.23
Taking orders	Number of orders	6,000	10,000	0.60
Calendar dispatch	Number sent	4,410	9,800	0.45
Customer complaints	Customer complaints	300	200	1.50
Total cost				3.58

At first glance, the blanket marketing cost of £3.00 per calendar does not look very different from the cost driver rate of £3.58 shown in the table. However, the reality is that the operation is costing £3.58 per calendar and this is reducing predicted profit by 58p per calendar. It also means that as the market is competitive management needs to make decisions about the future of the operation.

With the above information, management can consider each activity and determine whether savings can be made. For example, instead of sending leaflets to an existing customer mailing list, it may be more effective and less costly to have advertisements in appropriate magazines. As far as taking orders is concerned, management may decide to accept Internet orders only or to outsource the entire operation.

14.7   Advantages and disadvantages of activity-based costing

You may be wondering why every business has not adopted ABC, if it is such a good system. One of the main reasons is the question of cost and the problems associated with change. There is little inducement to undertake the substantial changes required to introduce a new system if the business already produces product costing information that meets their needs. Even if the business is not entirely satisfied with its present system, the cost of implementing and managing a new system may seem too large to make it worthwhile.

ABC is probably best suited for businesses that operate in highly competitive markets and have many different products that require complex production processes. In such organizations the arbitrary process of traditional absorption costing does not generate sufficiently specific information to aid managers in planning, controlling and decision making.

The main *advantages* of ABC are as follows:

- It provides more comprehensive detail about product costs.
- It generates data that are more specific and reliable than traditional costing.
- Because it does not distinguish between production overheads and general overheads, it overcomes the problem of finding a meaningful relationship between these non-production overheads and the production activity.
- It provides better information about the costs of activities, thus allowing managers to make more informed decisions.
- It improves cost control by identifying the costs incurred by specific activities.

The main *disadvantages* of ABC are:

- It can be costly and difficult to implement.
- Trained and experienced staff are required to operate the system.
- Substantial IT costs may be required.
- Managers may not find the information useful.
- It uses predetermined rates and therefore *underabsorption* or *overabsorption* of overheads will still occur as they do under absorption costing.

Information about the use of ABC internationally is relatively scarce. There is some evidence that adoption is more widespread in the UK and the USA than elsewhere, with growing use in continental Europe (CIMA, 2009). In the UK, a survey of 176

Table 14.1   Analysis of costing systems used in the UK

Business sector	ABC (%)	Absorption costing (%)	Direct costing system (%)	No costing system (%)	N
Manufacturing	20	52	21	7	91
Financial and commercial	68	9	9	14	22
Retail and other	22	26	35	17	23
Service	33	17	28	22	40
All sectors (%)	**29**	**35**	**23**	**13**	

N = 176
Source: Adapted from Al-Omiri and Drury (2007, p. 413).

large firms (Al-Omiri and Drury, 2007) found that 29% had adopted ABC systems and most of these firms were in the financial and commercial sector (see Table 14.1 on page 323). The majority of firms in the manufacturing sector used absorption costing and firms in the retail sector tended to use direct costing systems. Those that did not have not costing systems tended to be the smaller firms responding to the survey.

14.8 Conclusions

Activity-based costing has emerged as an alternative to absorption costing because of changes in manufacturing operations. The greater use of technology, the use of techniques such as JIT and the reduction and change in the nature of direct labour have meant that traditional costing methods are not providing sufficiently accurate information for decision-making purposes.

ABC is a costing system in which costs are first assigned to activities and then to products based on each product's use of activities. The principal assumption is that products consume activities and activities consume resources. There are four stages in implementing an activity-based costing system. These appear simple, but in practice they are complex and time-consuming. One of the major problems for companies is identifying those activities that consume resources and keeping this to a workable number. Once the activities have been identified and the costs assigned to them, a cost rate can be calculated by using the cost driver.

ABC offers the advantage of more accurate information than absorption costing because it looks for a closer relationship between overheads and the cause of these indirect costs. However, it suffers from the disadvantage that it is costly to implement and operate. It is most suitable for complex organizations with a range of products where absorption costing fails to provide costing information that is useful to management.

Practice questions

1 Discuss the reasons why accountants have developed ABC as an alternative to the traditional method of absorption costing for charging overheads to products or services.

2 Describe the four main stages in implementing a system of activity-based costing, defining all terms used.

3 Write a short report discussing the types of business where ABC might be appropriate and the advantages and disadvantages of implementing this type of cost accounting system.

4 Continental Communications Ltd manufactures two types of telephone: the standard and the advanced. The budget for the next financial year is as follows:

	Standard	Advanced
Production output	100,000	50,000
	£	£
Direct labour	200,000	100,000
Direct materials	50,000	20,000

The indirect overhead costs have been identified with three cost drivers as follows:

Cost driver	Cost assigned	Activity level	
		Standard	Advanced
Number of production runs	£150,000	40	10
Quality test performed	£40,000	8	12
Deliveries made	£20,000	80	20

Required
(a) Calculate the total cost per unit produced for each product.
(b) Prepare a presentation to be given to the board demonstrating the calculations and interpreting the results.

5 Parfums de Paris AG has a factory in France producing two aromatherapy oils. *Sweet Pea* is intended for the younger market and *Allure* is aimed at the more mature customer. The most significant costs incurred by the company relate to the packaging and advertising of the two products. The chief accountant has attended a seminar on ABC and has decided that it would be beneficial to implement it. The following information relates to the production in the current period:

	Sweet Pea	Allure
Number of litres produced	20,000	4,000
Number of purchasing orders	150	60
Quality inspection hours	1,000	750
Number of batches of materials	2,000	1,000
Cost of direct materials	€35,000	€12,000
Cost of direct labour	€25,000	€16,000

The budgeted cost pools and drivers for the financial year are as follows:

Activity	Cost driver	Predetermined annual overhead	Predetermined cost driver volume	Predetermined cost driver rate
		€		
Purchasing	No. of orders placed	180,000	15,000 orders	12 per order
Quality control	No. of inspection hours	50,000	12,500 hours	4 per hour
Material handling	Batches of materials	20,000	10,000 hours	2 per hour

Required

(a) Calculate the cost per unit for each of the two products.

(b) Discuss the decision of the chief accountant to implement the system in the context of the available information.

References

Al-Omiri, M. and Drury, M. (2007) A survey of factors influencing the choice of product costing systems in UK organizations. *Management Accounting Research* 18, 300–424.

CIMA (2005) *Management Accounting Official Terminology*. London: Chartered Institute of Management Accountants.

CIMA (2009) *Management Accounting Tools for Today and Tomorrow*. London: Chartered Institute of Management Accountants. Available at: http://www.cimaglobal.com/Thought-leadership/Research-topics/Recommended-reports/ (accessed 30 November 2011).

Johnson, H. T. and Kaplan, R. S. (1987) *Relevance Lost: The Rise and Fall of Management Accounting*. Boston: Harvard Business School Press.

Law, J. (ed.) (2010) *Dictionary of Accounting*, 4th edition. Oxford: Oxford University Press.

Weetman, P. (1999) *Financial and Management Accounting*, 2nd edition. Edinburgh: Pearson Education.

15 Marginal costing

Learning objectives

When you have studied this chapter, you should be able to:

- describe the main purposes of marginal costing
- construct a marginal cost statement and associated profit statement
- conduct breakeven analysis
- rank products using contribution analysis
- describe the limitations of marginal costing.

15.1 Introduction

In Chapter 13 we explained that absorption costing takes account of both the direct costs and a portion of the indirect costs when calculating the cost per unit. This chapter examines a costing technique known as *marginal costing* which only takes account of the variable costs of production when calculating the cost per unit; the fixed costs for the period are written off in full, without attempting to charge them to the cost units. The advantage of this is that marginal costing recognizes that costs behave differently as activity changes. Therefore, whereas absorption costing requires costs to be classified as direct or indirect costs, marginal costing requires costs to be classified as variable or fixed costs. In view of its focus on the variable costs of production, marginal costing is also known as *variable costing*.

Although it has some limitations, marginal costing is a widely used technique and the principles are simple to understand and easy to apply. In this chapter we explain how to construct a marginal cost statement to calculate the *contribution* made by the production and sale of a cost unit towards covering the fixed costs and, hence, profit.

We also examine how *breakeven analysis* and other types of *contribution analysis* using planned or actual figures can provide useful information to management for a number of short-term decisions.

15.2 Classifying costs by behaviour

Marginal costing meets the need for detailed information about costs in a business where production levels fluctuate. This costing method requires revenue expenditure to be classified into either *variable costs* or *fixed costs* according to their behaviour when the level of production or sales activity changes. The variable cost incurred in producing one unit is known as the *marginal cost*.

Key definitions

The marginal cost is the additional cost incurred as a result of the production of one additional unit of production. It usually equates to the direct costs plus the variable overhead costs.

A variable cost is an item of expenditure that, in total, varies directly with the level of activity achieved.

A fixcd cost is an item of expenditure that remains unchanged, in total, irrespective of changes in the levels of production or sales.

Source: Law (2010, pp. 275, 430 and 194 respectively).

The variable costs per unit are usually regarded as the direct costs plus any variable overheads and are assumed to be constant in the short term. Therefore, a characteristic of a variable cost is that it is incurred at a constant rate per unit; for example, the cost of direct materials will tend to double if output doubles.

From these definitions we can deduce that product direct costs will always be variable costs, whilst indirect costs tend to be fixed costs. Some indirect costs can be described as *semi-variable costs*. This means that they contain a variable element and a fixed element, each of which must be identified so that the variable element can be added to the other variable costs and the fixed element can be added to the other fixed costs. For example, the cost of electricity used to power machinery in a factory may consist of a standing charge (the fixed cost) plus a charge per kilowatt used (the variable cost).

Activity

Classify the following costs for a manufacturing business into variable and fixed costs:

- **depreciation on machinery**
- **direct materials**
- **direct labour**
- **factory rent and rates**

- **factory manager's salary**
- **commission paid to the sales team.**

Even if you do not have any experience of working in a manufacturing environment, you should have been able to identify these from the definitions of fixed and variable costs. Depreciation, rent and rates, and salaries (unless part of pay is related to productivity levels) are all examples of fixed costs. Direct materials, direct labour and commission paid to the sales team are usually considered as variable costs, because they change in accordance with changes in the level of production or sales activity.

In Chapter 11 we looked at Sam Reeve's taxi business, where the average mileage by a taxi in one quarter of the year was 15,000 miles and the quarterly costs, analysed by nature, were as follows:

Expense	Cost per quarter
	£
Driver's salary	2,670
Petrol and oil	1,050
Annual service	450
Tax and insurance	1,110
Depreciation	870

Sam wants to tender for a special job that will involve an additional 500 miles per quarter. This mileage can be done in the driver's current time allowance, so no additional salary will be incurred. Sam needs to know the cost of the additional 500 miles per quarter, so that he can submit a quotation for the job.

Activity

Explain how the following figures have been calculated and identify the correct cost of the additional 500 miles.

(a) £205
(b) £116
(c) £35

The total cost per mile is calculated by dividing the total cost for the quarter by the average mileage for the quarter:

$$\frac{£1,050}{15,000} = £0.07 \text{ (or 7p)}$$

Answer (a) is the result of multiplying the mileage of 500 miles by the total cost per mile of 41p. However, we know that no additional wages for the driver will be incurred, so it would be incorrect to take £205 as the cost of the additional 500 miles. The driver's wages, in this example, can be considered as a fixed cost. In our example, activity is measured in miles.

Answer (b) has been calculated by multiplying the 500 miles by 23.2p; that is, the total cost per mile less the driver's element. But this is not the correct answer to the question, because if you look at the list of costs, you will see that the driver's salary is not the only fixed cost. Certain other costs will not increase because of the additional 500 miles per quarter. Taking them in the order in which they are listed, the costs for petrol and oil will obviously rise with the increased mileage, so they are not fixed. With regard to servicing and repairs, some routine servicing will be carried out regardless of the mileage and this is therefore a fixed cost. However, other servicing and repair costs depend on the mileage. Clearly, tax and insurance are fixed costs and, like the driver's salary, should be excluded from our calculations of the cost for the additional 500 miles. Depreciation, to some extent, is influenced by the amount of mileage, but in a taxi business, depreciation depends mainly on the passage of time.

The above identification of fixed costs should help you with answer (c). The answer of £35 has been calculated by multiplying the 500 miles by 7p, the cost of petrol and oil per mile. In view of the information we have available, this is the best answer. If we are to be more precise, we will need more details of the service and repair costs so that we can identify which are fixed.

Activity

Circle the correct answer in the following statements:

(a) If activity increases, total fixed costs will increase/decrease/stay the same.
(b) If activity increases, the fixed costs per unit will increase/decrease/stay the same.
(c) If activity decreases, total fixed costs will increase/decrease/stay the same.
(d) If activity decreases, the fixed costs per unit will increase/decrease/stay the same.

You should have had little difficulty in deciding the answers to (a) and (c). These are drawn straight from the definition and in both cases the total fixed costs stay the same regardless of changes in the level of activity. You may have found the answers to (b) and (d) a little more difficult, and some simple figures may help. We will take as our example a factory where the rent is £8,000 per annum, a fixed cost. The output of the factory each year is 1,000 units. The cost for rent per unit is therefore £8. If the factory makes 1,500 units one year, what is the rent per unit? The total rent cost will stay the same at £8,000, so the cost per unit for rent will decrease to £5.33. Therefore, the answer to (b) is that if activity increases, the fixed cost per unit will decrease. The reasoning is similar with statement (d): if activity decreases the fixed cost per unit will increase.

Activity

Circle the correct answer in the following statements:

(a) If activity increases, total variable costs will increase/decrease/stay the same.
(b) If activity increases, the variable cost per unit will increase/decrease/stay the same.

(c) **If activity decreases, total variable costs will increase/decrease/stay the same.**
(d) **If activity decreases, the variable cost per unit will increase/decrease/stay the same.**

You should have found this activity fairly straightforward after the earlier example. The answer to statements (b) and (d) is that if activity increases or decreases, the variable cost per unit will stay the same. The answer to statement (a) is that when activity increases, the total variable cost will increase. Similarly, with statement (c), when activity decreases, the total variable cost decreases.

15.3   Calculating contribution

We saw in the previous section that in total the *variable costs* tend to increase or decrease in line with production or sales activity, whilst the *fixed costs* tend to remain the same, despite changes in the level of activity. *Semi-variable costs* contain both variable and fixed elements and must be analysed so that the variable elements can be added to the other variable costs and the fixed elements can be added to other fixed costs. Because some costs change and others stay the same when activity changes, the total cost per unit changes and the total cost for all production changes, but not directly.

Under marginal costing, only the variable costs are charged to the units. The difference between sales revenue and the variable costs is not the profit, since no allowance has been made for the fixed costs incurred; it is the *contribution* towards fixed costs.

> **Key definition**
>
> **Contribution is the additional profit that will be earned by an organization when the breakeven point production has been exceeded. The unit contribution is the difference between the selling price of a product and its marginal cost of production. This is based on the assumption that the marginal cost and the sales value will be constant.**
>
> *Source*: Law (2010, p. 110).

Contribution can be calculated for one unit or for any chosen level of sales. The *contribution per unit* is the selling price less the variable costs per unit. The *total contribution* is the contribution per unit multiplied by the number of units produced. Once the total fixed costs are exceeded by the total contribution, the business starts making a profit.

We will examine the concept of contribution by looking at an example. Mementos Ltd manufactures ceramic models of historic buildings for the tourist trade. The selling price of each model is £2.30. Direct materials cost 60p per unit, direct labour costs are 30p per unit and each model is packed in a presentation box which costs 15p per unit. The total fixed costs are the overheads for the business, which total £850 per week. The normal weekly output is 1,000 units. With this information we can draw up a *marginal cost statement*. The following statement calculates the total contribution and the net profit or loss for the week (assuming 1,000 units are produced and sold):

Mementos Ltd	
Marginal cost statement for one week	
	1,000 units
	£
Revenue	2,300
Variable costs	
Direct materials (60p × 1,000)	(600)
Direct labour (30p × 1,000)	(300)
Packaging (15p × 1,000)	(150)
	(1,050)
Contribution	1,250
Fixed costs	(850)
Profit for the period	400

Marginal costing forms the basis of a number of useful techniques for making short-term decisions and can be based on budgeted or actual costs. The theory is simple to understand and easy to apply.

15.4 Breakeven analysis

Marginal costing principles are used in *breakeven analysis* to identify the *breakeven point*, which gives management further useful information. The breakeven point is where the organization makes neither a profit nor a loss. It can be expressed as:

$$\text{Sales revenue} - \text{Variable costs} - \text{Fixed costs} = 0$$

or

$$\text{Sales revenue} = \text{Variable costs} + \text{Fixed costs}$$

or

$$\text{Contribution} = \text{Fixed costs}$$

Key definition

The breakeven point (BEP) is the level of production, sales volume, percentage of capacity, or sales revenue at which an organization makes neither a profit nor a loss.

Source: Law (2010, p. 65).

The breakeven point (BEP) can be measured in a number of different ways, which we will illustrate with the data for Mementos Ltd. The following marginal cost statement calculates the contribution per unit, together with the total contribution and the net profit, assuming that the production and sales capacity is 1,000 units for one week.

Mementos Ltd		
Marginal cost statement for one week		
	1 unit	1,000 units
	£	£
Revenue	2.30	2,300
Variable costs		
Direct materials	(0.60)	(600)
Direct labour	(0.30)	(300)
Packaging	(0.15)	(150)
	(1.05)	(1,050)
Contribution	1.25	1,250
Fixed costs		(850)
Profit for the period		400

The business can calculate the level of production and sales in number of *units* needed to break even by using the following formula:

$$\text{BEP (units)} = \frac{\text{Fixed costs}}{\text{Contribution per unit}} = \frac{£850}{£1.25} = 680 \text{ units}$$

Once you have found the breakeven point in units, you can use it to calculate the *sales revenue* at the breakeven point. The formula is:

BEP (sales revenue) = BEP in units × Selling price = 680 × £2.30 850 = £1,564

Further useful information can be gained by calculating the breakeven point as a *percentage of capacity* using the following formula:

$$\text{BEP (percentage of capacity)} = \frac{\text{BEP in units}}{\text{Capacity in units}} \times 100 = \frac{680}{1,000} \times 100 = 68\%$$

If the business has set a *target profit*, the level of activity needed to achieve the target profit can be found by using the following formula:

$$\text{Level of activity to achieve target profit} = \frac{\text{Fixed costs + Target profit}}{\text{Contribution per unit}}$$

Using the formula, we can work out how many models the company needs to sell to make a target profit of £200 per week:

$$\text{Level of activity to achieve target profit of £200} = \frac{£850 + £200}{£1.25} = 840 \text{ units}$$

The difference between the level of activity to achieve the target profit (in this case, 840 units) and the breakeven point (in this case, 680 units) is known as the *margin of safety*. This means that the company could miss its target of 840 units by 160 units before it goes below the breakeven point and starts making a loss.

All this information can be shown graphically. The procedure for constructing a *breakeven graph* is as follows:

1. Draw a horizontal axis to measure activity (in units).
2. Draw a vertical axis to measure costs and revenue (£).
3. Plot a fixed costs line that will be parallel to the horizontal axis.
4. Plot the total costs line by adding the variable costs to the fixed costs, remembering that at nil activity there will be no variable costs, but there will be total fixed costs.
5. Plot the revenue line. The breakeven point will be where the revenue line and the total costs line intercept.

Activity

Using graph paper, draw a breakeven graph for Mementos Ltd. Assume that the maximum level of activity is 900 models.

If you have drawn your graph accurately, you should have obtained the same breakeven point as you calculated using the formula and your graph should look Figure 15.1.

Although the breakeven point can be calculated by applying a formula or constructing a graph, the same answer would be arrived at by either method. However, the advantage of using a formula is that with more complex data it permits a greater degree of accuracy.

Figure 15.1 Mementos Ltd, breakeven graph

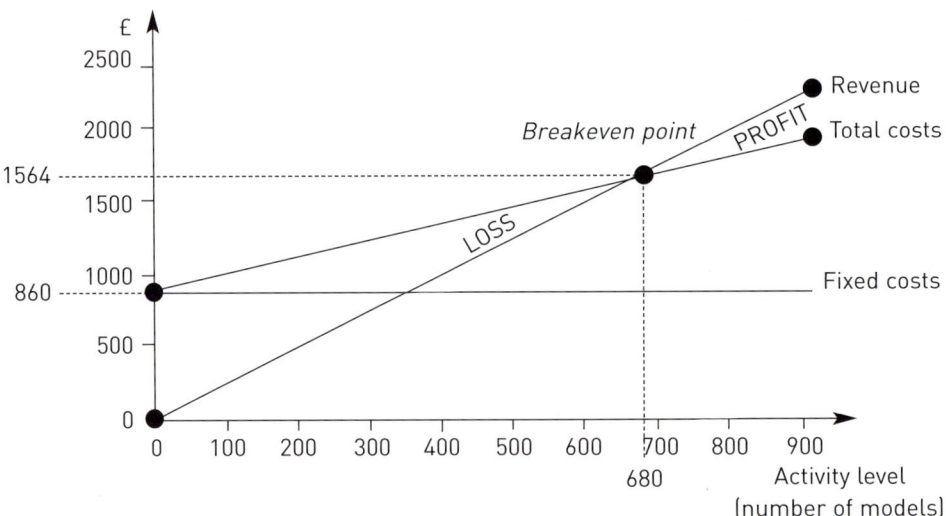

In this section we have concentrated on calculating the breakeven point. However, the same principles can be used for calculating the profit at different levels of activity. For this reason, accountants sometimes use the term *cost-volume-profit analysis*, as this focuses on what will happen to the financial results if the level of activity (such as the volume of products produced and sold) fluctuates.

15.5   Contribution analysis

Marginal costing principles are used in *contribution analysis* to provide management with information to help with other short-term decisions, such as:

- setting the minimum selling price of a product, particularly in times when the market is depressed and when introducing new products
- evaluating the proposed closure or temporary cessation of part of the business
- assessing whether to accept a special contract or order
- comparing the cost implications of different methods of manufacture
- choosing which of a range of products to make.

Perhaps the management at Mementos Ltd wants to know the minimum selling price that could be set for its models. If you look at the marginal cost statement, you will see that the answer is £1.05, which is the variable cost per unit; any lower than this amount would mean that the company would not recover the costs incurred in making the model. However, if the selling price was set at this price, the business would not obtain any contribution towards covering the fixed costs. This can be examined further by looking at another example.

Activity

Icetreats Ltd makes three types of ice lolly and shares its fixed overheads equally over the three types. A summary of the income statement for last month is shown below.

Icetreats Ltd				
	Fruit Ice	Choc Ice	Kool Ice	Total
Number of units produced	11,200	9,000	6,000	
	£	£	£	£
Sales	5,500	4,500	2,400	12,400
Variable costs	(2,400)	(1,800)	(1,300)	(5,500)
Contribution	3,100	2,700	1,100	6,900
Fixed costs	(2,000)	(2,000)	(2,000)	(6,000)
Profit/(loss) for the period	1,100	700	(900)	900

The sales director has suggested that as sales of all ice lollies are expected to decrease by 10% next month, production of Kool Ice should be stopped until demand picks up. Redraft the above statement, first showing what will happen if there is a 10% decrease in demand, and second, if production of Kool Ice is halted.

Check your answer against the following solution:

	Icetreats Ltd			
	Fruit Ice	Choc Ice	Kool Ice	**Total**
Number of units produced	10,080	8,100	5,400	
	£	£	£	£
Sales	4,950	4,050	2,160	11,160
Variable costs	(2,160)	(1,620)	(1,170)	(4,950)
Contribution	2,790	2,430	990	6,210
Fixed costs	(2,000)	(2,000)	(2,000)	(6,000)
Profit/(loss) for the period	790	430	(1,010)	210

The above statement shows the impact that the 10% decrease in sales will have on profit, as well as the fact that Kool Ice is making a contribution to fixed costs. If production of Kool Ice is stopped, then the net profit would turn into a net loss as, the following figures show:

	£
Contribution	
Fruit Ice	2,790
Choc Ice	2,430
Total contribution	5,220
Fixed costs	(6,000)
Loss for the period	(780)

The difference between the old profit of £210 and the new position (a loss of £780) is £990. This is the contribution lost if the business stops producing the Kool Ice product. The £780 loss is calculated on the basis of the assumption that the £6,000 of fixed costs will stay the same, at least in the short term, regardless of changes in activity or the cessation of one of the product lines. We can conclude from this that, in general, if a product or service makes a contribution towards fixed costs, it is financially worthwhile continuing to produce it. Of course, there may be other business reasons for dropping it, or it may be financially preferable to direct the activities of the organization in another direction. However, from a financial point of view, in this example it is advisable to continue production of Kool Ice.

Let us assume that a large hotel has approached Icetreats Ltd and offers to place an order for 600 Kool Ices per month, as long as the price is reduced from 40p to 30p per lolly. The order would restore demand, but should the company accept it in view of the low price offered? The general rule is that, if the business has spare production capacity, it is worthwhile accepting a special order, as long as it makes a contribution. The key figures for Kool Ice, calculated to the nearest penny, are as follows:

	Per unit £		Per unit £
Current selling price	0.40	Proposed selling price	0.30
Variable costs (1,300 ÷ 6,000)	(0.22)	Variable costs (1,300 ÷ 6,000)	(0.22)
Contribution	0.18	Contribution	0.08

As the special price will still give a contribution of 8p, it is worthwhile accepting, but there may be other factors that must be considered before making a final decision, such as the reaction of other customers who may learn of this discounted price.

Now the production manager says he can change the production method so that up to 12,000 Fruit Ices can be produced per month for an additional fixed cost of £500 per month. He estimates that this will save variable costs of 4p per Fruit Ice. Do you think this plan should be implemented? There is no need to do a full calculation again, but look instead at the maximum possible savings in variable costs and compare them with the fixed costs. The maximum savings will be 4p × 12,000 = £480. Since this is lower than the £500 additional fixed costs incurred, the proposal is not financially worthwhile.

Even when a business occupies a very specialist market, it is unlikely to rely solely on manufacturing a single product, as there is a strong demand in the developed world for a choice of products. Therefore, it is likely that at some stage the business will have more than one product and need cost accounting information to help management make decisions about which is the most profitable. This will then lead to a decision to concentrate production on the most profitable product until demand for that product has been met, and then the next most profitable, and so on. The information provided by marginal costing allows us to use contribution to *rank products*; we will explain this by turning back to the example of Mementos Ltd.

Activity

So far the business has only made one model: the Westminster Abbey. Direct materials for this model cost 60p, direct labour 30p, packaging 15p per unit and it sells for £2.30. It has now been suggested that they could also make a model of Windsor Castle. Direct materials for Windsor Castle will cost 90p, direct labour 35p and packaging 20p per unit and it will have a selling price of £3.00. The fixed costs of £850 per week would be unchanged by this proposal. Construct a marginal cost statement showing the marginal cost for 1 unit of each model and rank the two products according to the *contribution per unit*.

You should have had no difficulty with the first part of this activity if you have remembered the correct format for a marginal cost statement. Compare your answer with the following solution:

Marginal cost statement (1 unit)		
	Westminster Abbey	Windsor Castle
	£	£
Selling price	2.30	3.00
Variable costs		
Direct materials	0.60	0.90
Direct labour	0.30	0.35
Packing	0.15	0.20
Packaging	(1.05)	(1.45)
Contribution per unit	1.25	1.55
Ranking	2nd	1st

Interpreting the information is straightforward if you have recognized that the reason for constructing a marginal cost statement is to calculate the contribution. If you compare the contribution per unit for each model, you can see that the Windsor Castle model has the higher contribution. It contributes £1.55 towards the fixed costs compared to only £1.25 from the Westminster Abbey model. Assuming that it is just as easy to sell the Windsor Castle model as it is to sell the Westminster Abbey model and there are no limiting factors, the general rule for ranking products is to concentrate on making the product that gives the highest contribution first, in order to cover the fixed costs the fastest and start making the business a profit as quickly as possible. The fixed costs do not need to be considered in this decision because they remain unchanged by the choice of model produced.

The disadvantage of ranking products according to the contribution per unit is that we are ignoring differences in sales volume (the number of units sold) and, hence, differences in revenue generated. If 1,000 units of the Westminster Abbey model and 700 units of the Windsor Castle model can be sold in 1 week, the total contribution for each product will be:

Total contribution = Contribution per unit × Number of units sold

	Westminster Abbey	Windsor Castle
Total contribution	£1.25 × 1,000 = £1,250	£1.55 × 700 = £1,085
Ranking	1st	2nd

As you can see, ranking by *total contribution* reverses our earlier opinion and we can now recommend that the business concentrates on producing and selling the Westminster Abbey model.

15.6 Limiting factors

So far we have assumed that there is no factor present that would prevent the business from achieving the level of activity required to break even or achieve the desired level of profit. In reality, this is rarely the case and there is nearly always some *limiting factor*, such as shortages of materials or labour, a restriction on the sales demand at a particular price or the production capacity of machinery. Therefore, limiting factors are the last aspect we will consider in making decisions using contribution analysis.

Key definition

A limiting factor is a constraint that limits the business from achieving higher levels of performance and profitability.

The first step is to identify any limiting factor and arrange production so that the contribution per limiting factor is maximized. For example, perhaps the owner of Mementos Ltd is concerned about the supply of direct materials used in the products due to industrial action at the docks where they are imported. This could mean that the company will only be able to make a limited number of products. Management has a dilemma, since the same type of materials is used in both models, but we can see from the marginal cost statement in the previous section that the Windsor Castle model uses 50% more materials (direct materials are £0.90 per unit compared with £0.60 for the Westminster Abbey model). Under these circumstances, which model should the company make to obtain the maximum profit?

This is slightly more difficult than the decisions we have looked at so far. When a limiting factor is present, the general rule is to maximize production of the product with the highest *contribution per unit of limiting factor*. We do not know the amount of materials, but if we did, we could calculate the contribution per kilo by dividing the contribution per unit by the number of kilos per unit. However, we do know the cost of materials for each model. Therefore, we can calculate the contribution for each £1 spent on the limiting factor. The general formula for calculating the contribution per limiting factor is as follows:

$$\text{Contribution per limiting factor} = \frac{\text{Contribution per unit}}{\text{Limiting factor per unit}}$$

Substituting the figures for the words in the formula:

	Westminster Abbey	Windsor Castle
Contribution per limiting factor	$\frac{£1.25}{£0.60} = £2.08$	$\frac{£1.55}{£0.90} = £1.72$
Ranking	1st	2nd

If there is a shortage of direct materials, the management at Mementos Ltd should select the product that gives the greatest contribution for every £1 of direct materials used. This would be the model of Westminster Abbey, since you can see that it has the higher contribution per limiting factor. The results of our analysis show that for every £1 of direct materials used for making and selling Westminster Abbey models, the company would get a contribution of £2.08, but only £1.72 from selling Windsor Castle models.

The following table draws together the results of the three different methods we have used for ranking products, starting with the basic approach and increasing in level of sophistication until we find a method that takes account of factors that may constrain profitability.

	Westminster Abbey	Windsor Castle
Contribution per unit	£1.25	£1.55
Ranking	2nd	1st
Total contribution	£1,250	£1,085
Ranking	1st	2nd
Contribution per limiting factor	£2.08	£1.72
Ranking	1st	2nd

As you can see, our subsequent analysis shows that the company will need to reverse its first decision to focus production on the Windsor Castle model based on the contribution per unit, as it needs to take account of the sales volume for each product. We have also found out that if direct materials are in short supply, the Westminster Abbey model will still be the more profitable of the two products.

15.7   Limitations and the relevant range

The principles of marginal costing are based on assumptions about the behaviour of fixed and variable costs, but these rarely hold true over a complete range of activity or for any length of time. This leads to a number of limitations:

- Marginal costing is based on the assumption that variable costs will vary in direct proportion to changes in the level of activity, but they may also vary for other reasons. For example, variable costs may rise steeply in the early stages because production is not very efficient and rise again at the peak of activity due to pressure of work causing inefficiencies; a special discount on the price of direct materials for a short period may cause variable costs to fluctuate, whilst production levels remain constant.
- It is based on the assumption that fixed costs are not affected by changes in the level of activity, but they may change for other reasons. For example, the cost of electricity used to power machines used in the production process may decrease in steps as the level of consumption increases; other fixed costs may increase in steps as additional facilities – such as another machine, more factory space, etc. – become necessary as activity levels expand.
- Management may find it difficult to identify the variable and fixed elements of cost within semi-variable costs.
- Care must be taken when taking decisions based on contribution, since in the longer term the business will also need to recover the fixed costs.

- Like other accounting techniques, marginal costing does not take account of non-financial factors, such as changes in the motivation, skills and experience of employees that might affect activity levels.

In breakeven analysis, the limited range of activity over which the assumptions about the behaviour of costs hold true is known as the *relevant range*, and decisions should be restricted to this range unless investigations are conducted.

Key definition

The relevant range is the range of levels of activity between which valid conclusions can be drawn from the linear cost functions normally associated with a breakeven analysis. Outside this range it is recognized that the linear relationships between fixed costs, variable costs, and revenue do not apply.

Source: Law (2010, p. 355).

15.8 Conclusions

Marginal costing is a cost accounting technique that only takes account of the variable costs of production when calculating the cost per unit. In this chapter we have explained how a marginal cost statement is drawn up and how the contribution of various products is calculated. We have drawn a breakeven graph and used it to find the breakeven point as well as using a number of formulae. Finally, we have discussed the importance of limiting factors, which may constrain the growth of an organization and therefore affect the decision-making process. We have also explained the general rules for calculating which product will be more profitable to produce when limiting factors are present.

The principles upon which marginal costing techniques, such as breakeven analysis and contribution analysis, are based rest on the assumption that variable costs are not incurred unless production activity takes place, whilst fixed costs are incurred irrespective of the level of activity. However, the assumptions about the behaviour of variable and fixed costs in relation to changes in the level of activity are only reliable in the short term and over the relevant range of activity.

Practice questions

1 Describe the purposes of marginal costing and the importance of contribution.

2 Explain the impact of limiting factors and how you would allow for them. Use a worked example to illustrate your answer.

3 Funfair Engineering Ltd manufactures fairground equipment. The company uses absorption costing and has been experiencing falling demand for its products due to the economic recession. Steve Wrench, the production manager, is worried because the total cost per unit is increasing, despite strict cost controls. Diane Flowers, the marketing manager, is complaining that selling prices will have to be reduced to maintain sales levels. At a recent meeting they found that the selling

price suggested by Diane is lower than the total cost per unit calculated by Steve and they concluded that lowering the selling price to increase sales will only lead to even larger losses.

Required

Write a report addressed to Mr Wrench and Ms Flowers explaining:

(a) Why the total cost per unit increases as production decreases.

(b) Why marginal costing may be more appropriate than absorption costing for decision making in times of recession.

4 Edwards & Co Ltd manufactures teddy bears. The company's bears are in demand all year round and in the next financial year the sales manager plans to sell 12,000 teddies. The management accountant collects cost information for 1 unit of production (1 teddy bear). Based on last year's figures, each unit will sell for £10 and the variable costs will consist of direct materials, which will cost £1.00 per unit, and direct labour, which will cost £5.00 per unit. The fixed costs for the year are expected to be £32,000.

Required

You have been asked to provide information that will help the managing director consider the effect on profitability of changes in the level of sales activity next year.

(a) Draw up a marginal cost statement that calculates the contribution per unit.

(b) Draw up a marginal cost statement on the basis that 12,000 units will be sold and calculate the net profit or loss.

(c) Briefly explain what is meant by the breakeven point.

(d) Using the contribution per unit you have calculated in (a), calculate the following, showing the formulae in words and your workings:

   (i)   The breakeven point in number of units.

   (ii) The breakeven point in terms of total sales value.

   (iii) The level of sales activity to reach a target profit of £20,000.

   (iv) The margin of safety in units at the level of sales activity you have computed in (iii).

5 Audiomax Ltd manufactures three models of audio systems: Premier, Deluxe and Superior. When planning next year's production, the management team wants to make sure the most profitable mix of models is produced. The following table shows the selling price and variable costs per unit for each model.

	Premium	Deluxe	Superior
	£	£	£
Selling price	100	150	240
Direct materials	30	40	50
Direct labour	30	50	120
Direct expenses	10	25	24

Required

(a) Construct a marginal cost statement that calculates the contribution per unit for each model.

(b) Calculate the contribution per limiting factor for each model on the assumption that the supply of direct materials is limited, and rank the products accordingly. In addition, interpret your results by making a brief recommendation on the action management should take regarding prioritizing the production of these products.

(c) Calculate the contribution per limiting factor for each model on the assumption that the supply of direct labour is limited, and rank them accordingly. In addition, interpret your results by making brief recommendations on the action management should take regarding prioritizing the production of these products.

(d) Point out any other relevant matters that management should consider.

Reference

Law, J. (ed.) (2010) *Dictionary of Accounting*, 4th edition. Oxford: Oxford University Press.

16 Budgetary planning and control

Learning objectives

When you have studied this chapter, you should be able to:

- describe the main stages in budgetary control
- differentiate between fixed and flexible budgets
- explain the purpose of budgetary control and the requirements for an effective system
- describe the advantages and disadvantages of budgetary control.

16.1 Introduction

There are no rules and regulations governing management accounting because, unlike financial reporting, the information is intended for internal users. One advantage of this is that management accounting information can be produced about future accounting periods as well as for past periods. We have already seen that systems of cost accounting may use actual costs relating to a previous accounting period and budgeted costs based on estimates of future costs. In this chapter we introduce a major technique for planning and control known as *budgetary control* that uses budgeted figures for income and expenditure. Financial control is exercised by preparing detailed business plans for all aspects of the organization's activities, monitoring them against actual performance and taking any actions necessary to address any unfavourable deviations from the plan.

There are very few managers who do not encounter a budgetary control system during their careers. The technique of budgetary control is used in service and manufacturing businesses, as well as not-for-profit organizations. Apart from governments' budgets, some of the most publicly announced budgets are those of major films, where they are so important that the credits at the end show the name of the accountant.

In this chapter we explain the importance of budgetary control and the procedures for setting up the system. We also describe how it is used to generate valuable information that helps managers with the task of planning and controlling activities, and making decisions that ensure the business achieves its financial objectives.

16.2 Importance of business planning

Business planning is essential if the owners and managers of a business are to make a profit. In Chapter 1 we explained that some businesses pursue profit maximization strategies, whilst small businesses may pursue satisficing strategies that will give their owner-managers sufficient profit to maintain a certain lifestyle. The financial objectives of organizations in the not-for-profit sector are simply to break even; that is, they will be concerned with generating enough income to cover their total costs without making either a profit or a loss.

We will examine the importance of business planning by looking at an example. Cascade PLC manufactures bathroom fittings. Based on last year's production records, the production manager believes that 15,000 shower units will be needed and buys all the materials and stores them in a warehouse. The marketing manager has heard that the water companies are considering changing their charging methods from rates based on the value of the property where the water is used to a metered system based on the amount of water used. As a result, he has launched a large sales campaign and believes that 30,000 shower units will be sold. The financial accountant has received a letter from the bank stating that overdraft facilities will be withdrawn and has decided to stop any expenditure that is not absolutely necessary. The designer has come up with a new design that incorporates recycling waste water from the shower unit. The personnel manager believes the economic recession will get worse and has started issuing redundancy notices to the workforce. This illustrates how a lack of coordination of the various activities and managers following their own ideas can lead to resources not being matched to the demands made on them, which results in waste and inefficiency.

All this can be avoided if the business adopts a system of *budgetary control* to help them meet their financial objectives. Budgetary control is a major technique used in a wide range of organizations for planning and control. Traditionally, it took the form of a centralized and bureaucratic system of cost control, but it has evolved to meet the needs of modern business. In many organizations, it is a participative exercise that also involves managers at lower levels and the use of budgets to contribute directly to value creation. Cash flow forecasts (see Chapter 2) and financial year forecasts are amongst the most widely used tools for budgetary planning and control (CIMA, 2009).

Key definition

Budgetary control is the process by which financial control is exercised within an organization. Budgets for income and expenditure for each function of the

> organization are prepared in advance of an accounting period and are then compared with actual performance to establish any variances. Individual function managers are made responsible for the controllable costs within their budgets, and are expected to take remedial action if the adverse variances are regarded as excessive.
>
> *Source:* Law (2010, p. 67).

16.3 Main stages in budgetary control

The first stage in a system of *budgetary control* is for management to set out their *assumptions* about what is going to happen to the firm's markets and business environment.

Activity

Make a list of the factors that management should consider when arriving at their assumptions about what is going to happen to their markets and the business environment.

Depending on the type of organization you are thinking of, the sort of factors you may have included are as follows:

- changes in the size of the organization's market and its market share
- competitors' strategies
- changes in interest rates or sources of funding
- increases in costs and availability of energy, materials and labour
- changes in legislation or social pressures that will affect the organization
- the effects of the activities of other related organizations
- changes in climate, consumer demographics, social and environmental factors, etc.

Having set out their assumptions, management can then start making predictions about what is likely to happen in the year ahead. However, if they were to leave it at that, they would not be discharging their managerial responsibilities. For example, perhaps they forecast that the business will become insolvent and unable to pay its debts when they fall due. Although this might be an accurate prediction, it would not be acceptable and they must find ways of minimizing any threats to the organization and taking advantage of any opportunities. By setting out their *financial strategies* and the actions that must be taken in view of their predictions, they are making business plans that will help them meet their financial objectives.

The next step requires detailed plans (the *budgets*) to be drawn up with specific financial plans for each designated part of the business (the *budget centres*), thus covering every aspect of the organization's activities.

Key definitions

A budget is a financial or quantitative statement, prepared prior to a specified accounting period, containing the plans and policies to be pursued during that period. It is used as the basis for budgetary control.

A budget centre is a section or area of an organization under the responsibility of a manager for which budgets are prepared; these budgets are compared with actual performance as part of the budgetary control process.

Source: Law (2010, p. 67).

The budget period is usually one year and the budget is normally broken down into monthly figures. Initially, it may be expressed in quantitative terms (for example, the numbers of each type of product to be made and the quantity of materials to be ordered), but it will be converted into financial terms for the budgetary control system. A budget centre is typically a department or function in the business, a cost centre, an individual or any combination of these that management wishes to treat as a budget centre.

Activity

Give an example of a budget using the knowledge you have gained from your studies so far.

A cash flow forecast is a good example of a budget. You will be familiar with this from Chapter 2. A cash flow forecast is a statement that shows the amount of cash expected to come in and go out during some period in the future. It is usually drawn up for each month over a 12-month period, and shows the monthly cash inflows and outflows, the net cash flows and the cumulative cash position at the end of each month. A cash flow forecast is not a tool for control because it is only a plan. In order to achieve control, comparison must be made with the actual figures. In budgetary control, responsibility for monitoring and controlling items of income and expenditure is devolved to the managers of the budget centres. The management accounting system provides information to these managers on a regular basis (often monthly) that gives details of the budgeted figures and the actual figures achieved, so that they can compare their performance against the plan and take any actions deemed necessary. The provision of information to all levels of an organization based on responsibility of the individual managers is known as *responsibility accounting*.

The next stage involves translating the detailed plans into actions for each manager to pursue.

Activity

Both the production manager and the marketing manager of Cascade PLC need to know how many shower units they plan to sell in the coming year so they can ensure that the number of shower units to be made will meet the anticipated demand. What suggestions would you make if either of the following circumstances arose?

(a) Many more shower units are made than can be sold.
(b) Many more orders are received than the number of shower units made.

In situation (a) you may have decided that it is necessary to cut back severely on production. This could lead to redundancies, with machines and other resources not being used to their full capacity. Alternatively, you may have suggested that production continues at the same level and the excess production is stored, which could be very expensive. Finally, you may consider that the organization should boost sales through price reductions or increased marketing. Both these options could also be very expensive. Although you may think that situation (b) is a good position for the business to be in, it can lead to considerable problems. If the company attempts to boost production, it may need overtime working at a higher wage rate. More machines and larger premises may be required, which may require taking out a loan to pay for them. If the company fails to meet the orders, customers will become dissatisfied and the firm's reputation will be harmed; customers may go to competitors where the service is better.

Whichever of the above alternatives the company chooses, the policy will have to be communicated to all managers. This will ensure that detailed plans can be drawn up which minimize the potential damage to the company's financial performance. However, even if detailed plans are made available to all managers so that activities are coordinated, it does not mean that there is control. Because the plans are based on predictions, it is very likely that events such as the following may occur that prevent the plans from being achieved:

- prices may rise unexpectedly
- new competitors may enter the market and offer cheaper products
- machines may break down
- suppliers may not be able to deliver materials on time.

Once the period has commenced, regular financial statements are usually produced comparing actual performance with the budget. This is the final stage, where the individual managers responsible for the budget centres are expected to remedy any controllable adverse *variances* (differences) or revise the plan if necessary.

Key definition

In standard costing and budgetary control, a variance is the difference between the standard or budgetary levels of cost or income for an activity and the actual costs incurred or income achieved.

Source: Law (2010, p. 430).

Assumptions and predictions about what is going to happen to the firm's markets and business environment are normally made at the highest level, following consultation throughout the organization. Collecting information to measure actual performance is part of the accounting function and accountants are also responsible for issuing financial statements that compare the actual performance with the plan. At this stage, most managers find that they have a role in explaining any variances between the planned and actual figures, and in suggesting the appropriate course to pursue. If there is no formal system of planning and control, there will probably be an informal system. In a very small business, the owner-manager may be responsible for all the stages. In larger businesses, there is likely to be a formal system, with a greater division of responsibility at each stage. Figure 16.1 summarizes the main stages in budgetary control.

Figure 16.1 Main stages in budgetary control

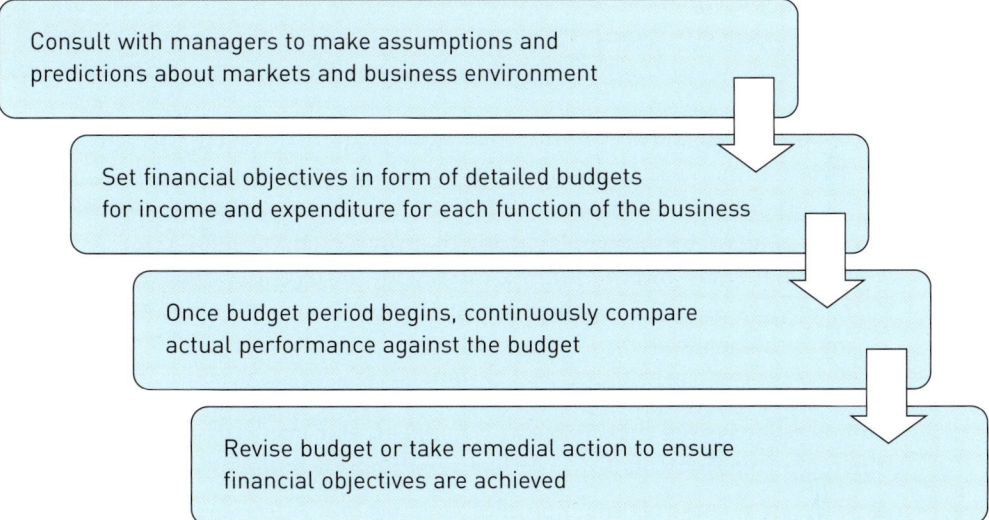

16.4   Purpose of budgetary control

Whilst the overall *purpose of budgetary control* is to help managers to plan and control the use of resources, there are a number of more specific purposes:

- A formal system of budgetary control enables an organization to carry out its planning in a systematic and logical manner.
- Control can be achieved only by setting a plan of what is to be accomplished in a specified time period and managers regularly monitoring progress against the plan, taking corrective action where necessary.
- By setting plans, the activities of the various functions and departments can be coordinated. For example, the production manager can ensure that the correct quantity is manufactured to meet the requirements of the sales team, or the accountant can

obtain sufficient funding to make adequate resources available to carry out the task, whether this is looking after children in care or running a railway network.

- A budgetary control system is a communication system that informs managers of the objectives of the organization and the constraints under which it is operating. The regular monitoring of performance helps keep management informed of the progress of the organization towards its objectives.
- By communicating detailed targets to individual managers, motivation is improved. Without a clear sense of direction, managers will become demotivated.
- By setting separate plans for individual departments and functions, managers are clear about their responsibilities. This allows them to make decisions within their budget responsibilities and avoids the need for every decision to be made at the top level.
- By comparing actual activity for a particular period of time with the original plan, any variance (difference), expressed in financial terms, is identified. This enables managers to assess their performance and decide what corrective action, if any, needs to be taken.
- By predicting future events, managers are encouraged to collect all the relevant information, analyse it and make decisions in good time.
- An organization is made up of a number of individuals with their own ambitions and goals. The budgetary control process encourages consensus by modifying personal goals and integrating them with the overall objectives of the organization. Managers can see how their personal aims fit into the overall context and how they might be achieved.

There is no single model of a perfect budgetary control system and each organization needs a system that meets its own particular needs. The following list summarizes the main requirements for an effective system of budgetary control:

- a sound and clearly defined organization with the managers' responsibilities clearly indicated
- effective accounting records and procedures which are understood and applied
- strong support and the commitment of top managers to the system of budgetary control
- the education and training of managers in the development, interpretation and use of budgets
- the revision of the original budgets where circumstances show that amendments are required to make them appropriate and useful
- the recognition throughout the organization that budgetary control is a management activity and not an accounting exercise
- the participation of managers in the budgetary control system
- an information system that provides data for managers so that they can make realistic predictions
- the correct integration of budgets and their effective communication to managers
- the setting of reasonable and achievable budgets.

16.5 Budget setting

There are two main methods for setting budgets:

- In *incremental budgeting* management adds a percentage to the current year's income and expenditure to take account of predicted changes in prices. However, this means that the budget will include non-recurring income or expenditure and will not be tailored to the conditions expected to prevail during the forthcoming budget period.
- In *zero-based budgeting* management starts from zero and builds in each budget figure where it can be justified from the policies and conditions that are likely to exist. This makes the budget much more relevant to the particular conditions expected in the budget period than incremental budgeting.

The budgets give details of the planned income and expenditure during a financial period that will achieve the given financial objective. In the first instance, the budgets may be measured in quantitative terms, such as the number of cost units to be produced or sold, the quantity of materials required or the number of employees needed. However, they will be converted into financial terms for the budgetary control system. Therefore, both *financial budgets* and *non-financial budgets* are normally prepared. Figure 16.2 shows an example of typical budgets prepared for a sales and marketing department (a budget centre).

Figure 16.2 Example of non-financial and financial budgets

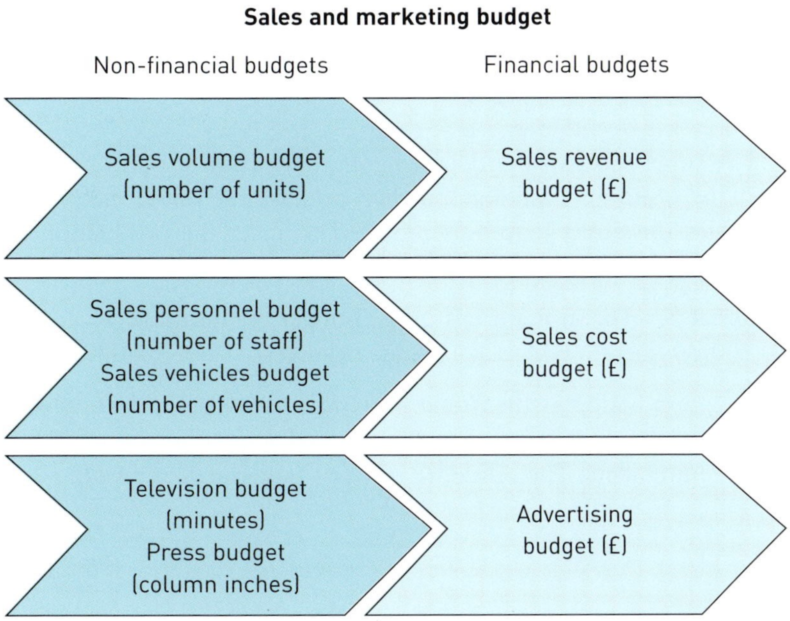

Sales and marketing budget

Non-financial budgets — Financial budgets

- Sales volume budget (number of units) → Sales revenue budget (£)
- Sales personnel budget (number of staff) / Sales vehicles budget (number of vehicles) → Sales cost budget (£)
- Television budget (minutes) / Press budget (column inches) → Advertising budget (£)

Budgets are drawn up for individual departments and functions, as well as for capital expenditure, inventory and cash flow. Therefore, both *functional budgets* and *non-functional budgets* are needed. Non-functional budgets are not the responsibility of a specific functional manager, but require contributions from various managers and the accountant. Non-functional budgets include the capital expenditure budget, which gives details of planned capital expenditure analysed by asset, project, functional area and budget period, the cash flow budget, the budgeted statement of comprehensive income, and the budgeted statement of financial position. The master budget incorporates all the budgets and is the final coordinated overall budget for the period.

We can illustrate the setting of budgets by looking at Portalite, which is a product made in China by Outdoor Lighting Ltd.

The *sales budget* forms the basis of all the other budgets and presents the range of products the company plans to sell during the period. It shows the estimated sales volume and the selling price of each product. It also shows the predicted revenue for the period. The company plans to sell 8,500 units of Portalite and each unit has a planned selling price of £100.

Sales revenue budget for Portalite
8,500 units to be sold × £100 = £850,000 sales revenue

The next stage is to prepare the *production budget*. The budget is expressed in quantity only and is the responsibility of the production manager. The objective is to ensure that production is sufficient to meet sales demand for the period.

Production budget for Portalite	
Units of product to be sold	8,500
Planned closing inventory	1,870
Total units of product required	10,370
Opening inventory	(170)
Units of product to be produced	10,200

The supervisors of the departments that produce Portalite and the other products made by Outdoor Lighting Ltd then prepare the *direct materials usage budget*. This estimates the direct materials required to meet the production budget. In this case, each Portalite uses 10 units of material X.

Material X – Direct materials usage budget for Portalite
10,200 production budget × 10 units of material X = 102,000 units of material X

The next budget is the *direct materials purchase budget*, which is prepared by the purchasing manager to ensure that enough materials are purchased to meet production requirements. The purchase price of material X is £1.50.

Material X – Direct materials purchase budget for Portalite	
Direct materials usage budget	102,000
Planned closing inventory	23,040
Total units of material required	125,040
Opening inventory	(9,600)
Units of material to be purchased	115,440
Total cost (x £1.50)	£173,160

The *direct labour budget* is the responsibility of the managers of the departments that produce the product. They will prepare estimates of the labour hours required by the department to meet the planned production. Each Portalite uses 3 hours of direct labour and the wage rate is £5 per hour.

Direct labour budget for Assembly Department for Portalite
10,200 production budget × 3 hours × £5 = £153,000 direct labour

The *factory overhead budgets* are the responsibility of the relevant departmental managers and show the assignment of overheads to each department, as well as indicating whether they are controllable or non-controllable for reporting purposes. The following simple example illustrates the principles. As the title of the budget suggests, in practice it would be factory wide.

Overhead budget for Production Department (only produces Portalite)	
	£
Controllable overheads	
Indirect materials	30,600
Indirect labour	15,300
Power	5,100
	51,000
Non-controllable overheads	
Depreciation	25,000
Supervision	25,000
Power (fixed proportion)	10,000
Maintenance	11,400
	71,400
Total overheads	122,400
Total labour hours	51,000
Budgeted overhead rate per labour hour	£2.40

In practice, separate *selling and administration budgets* will be produced by the managers responsible for sales, distribution and administration.

For cost control purposes the direct labour, material usage and factory overheads budgets are combined into separate *departmental budgets*. For responsibility accounting purposes, these budgets are compared with the actual results at the end of the period to assess how effective the departmental managers are in controlling the expenditure for which they are responsible.

The objective of the *cash budget* is to ensure that sufficient funds will be available throughout the period to cover the level of operations outlined in the various budgets. The cash budget may be prepared on a weekly, monthly or quarterly basis, as necessary, to identify any cash surplus or deficit as early as possible. The following example illustrates a cash budget for the first six months of the year.

Cash budget for the 6 months ending 30 June 2013	Quarter 1	Quarter 2
	£	£
Opening balance	8,500	28,500
Receipts from cash sales and trade receivables	250,000	300,000
	258,500	328,500
Payments		
Purchase of materials	(100,000)	(120,000)
Wages	(100,000)	(110,000)
Other costs	(30,000)	(125,000)
	(230,000)	(355,000)
Closing balance	28,500	(26,500)

The *budgeted statement of comprehensive income* and the *budgeted statement of financial position* are constructed to provide the overall picture of the planned financial performance for the budget period and the predicted financial position at the end of the budget period. These are prepared in accordance with financial accounting requirements but will be based on budgeted information.

When all the functional budgets, the capital budget, the cash flows budget, the budgeted statement of comprehensive income and the statement of financial position have been prepared, they form the *master budget*. The master budget is submitted by the accountant to the budget committee, together with a number of budgeted profitability, liquidity and gearing ratios. If the figures are acceptable, the budget will be approved.

Key definition

A master budget is the final coordinated overall budget for an organization as a whole, which brings together the functional budgets, the capital budget, and the cash flow budget, as well as the budgeted statement of comprehensive income and statement of financial position for the budget period.

Source: Adapted from Law (2010, p. 277).

We can illustrate the interrelationship of budgets by looking at the case of Portalite again, which is the product manufactured by Outdoor Lighting Ltd. The sales director has estimated that the following quantities will be sold over the next 6 months:

	January	February	March	April	May	June
Forecast sales volume	1,000	1,200	1,500	1,600	1,600	1,750

The production department will manufacture the torches in the month before the sales take place and it has been agreed that a buffer inventory of 200 torches will be maintained. On 1 December of the previous year there is an opening inventory of 100 torches.

Activity

Calculate the number of torches that must be manufactured each month.

The best way to tackle this problem is to draw up a table giving all the information.

	December	January	February	March	April	May	June
Opening inventory	100	1,200	1,400	1,700	1,800	1,800	1,950
Production	1,100	1,200	1,500	1,600	1,600	1,750	
Sales		1,000	1,200	1,500	1,600	1,600	1,750
Closing inventory	1,200	1,400	1,700	1,800	1,800	1,950	

We know that the opening inventory on 1 December was 100 torches. To find out how many torches need to be manufactured in December, you need to consider how many are expected to be needed to cover the sales volume of 1,000 in January and ensure that there is a buffer inventory of 200 torches on 31 December (1,000 + 200 = 1,200). Therefore, the December production volume needs to be the closing inventory less the opening inventory (1,200 – 100 = 1,100). You will remember that the closing inventory at the end of one month becomes the opening inventory at the beginning of the next. Therefore, on 1 January the opening inventory is the same as the closing inventory on 31 December (1,200 torches). We continued to use these principles to calculate the forecast production volumes for the rest of the period.

Having calculated the number of torches that must be produced, we now need to consider the decisions the production manager must take and which budgets will be affected. The most immediate decision concerns whether there is sufficient machine capacity and labour to make the torches. It may be that more machines and labour are required in the busy months and more space will be required in the factory; therefore all these budgets will be affected. The accountant will be concerned with the cash requirements for any changes and will want to ensure that the implications of these decisions are shown in the cash budget. It is because of the interrelated nature of budgets that a change in any one budget can affect the other budgets.

The process of preparing budgets for each of the functions and other activities in an organization and drawing up a master budget can take a number of months. The budgets must be communicated to managers before the start of the appropriate financial period, called the *budget period*, so they know what the plans are for their own departments and can implement them. Some organizations adopt a 'top-down' approach to budget setting, where the owners or senior management decide the individual plans for each department and function, and these plans are given to the individual managers to implement. Other organizations use a 'bottom-up' approach to budget setting, where individual managers construct their own budgets, which are given to the owners or senior managers, who then coordinate the individual budgets into a master budget. These are the two extremes, and most organizations fall somewhere between the two.

A *budget committee* may be formed, made up of the functional or departmental managers and chaired by the chief executive. The management accountant usually occupies the role of committee secretary, and he or she coordinates and assists in the preparation of the budget data provided by each manager. The budget committee reviews the budgets submitted by individual managers and ensures that each has the following characteristics:

- conforms to the policies formulated by the owners or directors
- shows how the objectives are going to be achieved, and recognizes any constraints under which the organization will be operating
- is realistic
- integrates with the other budgets
- reflects the responsibilities of the manager concerned.

If a budget does not display all these characteristics, it will need to be revised. This may affect other budgets and there may need to be negotiations between the managers concerned to introduce the necessary budget changes. When the budgets have been approved by the budget committee, they are submitted to the directors for approval prior to the commencement of the budget period. If the directors accept the budget, it is then adopted by the organization as a whole and becomes the working plan.

16.6   Fixed and flexible budgets

A *fixed budget* is a budget that is not changed once it has been established, even though there may be changes in the level of activity. It may be revised if the situation so demands, but not merely because the actual activity level differs from the planned level of activity. This can be a considerable disadvantage, because a fixed budget may show an adverse variance on costs which is simply due to an increase in variable costs because activity is higher than anticipated. As you will remember from Chapter 15, total variable costs increase or decrease in proportion with changes in activity level.

On the other hand, a *flexible budget* is designed to change with the level of activity. Therefore, in a flexible budget, any cost variance can be assumed to be due to an increase or decrease in fixed costs. A flexible budget may be used at the planning stage to illustrate the impact of achieving different activity levels. It can also be used at the control stage at the end of a month to compare the actual results with what they should have been.

Key definitions

A fixed budget is a budget that does not take into account any circumstances resulting in the actual levels of activity achieved being different from those on which the original budget was based. Consequently, in a fixed budget the budget cost allowances for each cost item are not changed for the variable items.

A flexible budget is a budget that takes into account the fact that values for income and expenditure on some items will change with changing circumstances. Consequently, in a flexible budget the budget cost allowances for each variable cost item will change to allow for the actual levels of activity achieved. A budget that has been adjusted in this way is known as a flexed budget.

Source: Law (2010, pp. 193 and 195).

We will illustrate the importance of flexible budgeting by returning to the example of Portalite Ltd. The budget for January is based on an output of 1,000 torches. The following budget report shows the budgeted and actual figures for the month when 1,100 torches were sold.

Portalite Ltd		
Budget report for January		
	Fixed budget	Actual
	£	£
Sales revenue (£1.50 × 1,000)	1,500	1,650
Variable costs (75p × 1,000)	(750)	(880)
Variable overheads (25p × 1,000)	(250)	(260)
Fixed overheads	(200)	(200)
Total costs	(1,200)	(1,340)
Profit for the period	300	310

The managing director has been sent the above budget statement and is delighted that the actual profit is £10 above the budget.

Activity

Write a brief report to the managing director explaining why he should not be so pleased with the results. Support your report with calculations.

After all the work you have done on marginal costing in Chapter 15, the words 'variable costs' should immediately have alerted you to the problem of comparing the actual results with the original budget when there has been a change in activity level. In this case the number of torches sold was 1,100 compared with the planned amount of 1,000. Although the sales department must be congratulated on achieving increased sales, the company needs to construct a flexible budget to see if they have controlled their variable costs. This is done by multiplying the planned variable costs per unit by the actual level of production.

The variable costs were originally set at £750 for 1,000 torches, which is 75p per torch. The variable overheads were originally set at £250 for 1,000 torches, which is 25p per torch. If we assume that as the number of torches manufactured increases, the total variable costs increase, the flexible budget compared with the actual results is as follows:

Portalite Ltd		
Budget report for January		
	Flexible budget	Actual
	£	£
Sales revenue (£1.50 × 1,100)	1,650	1,650
Variable costs (75p × 1,100)	(825)	(880)
Variable overheads (25p × 1,100)	(275)	(260)
Fixed overheads	(200)	(200)
Total costs	(1,300)	(1,340)
Profit for the period	350	310

The flexible budget shows that at an output level of 1,100 torches, a profit of £350 should have been made, but the business has only made a profit of £310. A comparison of the figures shows that although variable overheads have been reduced, there is an overspend on variable costs that must be investigated. This demonstrates the advantages of using a flexible budget, where the budget is amended if the actual activity level is not the same as planned. By comparing the actual results with what should have been achieved at that level of activity, a more accurate measure is given.

Variance analysis is the investigation of the factors that have caused the differences between the actual and the budgeted figures (the differences are known as variances). Actual progress is measured from the beginning of the budget period (usually one year). At the end of each month, the actual figures for all items of income and expenditure are compared with the plan and reported to the managers responsible. If actual income is higher than the budgeted income, there will be a favourable variance. On the other hand, if actual income is lower than budgeted income, there will be an adverse variance. There may also be cost variances. If actual costs are lower than the budgeted costs, there will be a *favourable variance*. If actual costs are higher than the budgeted expenditure, the variance is known as an *adverse variance*. Unless they can be remedied, adverse variances will result in a lower profit.

Activity

Richard Pillinger manages a farm that produces early crops by growing them in large polythene tunnels. Complete the following budget report for May by calculating the variances and indicating whether they are favourable or adverse.

	Early Crops Ltd Budget report for May		
	Budget	Actual	Variance
	£	£	£
Income			
Cucumbers	25,000	24,500	
Peppers	18,000	17,200	
Tomatoes	19,000	19,600	
	62,000	61,300	
Expenditure			
Salaries	28,400	29,000	
Expenses	12,500	12,000	
Administration	1,800	1,700	
Miscellaneous	700	300	
	43,400	43,000	
Profit for the period	18,600	18,300	

You should not have had too much difficulty with this, as it is simply a matter of subtracting the actual figures from the budgeted figures and remembering that an adverse variance is where actual revenue is lower than planned or actual costs are higher than planned. Compare your answer with the completed budget report below:

	Early Crops Ltd Budget report for May			
	Budget	Actual	Variance	
	£	£	£	
Income				
Cucumbers	25,000	24,500	(500)	Adverse
Peppers	18,000	17,200	(800)	Adverse
Tomatoes	19,000	19,600	600	Favourable
	62,000	61,300	(700)	Adverse
Expenditure				
Salaries	28,400	29,000	(600)	Adverse
Expenses	12,500	12,000	500	Favourable
Administration	1,800	1,700	100	Favourable
Miscellaneous	700	300	400	Favourable
	43,400	43,000	400	Favourable
Profit for the period	18,600	18,300	(300)	Adverse

The budget report shows that the business made a profit in May, which was £300 lower than planned. This was due to lower income from sales of cucumbers and peppers than planned, combined with higher salaries paid. If you had any problems with the calculations, you may find the spreadsheet formulae shown in Figure 16.3 helpful.

Now Richard must decide whether the adverse variances require any action on his part. The salary increase may not have been planned but is nevertheless necessary. The

Figure 16.3   Early Crops Ltd budget report for May

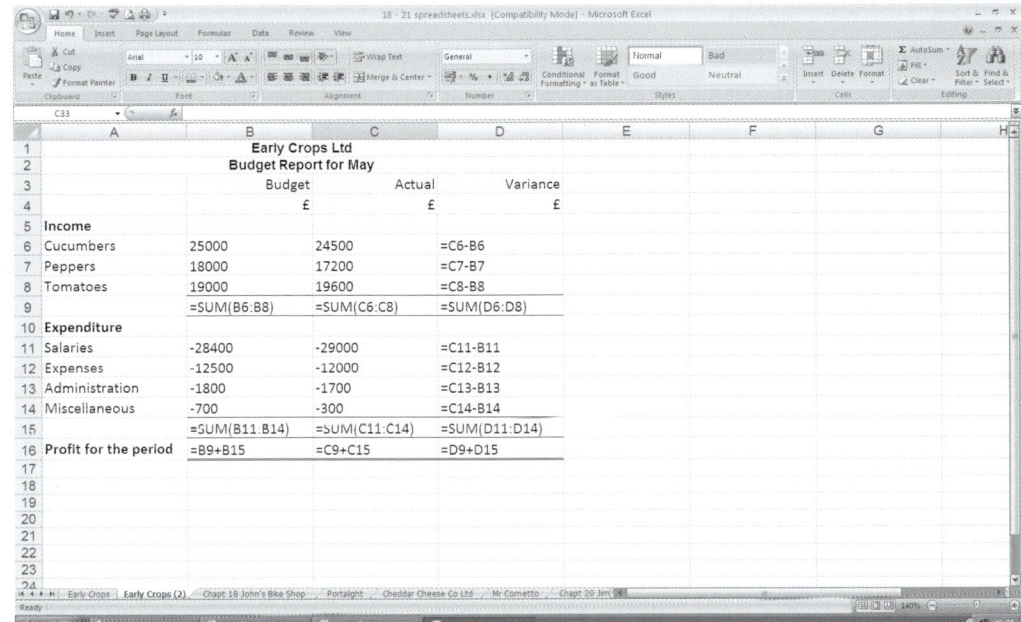

lower sales income may be due to factors beyond his control, such as unexpected bad weather affecting yield. Most businesses experience peaks and troughs during the year, especially where there are seasonal factors affecting production and demand. Therefore, these variations need to be reflected in the monthly budget figures. On the other hand, Richard may discover it is due to poor marketing or distribution problems. Therefore, before he can make any decision, Richard must first investigate the causes.

16.7   Advantages and disadvantages of budgetary control systems

Sometimes management implements a system of budgetary control, but becomes disillusioned with it because the disadvantages seem to outweigh the advantages.

Activity

When an organization has a budgetary control system, internal planning and control should be improved, which must be a considerable advantage. What other advantages might there be, and what are the disadvantages of a budgetary control system?

The main *advantages* of budgetary control systems are:

- Coordination – All the various functions and activities of the organization are coordinated.
- Responsibility accounting – Accounting information is provided to the managers responsible for income and expenditure budgets to allow them to conduct variance analysis.
- Utilization of resources – Capital and effort are used to achieve the financial objectives of the business.
- Motivation – Managers are motivated through the use of clearly defined objectives and the monitoring of achievement.
- Planning – Planning ahead gives time to take corrective action, since decisions are based on the examination of future problems.
- Establishing a system of control – Control is achieved if plans are reviewed regularly against performance.
- Transfer of authority – Authority for decisions is devolved to the individual managers.

There are quite a number of potential drawbacks associated with budgetary control systems. How serious these drawbacks are depends on the way the system is operated. The main *disadvantages* of budgetary control systems are:

- Set in stone – Managers may be constrained by the original budget and not take effective and sensible decisions when the circumstances warrant it (for example, they might make no attempt to spend less than maximum or make no attempt to exceed the target income).
- Time-consuming – Time spent on setting and controlling budgets may deflect managers from their prime responsibilities of running the business.
- Unrealistic – Plans may become unrealistic if fixed budgets are set and the activity level is not as planned. This can lead to poor control.
- Demotivating – Managers may become demotivated if budgets are imposed by top management without consultation or if fixed budgets cannot be achieved due to a lower levels of activity beyond their control.

The first letters of the above list of advantages and disadvantages of budgetary control form two mnemonics (CRUMPET and STUD) which some students find useful for remembering these points.

16.8 Conclusions

Budgetary control involves the preparation of detailed business plans for the forthcoming financial period. These plans take the form of *budgets* for income and expenditure, which are the responsibility of the managers of each *budget centre*. Financial control is achieved by these managers monitoring the actual performance of the budget centre against the budget on a regular basis, and taking whatever action is considered necessary to correct any adverse variances that are within their control.

In this chapter we have looked at the need for business planning and the cycle of planning and control in an organization. We have examined the way in which budgets are established for separate functions and how they are integrated into a master budget. We have seen how variance analysis is conducted and considered what organizational factors are required to operate an effective system of budgetary control. Finally, we have looked at the benefits of using flexible rather than fixed budgets in a business where activity levels are likely to fluctuate and examined the general advantages and disadvantages of budgetary control.

Practice questions

1 Describe the main stages in budgetary control and the specific purposes of a system of budgetary control.

2 Discuss the advantages and disadvantages associated with systems of budgetary control.

3 Explain the difference between a fixed budget and a flexible budget, using an example to illustrate your answer.

4 The managing director of Leisure Magazines Ltd has recently introduced a budgetary control system. The accountant drew up budgets for the advertising and editorial departments based on the actual results for the last 3 years. At the end of the first month of the new financial period, the actual income was higher than planned, but the actual total advertising department costs were higher than budgeted. The actual costs for the editorial department were the same as those budgeted and the actual profit for the period was higher. On receiving the first month's results, the managing director threatened to dismiss the advertising manager for exceeding the budgeted costs. The advertising manager retaliated by saying that he would resign unless the budgetary control system was scrapped. The accountant left to join another company.

You work for the firm of consultants that has been asked to advise the company. Prepare a preliminary report covering the following:
(a) An analysis of the problems, and how you think they have arisen.
(b) Guidelines for the operation of a successful and effective budgetary control system.
(c) Recommendations as to what action the director of the client company should take.

5 John Smith is planning to start a business selling bicycles on 1 January 2014. He has £25,000 capital to invest in the business and has arranged a bank loan of £25,000 over 5 years with a fixed interest rate of 6% per annum. Details of the anticipated income and expenditure for John's Bikes Ltd are as follows:

Cash sales	£30,000 per month
Credit sales	£5,000 per month (1 month's credit)
Purchases	£10,000 per month (2 months' credit)
Rent and rates	£24,000 per annum payable in full on 1 January
Insurance	£6,000 per annum payable monthly
Advertising	£1,000 quarterly, starting in January
Telephone and Internet	£100 per month
Salaries	£6,100 per month
Lighting and heating	£200 per month
Equipment	£12,000 payable in full on 1 January
Fixtures and fittings	£20,000 payable in full on 31 January

Interest on the bank loan will be paid in instalments at the end of each month. The equipment will be depreciated over 4 years and the fixtures and fittings over 5 years; neither is expected to have any residual value at the end of their respective useful economic lives. At the end of the first quarter, John expects to have £10,000 of inventory.

Required

Using a spreadsheet, construct the following budgeted financial statements for the first quarter:

(a) Cash flow budget for the 3 months 1 January to 31 March 2014.

(b) Budgeted statement of comprehensive income for the 3 months 1 January to 31 March 2014.

(c) Budgeted statement of financial position at 31 March 2014.

You can refresh your knowledge of the layouts of these financial statements by referring to Chapters 2, 6 and 7.

References

CIMA (2009) *Management accounting tools for today and tomorrow*. London: Chartered Institute of Management Accountants. Available from: http://www.cima-global.com/Thought-leadership/Research-topics/Recommended-reports/

Law, J. (ed.) (2010) *Dictionary of Accounting*, 4th edition. Oxford: Oxford University Press.

17 Standard costing

Learning objectives

When you have studied this chapter, you should be able to:

- describe the technique of standard costing
- calculate the direct materials variances
- calculate the direct labour variances
- describe the advantages and disadvantages of standard costing.

17.1 Introduction

This chapter introduces a method of financial control known as *standard costing* in which predetermined standard costs and standard revenues are compared with actual costs and actual revenues. Standard costing is closely associated with *budgetary control*, which we looked at in the previous chapter. Although either can be used without the other, it is unusual to find a standard costing system in operation without a budgetary control system also being present.

We have already seen that budgetary control is applied to budget centres and the organization as a whole, and can be used in any type of business or not-for-profit organization, such as a charity, university, hospital, government department, etc. On the other hand, standard costing is mainly applied to products and processes. Therefore, it is a technique that is more commonly used in manufacturing organizations, although it may also be useful in service industries. As in a budgetary control system, it allows the comparison of predetermined costs and income with the actual costs and income achieved. Any variances, or differences, can then be investigated. Managers within the organization can be held responsible for these variances and, by analysing the reasons for the variances, control can be achieved.

In this chapter we explain the principles that underpin standard costing and look at how the different variances associated with total direct costs are calculated. We also discuss the typical causes of any variances and describe the general advantages and disadvantages of standard costing.

17.2 Standard costs and revenues

Standard costing is a technique for controlling costs in which predetermined standard costs and revenues are compared with the actual costs and revenues to identify any variances. The predetermined costs and revenues are known as *standard costs* and *standard revenues*. Standards are set in defined working conditions and represent a benchmark of resource usage. They can be set on the following bases (CIMA, 2005):

- an ex ante estimate (before the event) of expected performance
- an ex post estimate (after the event) of attainable performance
- a prior period level of performance by the same organization
- the level of performance achieved by comparable organizations
- the level of performance required to meet organizational objectives.

> **Key definition**
>
> Standard costing is a system of cost ascertainment and control in which predetermined standard costs and income for products and operations are set and periodically compared with actual costs incurred and income generated in order to establish any variances.
>
> *Source*: Law (2010, p. 393).

Standards can be set at an ideal level or an attainable level, depending on the philosophy of the business. Ideal standards are based on the best possible working conditions, but attainable standards are more widely used because they are based on realistic efficient performance and allow for such problems as machine breakdowns, materials wastage, etc. Although ideal standards are useful for management decision making, there is some risk that employees will be demotivated by the impossibility of achieving them.

The standard cost is the planned unit of cost that is calculated from technical specifications. These specify the quantity of materials, labour and other elements of cost required, and relate them to the prices and wages that are expected to be in place during the period when the standard cost will be used. It is usual to measure the time in which it is planned to complete a certain volume of work in standard hours or standard minutes. This means that a standard hour is a measure of production output, rather than a measure of time.

Activity

A company has set one standard hour's production at 500 units. In a 7-hour day, 4,000 units are produced. What is this output in standard hours?

To answer this question, you will have needed to make the following calculation:

$$\frac{4{,}000 \text{ units}}{500 \text{ units per standard hour}} = 8 \text{ standard hours' production}$$

17.3 Variance analysis

You will remember from the previous chapter that *variance analysis* is the periodic investigation of the factors that have caused the differences between the actual and the budgeted figures. As in budgetary control, these differences are known as *variances*. At the end of each month of the budget period, the actual figures for all items of revenue and cost are compared with the plan and reported to the managers responsible. Timely reporting gives the opportunity for any *adverse variances* to be remedied if this is possible.

Key definition

In standard costing and budgetary control, a variance is the difference between the standard or budgetary levels of cost or income for an activity and the actual costs incurred or income achieved.

Source: Law (2010, p. 430–1).

Any variances are analysed to reveal their constituent parts, so that sufficient information is available to permit investigation by management. Favourable variances are those which improve the predetermined profit and adverse variances are those which reduce the predetermined profit.

Activity

In the Stitching Department of Jarvis Jackets Ltd 100 pockets can be made in one standard hour. In an 8-hour day, 950 pockets are produced. Determine whether this will give rise to a favourable or adverse variance.

The first step is to calculate how many pockets should be made in an 8-hour day:

100 units per standard hour × 8 actual hours = 800 standard hours' production

Next, you should have calculated the variance by subtracting the standard hours' production (800) from the actual production (950) to arrive at a figure of 150. This is a favourable variance because 150 more pockets are produced than the 800 planned. Now we are ready to make this part of the standard costing system, by expressing the variance in financial terms.

In a manufacturing business the *direct costs* associated with each cost unit are normally direct materials and direct labour. The reasons for overspending or underspending on either of these costs are based on the following simple concept:

Total cost of direct materials/labour = Quantity used × Unit price

Any variance in the total direct costs will be due to differences in the quantity used, the price per unit or a combination of both these factors, as shown in Figure 17.1.

Figure 17.1 Total direct costs variance

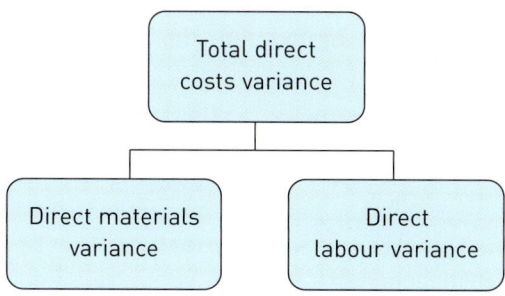

We will now look at the direct materials variance and the direct labour variance in a little more detail.

17.4 Direct materials variance

The above principles are applied to the cost of direct materials. Predetermined standards are set both for the usage level of direct materials for a given volume of production and the price allowed per unit of direct materials. The price standard is based on the price per unit expected to be paid or budgeted for the level of purchases projected over the period for which the standard is to be applied. In general, any price variance is considered to be the responsibility of the buyer or purchasing manager and any variation in the volume or quantity of materials consumed is considered to be the responsibility of the production manager. However, due to the interdependence of price and usage, it may be difficult to assign these responsibilities.

The *direct materials variance* is based on the following formula:

Total cost of direct materials = Quantity used × Price per unit

Standards are set for the quantity of materials to be used for a specific volume of production and the price to be paid per unit of direct materials. The *total direct materials variance* can be calculated using the following formula:

(Standard quantity used × Standard price per unit) − (Actual quantity used × Actual price per unit)

Activity

Jarvis Jackets Ltd has decided to extend its range to include denim jackets. One jacket requires a standard usage of 3 metres of direct materials which has been set at a standard price of £2.20 per metre. In the period, 80 jackets were made and 260 metres of materials consumed at a cost of £1.95 per metre. Using the above formula, calculate the total direct materials variance.

The first stage is to calculate the standard quantity of materials for the actual level of production. As 80 jackets were made and the company planned to use 3 metres of denim per jacket, the standard quantity for that level of production is 240 metres. Inserting the appropriate figures into the formula, the total direct materials variance is:

$$(240 \text{ metres} \times £2.20) - (260 \text{ metres} \times £1.95) = £528 - £507 = £21 \text{ favourable}$$

The difference of £21 between the planned cost and the actual cost is a favourable variance because we have spent less on our materials than we planned for that level of production. Although this information is useful, it needs to be more precise in order to enable the management to take any action required. The reason why the actual cost of materials can differ from the planned cost of materials for a given level of production is due to two factors. Either we have used more or less materials than planned and/or we have paid more or less per unit of materials than we planned.

The total direct materials variance can be divided into a usage variance and a price variance, as shown in Figure 17.2.

Figure 17.2 Total direct materials variance

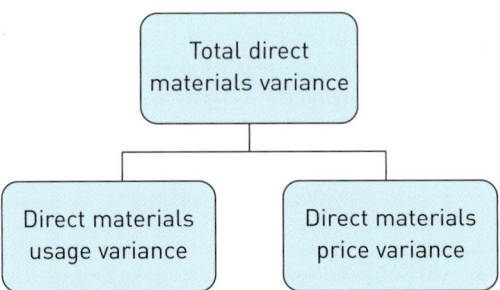

The *direct materials usage variance* is the difference between the standard quantity specified for the actual production and the actual quantity used at standard price per unit. The formula is:

(Standard quantity × Standard price per unit) − (Actual quantity × Standard price per unit)

If the data are available, you may find it more convenient to shorten this to:

(Standard quantity − Actual quantity) × Standard price per unit

Activity

Calculate the direct materials usage variance from the data for Jarvis Jackets Ltd.

Inserting the appropriate figures into the formula, the direct materials usage variance is:

$$(240 \text{ metres} - 260 \text{ metres}) \times £2.20 = (£44.00) \text{ adverse}$$

In this instance, there is an adverse variance because the company has used more materials than planned for that level of production.

The final stage is to find out the *direct materials price variance*. This is the difference between the standard and actual purchase price per unit for the actual quantity of materials purchased or used in production. The formula is:

(Standard price per unit × Actual quantity) − (Actual price per unit × Actual quantity)

If the data are available, you can use the following shortened formula:

(Standard price per unit − Actual price per unit) × Actual quantity

Activity

Calculate the direct materials price variance from the data for Jarvis Jackets Ltd.

Inserting the appropriate figures in the formula, the direct materials price variance is:

$$(£2.20 - £1.95) \times 260 \text{ metres} = £65.00 \text{ favourable}$$

The variance is favourable because the business has paid less for the materials than planned for that level of production. If you deduct the adverse usage variance of £44.00 from the favourable price variance of £65.00 you will arrive at the total direct materials variance of £21 favourable. Thus, the first two variances explain the last one you have calculated.

Of course, working out the figures is not the end of the task. Managers need to investigate the reasons for the variances and determine whether any corrective action is required. There are a number of reasons for the adverse usage variance. Perhaps inferior materials were used and this led to higher wastage than planned, or the labour force was inexperienced and this led to high levels of wastage. Alternatively, some materials may have been lost or stolen. One strong possibility for the price variance is that the company has used lower quality and therefore less expensive materials. This would tie in with the possible reason for the adverse usage variance. Other reasons may be that the business is using a different supplier than originally intended or has negotiated a bulk discount.

17.5 Direct labour variance

The same principles are applied to the cost of direct labour. Standards are established for the rate of pay to be paid for the production of particular products and the labour time taken for their production. The standard time taken is expressed in standard hours or standard minutes and becomes the measure of output. By comparing the standard hours allowed and the actual time taken, labour efficiency can be assessed. In practice, standard times are established by work, time and method study techniques.

The *direct labour variance* is based on the following formula:

$$\text{Total labour cost} = \text{Hours worked} \times \text{Rate per hour}$$

The total direct labour variance is calculated by using the following formula:

(Standard direct labour hours × Standard rate per hour) – (Actual direct labour hours × Actual rate per hour)

Activity

The management of Jarvis Jackets Ltd decides that it takes 6 standard hours to make 1 denim jacket and the standard rate paid to labour is £8.00 per hour. The actual production is 900 units and this took 5,100 hours at a rate of £8.30 per hour. Calculate the total direct labour hour variance.

With your knowledge of the calculation of materials variances, this activity should have caused you few problems. The first stage is to calculate the standard direct labour hours for this level of production:

$$900 \text{ jackets} \times 6 \text{ standard hours} = 5,400 \text{ standard hours}$$

The total direct labour hour variance can then be calculated as follows:

$$(5,400 \text{ standard hours} \times £8.00) - (5,100 \text{ actual hours} \times £8.30) = £43,200 - £42,330$$
$$= £870 \text{ favourable}$$

The variance is favourable because the actual total labour cost is less than the planned cost for that level of production.

The total direct labour variance can be divided into an efficiency variance and a rate variance, as shown in Figure 17.3.

The *direct labour efficiency variance* (sometimes referred to as the labour productivity variance) is the difference between the actual production achieved, measured in standard hours, and the actual hours worked, valued at the standard labour rate. The formula is:

(Standard hours × Standard rate per hour) – (Actual hours × Standard rate per hour)

Figure 17.3 Total direct labour variance

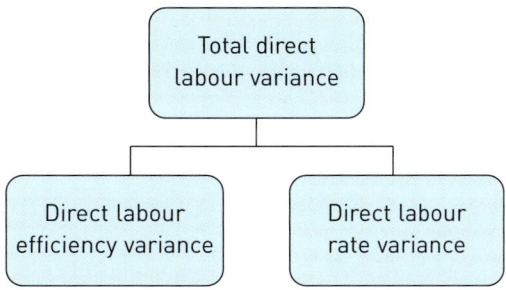

If the data are available, it may be more convenient to shorten the formula to:

(Standard hours – Actual hours) × Standard rate per hour

Activity

Calculate the direct labour efficiency variance from the data for Jarvis Jackets Ltd.

Inserting the appropriate figures into the formula, the direct labour efficiency variance is:

(5,400 standard hours – 5,100 actual hours) × £8.00 = £2,400 favourable

The *direct labour rate variance* is the difference between the standard and actual direct labour rate per hour for the actual hours worked. The formula is:

(Standard rate per hour × Actual hours) – (Actual rate per hour × Actual hours)

If the data are available, you can use the following shortened formula:

(Standard rate per hour – Actual rate per hour) × Actual hours

Activity

Calculate the direct labour rate variance from the data for Jarvis Jackets Ltd.

Once more, all you need to do is insert the appropriate figures into the formula and the direct labour rate variance is:

(£8.00 – £8.30) × 5,100 actual hours = (£1,530) adverse

The variance is adverse because employees have been paid more than planned for that level of production. If you deduct the adverse direct labour rate variance of £1,530 from the favourable efficiency variance of £2,400, you arrive at the favourable total direct labour variance of £870. Therefore, the first two variances explain the last one you have calculated.

The most likely reason for the labour rate and efficiency variances is that the company has used more highly skilled labour than originally planned. Therefore, the rate paid was higher and in addition the output was higher than planned. There are other possible reasons, such as the business may have given a pay rise or employees may have had to work overtime and been paid at higher rates. Further investigation would be required to identify the actual reasons and to determine whether any corrective action is required.

17.6 Advantages and disadvantages of standard costing

As with budgetary control, many of the benefits of standard costing are associated with the processes of planning. Control is improved and it compels managers to make decisions, coordinate activities and communicate with one another.

Activity

Make a list of advantages and disadvantages of standard costing.

With your knowledge of budgetary control, you should not have had many problems with this activity. The main *advantages* of standard costing are:

- Standard setting establishes a benchmark against which actual costs can be compared.
- The technique permits a thorough examination of the organization's production and operations activities.
- As the standards are based on future plans and expectations, the information provided to management is much more accurate than that based merely on past performance.
- By examining the reasons for any variances between standard and actual costs and income, management needs to concentrate only on the exceptions to the planned performance. This leads to greater managerial efficiency.
- Variance analysis may result in cost reductions, and control of costs is improved.

The main *disadvantages* of standard costing are:

- It may be difficult to set standards, particularly in a new or dynamic organization.
- The standard costing system may be expensive to maintain and the additional record keeping may become a burden to busy managers.
- Standards will naturally become out of date and require revision. In a very dynamic organization this may happen so quickly that managers lose confidence in the system.
- Information provided by the system is of value only if it is used by managers for control purposes. If the information has no credibility or is not understood, it has no value.

17.7   Conclusions

Standard costing is a method of financial control that is often used in organizations that have a system of budgetary control. Standard costing is mainly applied to products and processes and for this reason it is more commonly used in the manufacturing sector and can also be used in the service sector. Financial control is achieved by the individual managers responsible receiving accounting information on a regular basis that allows them to monitor actual performance against the standard performance. They must then investigate the cause of any adverse variances that are considered to be excessive and take action to correct any that are within their control. This is necessary to ensure that the business achieves its financial objectives.

In this chapter we have looked at standard costing and the calculation of variances. We have described how to calculate variances for both total materials costs and total labour costs. We have also examined the calculation of the sub-variances and considered the reasons why they have occurred. Finally, we have examined the advantages and disadvantages of a standard costing system.

Practice questions

1   Calculate and suggest possible reasons for the direct materials price variance from the following data:
   - Standard price is £4 per kilo
   - Standard usage is 5 kilos per unit
   - Actual price is £3 per kilo
   - Actual usage is 5 kilos per unit

2   Calculate and suggest possible reasons for the direct materials usage variance from the following data:
   - Standard price is £50 per tonne
   - Standard usage is 1,000 tonnes
   - Actual price is £50 per tonne
   - Actual usage is 995 tonnes

3   A manufacturing company has set a standard price for materials of £100 per kilo and anticipates that it will make 4 units from 1 kilo of materials. The actual production is 200 units and 52 kilos of materials are used at a price of £98 per kilo. Calculate all the materials variances and discuss the possible reasons for them.

4   A company plans to make 1 unit every 10 hours and the standard rate per hour is set at £9. In a financial period 50 units are made and this takes 460 hours. The total labour cost for the period is £5,060. Calculate all the labour variances and discuss the possible reasons for them.

5   Four years ago, your cousin Nikos set up Aphrodite Ltd, a small manufacturing company that manufactures shower screens. The business makes two models: Larnaca is the standard model and Paphos is the deluxe model. Both are made from frosted glass and have aluminium frames and fittings. Larnaca has plain glass and

silver finish to the frame and fittings, whereas Paphos has an attractive design etched on the glass and a gold finish to the frame and fittings.

Once a year Nikos comes back to spend Christmas with the family. This year, knowing that you are studying management accounting as part of your course, he asks for your advice. He explains that despite a buoyant market and excellent sales figures, his profits have been very disappointing and he wants to embark on a cost-cutting exercise. After discussions, you find that he does not operate a standard costing system and does not seem to know what it is. However, he is very keen to learn, but he is only staying a few days, so he asks you to write to him in Cyprus with full details.

Write a letter to Nikos explaining the advantages of a standard costing system, how it can be implemented and the information he can expect to obtain.

References

CIMA (2005) *Management Accounting Official Terminology*, London: Chartered Institute of Management Accountants.

Law, J. (ed.) (2010) *Dictionary of Accounting*, 4th edition. Oxford: Oxford University Press.

18 Capital investment appraisal

Learning objectives

When you have studied this chapter, you should be able to:

- explain the purpose of capital investment appraisal
- calculate and interpret the payback period for an investment project
- calculate and interpret the accounting rate of return for an investment project
- describe the advantages and disadvantages of these two techniques.

18.1 Introduction

Whilst the cost accounting techniques we have looked at in previous chapters provide detailed information to aid decisions about revenue expenditure, this chapter and the next focus on techniques that provide information to aid management decisions about capital expenditure. The process of appraising projects that involve the investment of large sums of capital is known as *capital investment appraisal* and a number of techniques have been developed to provide information that will help management choose between different long-term projects. For example, a business may want to invest capital in extending its premises, buying new delivery vehicles or adopting new technologies. In any major project that requires capital investment, there are a number of decisions that management needs to make. Some are important organizational and personnel decisions, but it is crucial that the financial implications of any such decisions are considered.

In this chapter and the next, we will be looking at the different approaches to capital investment appraisal and some of the commonly used techniques. We start with the *payback period*, which is a simple method that considers the project purely from the point of view of how long it takes to recover the initial capital invested. We then go on to examine the *accounting rate of return*, which focuses on profit rather than cash. In order to evaluate the usefulness of these methods, we also discuss the advantages and disadvantages of each. The next chapter examines techniques based on discounted cash flows.

18.2   Purpose of capital investment appraisal

The *purpose* of capital investment appraisal is to provide information to management that will help them decide which of several proposed capital investment projects is likely to yield the highest financial return. Capital expenditure is the outlay of a considerable amount of money on a project such as the purchase of a new fixed asset (for example, buying a new factory), the enhancement of an existing fixed asset (for example, extending the existing factory) or investment in a new business venture. You will remember from Chapter 7 that fixed assets are assets the business owns and plans to keep in the long term in order to generate future streams of revenue.

> **Key definition**
>
> Capital investment appraisal is the process by which an organization appraises a range of different investment projects with a view to determining which is likely to give the highest financial return.
>
> *Source:* Law (2010, p. 75).

Capital investment decisions are among the most important decisions made by management and are not only critical for the owners and managers of a business, but at the macro level they are also important for the country's economy. Research in innovative small, medium and large firms (Chittenden and Derregia, 2004) shows that some of these entrepreneurial businesses bypass the investment decision-making process by using operating leases, rental or hire contracts to obtain some of the fixed assets they require, such as land, buildings and capital equipment. This reduces the effect of uncertainty on decisions and increases the resources available to the business for a much lower initial outlay. However, not all fixed assets can be obtained like this and some are only available for outright purchase, hence the continuing need for methods to help management choose between different capital investment projects.

Capital investment decisions are very important to the long-term survival of the business and can be distinguished from short-term decisions. Table 18.1 compares the key characteristics of such decisions.

When a business is considering investing capital in a long-term project, management needs to be sure that the amount of money received during the life of the project will

Table 18.1   Short-term decisions and long-term capital investment decisions

Characteristic	Short-term decisions	Capital investment decisions
Time span	1–2 years	2+ years
Nature	Operational (e.g. whether to discontinue a product)	Strategic (e.g. whether to build or buy a new factory)
Level of expenditure	Low–medium	Medium–high
External factors	Generally of little importance	Very important (e.g. interest rates and rates of inflation)
Typical techniques	Contribution analysis Breakeven analysis	Payback period Accounting rate of return Discounted cash flow techniques

Source: Adapted from Jones (2002, p. 452).

be higher than the initial amount invested; at the very least, management needs to know that the business will get its money back. The annual profit and the distinction between fixed and variable costs is therefore of less importance than the timing and amount of the cash going in and out of the business. In some cases an investment is made to make a saving on costs, rather than to generate more cash. For example, a business may be deciding whether to replace an old machine with the latest model that will be less expensive to run. The question that the managers of the business need to answer is whether the saving on costs is likely to be sufficiently high that they make the investment worthwhile. Once again, cash is the most important factor.

Activity

The directors of The Cheddar Cheese Company Ltd are considering investing in a new packing machine. They have a choice of three suitable machines, each of which would cost £150,000 and each of which would have an estimated useful economic life of 5 years with no residual value. However, the net cash flows over that period (the difference between the cash coming in and going out each year) are expected to vary. The following table shows the budgeted annual net cash flows.

Year	Machine 1 £	Machine 2 £	Machine 3 £
1	60,000	20,000	10,000
2	50,000	30,000	20,000
3	40,000	40,000	30,000
4	30,000	50,000	40,000
5	20,000	60,000	150,000

Which machine should the company purchase?

One way to make the comparison is to total the annual net cash flows for each machine:

Year	Machine 1 £	Machine 2 £	Machine 3 £
1	60,000	20,000	10,000
2	50,000	30,000	20,000
3	40,000	40,000	30,000
4	30,000	50,000	40,000
5	20,000	60,000	150,000
Total	200,000	200,000	250,000

Both Machine 1 and Machine 2 are expected to give a total net cash flow of £200,000 over the 5-year period, which suggests that perhaps either would be a worthwhile investment. However, you may decide that Machine 1 is preferable because the cash comes in more quickly. Machine 3 looks better than the other two because the total net cash flow is £50,000 more than the other two machines. However, the directors would have to wait until year 5 before the business generates most of the cash and this means increased risk. Indeed, the net cash flows are forecast figures for all three machines and the further into the future the estimate is, the more unreliable the prediction is likely to be.

As you can see, it is difficult to decide which machine would be the best to buy, but accountants have developed a number of different investment appraisal techniques that can provide useful information to aid the decision. Figure 18.1 shows the methods we will examine in this chapter.

Figure 18.1 Non-discounting methods of investment appraisal

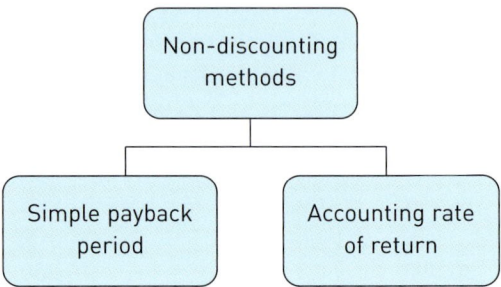

18.3 Simple payback period method

The *payback period method* is a widely used investment appraisal technique because it is very simple to apply and is easily understood by non-accountants. Each project is considered purely from the point of view of the cash flows and the time it takes to recover the capital that has been invested. Naturally, owners and managers will be very keen to know how long it will take to break even and the payback period of the proposed project is compared with the required payback period to determine whether the proposed project should be considered for approval.

Key definition

The payback period method is a method of capital investment appraisal in which the time required before the projected cash inflows for a project equal the investment expenditure is calculated.

Source: Law (2010, p. 315).

The project taking the shortest possible time is the one preferred. The payback period can be calculated using the following formula:

$$\text{Payback (years)} = \frac{\text{Initial capital invested}}{\text{Annual cash inflows}}$$

The following estimates are needed:

- the amount of capital required for the investment
- the annual cash inflows (based on the predicted cash inflows and outflows, including repayments of capital)
- the timing of the movements of cash.

We will illustrate the method with an example. Jimmy Chang is considering investing £15,000 in a hot dog van that will have an estimated useful economic life of 5 years, with no residual value after that time. He would employ someone to operate it from a single site in the marketplace in the centre of town. His accountant has done some research and estimates that annual cash flows will be as follows:

	£
Cash inflows	
Sales revenue	20,000
Cash outflows	
Purchases	(5,000)
Employee's salary	(8,000)
Motor expenses	(2,000)
	(15,000)
Net cash flow	5,000

We can now calculate the payback period:

Year	Cash flow £	Cumulative cash flow £
0	(15,000)	(15,000)
1	5,000	(10,000)
2	5,000	(5,000)
3	5,000	0
4	5,000	5,000
5	5,000	10,000

As you can see, depreciation of the van is not included because depreciation is not a cash flow; the cash flow relating to the van is the cash paid when the van was bought. There are several other things in this table which need explaining:

- Year 0 is the conventional way of referring to the start of Year 1. Year 1, 2, 3, etc. means the end of Year 1, 2, 3, etc.
- It is customary to assume that cash flows during a year will be received evenly throughout the year. Of course, this is not likely to be true, but it is one way of simplifying the calculation. It is possible to estimate cash flows on a quarterly or monthly basis, but this is seldom done in payback calculations, because forecasting to this degree of refinement is rarely possible.
- Cash outflows are shown in brackets.

The cumulative cash flows are shown as zero at the end of Year 3. This means that at the end of Year 3, the net cash flowing in from the investment has reached the figure of £15,000, which is the same as the initial cash outflow in payment for the van at the start of Year 1. Therefore, we can tell Jimmy that, based on his estimates, the payback period for this project will be exactly 3 years.

If the projected cash flows after the initial investment are constant annual sums, as in the above scenario, then you can also use a simple formula to calculate the payback period:

$$\frac{\text{Initial capital investment}}{\text{Annual cash inflows}} = \frac{£15,000}{£5,000} = 3 \text{ years}$$

However, this formula cannot be used when the projected annual cash flows vary from one year to another. We will illustrate this by continuing the example of our entrepreneur, Jimmy Chang.

Activity

At the same time as considering the hot dog van project, Jimmy is also considering investing £15,000 in the purchase of a fish and chip van. The van is expected to have an economic life of 5 years with no residual value after that time. The operator will drive the van around the main suburban areas of town and Jimmy's research suggests that it will take some time to build up a customer base. The following table shows how the estimated net cash flows for this project are expected to gradually build up over the period.

Year	Cash flow £
0	(15,000)
1	3,000
2	4,000
3	5,000
4	6,000
5	7,000

Calculate the simple payback period for the fish and chip van project.

The first step is to work out the cumulative net cash flows over the period. Check your answer against the following table.

Year	Cash flow £	Cumulative cash flow £
0	(15,000)	(15,000)
1	3,000	(12,000)
2	4,000	(8,000)
3	5,000	(3,000)
4	6,000	3,000
5	7,000	10,000

The cumulative cash flows show that the payback period lies somewhere between 3 years (when the cumulative position is expected to be a cash deficit of £3,000) and 4 years (when the cumulative position is expected to be a cash surplus of £3,000). Assuming the cash flow is regular throughout the year, we can calculate the part year by dividing the figure for the earlier year by the sum of the 2 years (ignoring the negative sign on the earlier year):

$$\frac{3,000}{3,000 + 3,000} = 0.5 \text{ of a year or 6 months}$$

Therefore, the payback period for the investment in the fish and chip van is 3 years and 6 months, compared with only 3 years for the hot dog van. Each project requires the same capital outlay, but on the basis of the time it will take to break even, Jimmy would be best advised to choose the hot dog van since he will recover his investment 6 months sooner.

18.4 Advantages and disadvantages of the simple payback method

The main *advantages* of the simple payback period method are as follows:

- It is simple to calculate and is understood by managers who are not very numerate.
- It is useful for comparing risky projects where the prediction of cash flows after the first few years is difficult, due to possible changes in the business environment. For example, changes in technology could make a product obsolete in a year or so, although the current market seems assured.
- It is useful where short-term cash flows are more important than long-term cash flows. For example, if the business has insufficient capital to sustain long-term objectives, it is little use aiming for long-term profitability if the business becomes insolvent 6 months later.
- It is useful if borrowing or gearing is a concern.

The main *disadvantages* of the payback period method are:

- It is difficult to estimate the amount and timing of future cash flows.
- It ignores cash flows after the payback period.
- It ignores profitability. Therefore the project with the shortest payback period might be chosen, even though an alternative project with a longer payback period might be more profitable.
- It ignores the size of the investment; therefore, the project with a smaller initial investment may have a shorter payback period than an alternative project that requires a larger investment but is more profitable in the long term.
- The simple payback period ignores the *time value of money* because it gives net cash flows in later years the same importance as those in Year 1, even though cash received this year is worth more than the same amount at a later date.

Activity

Returning to the example of The Cheddar Cheese Company Ltd, which packing machine would you recommend the directors purchase on the basis of the payback period method?

Your answer should be Machine 1, because this has a payback period of only 3 years compared with more than 4 years for the other two machines. Check your calculations against the following workings:

	Machine 1		Machine 2		Machine 3	
	Net cash flow	Cumulative net cash flow	Net cash flow	Cumulative net cash flow	Net cash flow	Cumulative net cash flow
Year	£	£	£	£	£	£
0	(150,000)	(150,000)	(150,000)	(150,000)	(150,000)	(150,000)
1	60,000	(90,000)	20,000	(130,000)	10,000	(140,000)
2	50,000	(40,000)	30,000	(100,000)	20,000	(120,000)
3	40,000	0	40,000	(60,000)	30,000	(90,000)
4	30,000	30,000	50,000	(10,000)	40,000	(50,000)
5	20,000	50,000	60,000	50,000	150,000	100,000

Payback period

$$\text{Machine 1} = 3 \text{ years}$$

$$\text{Machine 2} = 4 \text{ years} + \frac{10,000}{10,000 + 50,000} = 4.17 \text{ years}$$

$$\text{Machine 3} = 4 \text{ years} + \frac{50,000}{50,000 + 100,000} = 4.33 \text{ years}$$

However, if the directors relied solely on the payback period and chose Machine 1, they would not be taking account of the fact that Machine 3 is likely to give the greatest return of cash, which is what we observed when we first looked at this example in section 18.2. This illustrates the disadvantage of the payback period method due to the fact that it ignores any cash flows that occur after the initial investment has been recovered.

18.5 Accounting rate of return

Whereas the payback period method is concerned with cash flows, the focus of the *accounting rate of return (ARR)* is on profit. Not only is this a more conventional measure of success in business than cash, but it also takes account of depreciation, which spreads the capital costs of acquiring or enhancing tangible non-current assets over their useful life. The accounting rate of return is an accounting ratio that measures the relationship between profit and capital employed (equity plus non-current liabilities).

You will remember from previous chapters that there are a number of different ways in which profit can be defined and therefore we can only compare ratios that have been calculated on the same basis. We will define profit as the average annual profit before interest and tax that is expected to be generated over the life of the project. We will define capital employed as the average capital employed to finance the project. The formula is:

$$\frac{\text{Average profit before interest and tax}}{\text{Average capital employed}} \times 100$$

Key definition

The accounting rate of return (ARR) is an accounting ratio that expresses the profit of an organization before interest and taxation, usually for a year, as a percentage of the capital employed at the end of the period.

Source: Law (2010, p. 9).

The project with the highest ARR is the one preferred. We will now illustrate the ARR with an example. The owners of Cut Above Hairdressing are considering refurbishing the salon and are trying to decide between two different projects. Project A will require an initial investment of £19,000 (Year 0) but at the end of Year 1 the capital employed in the project will have increased to £21,000. Project B is more ambitious and will require an initial investment of £40,000 (Year 0) and by the end of Year 1 the capital employed in the project will have increased to £50,000. After a good deal of careful budgeting, the accountant has produced the following table showing the annual profits before interest and tax (PBIT) that the two projects are expected to generate.

Year	Project A £	Project B £
1	5,000	12,000
2	4,500	10,000
3	4,000	8,000
4	3,500	8,000
5	3,000	6,000

Before we can work out the accounting rate of return for the two projects, we need to calculate the averages:

	Year	Project A £	Project B £
Profit before interest	1	5,000	12,000
and tax (PBIT)	2	4,500	10,000
	3	4,000	8,000
	4	3,500	8,000
	5	3,000	6,000
		20,000	44,000
Average PBIT (÷ 5 years)		4,000	8,800
Capital employed (CE)	0	19,000	40,000
	1	21,000	50,000
		40,000	90,000
Average CE (÷ 2 years)		20,000	45,000

$$\frac{\text{Average PBIT}}{\text{Average CE}} \times 100 \qquad = \frac{4,000}{20,000} \times 100 \qquad = \frac{8,800}{45,000} \times 100$$

ARR $\qquad\qquad = 20\% \qquad\qquad = 20\%$

You can see from the results that although the average annual profit for Project B is a little more than twice as much as the average for Project A, both projects give a similar rate of return. This is because this technique also takes into account the average capital employed in the project, which for Project B is slightly more than twice the amount needed for Project A. However, both projects appear to be worthwhile and offer an accounting rate of return of 20%, which seems satisfactory when compared to an alternative, non-risky investment.

However, the accounting rate of return has not helped the owners of Cut Above Hairdressing to choose between the two projects, and they will need to take other factors into consideration, such as the cost of raising the larger sum of capital for Project B and the length of time that business will be disrupted by this more ambitious refurbishment. The most important thing to remember is that the calculation of the accounting rate of return is based on projected figures. Therefore the technique relies on assumptions and best estimates and, however careful the accountant is in preparing the figures, it is difficult to predict future profits with accuracy

Activity

Robbie Oliver already owns a successful restaurant in London. He is now considering opening a second restaurant in either Richmond or Hampton. Property is slightly cheaper in Hampton, but sales are likely to be lower than in Richmond. The following table shows financial estimates for the two locations.

	Richmond £	Hampton £
Average sales revenue	872,000	500,000
Average costs and expenses	656,000	340,500
Average capital employed	1,440,000	800,000

Calculate the ARR for each restaurant, and decide which investment is the more favourable of the two.

Before you can use the formula, you need to calculate the average profit. Drawing on your knowledge of financial accounting you should remember that profit is sales less all the costs of sales and expenses. Check your answer against the following:

	Richmond £	Hampton £
Average sales revenue	872,000	500,000
Average costs and expenses	(656,000)	(340,500)
Average PBIT	216,000	159,500
$\dfrac{\text{Average PBIT}}{\text{Average CE}} \times 100$	$\dfrac{216,000}{1,440,000} \times 100$	$\dfrac{159,500}{800,000} \times 100$
ARR	= 15%	= 20%

If we rank these projects by their ARR, the Hampton restaurant is ranked first, as the rate of return is 20% compared with 15% for the Richmond restaurant. However, Robbie would be well advised not to base his decision purely on this method of investment appraisal. For example, it would be useful to know what the payback period for each project would be. We cannot use this technique because the cash flow information is not available. Also, you can see that the Richmond restaurant requires more capital (an average of just under £1.5m compared with £800,000 for the Hampton restaurant), but the Richmond restaurant is likely to give a significantly higher average annual profit in absolute terms (£216,000 compared with £159,500 for the Hampton restaurant).

Assuming that the capital required for the Richmond restaurant is available for investment, and since the Hampton restaurant requires considerably less, what is Robbie going to do with the difference? He could deposit it in a bank or building society, but the return would be likely to be much less than the 15% for the Richmond restaurant. He might want to consider investing in a similar project, but this might not be possible.

Robbie may find it useful to calculate the ARR for each year of the project and examine the incremental effects. In the early years, a project tends to have a lower ARR (because revenues are growing and assets are new), whereas in later years, the ARR is likely to be higher (because revenues are higher but the net book value of assets is lower).

18.6   Advantages and disadvantages of the accounting rate of return

As you can see, the accounting rate of return is useful because it allows us to compare projects. However, it leaves many questions unanswered and is not sufficient on its own for making important capital investment decisions.

The main *advantages* of the accounting rate of return are as follows:

- The calculations are very simple and the results are easy to understand.
- The entire life of the project is taken into account.
- The technique is compatible with ROCE, a similar ratio used in financial accounting for assessing the financial performance of the business.

The main *disadvantages* of the accounting rate of return are:

- There is no standard definition of terms used in the formula, which makes comparison of ratios that have not used the same definitions unreliable.
- Averages can be misleading since they are hypothetical values; the actual figure in any year may be higher or lower.
- It does not take into account the benefit of earning a larger proportion of the total profit in the early years of the project.

- It is based on profit, yet the crucial factor in investment decisions is cash flow.
- It takes no account of the timing of profits or cash.
- There is no guidance on what is an acceptable rate of return.
- It takes no account of the time value of money, a topic we discuss in the next chapter.

Activity

The directors of The Cheddar Cheese Company Ltd have a choice of three cheese packing machines, each of which would cost £150,000 and have an estimated useful economic life of 5 years, with no residual value. Estimate the annual profits for each machine by deducting the annual depreciation charge from the annual cash flows, using the straight-line method. Then calculate the ARR for the three machines and consider this information with the payback periods you calculated in section 18.4.

The first step is to calculate the annual depreciation charge. You will remember that the formula for the straight-line method is:

$$\frac{\text{Cost}}{\text{Useful life}} = \frac{£150,000}{5 \text{ years}} = £30,000$$

The following table shows the deduction of the annual depreciation charge of £30,000 from the annual cash flows to calculate the annual profit or loss for each machine:

| | Machine 1 | | Machine 2 | | Machine 3 | |
| | Cash flow | Profit/ (loss) | Cash flow | Profit/ (loss) | Cash flow | Profit/ (loss) |
Year	£	£	£	£	£	£
1	60,000	30,000	20,000	(10,000)	10,000	(20,000)
2	50,000	20,000	30,000	0	20,000	(10,000)
3	40,000	10,000	40,000	10,000	30,000	0
4	30,000	0	50,000	20,000	40,000	10,000
5	20,000	(10,000)	60,000	30,000	150,000	120,000
Total		50,000		50,000		100,000
Average (÷ 5 years)		10,000		10,000		20,000
$\dfrac{\text{Average PBIT}}{\text{Capital employed}} \times 100$		$= \dfrac{10,000}{150,000} \times 100$		$= \dfrac{10,000}{150,000} \times 100$		$= \dfrac{20,000}{150,000} \times 100$
ARR		= 7%		= 7%		= 13%
Payback period		= 3 years		= 4.17 years		= 4.33 years

In section 18.2 we noted that both Machine 1 and Machine 2 are expected to give a total net cash flow of £200,000 over the 5-year period, which suggests that perhaps either would be a worthwhile investment. However, cash is not the same as profit and

Table 18.2 Comparison of non-discounting methods for capital investment appraisal

Characteristic	Simple payback period method	Accounting rate of return
Focus	Cash flows	Profits
Nature	Measures time taken to recover investment	Assesses profitability of investment
Assumptions	Value and amount of cash flows	Reliability of annual profits

you can now see that although both machines will generate an average profit of £10,000 over the life of the project, averages can be misleading. In the case of Machine 1, this project will stop making profits after Year 3 (breaking even in Year 4 and making a loss of £10,000 by Year 5). In the case of Machine 2, the project will make a loss of £10,000 in Year 1, break even in Year 2 and not start generating profits until Year 3. These differences are not revealed by the ARR, which shows the same low return over the life of the project for both machines.

The ARR for Machine 3 suggests that this would be the most favourable investment as it offers almost twice the return of either Machine 1 or Machine 2. However, when we calculated the payback periods in section 18.4, we ranked Machine 3 last because it would take the longest to recover the initial investment (4 years and 4 months compared to 3 years for Machine 1 and 4 years and 2 months for Machine 2). The directors of The Cheddar Cheese Company Ltd may want to take this into consideration when making a decision, as a short payback period is important if liquidity is a problem, gearing is a concern or borrowing is involved. For example, if debt finance is being used (see Chapter 2), a short payback period means less interest to pay and lower risk to the lender that the business will not be able to repay the loan.

Table 18.2 summarizes the key characteristics of the techniques we have examined in this chapter.

18.7 Conclusions

Capital investment appraisal is a process that provides management with accounting information that helps them choose between different long-term projects that involve the investment of large sums of money. In a business context, owners and managers need to evaluate potential projects carefully and select the investment that is likely to give the highest financial return. One of the main features of capital investment decisions is the difficulty in predicting events that could affect the future returns from an investment project; both financial and non-financial factors need to be considered.

In this chapter we have examined two techniques that provide information for capital investment appraisal. The payback period method focuses on early cash flows and gives information on how soon the capital invested is likely to be recovered by calculating the number of years it is expected for the project to break even. The accounting rate of return method focuses on profitability over the life of the project by expressing average profit as a percentage of the average capital employed. These techniques offer a number of different advantages and disadvantages, but the main drawback is that they do not take account of the time value of money. In the next chapter we will be looking at other methods that address this deficiency.

It is important to remember that the usefulness of the results of capital investment techniques depends on whether the financial estimates are based on realistic predictions. The further into the future the estimate is, the higher the level of uncertainty. We have mentioned a number of times in this book that accounting is not an exact science and you should be aware by now that much financial and management accounting information is based on estimated figures.

Practice questions

1 Explain the purpose of capital investment appraisal in general. In addition, explain the purpose of the payback period method and the accounting rate of return.

2 Describe the advantages and disadvantages of the payback period method and the accounting rate of return.

3 The managing director of Stuart's Boatyard Ltd has £500,000 to invest in a new marine project and has asked you to provide information that will help him choose which is the more favourable of two potential projects. Details of the annual net cash flows are as follows:

Year	Project 1 £	Project 2 £
1	80,000	90,000
2	100,000	110,000
3	180,000	190,000
4	140,000	110,000
5	100,000	80,000

(a) Calculate the payback period for each project.
(b) Recommend which of the two projects is likely to be the better investment, giving reasons to support your advice.
(c) Comment on any limitations of the technique you have used.

4 The owners of Film Animation Ltd wish to expand the business by investing in new technology. They have the necessary capital and have identified two potential projects, only one of which can be financed. The details are as follows:

	Project A £	Project B £
Average sales	318,500	358,000
Average cost of sales including expenses	240,500	264,400
Average capital employed	650,000	780,000

(a) Calculate the accounting rate of return for each project.
(b) Recommend which of the two projects is likely to be the better investment, giving reasons to support your advice.
(c) Comment on any limitations of the technique you have used.

5 Wren Electronics Ltd has capital available for investment in new equipment and the directors are considering two 5-year projects, only one of which can be financed. Details of the annual net cash flows are as follows:

Year	Equipment 1 £	Equipment 2 £
1	5,000	20,000
2	17,000	30,000
3	42,000	20,000
4	30,000	20,000
5	10,000	20,000

In both cases, the project will require an average investment of £50,000. Annual profit before interest and tax will be based on net cash flows less annual depreciation on the equipment. This will be based on the straight-line method over 5 years with no residual value at the end of the project. You should assume that the annual cash flows shown in the above table arise evenly throughout the year.
(a) Calculate the payback period for each project.
(b) Calculate the accounting rate of return for each project.
(c) Recommend which of the two projects is likely to be the better investment, giving reasons to support your advice.
(d) Comment on any limitations of the techniques you have used.

References

Chittenden, F. and Derregia, M. (2004) *Capital Investment Decision-Making: Some Results from Studying Entrepreneurial Businesses*, Briefing paper. London: ICAEW.
Jones, M. J. (2002) *Accounting for Non-Specialists*. Chichester: John Wiley & Sons.
Law, J. (ed.) (2010) *Dictionary of Accounting*, 4th edition. Oxford: Oxford University Press.

19 Discounting methods of investment appraisal

Learning objectives

When you have studied this chapter, you should be able to:

- explain the purpose of discounted cash flow techniques
- calculate and interpret the net present value for an investment project
- calculate and interpret the internal rate of return for an investment project
- calculate and interpret the discounted payback period for an investment project
- describe the advantages and disadvantages of these three techniques.

19.1 Introduction

In the previous chapter we looked at the usefulness of the simple payback period method and the accounting rate of return as tools for providing information when a long-term capital investment decision has to be taken. However, we concluded that both techniques suffer from the serious limitation that they do not take account of the *time value of money*. Since decisions concerning the investment of large amounts of capital in potential projects are crucial in business, *discounted cash flow* methods have been developed to provide managers with sophisticated discounting techniques.[1]

We start by explaining the concept of the time value of money. This is a fairly straightforward principle and, once you have mastered it, you will find the calculations in this chapter relatively simple. We introduce you to three discounted cash flow

---

1. The principle of discounting is now so important that it is also being used in financial accounting.

methods used in investment appraisal. These are the *net present value*, the *internal rate of return* and the *discounted payback period*. All three take account of the time value of money. The specific information required for discounted cash flow techniques presents some problems, but if it is available, this choice of method greatly assists management decision making.

19.2 Time value of money

In the last chapter we looked at two of the main methods used to support capital investment decisions. The simple payback period method focuses on early cash flows and calculates the time it is expected to take to recover the capital invested. The accounting rate of return is an accounting ratio that expresses the average profit over the life of the project as a percentage of the average capital employed in the investment. One of the main criticisms of these techniques is that they do not take account of the *time value of money*, so we are now going to look at three *discounted cash flow* techniques that address this deficiency. The main methods used for capital investment appraisal are summarized in Figure 19.1.

Figure 19.1   Main methods of investment appraisal

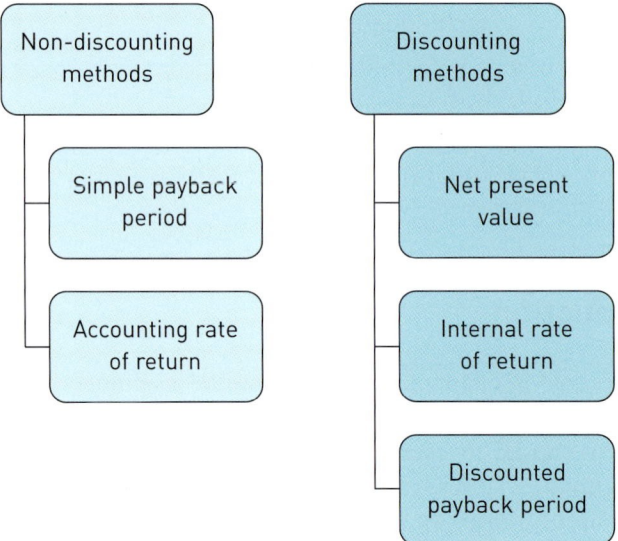

The *time value of money* is the concept that cash received at an earlier date is worth more than a similar amount of cash received later. This is because the cash received earlier can be invested to earn interest in the intervening period. The interest forgone in this way is known as the *opportunity cost of capital*. Similarly, because the cash paid out later is not available for investment today, it is worth less than a similar amount received at an earlier date.

Key definitions

The time value of money is the concept used as the basis for discounted cash flow calculations that cash received earlier is worth more than a similar sum received later, because the sum received earlier can be invested to earn interest in the intervening period.

The opportunity cost is the economic cost of an action measured in terms of the benefit foregone by not pursuing the best alternative course of action.

Source: Law (2010, pp. 415 and 306).

The longer we have to wait for the money, the less it is worth. For example, supposing someone wanted to borrow money from you now and promised to pay you £100 in a year's time, how much would you be willing to lend them if the usual interest rate is 10%? One concern you may have is whether you are likely to be paid the £100. If you consider it is doubtful, you may decide not to lend the money or you may decide to charge a high rate of interest because of the risk. If you consider the loan is very safe, you may be willing to lend £90.90. In a year's time this would give interest of £9.10 to make the sum of £100 which you are repaid.

Activity

How much would you be willing to lend now, if the interest rate is 15% and the borrower promises to repay £500 in 3 years' time?

You have probably had to make some complex calculations to arrive at the correct answer of £329. However, there is an easy method that makes use of the present value table in the Appendix, which shows the *present value factors* for future years at a range of different interest rates. For convenience, Table 19.1 shows an extract.

The question we are trying to answer is: What is the present value of £500 received in 3 years' time, if the interest rate is 15%? Look down the left-hand column until you reach future years 3 and then look along the row to the 15% interest column. The

Table 19.1   Present value table for £1 at compound interest (extract)

Future	Interest rate			
years	1%	5%	10%	15%
1	0.990	0.952	0.909	0.870
2	0.980	0.907	0.826	0.756
3	0.971	0.864	0.751	0.658
4	0.961	0.823	0.683	0.572
5	0.951	0.784	0.621	0.497
6	0.942	0.746	0.564	0.432
7	0.933	0.711	0.513	0.376
8	0.923	0.677	0.467	0.327
9	0.914	0.645	0.424	0.284
10	0.905	0.614	0.386	0.247

discount factor is 0.658, which is the discount factor for £1. It means that the present value of £1 received in 3 years' time is only £0.658. If you multiply £500 by the discount factor of 0.658, the result is £329, which is the amount you would be willing to lend now. You can check this by working out 15% compound interest on £329 for 3 years:

Year		£
0	Principal	329.00
1	Interest 15%	49.35
		378.35
2	Interest 15%	56.75
		435.10
3	Interest 15%	65.27
	Total	500.37

The time value of money underpins all discounted cash flow techniques, which makes them much more sophisticated tools for appraising capital investment projects. Such techniques convert future cash flows into present-day values and this is known as *discounting*.

Key definition

Discounted cash flow (DCF) is a method used in capital budgeting, capital expenditure appraisal, and decision appraisal that predicts the stream of cash flows, both inflows and outflows, over time and discounts them, using a cost of capital or hurdle rate, to present values in order to determine whether the project or decision is likely to be financially feasible.

Source: Law (2010, p. 151).

The basic assumptions of discounted cash flow are as follows:

- Cash is invested at the start of the year (Year 0).
- Future annual cash flows are certain (but in reality they are estimates).
- There is no inflation.
- Interest rates for lending and borrowing are the same.
- The interest rate is constant throughout the period.

We are now ready to look at the first technique.

19.3 Net present value

The *net present value (NPV)* technique uses discounting to convert the future cash flows of a project into present-day values. The *discount factor* is chosen on the basis of the required interest rate. Therefore, the net present value tells us how much better the return on a capital investment project will be than an alternative low-risk investment.

Key definition

Net present value (NPV) is a method of capital budgeting in which the value of an investment is calculated as the total present value of all cash inflows and cash outflow minus the cost of the initial investment.

Source: Law (2010, p. 293).

When comparing capital investment projects, the project with the largest positive net present value is the one preferred.

Activity

Keith Hackett is considering whether to buy computer-aided design equipment that will improve his cash flows by £30,000 per annum for the next 5 years. At the end of this time, the equipment will have reached the end of its useful economic life as it will be out of date and have no residual value. The equipment will cost £75,000 and will be bought for cash. The interest rate that Keith thinks is suitable is 15%. Calculate the NPV of this investment project using the following pro forma and the present value factors in the Appendix.

Year	Cash flow £	Discount factor 15%	Present value £
0	(75,000)	1.000	(75,000)
1			
2			
3			
4			
5			
		NPV	

If you had problems with this activity, you may find the following comments helpful:

- The initial investment takes place in Year 0, which refers to the start of Year 1. It is shown in brackets because it is a negative cash flow.
- The discount factor is 1.000 in Year 0 because this is the present year and not a future year.
- The NPV is the difference between the total of the present value (PV) of the future cash flows expected from the project (the discounted cash flows) and the initial capital invested ('net' always means something has been deducted).

The solution is as follows:

Year	Cash flow £	Discount factor 15%	Present value £
0	(75,000)	1.000	(75,000)
1	30,000	0.870	26,100
2	30,000	0.756	22,680
3	30,000	0.658	19,740
4	30,000	0.572	17,160
5	30,000	0.497	14,910
		NPV	25,590

The results show that the NPV of the project is a positive £25,590, which means that Keith will be getting a return on his investment of 15% plus this amount. If the NPV had been 0, his return would be 15%. If the project had shown a negative NPV, the return would be less than 15%. If 15% represented the return on an alternative low-risk investment, a negative NPV would indicate that the project under consideration would not be worthwhile. Therefore, the decision rule is to accept the project with the highest positive NPV.

19.4 Internal rate of return

The *internal rate of return* (IRR) uses the same principles as the NPV method, but the aim is to find the interest rate which gives a NPV of zero for the project. This is the rate at which the sum of the discounted values of the predicted cash flows is equal to the capital invested in a proposed investment project. The IRR allows us to show the return on the investment entirely as a percentage instead of measuring it partly as a percentage and partly as a financial figure.

Key definition

The internal rate of return (IRR) is an interest rate that gives a net present value of zero when applied to a projected cash flow of an asset, liability, or financial decision.

Source: Law (2010, p. 242).

When evaluating a single project, the IRR will be chosen when it is higher than the cost of capital. When comparing projects, the project with the highest IRR is preferred.

Activity

In the previous example we concluded that at an interest rate of 15%, a positive NPV of £25,560 made Keith's investment worthwhile. In other words, Keith would be getting a return on the project in excess of 15%. Using the following pro forma and the present value factors in the Appendix, calculate the net present value for the project using interest rates of 20%, 25% and 30%.

Year	Cash flow £	Discount factor 20%	Present value £	Discount factor 25%	Present value £	Discount factor 30%	Present value £
0	(75,000)	1.000	(75,000)	1.000	(75,000)	1.000	(75,000)
1	30,000						
2	30,000						
3	30,000						
4	30,000						
5	30,000						
		NPV	_____		NPV _____		NPV _____

Check your answer against the following solution:

Year	Cash flow £	Discount factor 20%	Present value £	Discount factor 25%	Present value £	Discount factor 30%	Present value £
0	(75,000)	1.000	(75,000)	1.000	(75,000)	1.000	(75,000)
1	30,000	0.833	24,990	0.800	24,000	0.769	23,070
2	30,000	0.694	20,820	0.640	19,200	0.592	17,760
3	30,000	0.579	17,370	0.512	15,360	0.455	13,650
4	30,000	0.482	14,460	0.410	12,300	0.350	10,500
5	30,000	0.402	12,060	0.328	9,840	0.269	8,070
		NPV	14,700	NPV	5,700	NPV	(1,950)

The information we now have can be summarized as follows:

- Using an interest rate of 15%, the NPV is a positive £25,590.
- Using an interest rate of 20%, the NPV is a positive £14,700.
- Using an interest rate of 25%, the NPV is a positive £5,700.
- Using an interest rate of 30%, the NPV is a negative (£1,950).

Looking at this, you can see that the higher the interest rate used to discount the future cash flows, the smaller the NPV becomes, until it eventually becomes negative somewhere between 25% and 30%. The IRR lies at the point where the net present value changes from positive to negative, which is where the NPV is 0. This is illustrated in Figure 19.2 by plotting the NPVs on a graph against the appropriate interest rates. The interest rates are marked on the x axis, and net present values on the y axis.

You will see that the line joining the four points is a slight curve, but for all practical purposes, we can assume that it is a straight line, provided the points are not too far apart. We shall use the data at 25% and 30% interest rates. The interest rate at which the line crosses the x axis, where NPV is 0, is somewhere between 25% and 30%; in other words, 25 + a number between 0 and 5 (30 − 25). The calculation of the IRR involves linear interpolation (linear, because it assumes a straight line) and the formula is as follows:

Figure 19.2 Keith Hackett: Internal rate of return

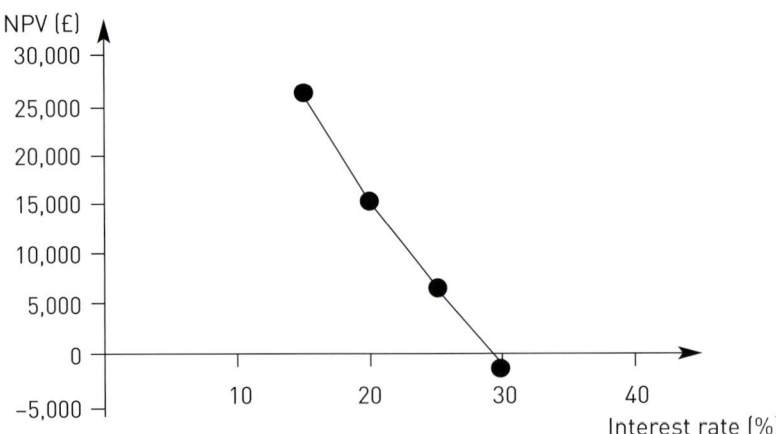

$$\text{Positive rate} + \left(\frac{\text{Positive NPV}}{\text{Positive NPV} + \text{Negative NPV}} \times \text{Range of rates} \right)$$

$$= 25 + \left(\frac{5,700}{5,700 + 1,950} \times (30 - 25) \right)$$

$$= 25 + (0.745098 \times 5) = 28.73\%$$

As you can see, Keith will get a return of 28.73% on the project. The figures in brackets represent the proportion of 5 that we require to be added to 25. The difference between the two NPVs (£5,700 positive and £1,950 negative) is actually the sum of the two figures, because we are ignoring the fact that the second figure is negative. If you find this difficult to understand, the following explanation may help. If you had £100 in the bank yesterday (a positive figure), and today find that you have an overdraft of £50 (a negative figure), how much money have you drawn out of the bank since yesterday? The answer is:

$$£100 + £50 = £150$$

19.5   Discounted payback period method

In the previous chapter we explained that the simple payback period method is widely used because it is important for the owners and managers of a business who are considering an investment project to know how long it will take before the capital invested has been recovered and the project begins to pay for itself. However, the drawback of the simple method is that it ignores the time value of money. This can be overcome by discounting the future cash flows.

Key definition

The discounted payback period method is a method of capital budgeting in which managers calculate the time required before the forecast discounted cash inflows from an investment will equal the initial investment.

Source: Law (2010, p. 151).

The discounted payback period is the time required for the predicted discounted cash flows to equal the capital invested in a proposed investment project. The project taking the shortest possible time is the one preferred.

Activity

Return to the example of The Cheddar Cheese Company Ltd in the previous chapter where we compared the simple payback period for three projects that involved investment in a packing machine. Using a spreadsheet and the following layout, calculate the discounted payback periods for each project. Then compare them with your earlier results and make recommendations to the directors.

		Machine X		
	Cash flow	Discount factor	Present value	Cumulative cash flow
Year	£	10%	£	£
0				
1				
2				
3				
4				
5				

Check your calculations against the following:

		Machine 1		
	Cash flow	Discount factor	Present value	Cumulative cash flow
Year	£	at 10%	£	£
0	(150,000)	1.000	(150,000)	(150,000)
1	60,000	0.909	54,540	(95,460)
2	50,000	0.826	41,300	(54,160)
3	40,000	0.751	30,040	(24,120)
4	30,000	0.683	20,490	(3,630)
5	20,000	0.621	12,420	8,790

$$\text{Discounted payback period} = 4 \text{ years} + \frac{3,630}{3,630 + 8,790}$$

$$= 4.29 \text{ years}$$

Simple payback period   = 3 years

Machine 2

Year	Cash flow £	Discount factor at 10%	Present value £	Cumulative cash flow £
0	(150,000)	1.000	(150,000)	(150,000)
1	20,000	0.909	18,180	(131,820)
2	30,000	0.826	24,780	(107,040)
3	40,000	0.751	30,040	(77,000)
4	50,000	0.683	34,150	(42,850)
5	60,000	0.621	37,260	(5,590)

Discounted payback period = Investment not recovered
Simple payback period = 4.17 years

Machine 3

Year	Cash flow £	Discount factor 10%	Present value £	Cumulative cash flow £
0	(150,000)	1.000	(150,000)	(150,000)
1	10,000	0.909	9,090	(140,910)
2	20,000	0.826	16,520	(124,390)
3	30,000	0.751	22,530	(101,860)
4	40,000	0.683	27,320	(74,540)
5	150,000	0.621	93,150	18,610

$$\textbf{Discounted payback period} = 4 \text{ years} + \frac{74,540}{74,540 + 18,610}$$

$$= 4.8 \text{ years}$$

Simple payback period = 4.33 years

This exercise illustrates the difference it makes to the choice of project when the time value of money is taken into consideration in the calculation of the payback period. With an interest rate of 10%, you can see that the investment in Machine 1 will not be recovered at the end of Year 3 after all; instead, the directors will have to wait for 4 years and 3½ months (4.29 years), which is into the second quarter of Year 5. If you look at the results for Machine 2, the simple payback period was 4 years and 2 months (4.17 years), but now you can see that once the annual cash flows are discounted, the capital will not be recovered at all. Finally, the results for Machine 3 show that instead of being paid back in 4 years and 4 months (4.33 years), the discounted payback period shows it will not be paid pack for 4 years and 9½ months (4.8 years) and the company will have to wait until the last quarter of Year 5 to recover the capital.

You should have recommended Machine 1 as being the most favourable project in terms of its discounted payback period. Not only does this method consider the time value of money, but it also takes account of more of the future cash flows, since the discounted payback period is always longer than the payback period using the simple method.

19.6 Advantages and disadvantages of discounted cash flow methods

The main *advantages* of discounted cash flow methods are as follows:

- They use the concept of the time value of money.
- The NPV and IRR methods take account of the entire life of the project (the discounted payback period only considers the project up to the payback period).
- They permit comparisons to be made with other opportunities.

The main *disadvantages* are:

- It is difficult to determine the appropriate interest rate to use and predict the cash flows over the life of the project.
- The calculations are complex.
- They do not take account of non-financial factors such as the flexibility of plant and equipment purchased.
- Some managers may have difficulty in understanding the results.

We can conclude that although the net present value, internal rate of return and discounted payback period are useful techniques, they are also complex and managers with little knowledge of accounting may have difficulty in understanding them. The main purpose of management accounting is to assist managers by providing information that will help them carry out their responsibilities of planning, controlling and decision making. Therefore, giving information that is hard to interpret makes it less useful.

Activity

What sort of problems do you think might be associated with investment appraisal techniques based on discounted cash flows?

As well as the management team having problems in understanding the results of the calculations, the accountant may have difficulty in obtaining the figures to do the calculations. Indeed, this is a problem that is common to all investment appraisal techniques. As far as discounted cash flow methods are concerned, the difficulty lies in predicting the amount of cash inflows and outflows over the life of the project. Some projects last for many years and it will not be possible for the accountant to forecast the amounts with any certainty. For this reason, many firms prefer the payback period, because it is based on the earliest cash flows. One cash flow that can arise at the end of a project is the sale of the machinery and equipment that was originally purchased for the project. With a large investment in machinery, the *residual value* (the second-hand or scrap value) may be very high, even after many years of use. The expected proceeds from the sale of such assets must be shown as a cash inflow in the calculations.

Another problem is the choice of *discount factor*. In this chapter we have used a number of different rates as illustrations, but management (with advice from the

Table 19.2   Comparison of discounted cash flow methods of investment appraisal

Characteristic	Net present value	Internal rate of return	Discounted payback period
Focus	Cash flows	Cash flows	Cash flows
Nature	Measures present value of cash flows	Determines rate of return at which investment breaks even	Measures time taken to recover investment
Assumptions	Value and amount of cash flows, and the interest rate	Value and amount of cash flows, and the interest rate	Value and amount of cash flows, and the interest rate

accountant) must decide which rate to use. You will appreciate that the choice of discount factor is critical to the results. Most commonly, businesses base their choice on the current rate of return received on capital employed, the current cost of capital, the return on other projects available or the rate that could be received if the business were to invest the capital externally. When answering questions on capital appraisal, it is easy for students to concentrate on the calculations and forget these other aspects. The calculations are relatively easy, but the above issues make capital investment appraisal techniques complex. However, it is vital that the management accountant makes use of them, as they assist management in determining the likely return they will get from a long-term project and deciding whether it is acceptable in view of the risks involved.

A survey of UK and international members of CIMA (2009) showed that of range of methods we have discussed, the most widely used is net present value, followed by the simple payback method, the internal rate of return, the discounted payback method and accounting rate of return. The use of leasing, renting, outsourcing and subcontracting reduces the effect of uncertainty on decisions, increases the resources available for a much lower initial outlay and in some cases avoids capital investment decisions altogether. Table 19.2 summarizes the key characteristics of the techniques we have examined in this chapter.

19.7   Conclusions

There are a number of different investment appraisal techniques that can provide useful information to aid capital investment decisions. In the last chapter we introduced the simple payback period method and the accounting rate of return. In this chapter we have described three techniques that are based on discounting projected cash flows: net present value, internal rate of return and discounted payback period. Each technique provides different information and offers different advantages and disadvantages. The specific information required for discounted cash flow techniques presents some problems, but, if available, these more sophisticated methods offer the advantage of incorporating the time value of money in the calculation of return.

Guided by the accountant, management will have to decide which methods are appropriate to aid decisions. In many companies, multiple methods will be used to overcome the individual weaknesses inherent in each method.

Practice questions

1 Describe the advantages and disadvantages of using discounted cash flow methods for capital investment appraisal.

2 Compare the net present value method with the internal rate of return.

3 Kerry Melrose is considering an investment in audiovisual equipment costing £10,000 for her training business, Melrose Events. With the help of her accountant, Kerry has done her calculations on a cash basis and is assuming that the following annual cash flows will take place evenly throughout the year. She anticipates that the project will require the business to spend £5,000 on advertising in the first year, but it should generate £1,000 in revenue. The advertising costs are expected to reduce to £3,000 in the second year and generate £2,000 worth of business. In the third and fourth years, no advertising will be required and the revenue generated is expected to be £3,000 in Year 3 and £6,000 in Year 4. In Year 5 the project will generate £8,000 worth of business, but by the end of the year she expects that the equipment will be obsolete, with no residual value.

(a) Calculate the simple payback period and the net present value for the project using an interest rate of 12%.

(b) Interpret your results and recommend whether Kerry should go ahead with the project, giving reasons to support your advice.

(c) Comment on any financial considerations Kerry should bear in mind.

4 The managing director of Stuart's Boatyard Ltd has £500,000 to invest in a new marine project and has asked you to provide information that will help him choose which is the more favourable of two projects. Details of the annual cash flows are as follows and these are assumed to arise evenly throughout the year:

Year	Project 1	Project 2
	£	£
1	80,000	90,000
2	100,000	110,000
3	180,000	190,000
4	140,000	110,000
5	100,000	80,000

(a) Calculate the discounted payback period for each project and the net present value of each project using an interest rate of 6%.

(b) Recommend which of the two projects should be chosen, giving reasons to support your advice.

(c) Comment on any limitations of the techniques you have used.

5 Your Aunt Laura owns Bloomfield Laundry Ltd and has £50,000 to invest in new dryers. She has asked you to advise her on the financial viability of the project and tells you that she requires a 15% rate of return. The following projected annual cash flows are expected to arise evenly throughout each year:

Year	£
1	10,000
2	25,000
3	25,000
4	20,000
5	10,000

(a) Calculate the discounted payback period, the net present value and the internal rate of return from the purchase of the new dryers.

(b) Interpret your results and advise your aunt.

(c) Comment on any limitations of the techniques you have used.

References

CIMA (2009) *Management accounting tools for today and tomorrow*. London: Chartered Institute of Management Accountants. Available at: http://www.cima-global.com/Thought-leadership/Research-topics/Recommended-reports/ (accessed 1 December 2011).

Law, J. (ed.) (2010) *Dictionary of Accounting*, 4th edition. Oxford: Oxford University Press.

20 Issues in management accounting

Learning objectives

When you have studied this chapter, you should be able to:

- discuss the limitations of traditional management accounting
- describe the main management accounting techniques used to monitor the strategic process
- explain the four perspectives of the balanced scorecard method
- describe the role of accounting in the management of quality
- describe the role of environmental accounting.

20.1 Introduction

In Part III of this book we have looked at how traditional cost and management accounting methods can be used to provide detailed information for cost control and managerial decision making. However, we have also pointed out that some techniques can be criticized for their lack of relevance to modern business. For example, in Chapter 14 we explained how the limitations of absorption costing led to the development of activity-based costing and the need for other techniques to provide information for managing the competitive, strategic and operational issues that businesses face. Management accounting continues to evolve and in this chapter we describe a number of current issues in the subject.

We start by discussing the need for *strategic management accounting* and describe the range of techniques that can be used to produce more strategically relevant financial information. We then discuss the role of management accounting as an aid to managing quality and reducing the impact of the business on the environment.

20.2 Strategic management accounting

A strategy is a plan of action devised by management to achieve the financial objectives of the business. Choices are made about what products and services to produce and/or sell, how they will be priced and marketed, and what technologies, resources, organizational structures and supply arrangements are needed. *Strategic management accounting (SMA)* is a management accounting system that supplies the information for the strategic management decisions needed to achieve the long-term goals of the business. For management accounting to play a role in strategic management, the system must not only provide information that focuses on internal operations, but also information about the external business environment such as information about competitors' products that will assist in the pricing strategy of new products and decisions relating to expansion.

Key definition

Strategic management accounting is a management accounting system organized so that it is capable of providing the information needed for long-term strategic decision making, as opposed to the more traditional approach of providing short-term costs.

Source: Law (2010, p. 401).

The three main stages of SMA are:

1. Assess the current position of the business through techniques such as value chain analysis.
2. Evaluate the current position of the business through techniques such as an analysis of strengths, weaknesses, opportunities and threats (SWOT), the balanced scorecard and benchmarking.
3. Make a strategic choice for the future direction of the business based on factors such as the strength of its existing products or customer base, or diversification of products and markets.

Activity

Consider whether any of the management accounting techniques described in this book could be used to provide information about a business's competitive environment. Do any of these techniques provide non-financial information?

There are a number of problems with using traditional management accounting methods for strategic management purposes because they focus on the internal operations of the business and do not consider factors such as the production costs of competitors or whether products or services are competitive in the market. Although traditional management accounting methods are useful for measuring and controlling costs, and helping to improve internal decision making, they fail to provide benchmarks for

Table 20.1   Characteristics of traditional and strategic management accounting

Traditional management accounting	Strategic management accounting
Historical	Forward looking
Introspective	Outward looking
Narrow scope	Broad scope
Internal performance	Performance relative to competitors
Single period	Multiple periods
Manufacturing focus	Competitive focus
Existing activities	Possibilities
Reactive	Proactive
Programmed (often)	Unprogrammed
Overlooks linkages	Exploits linkages
Based on existing systems	Unconstrained by existing systems
Built on conventions	Ignores conventions
Financial measures	Financial and non-financial measures
Exact figures	Approximations

Source: Lord (2007, p. 137).

comparing the organization's performance with that of its competitors. Table 20.1 compares the characteristics of traditional management accounting techniques with those of SMA.

Traditional management accounting adopts an internally focused historical perspective where the focus is on single decisions, single periods and single products. Most of the information is financial in nature and therefore its techniques fail to consider performance that cannot be measured in monetary terms, such as the number of defective products or the level of customer satisfaction. By contrast, SMA is future orientated and has an external focus on the strategic and competitive position of the business and its products in the market. SMA provides subjective non-financial information as well as objective financial information, and its prime focus is on providing information about the success or failure of the entity's business strategy.

In addition to requiring external information about customers, suppliers and competitors, strategic management requires internal information relating to what Porter (1985, p. 48) describes as the firm's *value chain*. This value chain consists of a set of value-creating primary and support activities that are necessary to provide a competitive product or service to customers. Support activities include the firm's infrastructure (e.g. its organizational structure and management control systems), human resource management, research and development processes and procurement. The firm's primary activities are a chain of business activities in which value is added to the product or services of the organization. These may include:

- inbound logistics, which involve handling the delivery, warehousing and distribution of raw materials
- operations, which are the activities needed for producing a product or delivering a service

- outbound logistics, which involve the storage and distribution of finished goods to customers
- marketing and sales, which comprise activities to identify the product or service attributes that customers require and to generate sales
- customer service, which is the support offered to customers after products and services are sold.

A firm's profit margin depends on its ability to perform these activities efficiently, so that the price that a customer is willing to pay for the product or service exceeds the cost of the activities within the value chain. Thus, a firm must focus on only incurring expenditure on those 'value added' activities for which customers will pay for. For example, there is little point marketing a personal computer with a 3-year warranty and customer service package if customers are only willing to pay for a computer with a 1-year warranty.

Understanding the links within the value chain of activities is critical, since identifying the relationships between the way one activity is performed and the cost of performing another provides opportunities for improving efficiency by redesigning or re-engineering these activities. As an organization's own value chain is linked to the value chains of suppliers and customers, it is also important for SMA to investigate ways in which collaborations between suppliers and customers may reduce costs and increase value added for all parties. For example, an organization may obtain cost savings from having suppliers deliver components to its site with less polystyrene packaging, as such protective materials are costly and after use must be sent for disposal.

As SMA supports strategic decision making, it must provide information to help the business determine its strategic position in the market and analyse whether its position is sustainable in the level of competition in the market. Porter (1985) describes strategy as an analytical process which calculates and selects the optimum strategic position for an organization by balancing the competitive forces within an industry against the distinctive internal abilities of the firm. *Porter's five forces model* (1985, p. 5) can be used to determine the level of competition in an industry, which reflects its attractiveness in terms of the likelihood of being able to achieve above-normal profits. The five forces that drive competiveness are:

- the threat of new entrants to the market
- the threat of substitute products or services
- the bargaining power of customers
- the bargaining power of suppliers
- the intensity of rivalry among existing firms in the industry.

As you can see, the first and the last of these competitive forces are external sources of competition. Government intervention is not included as a competitive force, but government can limit or prevent new entrants to a market through state controls.

SMA techniques can be used to support this positioning process by analysing the strengths and weaknesses of the business, its opportunities and the threats it faces (SWOT analysis). This may involve monitoring the cost and pricing policies of competitors, comparing the performance of the business with its competitors, analysing the barriers to entry in its product markets and evaluating the net cost of strategic options such as establishing long-term relationships with suppliers. Some of the SMA information required will be based on estimates (for example, data used to assess whether the costs of competitors are higher than those of the business), and industry benchmarks may be available.

When an organization has found a sustainable strategic position within a market, it must develop a strategy for securing a sustainable competitive advantage over its rivals. According to Porter (1985), an organization can choose between the following options, which can be applied to an entire market or a niche area within a market.

- A product differentiation strategy is where the business provides unique products that offer value not found in competing products, and competitive advantage is secured through being able to charge a high market price and to innovate in a cost-effective manner.
- A cost leadership strategy is where the business produces its products at a lower cost than its competitors.

Activity

Identify some well-known companies that adopt product differentiation or cost leadership strategies.

Apple Inc is a good example of a company that adopts a product differentiation strategy, as its unique products such as the Mac computer, the iPhone and the iPad are sold at premium prices to a loyal customer base. On the other hand, Tesco PLC and Wal-Mart Stores Inc are examples of companies that have adopted a cost leadership strategy.

We will now look at a case study that will help you understand the importance of SMA information. Euro Cars GmbH was founded in 1999 and operates in a niche market manufacturing three models of car for the European car market. The company's long-term strategy has been to design and make high-quality cars and simply price above total cost using cost-plus pricing. For many years this approach has proved profitable and allowed the company to win at least one annual consumer award for best motor vehicle.

The company prides itself on being the most cost efficient in the European motor industry, but cost management has never been a primary strategic or operational concern. The company's managers have never undertaken a comparative analysis with competitors' cost structures and believe they are already following best practice in terms of cost control and operational efficiency. As a result of its reputation for engineering excellence and its perceived cost advantage over its rivals, Euro Cars GmbH has always adopted a cost-plus pricing policy. Each car is routinely priced at approximately 7% above its total variable production cost.

Since the start of 2012, Euro Cars GmbH faced strong market competition for the first time and revenue fell sharply. Further analysis revealed that sales of their Cyclone model had suffered most. Cyclone is a sleekly styled sports car aimed at the professional person market. The company anticipated producing and selling 2,000 Cyclones during 2012, but the actual figures showed sales were 25% below this target. Further bad news came when the company failed to win any honours at the 2012 European Car of the Year Awards.

Prior to this crisis, Euro Cars GmbH had established a competitive advantage by selling the Cyclone at a lower price than similar models produced by rival companies. However, two low-cost competitors entered the market in 2012: China Motors with the SU4 sports car and Indian Cars with the Chita sports car, both with a selling price of €28,000, which was €2,000 less than Euro Car's Cyclone. Furthermore, the SU4 won the 2012 European Sports Car of Year Award. The following table compares the specifications for the three competing models.

Specifications of Cyclone and competing models

	Cyclone	SU4	Chita	Audi TT
Engine size (litres)	3.2	3.2	3.2	3.2
Engine power in kilowatts (kW)	201	200	199	203
Top speed: kilometres (km) per hour (km/h)	252	248	248	250
0–100 km/h acceleration (seconds)	5.5	5.6	5.7	5.5
Litres of fuel per 100 km	9.7	9.4	9	9.4
CO_2 emissions (grams per km)	179	169	165	175
Insurance group (1–50)	36	34	34	38
Last award won	2011	2012	None	2011
Automatic gearbox	Yes	Yes	No	Yes
Automatic roof	Yes	Yes	Yes	Yes
Leather upholstery	Yes	Yes	Yes	Yes
ABS anti-lock brakes	No	Yes	Yes	Yes
Satellite navigation system	No	No	No	Yes
Premium Sound system	Yes	No	No	Yes
Warranty	5 years or 140,000 km	4 years or 120,000 km	4 years or 120,000 km	2 years or 100,000 km
Selling price	€30,000	€28,000	€28,000	€36,518

Activity

(a) Explain whether the company is following a product differentiation strategy or cost leadership strategy and any problems associated with following such a strategy.

(b) Explain how Euro Cars GmbH could use Porter's (1985) model of strategic positioning to assess the current strategy and competitive advantage of the firm.

(c) Identify the types of financial and non-financial information that could be used to improve strategic decision making at the company.

The company appears to be pursuing a product differentiation strategy for the Cyclone, but has failed to assess its current strategic position in the context of new entrants into the market or the relative value of its product compared with competing products. The comparative table of product attributes suggests that Euro Cars GmbH is charging a premium price of €30,000 for the Cyclone, which is €2,000 more than competing products, which have similar attributes.

Management could use Porter's five forces model to assess the company's current strategic position and suggest how it could secure competitive advantage over its new rivals. The case study contains no information about suppliers, but many car manufacturers try to establish long-term contracts with suppliers to obtain lower prices and/or higher quality materials, components and services.

Because of the threat posed by the low-cost competitors, Euro Cars GmbH urgently needs to obtain SMA information such as data on competitors' costs, volumes, market shares and customer satisfaction. Furthermore, efficiency of the production operations needs to be compared with competitors or industry benchmarks. Such an exercise will allow the standard costs to be revised in line with best practice. Finally, if the company is to continue its product differentiation strategy, the management accounting system should focus on the marketing costs and on establishing the value-added activities that customers are willing to pay for in respect of the Cyclone model.

Whichever strategy is chosen, the exact functioning and content of a supporting SMA system will reflect this choice. A cost leadership strategy will require an SMA system that emphasizes the role of standard and product costs in assessing performance and pricing decisions, and the SMA system will emphasize marketing costs and benchmark products on a continuous basis. Research shows that many of the techniques for generating and using this information are already part of the operational management of firms without the involvement of the management accountant or a need for accounting data (Lord, 2007). This also applies to environmental management accounting, which we discuss later in the chapter.

The debate over the need for SMA has led to a range of new and modified accounting techniques. We will now review three of the main approaches: market-orientated accounting, target costing and the balanced scorecard.

20.3 Market-orientated accounting

Market-orientated accounting (MOA) is a form of SMA that provides information about the specific attributes that products and services offer customers and monitors how these benefits contribute to securing a competitive advantage. This approach was developed by Bromwich (1990), who suggests that economic goods are desired for the underlying bundle of product attributes they provide rather than their price, as these are the characteristics that give the products their market value. They include a variety of quality elements, such as operating performance variables, reliability and warranty arrangements, physical items (such as the degree of finish and trim), and service factors (such as the assurance of supply and after sales service. Once the bundle of attributes desired by customers has been identified, the success of the business depends on its ability to produce goods that provide those attributes at a competitive cost level.

Activity

Identify the product attributes of a tube of toothpaste. Hint: Think about the benefits that consumers require.

You may have thought of some of the following attributes:

- protection from plaque and decay
- reduced sensitivity
- stain removal and whitening
- fresher breath
- pleasant smell, taste, texture and colour.

The following cost information for a 100 ml tube of toothpaste is taken from a traditional absorption costing system:

	£
	£
Direct materials	0.50
Direct labour	0.05
Overhead allocated	0.95
Total cost	1.50
Profit	0.15
Selling price	1.65

This information has little value from an SMA perspective as it is cannot be used to benchmark the relative efficiency of the product's manufacture or whether its price is competitive. In addition, there is no information about the attributes that the toothpaste provides or the cost of including them in the product. The detailed strategic cost analysis shown in the table on page 413 addresses these deficiencies. With the help of the marketing and manufacturing staff, the accountant has been able to identify and allocate £1.35 of the total production cost to the product attributes identified by consumers. It was not possible to allocate the remaining £0.15.

The analysis of costs is extremely useful from a benchmarking perspective, and is extended by the analysis of the relative importance of the attributes to consumers, taken from a customer survey. The results show that protection from decay was the most important attribute and the use of organic ingredients was the least important. By comparing the percentage cost of providing the attribute with the percentage importance it is given by consumers, the management accountant can determine whether the cost is justified. The table suggests that protection from decay is inexpensive and consumers consider it the most important factor in their buying decision.

Strategic cost analysis for a 100 ml tube of toothpaste				
Product attributes	Cost £	% of total cost	Importance to consumers [%]	Strategic cost index
Protection from decay	0.23	15.33	26.00	1.70
Protection from plaque	0.11	7.33	23.00	3.14
General teeth cleaning	0.10	6.67	17.00	2.55
Whitening capability	0.20	13.33	12.00	0.90
Breath freshening	0.10	6.67	8.00	1.20
Reduced sensitivity	0.11	7.33	4.00	0.55
Taste/texture	0.05	3.33	7.00	2.10
Appearance/colour	0.10	6.67	1.00	0.15
Use of organic ingredients	0.18	12.00	0.80	0.07
Other attributes				
Ethical and green production	0.12	8.00	1.00	0.13
Advertising	0.05	3.33	0.20	0.06
Costs attributable to consumer benefits	1.35	90.00	100.00	
Cost not attributable to consumer benefits	0.15	10.00		
Total cost	1.50	100.00		

However, the cost of providing organic ingredients outweighs the benefits. The final column in the table shows the *strategic cost index* (SCI), which is calculated as the relative importance of the attribute divided by the cost of providing that attribute (column 3 divided by column 2). Management should redesign or re-engineer products to focus on the attributes with the highest SCI results and consider ways of eliminating attributes with very low SCI scores.

Thus the aim of MOA is to determine the cost of providing product features to consumers given operating conditions that continuously seek improvement. For survival in a competitive market, a firm must offer a product which is not dominated by other products – so the business must offer the cheapest way for a consumer to obtain the bundle of characteristics being offered, or yield at least the same amount of each characteristic as its competitors unless it generates sufficient extra of one or more characteristics to offset the lower amount of one or more of the other characteristics. The cost structure of the business relative to that of its actual and potential rivals is the key factor in ensuring the sustainability of the firm's market strategy. It must possess cost advantages over rivals and expect to retain these in the future. For example, even a product differentiator has to adopt a cost leader-like pursuit of cost containment. As a result, a better understanding of cost behaviour within the firm is a fundamental goal of SMA.

Returning to the case of Euro Cars GmbH, imagine that the management accountant has been given the results of a customer survey that show the important product attributes of a sports car and their relative importance:

- safety 25%
- comfort 20%
- economy 5%
- performance 20%
- styling 30%

This enables the accountant to construct the next table, which estimates how the different components of the car contribute to the product attributes. The importance index in the last column incorporates the customer survey data and measures the relative importance of each component in providing the desired product attributes. For example, the importance index for the chassis and wheels is calculated by multiplying the line item value by the weighting of the product attribute from the consumer survey and summing the results:

$$(0.45 \times 0.25) + (0.20 \times 0.20) + (0.10 \times 0.05) + (0.15 \times 0.20) + (0.15 \times 0.30) = 0.2325 \times 100 = 23.25\%$$

This tells us that the chassis and wheels provide 23% of the characteristics of the product that consumers consider are important. Together with the engine, suspension and brakes, these components provide nearly 56% of highly rated characteristics, whereas the air conditioning system provides only 2%.

Importance index for components of a sports car						
Component group	Safety 25%	Comfort 20%	Economy 5%	Performance 20%	Styling 30%	Importance to consumers (%)
Chassis and wheels	0.45	0.20	0.10	0.15	0.15	23.25
Engine, suspension and brakes	0.35	0.30	0.50	0.75	–	32.25
Electrical systems	0.5	–	0.10	0.05	0.05	4.25
Interior fittings	0.5	0.25	–	–	0.30	15.25
Air conditioning	–	0.10	–	–	–	2.00
Other systems	0.10	0.15	0.30	0.05	0.50	23.00
Total	1.00	1.00	1.00	1.00	1.00	100.00

The management accountant has also prepared the following statement of total standard costs for each component group:

Statement of total standard costs	
Component group	% of total standard cost
Chassis and wheels	22.4
Engine, suspension and brakes	23.7
Electrical systems	6.7
Interior fittings	7.9
Air conditioning	6.4
Other systems	32.9
Total	100.0

Activity

Prepare a strategic cost index for each component group of the Cyclone car and suggest how the company could redesign it to make its attributes more appealing to customers.

Your answer should reveal some interesting results about the product. As you can see from the following solution, the air conditioning is the function that is relatively costly to provide (6.4% of the total cost of the Cyclone) when one compares it to the relative importance it has to consumers (only provides 10% of the comfort attribute). A recommendation is for the company to source a less expensive air conditioning unit or even offer a less expensive version of the Cyclone without this function. Other key component groups that require investigation during the product redesign are the electrical and other systems, as they also have an SCI below 1. By contrast, the interior fittings have an SCI of 1.94, indicating that they provide a required product attribute in a cost-effective manner.

Strategic cost analysis for car component groups			
Component group	Importance to consumers (%)	% of total standard cost	Strategic cost index
Chassis and wheels	23.25	22.40	1.04
Engine, suspension and brakes	32.25	23.70	1.36
Electrical systems	4.25	6.70	0.63
Interior fittings	15.25	7.90	1.94
Air conditioning	2.00	6.40	0.31
Other systems	23.00	32.90	0.70
Total	100.00	100.00	

While the costing of product attributes that market-orientated accounting requires can be complex and time-consuming, this type of analysis provides an invaluable source of strategically relevant information about the relative competitiveness of products. The provision of this type of accounting information may require input from many functional areas within an organization, most notably the marketing and production departments, and requires a strategic dialogue between accountants and non-accountants.

20.4 Target costing

Target costing is a strategic technique that relies on market data to provide an externally orientated approach to pricing, profit planning and cost management. It was developed in the Japanese car industry and is now used extensively by US and European manufacturing companies (Ansari et al., 2007). In a target costing framework, the selling price of a product or service is constrained by the product market and is determined by analysis of the entire industry value chain and across all functions in the organization. In contrast to cost-plus pricing, the cost of producing the product or service does not dictate the selling price. Instead, the target cost is the goal that an organization must achieve to meet its strategic objectives. The notion can be expressed mathematically as follows:

$$\text{Target cost} = \text{Target price} - \text{Target profit}$$

In this equation, market price and profit are independent variables as both are determined by competitive forces within the product and capital markets. As illustrated by MOA, price is determined by what customers are willing to pay for the attributes that the product or service offers, and profit is determined by what financial markets expect as a return from operating in a particular industry. The dependent variable is cost, which implies that an organization must manage its costs to meet the external market constraints that it faces.

Key definition

Target costing is a method of costing products or services to reflect the price that customers are willing to pay.

Source: Law (2010, p. 408).

The main steps in target costing are as follows:

1. Develop a product that satisfies the needs of customers. As we illustrated in the last section on MOA, it is vital that each product or service provides attributes that consumers demand. When designing a new product it is essential that it offer a bundle of attributes superior to the market competition.
2. Determine an appropriate target price for the product based upon customers' perceived value of its attributes and the price of competing products, and the target profit per unit. For each product, an assessment is needed of the market price that is appropriate for the bundle of attributes it offers and the competition it faces.
3. Calculate the target cost after allowing for target profit (target price – target profit). An organization must provide a return that is appropriate for the level of risk inherent in the business. This target profit per unit can be calculated in a number of different ways, but is deducted from the target price to obtain the target cost per unit.
4. Use value engineering and SMA techniques to achieve the target cost per unit.

Value engineering is an activity that creates products that meet customer needs at the lowest cost. It supports the target costing process by evaluating the value chain of business functions, with the objective of identifying cost reduction opportunities that help to achieve each product's target cost per unit while still satisfying customer needs. If the actual cost of production exceeds this target cost, products can be re-engineered or redesigned to reduce cost. Target costing is an incremental process that must be repeated on a continuous basis over a product's life cycle.

We will return to the case of Euro Cars GmbH to illustrate the principles for establishing a target cost for the Cyclone sports car that will allow it to survive against its rivals, the Su4 and the Chita. You will remember that both rival cars have the same product attributes as the Cyclone, but the SU4 and the Chita have a selling price of €28,000, whereas the Cyclone has a premium selling price of €30,000. Unless the

Cyclone can be redesigned to offer extra attributes or features, its target price must match that of its competitors.

The accountant predicts that the company needs to make a target profit of 10% or €2,800 per unit in order to cover the cost of capital for running the production operation. As a result, the target cost per Cyclone sold is €25,200 (€28,000 – €2,800), which is substantially lower than the Cyclone's existing unit cost. During the last production period, the total standard cost for production of a Cyclone was €28,500 per unit, which included €28,000 of variable production costs and €500 of fixed manufacturing overheads. The challenge for Euro Cars GmbH is to achieve the target cost of €25,200 through value engineering and finding ways to save costs totalling €3,300 per unit (current standard cost per unit – target cost per unit).

Activity

Explain how Euro Cars GmbH could reduce the cost of the Cyclone through value engineering and improved cost efficiency.

You may have decided that the company should investigate the potential for cost-saving opportunities in its manufacturing operations and processes. However, any cost reduction exercise must target those costs that do not provide value to the customer, whether these are located within the firm's value chain of business functions or the functions of the car itself. As was identified in the strategic cost analysis for the Cyclone in section 20.3, the firm could reduce the expenditure on the air conditioning and electrical systems without harming customer satisfaction levels. In addition, the management accountant should investigate the waste tolerances and allowable variances contained within the standard cost estimates in order to ascertain whether they reflect attainable best practice in the industry.

After completing its value engineering process, the company was able to match the target cost of €25,200 per Cyclone by achieving cost reductions by entering into long-term contracts for the supply of utilities and materials, sourcing a cheaper air conditioning unit of the same quality and retraining the staff to reduce the assembly time required.

The main strength of target costing is that it considers the pricing of products and services in terms of their relative market desirability, and forces an organization to focus on identifying cost-saving opportunities that enhance and sustain its competitive advantage over rivals. Its other advantages include the following:

- It reduces the total time for product development, through improved coordination of design, manufacturing and marketing.
- It promotes a culture of cost awareness throughout an organization.
- It increases customer satisfaction, as design is focused on customer values.
- It improves product quality, as design is carefully developed and manufacturing issues are considered explicitly in the design phase.
- It creates cross-functional teams that enhance the dialogue about product development and cost control.
- It can be combined with MOA techniques.

20.5 Balanced scorecard

The *balanced scorecard* (BSC) was developed by Kaplan and Norton (1996) as a strategic performance measurement system and is now widely used in organizations of all sizes throughout the world. Its popularity stems from its ability to translate an organization's vision and strategy into a comprehensive set of performance measures that provides a framework for implementing and monitoring its strategy.

> **Key definition**
>
> The balanced scorecard (BSC) is an approach to management that integrates both financial and non-financial performance measures into a framework proposed by Professors Kaplan and Norton ... in the *Harvard Business Review* in 1992 and has since been adopted by a wide range of organizations. It is considered one of the most significant recent developments in management accounting.
>
> *Source:* Law (2010, p. 46).

In contrast to traditional performance measurement systems that focus solely on the achievement of financial objectives, the BSC attempts to balance or integrate financial and non-financial performance measures to evaluate both short-run and long-run performance measures in a single combined report. As a result, the technique focuses on the non-financial objectives that an organization must achieve in order to meet its financial objectives. The logic for this is that non-financial and operational indicators can capture improvements in performance that cannot be found in short-term financial measures. For example, a customer survey in 2012 shows a 20% increase in highly satisfied customers compared with 2011. While this improvement in non-financial performance may lead to increased sales in the future, it is unlikely to have any impact on the income reported for 2012. Because of this assumed relationship between non-financial and financial performance, a BSC incorporates two different types of performance measure:

- *leading drivers of performance*, which are non-financial performance indicators that drive future financial performance (e.g. order execution/fulfilment time)
- *lagging measures of performance*, which are financial measures of outcomes (e.g. revenue or operating profit from growth).

The BSC model shown in Figure 20.1 uses an appropriate mix of these leading and lagging performance indicators to measure performance across four key perspectives:

- *Financial* – What are the financial goals of our strategy?
- *Customer* – What customers do we intend to serve and how are we going to win and retain them?
- *Internal business processes* – What internal processes are critical to providing value to customers?
- *Learning and growth* – What capabilities and skills must we excel at to achieve superior internal business processes that create value for customers and shareholders?

Internal business processes are the activities an organization undertakes to satisfy its customers. For example, in a manufacturing organization, assembly of a product is

Figure 20.1 Four perspectives of the balanced scorecard

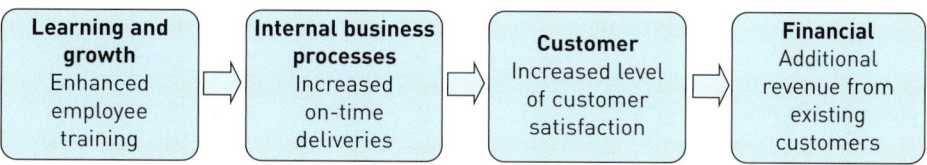

Source: Adapted from Kaplan and Norton (1996, p. 76).

an internal business process. For an airline, baggage handling is an internal business process. For each of the perspectives within its BSC, an organization must establish specific objectives, performance measures, targets and initiatives that help it to achieve its overall strategy.

A critical assumption of the BSC is that each performance measure is part of a cause-and-effect relationship involving a link from strategy formulation to financial outcomes. Improved learning and growth performance is necessary for improving internal business processes, and these in turn drive performance measures within the customer perspective. Finally, improved measures of customer satisfaction will eventually lead to increased financial returns. Figure 20.2 illustrates the cause-and-effect relationship for a delivery company whose strategic objective is to grow by obtaining additional orders from existing customers. If the company invests in enhanced training of its delivery staff, these improvements should result in higher levels of on-time deliveries, which should lead to increased customer satisfaction and extra orders from existing customers. Whether the cause-and-effect relationship implicit within the BSC always applies is open to debate and will be discussed later, in the critique of the technique.

The measurements used to monitor performance within each of the four perspectives in the BSC typically include:

Figure 20.2 Cause-and-effect relationships within the balanced scorecard

Learning and growth	Internal business processes	Customer	Financial
Enhanced employee training	Increased on-time deliveries	Increased level of customer satisfaction	Additional revenue from existing customers

- *Financial*: revenue growth, revenue from new products, cost reductions in key areas, profit increase from productivity gains, operating profit changes from price recovery (i.e. the net impact of changes in input costs and output prices from the previous period).
- *Customer*: market share of a specific type of customer or market, customer satisfaction levels.
- *Internal business processes*: innovation process: number of new products; operations process: yield, defect rate, on-time deliveries; after-sales service: time taken to replace defective product.
- *Learning and growth*: employee education and skill level, employee satisfaction and retention rates, percentage of processes using advanced controls.

Figure 20.3 illustrates the BSC used by Southwest Airlines. As the company operates within the low-cost sector of the market, its strategic theme was to increase its

Figure 20.3 Balanced scorecard for Southwest Airlines

Strategic theme: Operating efficiency		Objectives	Measures	Targets	Initiatives
Financial		Profitability	Market value	30% CAGR*	
		More customers	Seat revenue	20% CAGR*	
		Fewer aircraft	Plane lease cost	5% CAGR*	
Customer		Flight on time	On-time rating	Be number 1	Quality management
		Lowest price	Customer ranking	Be number 1	Loyalty scheme
Internal		Fast ground turnaround	On-ground time	30 minutes	Cycle time optimization
			On-time departure	90%	
Learning and growth		Ground crew aligned with strategy	% ground crew trained	Year 1: 70% / Year 2: 90% / Year 3: 100%	Training programme
			% ground crew shareholders	Year 1: 70% / Year 2: 90% / Year 3: 100%	Employee share scheme

* Compound annual growth rate

Source: Adapted from Kaplan and Norton (2004, p. 53).

operating efficiency. For each of the perspectives within the BSC, the company undertook an investigation as to how each influenced its overall operating efficiency. The following issues were discovered and used to produce a strategy map of the cause-and-effect relationship between each perspective:

- *Financial:* operating efficiency and profitability were influenced by having increased passengers on fewer planes.
- *Customer:* customers desired the lowest prices and on-time arrival, and it was these factors that were critical to attracting new customers.
- *Internal business processes:* through faster turnaround of aircraft it was possible to reduce the number of aircraft needed for a daily schedule of flights. Aircraft turnaround was the also found to be the major driver of on-time arrivals and departures and directly influenced the price per ticket.
- *Learning and growth:* fast ground turnaround was found to require a motivated and committed ground crew. Through dialogue with the ground crew, management established that these workers could be 'aligned' towards the achievement of strategy if they were educated and compensated in an appropriate manner.

The strategic map for Southwest Airlines is shown in the first column within Figure 20.3 and it illustrates the key role of ground crew alignment in driving operating efficiency at the airline. Using this, management devised objectives for each of the four BSC perspectives and formulated performance measures for tracking their achievement. Target performance measures were then established in order to benchmark periodic performance, and a range of initiatives introduced to further encourage performance improvements. The BSC for Southwest Airlines shows that employing well-trained ground crews who are shareholders in the company leads to faster turnaround and more on-time flights, which lead to higher customer satisfaction, lower costs and greater profits. This example clearly shows the power of a well designed and implemented BSC.

We will now use the example of Euro Cars GmbH to illustrate the preparation of a BSC. Since the low-cost competitors entered the sports car market, the company's market share has fallen from 15% to 10%. As a response, the company has devised a new strategy for the Cyclone, which is to restore its share of the sports car market and profitability by producing a market-leading product with world-class levels of operating efficiency. In order to measure the success of this strategy, the company wants to create a BSC from the following information.

- In terms of the learning and growth perspective, it was discovered that each of the plant's 30 production processes could be improved by implementing advanced software systems. In addition, current levels of employee training were found to be deficient. Production employees currently attend an average of 2 hours of training seminars and meetings per month. If training is increased to 5 hours per month, it is believed that both product quality and operational efficiency will increase. This increased training should also raise awareness of the need for continuous improvement and encourage employees to provide suggestions for cost reductions or product redesign.

- Following an audit of its internal business processes, the company discovered the following problems that must be corrected before the Cyclone can be a competitive and profitable product:

  o In terms of raw materials (i.e. aluminium, steel, plastic, glass, rubber and paint), the company only achieves an average yield of 85%, with the 15% of waste being sent to landfill. With increased training, recycling and process improvements, materials yield could be increased to 96%.

  o The company only uses virgin sources of raw materials. The vast majority of vehicle manufacturers utilize at least 40% recycled materials in their products and these can be purchased for 20% less than virgin-quality materials.

  o During the last production year, Euro Cars GmbH used 1,980 kWh of electricity to manufacture each Cyclone. The target for energy use is to be reduced to 1,200 kWh per car.

  o Average production downtime due to machine breakdowns is currently 30 minutes per day and the aim is to reduce this to 5 minutes. Average production time per car is currently 80 hours and the new target is 70 hours.

  o Typically, 10% of Cyclones produced fail the quality inspection and require rework. The target is to reduce this to zero failure and reduce warranty claims from an average of 50 per month to 10.

  o On average, two of the Cyclone's main components are redesigned every 3 months. The new target is to re-engineer a minimum of five components per quarter in order to further differentiate the product from its competition.

- From a customer perspective, to restore its market share to the original 15%, the company must win industry awards for quality, reduce customer complaints and improve customer satisfaction rates. Yearly targets include winning two awards, receiving fewer than 20 complaints and having a customer satisfaction level of 96%.

- From a financial perspective, the company's new strategy should eventually lead to increased shareholder returns through increased operating profit from sales growth, price recovery (i.e. the profit impact of changes in input and output prices from the prior period) and enhanced operational efficiency. The company has established 3-year targets for increased operating profit of €800,000 from growth, €200,000 from price recovery and €300,000 from enhanced operating efficiency.

Activity

Using the above information, design a BSC for Euro Cars GmbH that provides suitable objectives, performance measures, targets and initiatives that support the company's strategy.

Your BSC may differ from the example below, but should share the main features. You will see that it suggests that employing well-trained production staff and using improved production processes lead to increased operational efficiency and a better designed car. In turn, this leads to higher customer satisfaction, increased market share, lower costs and increased operating profit.

Objectives	Measures	Targets	Initiatives
Financial			
Increase shareholder value	Operating profit changes from growth	€800,000	
	Operating profit changes from price recovery	€200,000	Long-term contracts with suppliers
	Operating profit changes from operating efficiency	€300,000	
Customer			
Reclaim market share	Market share of the sports car market	15%	Owners club
	Number of customer complaints	20	Customer hotline
	Customer satisfaction level	96%	
	Number of industry awards	2	Media day at plant
Internal business processes			
Improve operational efficiency	Average yield on raw materials	96%	Review and audit of procurement, production and quality control procedures
	Use of recycled materials	40%	
	Energy use per vehicle	1,200 kWh	
	Average production downtime per day	5 minutes	
	Average production time per vehicle	70 hours	
	Output failing final inspection	0%	
	Number of warranty claims	10	
Improve product design	Components redesigned per quarter	5	Quarterly audit of product design
Learning and growth			
Increase employee alignment and training	Average number of training hours per employee per month	5 hours	Training schemes
	Number of employee suggestions received	10	Bonus paid if suggestion implemented
Improve production processes	Production processes using advanced software systems	100%	

As we identified in our earlier discussion of strategy and SMA, a BSC must be appropriately designed and modified for the specific strategy that an organization chooses to adopt. For example, a *product differentiation strategy* will require a BSC that includes:

- a financial perspective that isolates the operating income that comes from charging for a premium product

- a customer perspective that measures the percentage of revenue from new products or customers
- an internal business perspective that measures an organization's ability to develop technologies or processes for producing custom products
- a learning and growth perspective that measures the number of employee suggestions for new or re-engineered products.

For a BSC to operate effectively it must be designed to:

- use objectives, measures, initiatives and targets that link each of the four perspectives to the achievement of strategic objectives
- communicate strategy to employees by translating it into performance measures that they understand and can influence
- provide an appropriate balance and linkage between non-financial and financial performance measures
- prevent suboptimal trade-offs and inappropriate cost cutting (i.e. cut R&D expenditure during a recession)
- focus on the critical measures of performance – does not use too many measurements.

Despite the supposed benefits of using the BSC, there has been much debate about whether cause-and-effect relationship actually exists between each of its four perspectives. For example, the production of high-quality products does not always result in increased profit, especially when customers are unwilling to pay for such improvements. Furthermore, in many instances, a loyal and highly satisfied customer may not be a profitable one, as they may require many hours of costly support and customer service time. A further criticism of the BSC surrounds the choice about the number of performance measures to be used. Using too many may result in a BSC that produces confusing performance measurement data that could increase the risk of corporate failure because attention may focus on incorrect measures and provide a distorted view of strategy. Other limitations of the BSC include these:

- As managers are normally evaluated using financial measures of performance, they may attach less importance to improving non-financial performance.
- Certain perspectives, such as other stakeholders, suppliers and the employees, are excluded from Kaplan and Norton's BSC.
- As with any technique, a BSC needs to fit the adopting organization's culture.
- It can be costly to implement, both in terms of resources and management time.

Despite these potential limitations, widespread use of the BSC in Europe and the USA is evidence of its value to many different types of organization (Bhimani and Bromwich, 2009).

20.6   Accounting for quality

In this chapter we have highlighted the point that providing customers with desirable products and services is a primary strategic objective. Quality is an essential element of a product's desirability and it is important that management accounting provides information that supports the management of quality. Quality refers to factors such as the product's fitness for use and the degree to which it satisfies customer needs and conforms to design specification requirements. For example, a business customer buying an iPhone would expect it to offer a wireless connection to the Internet, fast processing, sufficient memory, a long-life rechargeable battery, an operating system and application software.

Total quality management (TQM) is an approach to managing people and business processes that emphasizes the importance of customer satisfaction and sees continuous improvement as the means by which this is achieved (Law, 2010). For example, washing machine manufacturers can save money by continuously improving the quality of their products to reduce the number of faulty goods returned for repair. Some companies even have specific quality management systems certified by the International Organization for Standardization (ISO) under the ISO 9001 Quality Management Systems programme (see BSI, 2008). As quality-related costs can often equal 20% of revenue, quality improvement programmes may result in substantial savings and help increase customer demand (Bhimani and Bromwich, 2009). From a strategic perspective, if competitors are improving their quality, an organization has no choice but to do the same or lose customers. Management accounting can help an organization to achieve its quality goals by providing a variety of reports and performance measures that motivate and evaluate managerial efforts to improve quality. As with the collection of SMA information, such information may include non-financial and financial information. Managers need to know the *costs of quality* and how they are changing over time. The costs of quality represent the costs incurred in defect prevention and appraisal activities, and the losses from the internal and external failure of a product or service to meet agreed quality requirements (Bromwich and Bhimani, 1994).

> **Key definition**
>
> **Total quality management (TQM) is an integrated and comprehensive system of planning and controlling all business functions so that products or services are produced which meet or exceed customer expectations.**
>
> *Source*: CIMA (2005, p. 54).

A cost of quality report can be prepared to measure the total cost to the organization of producing products or services that do not conform to quality standards. Four categories of costs are typically reported:

- *Prevention costs* – costs incurred in preventing or reducing the production of defective products that do not conform to specification. These may include the cost of undertaking supplier reviews, field trials, quality training or investment in new production technology.

- *Appraisal costs* – costs incurred in monitoring and inspecting products and material to ensure that they meet quality conformance standards. Examples include the cost of measurement equipment, inspection, testing and audits.
- *Internal failure costs* – costs that arise from the production of products and components that fail to meet internal quality standards. These may include rework costs, and the net cost of scrap and disposal costs.
- *External failure costs* – costs incurred when the product or service fails to conform to requirements after it is supplied to the customer. These may include the cost of dealing with warranty claims, product recalls and the cost of lost sales.

Many of the items within a cost quality report have to be estimated and such documents typically exclude the opportunity costs associated with poor quality, such as the lower prices that result from a lack of quality.

We will use the example of Euro Cars GmbH to illustrate the preparation of a cost of quality report. It is now the end of 2012, and a year has passed since the low-cost competitors entered the market. The total revenue for 2012 was €48,000,000 (€50,000,000 in 2011), and the company has made considerable effort to strengthen its quality control system in the hope that enhanced quality will restore the company's competitive position and reduce warranty and servicing costs. Costs relating to quality management and control for 2012 and 2011 are shown in the following table:

Quality management costs	2012	2011
	€	€
Depreciation of testing equipment	133,000	86,000
Disposal of defective products	296,000	211,000
Field servicing	468,000	702,000
Inspection	468,000	296,000
Net cost of scrap	484,000	335,000
Product recalls	320,000	1,326,000
Product testing	624,000	382,000
Quality engineering	312,000	218,000
Rework labour	780,000	546,000
Supplies used in testing	23,000	16,000
System development	413,000	250,000
Warranty repairs	546,000	1,638,000
Warranty replacements	70,000	234,000

Activity

Decide whether the quality management costs in the above table should be classified as prevention, appraisal, internal failure or external failure cost and use your analysis as the basis for a cost of quality report for 2012 and 2011.

Check your report against the following solution where each cost category has been expressed as a percentage of revenue for 2012 and 2011 to aid comparison with previous periods.

Cost of quality report for Euro Cars GmbH				
	2012		2011	
	€	% of revenue	€	% of revenue
Prevention costs				
Systems development	413,000		250,000	
Quality engineering	312,000		218,000	
Total	725,000	1.51%	468,000	0.94%
Appraisal costs				
Product testing	624,000		382,000	
Supplies used in testing	23,000		16,000	
Inspection	468,000		296,000	
Depreciation of testing equipment	133,000		86,000	
Total	1,248,000	2.60%	780,000	1.56%
Internal failure costs				
Rework labour	780,000		546,000	
Net cost of scrap	484,000		335,000	
Disposal of defective products	296,000		211,000	
Total	1,560,000	3.25%	1,092,000	2.18%
External failure costs				
Warranty repairs	546,000		1,638,000	
Field servicing	468,000		702,000	
Warranty replacements	70,000		234,000	
Product recalls	320,000		1,326,000	
Total	1,404,000	2.93%	3,900,000	7.80%
Total cost of quality	4,937,000	10.29%	6,240,000	12.48%

Activity

Compare the costs of quality for the 2 years. What do the results reveal about the management of quality at Euro Cars GmbH?

During 2012 the company significantly increased its expenditure on prevention costs and appraisal costs. This has led to considerably lower costs related to external failure costs and total quality costs have declined. Despite this improvement, the company still has a poor distribution of quality costs and most costs are identified with internal and external failure, rather than to prevention and appraisal. However, as continued emphasis is given to prevention and appraisal activities in the future, this situation should improve and internal and external failure costs should reduce.

Due to the increased spending on prevention and appraisal activities this year, internal failure costs have increased. The reason internal failure costs have gone up is that, through increased appraisal activity, defects are being caught and corrected before products are shipped to customers. Thus, the company is incurring more cost for scrap and rework, but is saving considerable amounts on warranty repairs, field servicing and product recalls. External failure costs have fallen considerably and represent only 3% of revenue in 2012. If the company continues to focus on prevention activities in future years, then appraisal costs and internal failure costs should begin to decline. As quality is built into products through better engineering and design, and process control is improved, the number of defects should decrease. Thus, internal failures – and the need to detect these failures through appraisal activities – should also decrease.

20.7 Environmental management accounting

Not only does traditional management accounting fail to provide strategically relevant information, but it can also be criticized for failing to systematically monitor the environmental cost of organizational operations. As a result, the literature is full of competing ideas for developing a form of *environmental management accounting* (EMA). Environmental management accounting involves the identification, collection, analysis and use of non-financial and financial information for managing the environmental costs and impacts of business operations.

Key definition

Environmental management accounting is the identification, collection, analysis and the use of two types of information for internal decision-making:

- physical information on the use, flows and fates of energy, water, and materials (including wastes) and
- monetary information on environment-related costs, earnings and savings.

Source: United Nations Division for Sustainable Development (2001, p. 2).

The premise behind the need for EMA is that traditional management accounting systems cannot be used to measure environmental issues as they effectively 'hide' environmental costs as overheads, thereby obscuring their size and origin. Such environmental costs are not typically allocated or apportioned in an appropriate manner because they are not made the responsibility of the department or product that causes them. EMA aims to make environmental issues visible in all areas of organizational and operational decision making, and thus permit them to be managed effectively.

Activity

Identify five costs related to the production of vehicles that Euro Cars GmbH could classify as environmental costs. Are these costs borne by the company, society in general or the local community in particular?

You have probably identified a range of environmental costs as a subset of the costs of operating a business. In terms of manufacturing costs, such as the usage of electricity and materials, the manufacturer pays a market price for these commodities. However, such costs are also environmental in nature as their total stock in the natural environment may be limited and their use may cause social cost externalities in the form of environmental pollution to the local community. Other types of environmental cost include:

- regulatory compliance costs associated with the purchase of testing and monitoring equipment for effluent
- environmental taxes payable on waste materials sent to landfill and on carbon emissions
- fines payable for non-compliance with environmental legislation
- back-end costs associated with decommissioning a plant that uses hazardous materials
- image and relationship costs associated with producing an environmental report for the local community
- social costs resulting from the impact of manufacturing activity, including the impact on human life and environmental degradation.

Chapter 10 outlined the way that certain businesses publish reports on their environmental and social impacts. EMA may have a role within the provision of this type of information but its primary focus is on the internal management and control of environmental impacts of the organization. There is no agreed conceptual framework for the scope and extent of EMA, so the term is used to describe many different techniques and practices, including those already practised as part of traditional management accounting. It is unclear whether EMA is seen as an entirely new system or simply integrated within traditional management accounting. While this is a problem, the more pressing problem may be how this environmental information is generated and used within decision making, and whether management accountants are the ones to supply this information. While it is clear that traditional management accounting techniques, such as activity-based costing, could be used to manage environmental costs, there is some debate over the need to develop specific techniques for measuring environmental performance. Part of this debate is the argument that management accounting is the cause of the environmental problem by rendering issues such as manufacturing profit and standard cost 'visible' and the social costs of pollution 'invisible'.

A critical issue that is often overlooked by proponents of EMA is that traditional management accounting should be actively managing many environmental costs as part of normal efficient management. The creation of excess waste and the inefficient use of energy have resulted in costs to manufacturing organizations long before they were given an additional environmental dimension through concern for the preservation of the natural environment. However, the management accounting systems of many organizations fail to systematically manage or reduce these types of costs. It is through increased social interest in environmental issues that accountants are encouraged to focus on the control of costs that should already be part of everyday cost management. Furthermore, despite calls for EMA, evidence suggests that management accountants and accounting are normally uninvolved in the day-to-day management of environmental issues.

Corporate responses to green pressures largely involve the use of non-accounting expertise and non-financial information systems. Indicative of the current use of 'non-accounting' methods to tackle internal environmental issues is the way that many organizations have implemented environmental management systems (EMSs) certified to the ISO 14001 standard (BSI, 2004). Such EMSs are typically structured as an extension of existing health and safety or TQM systems, rather than becoming a routine part of the finance function. Furthermore, as we have found in our own empirical work, the manager in charge of the EMS is very rarely, if ever, a qualified accountant. Unsurprisingly, EMA information is typically generated with little direct input from management accountants, and, at best, is used in an ad hoc manner by accountants within decision making. It is only when there is a major environmental problem that the management accounting function needs to confer directly with the environmental management unit, seeking its help as a specialized consultant.

We will now use Euro Cars GmbH to illustrate the use of EMA. Production takes place in three departments: Assembly 1, Assembly 2 and Quality Control. Each department uses water that is transformed into special waste during operations. The special waste is collected by tanker on a regular basis by a local waste management firm. During the last production period, the total charge for special waste collection at the site was €500,000. Site overheads are currently apportioned to departments based on area. The total area occupied by the three departments is 25,000 square metres (m²) and the overhead apportionment rate for special waste is €20 per m² occupied. The following table provides further details.

	m² occupied	Total overhead apportionment for special waste (€)	Total Cyclones processed (units)	Other products processed (units)
Assembly 1	4,500	90,000	1,500	0
Assembly 2	10,500	210,000	0 3,500	
Quality Control	10,000	200,000	1,500	3,500
Total	25,000	500,000		

Using new metering equipment, assume that the site's environmental manager can provide a detailed EMA analysis of special waste generation at the site. The following information is made available:

	Meter reading for special waste generation (m³)	% of special waste
Assembly 1	300	3%
Assembly 2	7,700	77%
Quality Control	2,000	20%
Total	10,000	100%

Activity

(a) Using the original overhead apportionment basis, calculate the total amount of special waste overhead that would be allocated to the unit cost of a Cyclone.

(b) Discuss whether the EMA information prepared by the company's environmental manager helps to improve the management and control of special waste costs at the site.

(c) Use the EMA information to recalculate the amount of special waste allocated to each Cyclone.

Under the original apportionment basis, each Cyclone product will be charged with a proportion of the special waste overhead allocated to the Assembly 1 and Quality Control departments. In total, each Cyclone should be charged with €100 of special waste overhead, with €60 per unit in the Assembly 1 department (€90,000 total overhead/1,500 units of output) and €40 in the Quality Control department (€200,000 total overhead/5,000 total vehicles processed).

The EMA metering data reveal invaluable information for the management and control of environmental overheads. The special waste overhead is clearly influenced by the amount of waste generated in each building rather than its total size. Once the metering equipment was operational, the site accountant no longer had to estimate cost causality and could identify the buildings and products that created the most waste. As 77% of special waste was generated by Assembly 2, the work undertaken there should be allocated €385,000 of special waste overhead (77% of €500,000). As only non-Cyclone products are produced in Assembly 2, it is clear that these models, rather than the Cyclone, are the biggest generators of special waste. Ultimately, a decision could be made to switch production towards more environmentally friendly models. If overhead allocation is based upon the EMA metering data, each Cyclone will be allocated only €30 of special waste overhead, with €10 per unit in Assembly 1 (3% × €500,000 total overhead/1,500 units of output) and €20 in the Quality Control department (20% × €500,000 total overhead/5,000 total vehicles processed).

20.8 Conclusions

In this chapter we have highlighted a number of emerging issues within management accounting. Traditional management accounting practices and techniques have a long history and are subject to frequent criticism for failing to provide relevant information for decision making in the modern business environment. We commenced this chapter by describing how strategic decision making requires a management accounting system that provides not only financial information that focuses on internal operations, but also information, both financial and non-financial in nature, about the environment and markets in which the organization operates. From this starting point, we explained the concept of strategy and the case for developing SMA. A range of SMA techniques and perspectives were then reviewed to illustrate how management accountants, with the assistance of cross-functional expertise from non-accountants, can be involved in the provision of strategic information for decision making.

In the final sections of the chapter we considered the related issues of how to account for product and service quality and whether management accountants have a role within the provision of EMA information about the environmental impacts of products and services. From this analysis it is clear that management accounting techniques and practices continue to evolve as organizations, markets, production technologies and customer demands change.

Practice questions

1 Describe the target costing process. Explain its advantages over a cost-plus approach to product or service pricing.

2 Explain the purpose of environmental management accounting and explain how it can be used to assist in the management and control of environmental costs.

3 Stunt Ltd is a manufacturer of stunt scooters used for performing tricks and stunts in skate parks. A customer survey reveals that customers look for the following product attributes when purchasing a stunt scooter:

Attribute	Relative importance %
Safety	10
Style	40
Performance	50
Total	100

The company is designing a new model called the Slammer. Each Slammer consists of three components, whose target costs are estimated below:

Components	Target cost per scooter £	% of total cost
Handlebars and steering column	20	33.33
Painted aluminium footplate	30	50.00
Wheels and suspension	10	16.67
	60	100.00

With the help of the production and design staff, the management accountant uses the above information to construct the following matrix of the product attributes. This shows how each component of the Slammer contributes to the supply of product attributes:

	Attributes supplied by a stunt scooter		
	Safety 10%	Style 40%	Performance 50%
Components of a slammer scooter			
Handlebars and steering column	40%	20%	40%
Painted aluminium footplate	40%	60%	20%
Wheels and suspension	20%	20%	40%
Total	100%	100%	100%

Required

(a) Calculate an importance index for each of the Slammer scooter's three components. What does it indicate about the relative importance of each component in providing the attributes that customers require?

(b) Using the target cost information, prepare a strategic cost index for each of the Slammer's three components. Discuss whether this design incurs too much expenditure on any component.

4 Electro Ltd manufactures a single electronic circuit board for the telecommunications industry. At the end of December 2011 the company received a letter of complaint from Telecom International PLC, its largest customer, about the poor quality of recent component shipments. As a result, in January 2012 the directors of Electro Ltd implemented a TQM system and this has been used to estimate the following costs of quality for 2012 and 2011:

	2012 £	2011 £
Operating costs of the customer complaints department	270,000	480,000
Depreciation of test equipment	370,000	270,000
Inspection	150,000	80,000
Forgone contribution from lost sales	823,000	1,790,000
Product recall	360,000	920,000
Product testing	670,000	700,000
Quality engineering	770,000	520,000
Quality training	1,100,000	700,000
Retesting	480,000	1,250,000
Rework	580,000	770,000
Supplier reviews	200,000	50,000
Cost of warranty repairs	240,000	320,000

Electro Ltd's total revenue for 2012 was £62,000,000 (£56,700,000 in 2011).

Required

(a) Decide whether the quality management costs above should be classified as prevention, appraisal, internal failure or external failure cost and use your analysis as the basis for preparing a cost of quality report for 2012 and 2011.

(b) Compare the costs of quality for the two years. What do the results reveal about the management of quality at Electro Ltd?

5 Contain Ltd produces aluminium transport containers for the airline industry, and faces intense competition from three competitors whose containers provide identical product attributes. As of 1 January 2012, the company's strategic objective is to increase shareholder value by increasing market share and reducing production costs. It is thought that new customers can be attracted by producing low-price, high-quality containers that are delivered within 10 days of receiving a customer's order. In order to achieve its new objective, the company must seek to increase customer satisfaction, product quality, productivity and employee training and retention.

During 2011 the following events occurred:

- 20% of employees underwent training in total quality management techniques.
- 15% of employees resigned and left the company's employment during the year.
- It took an average of 12 days to process and fulfil customer orders.
- The yield on the usage of aluminium was 85% and 800 containers were produced per employee.
- 10% of containers were returned by consumers due to defective hinges.
- A survey revealed that 18% of customers were dissatisfied with the company's products during 2011.
- No new customers were recruited during 2011. The company's market share of the 'low-price' container market fell 1% to 9%. Its share of the total container market fell 5% to 6%.
- Annual turnover fell 2% to £8,000,000. Total operating income for the year also fell 2% to £600,000.
- The company has targeted productivity and process improvements equal to £150,000 of operating profit by 2015. Furthermore, it plans to obtain cost reductions equal to £50,000 per year from increasing its yield on the factory's usage of aluminium.
- The company has also established a 5-year financial target to achieve a total of £300,000 of additional operating income from growth.

Required

(a) Identify the type of strategy that Contain Ltd plans to implement during 2012.

(b) Using your answer from (a) and the question data, identify, for each of the four perspectives within Contain Ltd's balanced scorecard for 2012, two performance measures that are consistent with, and follow from, the company's strategy.

(c) Briefly explain the cause-and-effect relationship between your eight performance measures identified in part (b).

   (d) Acting as the accountant for Contain Ltd, discuss the benefits and problems in implementing and using a balanced scorecard performance measurement system.

References

Ansari, S., Bell, J. and Okano, H. (2007) Target costing: uncharted research territory. In Chapman C., Hopwood, A. and Shields, M. (eds), *Handbook of Management Accounting Research*. Amsterdam: Elsevier, pp. 507–29.

Bhimani, A. and Bromwich, M. (2009) *Management Accounting: Retrospect and Prospect*. London: CIMA Publishing.

Bromwich, M. (1990) The case for strategic management accounting: the role of accounting information for strategy in competitive markets. *Accounting, Organizations and Society* 15(1/2), 27–46.

Bromwich, M. and Bhimani, A. (1994) *Management Accounting: Pathways to Progress*. London: CIMA Publications.

BSI (2004) *ISO 14001 Environmental Management Systems – Requirements*. Chiswick: BSI.

BSI (2008) *ISO 9001 Quality Management Systems – Requirements*. Chiswick: BSI.

CIMA (2005) *CIMA Official Terminology*. Oxford: CIMA Publishing.

Kaplan, R. and Norton, D. (1996) Using the balanced scorecard as a strategic management system. *Harvard Business Review*, January–February, pp. 75–85.

Kaplan, R. and Norton, D. (2004) *Strategy Maps: Converting Intangible Assets into Tangible Outcomes*. Boston: Harvard Business School Press.

Law, J. L. (2010) *Dictionary of Accounting*, 4th edition. Oxford: Oxford University Press.

Lord, B. (2007) Strategic management accounting. In T. Hopper, D. Northcott and R. Scapens (eds), *Issues in Management Accounting*, 3rd edition. Harlow: Prentice Hall, pp. 135–53.

Porter, M. (1985) *Competitive Advantage: Creating and Sustaining Superior Performance*. New York: Free Press.

United Nations Division for Sustainable Development (2001) *Environmental Management Accounting, Procedures and Principles*. New York: UNDSD.

Appendix

Present value table for £1 at compound interest

Future years	Interest rate 1%	2%	3%	4%	5%	6%	7%	8%	9%	10%	11%	12%	13%	14%	15%
1	0.990	0.980	0.971	0.962	0.952	0.943	0.935	0.926	0.917	0.909	0.901	0.893	0.885	0.877	0.870
2	0.980	0.961	0.943	0.925	0.907	0.890	0.873	0.857	0.842	0.826	0.812	0.797	0.783	0.769	0.756
3	0.971	0.942	0.915	0.889	0.864	0.840	0.816	0.794	0.772	0.751	0.731	0.712	0.693	0.675	0.658
4	0.961	0.924	0.888	0.855	0.823	0.792	0.763	0.735	0.708	0.683	0.659	0.636	0.613	0.592	0.572
5	0.951	0.906	0.863	0.822	0.784	0.747	0.713	0.681	0.650	0.621	0.593	0.567	0.543	0.519	0.497
6	0.942	0.888	0.837	0.790	0.746	0.705	0.666	0.630	0.596	0.564	0.535	0.507	0.480	0.456	0.432
7	0.933	0.871	0.813	0.760	0.711	0.665	0.623	0.583	0.547	0.513	0.482	0.452	0.425	0.400	0.376
8	0.923	0.853	0.789	0.731	0.677	0.627	0.582	0.540	0.502	0.467	0.434	0.404	0.376	0.351	0.327
9	0.914	0.837	0.766	0.703	0.645	0.592	0.544	0.500	0.406	0.424	0.391	0.361	0.333	0.308	0.284
10	0.905	0.820	0.744	0.676	0.614	0.558	0.508	0.463	0.422	0.386	0.352	0.322	0.295	0.270	0.247

Future years	Interest rate 16%	17%	18%	19%	20%	21%	22%	23%	24%	25%	26%	28%	30%	40%	50%
1	0.862	0.855	0.847	0.840	0.833	0.826	0.820	0.813	0.806	0.800	0.794	0.781	0.769	0.714	0.667
2	0.743	0.731	0.718	0.706	0.694	0.683	0.672	0.661	0.650	0.640	0.630	0.610	0.592	0.510	0.444
3	0.641	0.624	0.609	0.593	0.579	0.565	0.551	0.537	0.524	0.512	0.500	0.477	0.455	0.364	0.296
4	0.552	0.534	0.516	0.499	0.482	0.467	0.451	0.437	0.423	0.410	0.397	0.373	0.350	0.260	0.198
5	0.476	0.456	0.437	0.419	0.402	0.386	0.370	0.355	0.341	0.328	0.315	0.291	0.269	0.186	0.132
6	0.410	0.390	0.370	0.352	0.335	0.319	0.303	0.289	0.275	0.262	0.250	0.227	0.207	0.133	0.088
7	0.354	0.333	0.314	0.296	0.279	0.263	0.249	0.235	0.222	0.210	0.198	0.178	0.159	0.095	0.059
8	0.305	0.285	0.266	0.249	0.233	0.218	0.204	0.191	0.179	0.168	0.157	0.139	0.123	0.068	0.039
9	0.263	0.243	0.225	0.209	0.194	0.180	0.167	0.155	0.144	0.134	0.125	0.108	0.094	0.048	0.026
10	0.227	0.208	0.191	0.176	0.162	0.149	0.137	0.126	0.116	0.107	0.099	0.085	0.073	0.035	0.017

Glossary of terms

Absorption costing	The cost accounting system in which the overheads of an organization are charged to the production by means of the process of absorption. Costs are first allocated or apportioned to the cost centres, where they are absorbed into the cost unit using absorption rates (Law, 2010, p. 2).
Accounting	The process of identifying, measuring, recording and communicating economic transactions (Law, 2010, p. 6).
Accounting rate of return (ARR)	An accounting ratio that expresses the profit of an organization before interest and taxation, usually for a year, as a percentage of the capital employed at the end of the period (Law, 2010, p. 9).
Accounting standard	An authoritative statement on how a particular type of transaction or other event should be reflected in the financial statements. In the UK, compliance with accounting standards is normally necessary for the financial statements to give a true and fair view.
Accrual	An estimate of a liability that is not supported by an invoice or a request for payment at the time when the accounts are prepared (Law, 2010, p. 11).
Accrual accounting	Accounting based on the principle that revenue and costs are recognized as they are earned and incurred irrespective of when cash (or its equivalent) is received or paid (the *realization principle*), and they are matched with one another (the *matching principle*) and dealt with in the income statement of the period to which they relate (the *period principle*).
Activity cost pool	A collection of indirect costs grouped according to the activity involved (Law, 2010, p. 15).
Activity-based costing (ABC)	A system of costing … that recognizes that costs are incurred by each activity that takes place within an organization and that products (or customers) should bear costs according to the activities they use. Cost drivers are identified, together with the appropriate activity cost pools, which are used to charge cost to products (Law, 2010, p. 15).

Allowance for doubtful receivables	An amount charged against profit and deducted from receivables to allow for the estimated non-recovery of a proportion of debts.
Asset	A resource controlled by the entity as a result of past events and from which future economic benefits are expected to flow to the entity (IASB Framework, 2010, para 4.4).
Associate	An entity over which the investor has significant influence (IAS 28, 2011, para 3).
Audit	An independent examination of, and the subsequent expression of opinion on, the financial statements of an organization. This involves the auditor in collecting evidence by means of compliance tests (tests of control) and substantive tests (tests of detail) (Law, 2010, p. 37)
Bad debt	An amount owed to the entity that is considered to be irrecoverable. It is written off as a charge against profit or against an existing allowance for doubtful receivables.
Balanced scorecard (BSC)	An approach to management that integrates both financial and non-financial performance measures into a framework proposed by Professors Kaplan and Norton … in the *Harvard Business Review* in 1992 and has since been adopted by a wide range of organizations. It is considered one of the most significant recent developments in management accounting (Law, 2010, p. 46).
Breakeven point (BEP)	The level of production, sales volume, percentage of capacity, or sales revenue at which an organization makes neither a profit nor a loss (Law, 2010, p. 65).
Budget	A financial or quantitative statement, prepared prior to a specified accounting period, containing the plans and policies to be pursued during that period. It is used as the basis for budgetary control (Law, 2010, p. 67).
Budget centre	A section or area of an organization under the responsibility of a manager for which budgets are prepared; these budgets are compared with actual performance as part of the budgetary control process (Law, 2010, p. 67).
Budgetary control	The process by which financial control is exercised within an organization. Budgets for income and expenditure for each function of the organization are prepared in advance of an accounting period and are then compared with actual

performance to establish any variances. Individual function managers are made responsible for the controllable costs within their budgets, and are expected to take remedial action if the adverse variances are regarded as excessive (Law, 2010, p. 67).

Capital	The money contributed by the proprietors to an organization to enable it to function (Law, 2010, p. 74).
Capital investment appraisal	The process by which an organization appraises a range of different investment projects with a view to determining which is likely to give the highest financial return (Law, 2010, p. 75).
Cash deficit	The cash position at the end of the accounting period when the cash outflows exceed the accumulated cash in the business.
Cash inflows	Cash inflows are cash transactions that bring money into the business.
Cash outflows	Cash transactions that take money out of the business.
Cash surplus	The cash position at the end of the accounting period when the accumulated cash in the business exceeds the cash outflows.
Comprehensive income	The total of all profits and gains made over the period.
Conceptual framework	A statement of theoretical principles that provides guidance for financial accounting and reporting (Law, 2010, p. 102).
Consolidated financial statements	The financial statements of a group in which the assets, liabilities, equity, income, expenses and cash flows of the parent and its subsidiaries are presented as those of a single economic entity (IFRS 10, 2011, Appendix A).
Continuous weighted average (CWA) cost	A method of valuing units of raw materials or finished goods issued from inventory based on the weighted-average price, which is recalculated every time a new consignment is received.
Contribution	The additional profit that will be earned by an organization when the breakeven point production has been exceeded. The unit contribution is the difference between the selling price of a product and its marginal cost of production. This is based on the assumption that the marginal cost and the sales value will be constant (Law, 2010, p. 110).

Control [of an investee]	Achieved when the investor is exposed, or has rights, to variable returns from its involvement with the investee and has the ability to affect those returns through its power over the investee (IFRS 10, 2011, Appendix A).
Corporate governance	The manner in which organizations, particularly limited companies, are managed and the nature of accountability of the managers to the owners (Law, 2010, p. 113).
Cost	Expenditure on goods and services required to carry out the operations of an organization (Law, 2010, p. 115).
Cost accounting	The techniques used in collecting, processing and presenting financial and quantitative data within an organization to ascertain the cost of the cost centres, cost units and the various operations (Law, 2010, p. 115).
Cost centre	Area of an organization for which costs are collected for the purpose of cost ascertainment, planning, decision making, and control (Law, 2010, p. 116).
Cost driver	Any factor such as number of units, number of transactions, or duration of transactions that drives the costs arising from a particular activity. When such factors can be clearly identified and measured, they will be used as a basis for allocating costs to cost objects (Law, 2010, p. 117).
Cost unit	A unit of production for which the management of an organization wishes to collect the costs incurred (Law, 2010, p. 119).
Cumulative cash brought forward (b/f)	The cash surplus or deficit at the start of the accounting period that has been brought forward from the previous period.
Cumulative cash carried forward (c/f)	The cash surplus or deficit at the end of the accounting period that is carried forward to the next period.
Depreciable amount	The cost of an asset, or other amount substituted for cost, less its residual value (IAS 16, 2008, para 6).
Depreciation	The systematic allocation of the depreciable amount of an asset over its useful life (IAS 16, 2008, para 6).
Direct costs	Product costs that can be traced directly to a product or cost unit (Law, 2010, p. 145).
Discounted cash flow (DCF)	A method used in capital budgeting, capital expenditure appraisal, and decision appraisal that predicts the stream of cash flows, both inflows and outflows, over time and

discounts them, using a cost of capital or hurdle rate, to present values in order to determine whether the project or decision is likely to be financially feasible.

Discounted payback period method

A method of capital budgeting in which managers calculate the time required before the forecast discounted cash inflows from an investment will equal the initial investment (Law, 2010, p. 151).

Double-entry bookkeeping

A method of recording the transactions of a business in a set of accounts, such that every transaction has a dual aspect and therefore needs to be recorded in at least two accounts (Law, 2010, p. 158).

Environmental management accounting

The identification, collection, analysis and the use of two types of information for internal decision making: physical information on the use, flows and fates of energy, water, and materials (including wastes) and monetary information on environment-related costs, earnings and savings (UNDSD, 2001, p. 2).

Equity

The residual interest in the assets of the entity after deducting all its liabilities (IASB Framework, 2010, para 4.4).

Expenses

Decreases in economic benefits during the accounting period in the form of outflows or depletions of assets or incurrences of liabilities that result in decreases in equity, other than those relating to distributions to equity participants (IASB Framework, 2010, para 4.25).

Fair value

The price that would be received to sell an asset or paid to transfer a liability in an orderly transaction between market participants at the measurement date (IFRS 13, 2011, Appendix A).

Finance

1. The practice of manipulating and managing money.
2. The capital involved in a project, especially the capital needed to start a new business.
3. A loan of money for a particular purpose, especially by a financial house (Law, 2010, p. 185).

First in, first out (FIFO) cost

A method of valuing units of raw materials or finished goods issued from [inventory] based on using the earliest unit value for pricing the issues until all [inventory] received at that price has been used up. The next latest price is then used for pricing the issues, and so on. Because the issues are based on a FIFO cost, the valuation of closing [inventory] is described as being on the same FIFO basis (Law, 2010, p. 192).

Fixed budget

A budget that does not take into account any circumstances resulting in the actual levels of activity achieved being different from those on which the original budget was based. Consequently, in a fixed budget the budget cost allowances for each cost item are not changed for the variable items (Law, 2010, p. 193).

Flexible budget

A budget that takes into account the fact that values for income and expenditure on some items will change with changing circumstances. Consequently, in a flexible budget the budget cost allowances for each variable cost item will change to allow for the actual levels of activity achieved. A budget that has been adjusted in this way is known as a flexed budget (Law, 2010, p. 195).

Goodwill

An asset representing the future economic benefits arising from other assets acquired in a business combination that are not individually identified and separately recognized (IFRS 3, 2010, Appendix A).

Gross profit

The difference between the revenue and the cost of goods sold during the period.

Income

Increases in economic benefits during the accounting period in the form of inflows or enhancements of assets or decreases of liabilities that result in increases in equity, other than those relating to contributions from equity participants (IASB Framework, 2010, para 4.25).

Indirect costs

Indirect costs are expenses that cannot be traced directly to a product or cost unit and are therefore overheads (Law, 2010, p. 230).

Internal rate of return (IRR)

An interest rate that gives a net present value of zero when applied to a projected cash flow of an asset, liability, or financial decision (Law, 2010, p. 242).

Joint control

The contractually agreed sharing of control of an arrangement, which exists only when decisions about the relevant activities over an economic activity require the unanimous consent of the parties sharing control (IFRS 11, 2011, Appendix A).

Joint operation

A joint arrangement whereby the parties that have joint control of the arrangement have rights to the assets, and obligations for the liabilities, relating to the arrangement (IFRS 11, 2011, Appendix A).

Joint venture	A joint arrangement whereby the parties that have joint control of the arrangement have rights to the net assets of the arrangement (IFRS 11, 2011, Appendix A).
Liability	A present obligation of the entity resulting from past events, the settlement of which is expected to result in an outflow from the entity of resources embodying economic benefits (IASB Framework, 2010, para 4.4).
Limiting factor	A constraint that limits the business from achieving higher levels of performance and profitability.
Master budget	The final coordinated overall budget for an organization as a whole, which brings together the functional budgets, the capital budget, and the cash flow budget, as well as the budgeted statement of comprehensive income and statement of financial position for the budget period (adapted from Law, 2010, p. 277).
Material	The production supplies of an organization that feature as revenue expenditure purchased from a third party ... Materials are not necessarily raw materials, but can include components and sub-assemblies used in the finished product (Law, 2010, p. 278).
Net present value (NPV)	A method of capital budgeting in which the value of an investment is calculated as the total present value of all cash inflows and cash outflow minus the cost of the initial investment (Law, 2010, p. 293).
Net realizable value (NRV)	The sales value of the [inventory] less any additional costs likely to be incurred in getting the [inventories] into the hands of the customer (Law, 2010, p. 294).
Non-controlling interest	The equity in a subsidiary not attributable, directly or indirectly, to a parent (IFRS 3, 2010, Appendix A).
Operating profit	The difference between the operating income and revenue expenditure for the period.
Opportunity cost	The economic cost of an action measured in terms of the benefit foregone by not pursuing the best alternative course of action (Law, 2010, p. 306).
Overhead absorption rate (OAR)	The rate or rates calculated in an absorption costing system in advance of an accounting period for the purpose of charging the overheads to the production of that period (Law, 2010, p. 2).

Parent	An entity that controls one or more entities (IFRS 10, 2011, Appendix A).
Payback period method	A method of capital investment appraisal in which the time required before the projected cash inflows for a project equal the investment expenditure is calculated (Law, 2010, p. 315).
Power	The existing rights [of the investor] that give the current ability to direct the relevant activities [or the investee] (IFRS 10, 2011, Appendix A).
Prepayment	A payment made for goods or services before they are received (Law, 2010, p. 328).
Property, plant and equipment	Tangible assets that are held for use in the production of supply of goods or services, for rental to others, or for administrative purposes, and are expected to be used during more than one period (IAS 16, 2008, para 7).
Protective rights	Rights designed to protect the interest of the party holding those rights without giving that party power over the entity to which those rights relate (IFRS 10, 2011, Appendix A).
Ratio analysis	The use of accounting ratios to evaluate a company's operating performance and financial stability … In conducting an analysis comparisons will be made with other companies and with industry averages over a period of time. The analysis of ratios can indicate how well a company is run, the risks of financial insolvency, and the financial returns provided (Law, 2010, p. 345).
Relevant activities	Activities of the investee that significantly affect the investee's returns (IFRS 10, 2011, Appendix A).
Relevant range	The range of levels of activity levels between which valid conclusions can be drawn from the linear cost functions normally associated with a breakeven analysis. Outside this range it is recognized that the linear relationships between fixed costs, variable costs, and revenue do not apply (Law, 2010, p. 355).
Residual value	The estimated amount that an entity would currently obtain from disposal of the asset, after deducting the estimated costs of disposal, if the asset were already of the age and in the condition expected at the end of its useful life (IAS 16, 2008, para 6).

Significant influence	The power to participate in the financial and operating policy decisions of the investee but is not control or joint control of those policies (IAS 28, 2011, para 3).
Stakeholders	All those with interests in an organization; for example, as shareholders, employees, suppliers, customers, or members of the wider community (who could be affected by the social or environmental consequences of an organization's activities) (Law, 2010, p. 390).
Standard costing	A system of cost ascertainment and control in which predetermined standard costs and income for products and operations are set and periodically compared with actual costs incurred and income generated in order to establish any variances (Law, 2010, p. 393).
Stewardship	A traditional approach to accounting that placed an obligation on stewards or agents, such as directors, to provide relevant and reliable financial information relating to the resources over which they have control but which are owned by others, such as shareholders (Law, 2010, p. 398).
Strategic management accounting	A management accounting system organized so that it is capable of providing the information needed for long-term strategic decision making, as opposed to the more traditional approach of providing short-term costs (Law, 2010, p. 401).
Time value of money	The concept used as the basis for discounted cash flow calculations that cash received earlier is worth more than a similar sum received later, because the sum received earlier can be invested to earn interest in the intervening period (Law, 2010, p. 415).
Total quality management (TQM)	An integrated and comprehensive system of planning and controlling all business functions so that products or services are produced which meet or exceed customer expectations (CIMA, 2005, p. 54).
Trial balance	A listing of the balances on all the accounts of an organization with debit balances in one column and credit balances in the other. If the rules of double-entry bookkeeping have been accurately applied, the totals of each column should be the same (Law, 2010, p. 420).
Useful life	The period over which an asset is expected to be available for use by an entity ... or the number of production or similar

units expected to be obtained from the asset by the entity (IAS 16, 2008, para 6).

Variance

In standard costing and budgetary control, a variance is the difference between the standard or budgetary levels of cost or income for an activity and the actual costs incurred or income achieved (Law, 2010, p. 430).

Index

abbreviated accounts, 97
absorption costing, 298–313, 318
accountability, 82
Accountancy and Actuarial Discipline Board (AADB), 247
accountancy profession, 12
accounting equation, 61, 158
accounting for quality, 425
accounting principles, 23
accounting rate of return (ARR), 383, 386
accounting standards, 93
  international, 101
  UK, 98
accounting system
  double-entry booking, 57–80
accounting
  nature and purpose, 13
accrual accounting, 24, 130
accruals, 143, 169
accruals concept, 24
acid test, 228
activity cost pool, 316
activity-based costing (ABC), 314–26
administrative expenses, 134
Alternative Investment Market (AIM), 37
amortization, 145
annual report and accounts, 16, 84
apportioning
  production cost centre overheads, 301
  service cost centre overheads, 307

assets, 62, 123
associates, 201
  equity method, 201
Association of Chartered Certified Accountants (ACCA), 12
audit, 16, 83
audit exemption, 97
Auditing Practices Board (APB), 247

bad debts, 148
balanced scorecard (BSC), 418
balancing the accounts, 71
bankruptcy, 39
big GAAP, 95
bookkeeping, 16, 57–80
breakeven analysis, 332
breakeven point, 332
budget centre, 347
budgetary planning and control, 344–63
budgets, 347
  setting, 351
business angels, 37
business entities, 4
business entity concept, 25
business planning, 18, 48, 345

Cadbury Report, 246
capital, 34
capital and capital maintenance concepts, 125
capital investment appraisal, 375–90, 391–404
capital turnover, 224

carriage inward and outward, 75
cash deficit, 42, 44
cash flow forecast, 41, 46
cash flow information, 39
cash flow statement for management, 48
cash inflows and outflows, 42, 44
cash surplus, 42, 44
Chartered Institute of Management Accountants (CIMA), 12
Code of Ethics for Professional Accountants, 242
Combined Code on Corporate Governance, 249, 250
Companies Act 2006, 10, 93
companies, 4, 8
company law, 93
comparability, 119
comprehensive income, 134
Conceptual Framework for Financial Reporting, 16, 112–28
consistency concept, 26
consolidated financial statements, 183–211
consolidated statement of changes in equity, 200
consolidated statement of comprehensive income, 198
consolidated statement of financial position
  after acquisition, 196
  acquisition method, 188

continuous weighted average (CWA) cost, 286, 291
contribution, 331
contribution analysis, 335
limiting factors, 338
control of an investee, 186
convergence of financial reporting, 89
corporate governance, 246
developments in the UK, 248, 250
international developments, 253
corporate social responsibility (CSR), 255
cost, 268, 269, 277
classifying in total costing, 273, in marginal costing, 328
continuous weighted average (CWA), 286, 291
first in, first out (FIFO), 286, 291
cost accounting, 21, 267, 270
indirect costs 298–313
product direct costs, 283–97
cost centre, 273
cost driver, 316, 318
rate, 317
cost of sales, 133
cost of quality, 426
cost pool, 316
cost unit, 272
costing direct expenses, 295
costing direct labour, 292
costing direct materials, 286, 291
costing for indirect costs, 298–313
costing for product direct costs, 283–97

credit transactions, recording, 69
cumulative cash, 42, 44
current cost, 125
current ratio, 227

debentures, 37
debt finance, 37
debt/equity ratio, 231
depreciable amount, 145
depreciation, 145
property, plant and equipment, 143, 169
differential reporting, 96
direct costs, 278
costing methods, 283–97
direct labour variance, 370
direct labour efficiency variance, 370
direct labour rate variance, 371
direct materials variance, 367
direct materials price variance, 369
direct materials usage variance, 368
discounted cash flow (DCF), 394, 401
discounted payback period, 398, 401
discounts allowed and received, 75
distribution costs, 134
dividend per share, 219
dividend yield, 220
double-entry bookkeeping, 59
assets, liabilities and equity, 62
carriage, discounts and petty cash, 75
credit transactions, 69
non-sales revenue, 76
purchases, sales and inventory, 66
revenue and expenses, 64

doubtful receivables allowance, 148, 172

earnings per share, 220
efficiency ratios, 215
inventory holding period, 228
trade payables payment period, 230
trade receivables collection period, 229
elements of financial statements, 121–24
recognition and measurement, 124
enhancing qualities of usefulness, 119
environmental and corporate social responsibility, 255
environmental management accounting (EMA), 428
equity, 62, 123
equity finance, 36, 37
equity method for an associate, 201
ethics and the professional accountant, 242
expenses, 64, 121, 130

factoring, 35
fair value, 190
faithful representation, 119
finance, 31
finance gap, 31
main sources, 34
financial accounting overview, 15
financial and non-financial budgets, 351
financial performance, 122
financial position, 123
financial reporting, 16, 81
harmonization and convergence, 89
international differences, 91

objective of general purpose, 115
Financial Reporting Council (FRC), 99–101
Financial Reporting Standard for Smaller Entities (FRSSE), 100
Financial Services and Markets Act 2000, 249
financial statement analysis, 214–36
  limitations, 234
  trend analysis, 233
financial statements, 184
  elements of, 121
first in, first out (FIFO) cost, 286, 291
fixed budget, 356
fixed cost, 328
flexible budget, 357
Fourth, Seventh and Eighth Directives, 96
functional and non-functional budgets, 352
fundamental qualities of usefulness, 118

gearing ratios, 215
  debt/equity ratio, 231
  interest cover, 232
general purpose financial reporting, 115
Generally Accepted Accounting Practice (GAAP), 82
going concern concept, 23, 121
goodwill, 189, 190
Greenbury Report, 249
gross profit, 134
gross profit margin, 226
group accounting, 183–211

Hampel Report, 249
harmonization of financial reporting, 89

Higgs Review, 249
hire purchase, 36
historical cost concept, 26, 125

IAS 1, *Presentation of Financial Statements*, 121, 134
IAS 2, *Inventories*, 142, 286
IAS 16, *Property, Plant and Equipment*, 143
IAS 28, *Investments in Associates and Joint Ventures*, 201
IAS 36, *Impairment of Assets*, 190
IFRS 3, *Business Combinations*, 188
IFRS 10, *Consolidated Financial Statements*, 184
IFRS 11, *Joint Arrangements*, 205
IFRS 12, *Disclosure of Interests in Other Entities*, 206
IFRS for SMEs, 105–6
IFRS Foundation, 102, 103
income, 64, 121, 130
incremental budgeting, 351
indirect costs, 278
  absorption costing 298–313
initial public offering (IPO), 10
Institute of Chartered Accountant in Ireland (ICAI), 12
Institute of Chartered Accountants in England and Wales (ICAEW), 12, 98
Institute of Chartered Accountants in Scotland (ICAS), 12
interest cover, 232

internal rate of return (IRR), 396, 401
International Accounting Standards Board (IASB), 102
  standard setting process, 106
International Ethics Standards Board for Accountants (IESBA), 242
International Federation of Accountants (IFAC), 242
International Financial Reporting Standard for SMEs (IFRS for SMEs), 105–6
International Financial Reporting Standards (IFRSs), 101–6
inventory, 66, 74, 168
inventory holding period, 228
investment ratios, 215, 216
  dividend per share, 219
  dividend yield, 220
  earnings per share, 220
  price earnings ratio, 221
invoice discounting, 35, 36
invoice finance, 35

joint arrangements, 205
joint control, 205
joint operations, 205, 206
joint ventures, 205
just-in-time (JIT) manufacturing, 284, 316

leasing, 36
ledgers, 61
liabilities, 62, 123
limitations
  marginal costing, 340
  ratio analysis, 234
  trial balance 77

limited companies, 8
limited liability concept, 9
Limited Liability Partnership
    Act 2000, 8
limited liability partnerships,
    8
limiting factors, 338
liquidation, 39
liquidity ratios, 215
    acid test, 228
    current ratio, 227
little GAAP, 96
loans, 35
London Stock Exchange
    (LSE), 11, 37

management accounting, 18
    issues in, 405–35
management buyout (MBO),
    37
managerial accounting, 22
marginal cost, 328
marginal cost statement,
    332
marginal costing, 327–41
    limitations and the
        relevant range, 340
market-orientated
    accounting (MOA), 411
master budget, 354
material, 284
    costing direct materials,
        286
material control 284
materiality concept, 26, 118
monetary measurement
    concept, 25
mortgages, 36

net cash flow, 42
net present value (NPV),
    394, 401
net realizable value, 136
non-controlling interest, 189,
    190
non-sales revenue, 76

operating profit, 134
operating profit margin, 225
opportunity cost, 392, 393
Organization for Economic
    Cooperation and
    Development (OECD),
    253
other income, 134
overdraft, 34
overhead absorption rate
    (OAR), 298, 310

parent entity, 184
Partnership Act 1890, 7
partnerships, 4, 6
payback period
    simple method, 378, 382
    discounted method, 399
petty cash, 75
Porter's five forces model,
    408
post trial balance
    adjustments, 141–9
power of an investor, 186
predetermined overhead
    absorption rate, 310
prepayments, 143, 169
present value, 125
price earnings ratio, 221
prime cost, 277
private company, 10
product direct costs, 283–97
production cost
    in total, 277
    per unit, 306
Professional Oversight Board
    (POB), 247
profit for the year, 134
profitability ratios, 215
    return on capital
        employed, 223
    return on equity, 222
    capital turnover, 224
    gross profit margin, 226
    operating profit margin,
        225

property, plant and
    equipment, 145
    depreciation, 143, 169
protective rights, 186
prudence concept, 26
public company, 10
purchases, 66, 133

qualitative characteristics of
    usefulness, 118–21
quality
    accounting for, 425

ratio analysis, 214–40
    gearing ratios, 231
    investment ratios, 216
    limitations, 234
    liquidity and efficiency
        ratios, 227
    profitability ratios, 222
    trend analysis, 233
realizable value, 125
regulatory framework for
    financial reporting,
    81–111
relevance, 118
relevant activities, 186
relevant range, 310
residual value, 36, 145
return on capital employed,
    223
return on equity, 222
revenue expenditure, 134
revenue, 64, 76, 133
    standard, 365

sales, 66
Sarbanes-Oxley Act, 249,
    253
Securities and Exchange
    Commission (SEC), 249
semi-variable cost, 328
significant influence, 201
small and medium-sized
    entities (SMEs), 4, 37
Smith Report, 249